The Values Divide
American Politics and Culture in Transition

by

John Kenneth White
Catholic University of America

CHATHAM HOUSE PUBLISHERS

SEVEN BRIDGES PRESS, LLC

NEW YORK · LONDON

Seven Bridges Press
135 Fifth Avenue
New York, NY 10010-7101

Publisher: Ted Bolen
Managing Editor: Katharine Miller
Composition: Rachel Hegarty
Cover design: Stefan Killen
Cover photo: PhotoDisc, Inc.
Printing and Binding: Victor Graphics, Inc.

LIBRARY OF CONGRESS CATALOGING-IN-PUBLICATION DATA

White, John Kenneth.
    The values divide : American politics and culture in transition / by
John Kenneth White.
        p.   cm.
Includes bibliographical references and index.
    ISBN 1-889119-75-X
    1. Social values—United States.   2. Social ethics—United States.   3.
Culture conflict—United States.   4. United States—Politics and
government—1993–2001.   5. Presidents—United States—Election—2000.
6. Political campaigns--United States--History--20th century. 7.
United States--Social policy--1993- I. Title.
    HN90.M6 W54 2002
    303.3'72'0973—dc21

                                2002003727

Manufactured in the United States of America
10   9   8   7   6   5   4   3   2   1

For Jeanette Brigitte Prevost White,
who is destined to live the politics
described in these pages.

Contents

List of Tables

Foreword

by John J. Zogby

WE AMERICANS KNOW so little about ourselves. Oddly enough for a nation that conducts, reads, argues over, and bashes polls, we still seem to have difficulty understanding who we really are.

Every generation or so there have been attempts at a definition of what it means to be an American. The astute French aristocrat Alexis de Tocqueville loved the classlessness of American life and the engagement of ordinary citizens in civic and political life. The iconoclast poet Walt Whitman championed our democratic institutions. Later in the nineteenth century Henry Adams bemoaned the very democratic elements that earlier pundits reveled in. And by the twentieth century two of our greatest observers, W.E.B. DuBois and Gunnar Myrdal, could not see past the "color line"—race and racism—as the force which has held (and continues to hold) us back from the greatness to which we aspire.

Just who are we Americans? What, if anything, makes us different from citizens of anywhere else? We know well the factors that determine the values we cherish as human beings. And, as Americans, we know the sources of many of these values, whether they derive from Christianity, Judaism, Islam, or other religious backgrounds. We also know that certain ethnic values enter the picture for many of us. Do we live in cities, suburbs, or rural towns? Self-help guru John Gray tells us that men are from Mars, while women see the world colored by glasses made on Venus. These are all determinants of the values that many Americans hold.

But what makes us all different as Americans? What actually makes us Americans? What is it that we all share?

Answering these questions is not a new pursuit. Nor has the pursuit been without debate and controversy. In the 1790s, the Federalists and Jeffersonian Democratic-Republicans waged a holy war over which party truly represented the spirit of the American Revolution. Anyone reading the party newspapers and pamphlets of that time can easily see the similarities between that era and the hyper-partisan rhetoric of the religious right and the liberal left of today. For the party of Jefferson, the Revolution was defined by the principles of freedom, tolerance, equality, and no taxation without representation. For the party of Hamilton, principles mattered, but the Revolution was for naught if a strong government could not be established to protect them and the people it served. Both sides fought as if the election of the other would be followed by Armageddon.

The fact is that America and Americans have survived the early years of partisan bickering, the Civil War, the Great Depression, the civil rights struggle, assassinations, and a couple of impeachment efforts. The reason for this survival is simple—we all share a common set of values that make us Americans.

Too often our politics (both in the past and today) is not about what we all hold together but what splits us apart. But lost in all of this is the fact that the same American electorate chose both Lyndon B. Johnson and Ronald Reagan, Jimmy Carter and George H.W. Bush, Richard Nixon and Bill Clinton. Each man won because each addressed the dominant values of that year. Johnson promised to expand civil rights and opportunity as Americans watched riots on television. Nixon promised law and order when urban crime and antiwar protests reached a boiling point. Carter promised to restore decency and honor to the shattered presidency following Watergate, and Reagan promised to bring dignity back to an America held hostage during the Iran crisis. Bush used simple values such as patriotism and punishment of violent criminals in his campaign against Michael Dukakis, and Clinton defeated Bush four years later because he promised change. If the bitter partisans were right, how could there ever be enough votes to persuade a majority one way or another? And how would Americans continue to thrive with the victory of one side over the other?

James Carville is a very smart man and an extremely savvy political consultant. His most famous dictum is from the 1992 campaign when he hung a sign on the wall of the Clinton campaign headquarters in Little Rock, proclaiming, "It's the economy, stupid!" Campaigns are won with the right message and the right timing, and Carville's warning to Bill Clinton was right on the mark. At the tail end of a recession, the challenger would defeat the incumbent by focusing on what voters cared about the most.

But Carville's words have been misunderstood and misused ever since. The common mistake is viewing voters as one-dimensional beasts who vote only from their pocketbooks. Stated simply, if the economy is good, the incumbent party wins. If the economy is bad, the incumbent party loses. What this interpretation does not take into account is the role values play in our lives and politics. While the state of the economy is certainly a very important factor in explaining voting behavior, two things must first be clarified. First, voters ultimately vote for the candidate or party with whom they most closely identify. That normally means supporting the candidate whose message most truly represents what the voters believe. Second, putting food on the table and keeping a job are key values.

So, in short and for all time, it is not the economy, stupid. It is who we are, what we want to be, what we want for our children, and whichever candidate or party best represents these values that wins an election. In the words of former Lyndon Johnson aide and American Enterprise Institute fellow Ben Wattenberg, "values matter most."

Values are not fleeting, they are sacrosanct. At times, many voters cannot express them and look to the candidates and parties to articulate them by proxy in a given campaign and specific context. These values are simple—they are the Bill of Rights. We are the people of rights. That is what defines us. Unlike any other nation or people we are defined by the rights we have, not by geography, by the arts and letters, not by our cuisine or sensibilities, not religion or civilization, not by war. Our rights are our history, why the first European settlers came here and why millions more have come here since. It is what we all aspire to. It is what we are about.

Our rights are the constant in the American experience. Even though they have been challenged many times in American history, they still override the dark moments. There have been wars. Under John Adams, French sympathizers were jailed and fined for violating the Alien and Sedition Acts. Abraham Lincoln suppressed civil liberties during the Civil War. German-Americans were victimized during World War I; Japanese-Americans were interned during World War II.

There have been xenophobic moments as well. Chinese were excluded from immigration to the United States from the 1880s through the 1940s. Japanese were prevented after 1905. After World War II, severe limits were placed on immigration from southern and eastern Europe and the Middle East. California has moved to limit rights and services to illegal immigrants. Arabs and Arab Americans are profiled at airports.

But, importantly, no one looks at any of these events as proud chapters in our history. We are the people of rights and see such actions as historical aberrations in times of crisis. They were, at best, awful means to a better end—the protection of our freedom and our rights.

Throughout our history we have disagreed about the meaning of these rights and how far they should be extended. But at the same time we have all internalized these rights as our own. Does a woman have a right to choose on matters of abortion? Is the death penalty cruel and unusual punishment? Are special measures such as racial profiling and obtaining secret evidence necessary measures in a time of high national security risk? Should same-sex unions have the same rights and privileges as those accorded to traditional marriages? Should embryonic stem cells be cloned to prevent or cure disease?

These are some of the core debates of our time. Both left and right dig in and debate these hot-button topics as if everyone were on the same page. Both sides speak the loudest, have the greatest intensity, and thus dominate the thoughts and strategies of the two major parties. But what is so fascinating about this "values divide" is that both sides claim to speak for America, its core values, and a silent majority of Americans. Oddly, both sides are right. When we cut through the rhetoric of "choice" versus "life," the death penalty versus life without parole, the rights of the accused versus national security, or gay rights versus the traditional family, both sides claim correctly to be representing the Constitution and its first ten amendments. Regardless of the rhetoric and the ugly partisanship that has dominated our politics of late, the two sides are equally American. Sometimes the loudest voices forget that.

Both sides are battling to win the hearts and minds of the center—the growing number of registered independents, those who choose not to identify with a party, or those who want to vote for the candidate or party that best addresses their concerns. While the "values divide" dominates party politics, this vital center listens and votes, or chooses to turn off and not vote.

This brings us to John Kenneth White's discussion of the cultural war that dominates much of the "inside-the-Beltway" debate of the past few decades. In these pages we relive the major elections and policy debates of recent years. White ably chronicles the polarities that have come to dominate discussion on many of the major issues, and he reminds us that there are few heroes in our recent political past. Gone are bipartisan congressional leaders. In their place are the spokespersons, both within and outside the walls of Congress, from of a myriad of special interest groups. One cannot but think of poor James Madison, who eloquently warned us about selfish interests.

Both sides claim to represent the best of American values. Both shout about the Bill of Rights and the Constitution. Meanwhile, voter turnouts and voter interest are at an all-time low. Before terrorists attacked the World Trade Center in New York and the Pentagon in Washington, voters were disconnected from their government and its leaders. How could this be? How could voter turnouts and interest be so diminished when the opportunities to reach citizens via old and new forms of media are greater than ever before? Is anybody listening?

One thing is certain. Whichever side appears to be intolerant of opposing views is most likely to alienate a majority of voters. Democrats and the left suffered that fate in the 1980s. Republicans got pounded in the election of 1998 after their campaign to expose the sexual exploits of President Clinton. The vast majority of voters, as Boston College sociologist Alan Wolfe has pointed out, are tolerant of the views of others.

Our political system is filled with numerous ironies. As the debates become more polarized and partisan and twenty-four-hour news channels proliferate on cable television, fewer people are watching. There are several explanations. First and foremost, many voters have bought into the conservative Republican argument presented by Ronald Reagan in the 1980s: government is steeped in debt, it has no money to spend on new programs, and it is not a problem-solver in our lives. This certainly explains the great turnoff among those in the $25,000 to $50,000 income category who pay too much in taxes and have few government programs or tax cuts designed to meet their needs—the group Harvard political science professor Theda Skocpol calls "the missing middle."

Second, more and more voters consider themselves to be in the political center—without any dominant political ideology. This is a phenomenon that needs some explanation. For many years we have tried to understand the center as socially liberal and fiscally conservative. But my Values Polls series suggests the opposite. Indeed, in recent years, many in the center seem to be liberal on issues such as government spending for the poor and middle class, a higher minimum wage, a federal program covering prescription drugs, universal health care coverage, and government regulation of the environment. On the other hand, they lean conservative on the death penalty, late-term abortion, treating juveniles as adults in criminal courts, and teaching traditional values in schools.

Even so, their positions on these issues can be flipped depending on how the debate is framed. Many who initially support the death penalty change their minds when they learn that a conviction in a capital punishment case can result from racial discrimination or from a faulty and incompetent defense, or when DNA evidence leads to exoneration. The same holds true for late-term abortion. Not only the same group, but the same individual who believes that destroying a fetus is tantamount to manslaughter can at the same time believe in a woman's right to choose. Many voters in this political center share conflicting values. In addition to the above, they can also believe that a president is morally wrong for having sex with a student intern but feel that one is entitled to privacy on such matters.

That is just the point. As Americans we feel free to make our own choices, respond to each situation, and refuse to be locked into a single ideology or party label. Depending on the news agenda, a cataclysmic event, a dynamic leader, or a persuasive television advertisement, one value can trump another, even if both are deeply felt.

On 11 September 2001, America was attacked by terrorists. In the immediate aftermath of this invasion, my polls showed some significant changes in the public mood. We are more fearful than before. Many have stopped or limited their travel, not only because of safety concerns but also to be closer to their families. Some are willing to give up some civil liberties and restrict the freedoms of others. And we are much more spiritual in both our behavior and our aspirations. Significantly, we did not clamor for General Motors or Microsoft to lead us out of this crisis and fear. Instead, Americans looked to government as the only force that could mobilize the military, provide spiritual comfort and safety, and command the physical and spiritual resources to win this new war.

Polls conducted since 11 September 2001 have shown a renewed faith in government at all levels and an almost record-high job performance rating for President George W. Bush and most incumbents. This is something more than Americans merely rallying around the flag in a time of crisis. It is, instead, a kind of nationwide bonding. Whether the events of 11 September portend any lasting seismic changes in the American psyche is hard to predict. Much will depend on future terrorist attacks and our reaction to the menu of choices that terrorists now have before them—nuclear, cybernetic, biological, and so on. Will Americans continue their renewed faith in government? Will they vote in greater numbers? Which way will the center turn in the near future, to the right for defense and national security or to the left to protect our freedoms against these terrifying challenges? Of course, we cannot predict.

Clearly, however, we live in a new world. But we live with old values. Despite the great values divide that White presents in the following pages, those rights will persist—because that is who we are.

Acknowledgments

IT IS CUSTOMARY for authors to say that in writing their books they have incurred more than the usual number of obligations. In this case, such an admission is particularly true. I am especially indebted to Bob Gormley, formerly of Chatham House, who saw value in this book and kept the author plied with encouraging comments. Beatrice Gormley was also kind enough to let me read her children's book manuscripts on George W. Bush and Al Gore. I also owe a considerable debt of thanks to Ted Bolen, managing partner and publisher at Chatham House, who understood the importance of what I was trying to say and continuously offered his support. Glenn Perkins ably edited the manuscript, and his efforts are much appreciated. Wilson Carey McWilliams of Rutgers University also provided much inspiration and voraciously read each of the chapters, offering his usual penetrating insights. Over the years, I have gained a great deal of insight about American politics from James Reichley of Georgetown University. His careful reading of this manuscript helped provide additional clarity to the argument. John Zogby and I have met on numerous occasions to share our thoughts about contemporary politics, and he generously agreed to write the Foreword to this book, for which I am especially grateful.

I am indebted to my colleagues at the Catholic University of America, with whom I have shared my observations about American politics for the past dozen years. The Research Foundation of the Catholic University of America provided much-needed financial assistance that allowed me to travel to the Roper Center at the University of Connecticut and obtain hundreds of polls from its vast archive. I am particularly grateful to Lois Timms-Ferrara, associate director of the Roper Center, who graciously invited me and my family to stay with her while I examined the hundreds of values-related polls in the Roper Center's treasure trove of survey research data. Other members of the Roper Center staff also provided valuable assistance, especially Marilyn Milliken and Lisa Ferraro Parmelee. I also wish to express my appreciation to the Mullen Library staff at the Catholic University of America, particularly reference librarian Anne Lesher, for responding to my many requests for books and articles. Finally, Arizona legislator Steve May, pollster

John Zogby, and congresspersons Constance Morella, David Price, and Barney Frank consented to interviews for this book, and I appreciate the time they took to answer my many questions.

My greatest debt of gratitude, however, is to my family. My wife, Yvonne Prevost, strongly encouraged me to write this book and was unfailing in her support. She spent many hours taking notes, fulfilling research requests, reading the manuscript, and creating an environment of love that greatly facilitated my work. My daughter, Jeannette, though a toddler, did her part by foregoing time with Papa so that he could think and write. It is to her that I dedicate this book because she is destined to live the values debates of the twenty-first century.

—John Kenneth White

The paradox of our time in history is that we have taller buildings, but shorter tempers; wider freeways, but narrower viewpoints; we spend more, but we have less; we buy more, but enjoy it less.

We have bigger houses and smaller families; more conveniences, but less time; we have more degrees, but less sense; more knowledge, but less judgment; more experts, but more problems; more medicine, but less wellness.

We have multiplied our possessions, but reduced our values. We talk too much, love too seldom, and hate too often. We've learned how to make a living, but not a life; we've added years to life, not life to years.

We've been all the way to the moon and back, but have trouble crossing the street to meet the new neighbor.

We've conquered outer space, but not inner space;

We've cleaned up the air, but polluted the soul;

We've split the atom, but not our prejudice.

We have higher incomes, but lower morals;

We've become long on quantity, but short on quality.

These are times of tall men, and short character; steep profits, and shallow relationships.

These are the times of world peace, but domestic warfare; more leisure, but less fun; more kinds of food, but less nutrition.

These are the days of two incomes, but more divorce; of fancier houses, but broken homes.

It is a time when there is much in the shop window and nothing in the stockroom;

A time when technology can bring this letter to you, and a time when you can choose either to make a difference . . . or just hit delete.

—An anonymous Columbine High School student

Introduction

Making values explicit is an activity that has been devalued and corrupted.
—Students for a Democratic Society,
"Port Huron Statement," 11–15 June 1963

SOMETHING IMPORTANT HAS HAPPENED in the everyday lives of ordinary Americans. The once predominant two-parent, mostly white household with two or more children under age eighteen is giving way to several new family forms. That transformation, coupled with a multiplication of non-whites who are rapidly becoming a majority in many places, is changing how Americans live and think of each other. Almost overnight, the 1950s era with its Working Dad and Stay-at-Home Mom (forever symbolized by television's Ozzie and Harriet Nelson and Ward and June Cleaver) is relegated to reruns on the Nickelodeon cable channel. Today, the family next door might include a single mother who has never married and is raising one or more children; live-in partners who are unmarried heterosexuals; a blended family trying to rear children and stepchildren; a two-parent family with adopted children of different racial backgrounds; a working mother and father with independent careers outside the household; or a gay couple. With every turn of the calendar page, the distance from the stereotypical post–World War II families like the Nelsons and Cleavers grows. Consider the following statistics:

- The traditional married couple—an employed husband and a wife keeping house and tending to the children at home—declined from 60 percent of U.S. households in 1972 to 27 percent in 1998. Today, in two-thirds of all married couples, both spouses go to work.[1]
- Since 1960, the divorce rate has more than doubled. Forty years ago there was a one-in-four chance that a child would witness his or her parents split apart; today, the odds are one in two.[2]
- In 1996, 32 percent of all births were to unmarried mothers, compared to just 5 percent in 1960. For whites, the percentage expanded tenfold,

from 2 percent to 26 percent, while among blacks the ratio grew three-fold, from 22 percent to 70 percent.[3]

- Between 1972 and 1998, the number of single-parent families—most of them headed by single mothers—grew from 5 percent to 18 percent. More than one-third of American children are living apart from their biological fathers, and 40 percent of them have not seen their fathers in at least a year.[4]
- The number of couples cohabiting increased from fewer than 500,000 to 5.5 million between 1960 and 2000. Two-thirds of those born between the years 1963 and 1974 say that their first union was a cohabitation.[5]
- California has seen its non-Hispanic whites become a minority of the state's population (49.9%). California, New Mexico, Hawaii, Houston, Boston, New York City, and Washington, D.C., comprise a growing list of places where whites are a minority. By 2010, Florida and Texas are likely to be added to the roster of states with non-white majorities.[6]

Years ago, political scientists Richard M. Scammon and Ben J. Wattenberg described a nation that was mostly "*un*young, *un*poor, and *un*black."[7] The white, middle-class, middle-aged world of suburbanites they described formed "the real majority," best typified by the mythical wife of a machinist living in Dayton, Ohio. Across the country, one could easily spot husbands and wives like the lady from Dayton living lives of amazing sameness in their Levittown-like suburbs. In 1967, political scientist James Q. Wilson described his boyhood home in Southern California: "Each family had a house; there it was for all to see and inspect. With a practiced glance, one could tell how much it cost, how well it was cared for, how good a lawn had been coaxed into uncertain life, and how tastefully plants and shrubs had been set out."[8] It was these folks who did the country's work and voted on Election Day. This was, said Wilson, Ronald Reagan country.

I, too, was once a member of that real majority. Of the dozen or so white, ethnic, and mostly Roman Catholic families living on my street in Rhode Island when I was growing up in the 1950s, only one had a working mother. Even when inflation prompted more moms to enter the workplace a decade later, their roles inside the household did not change much. When my own mother went back to work in the mid–1960s, for example, she took a job at a local public school so that her working hours and vacations coincided with those times when my sister and I were in the classroom or at home. But even as she worked outside the home, Mom still bore the primary responsibility for preparing the family meals and making sure the children got to bed on time. Meanwhile, my father's authority remained firm, and his roles as principal breadwinner and home handyman went largely unquestioned.

The popular culture helped reinforce this stereotypical image of the real majority. Television comedies such as *The Adventures of Ozzie and Harriet, Father Knows Best,* and *Leave It to Beaver* featured two-parent suburban families that lived in Any Town, USA. While the siblings often got into humorous situations, the traditional roles imposed on husbands and wives formed the basis for the unambiguous moral lessons conveyed in each program's closing moments. Thus, when Ward Cleaver asked wife June, "What type of girl would you have Wally [their older son] marry?" "Oh," answered June, "Some very sensible girl from a nice family . . . one with both feet on the ground, who's a good cook, and can keep a nice house, and see that he's happy."9 Even Lucy Ricardo of *I Love Lucy* was forced to conform to the traditional family norms of the 1950s, as she battled unsuccessfully with husband Ricky for a job at his Tropicana nightclub. When Lucy, Ricky, and their infant son finally moved to the Connecticut suburbs at the series end, all hopes she had for working at the Tropicana evaporated.

The traditional nuclear family with its Stay-At-Home Mom and Working Dad no longer represents the real majority. In the suburban Maryland neighborhood where I currently reside, there are plenty of single moms and single dads, lots of blended families, interracial couples, couples with adopted children of different races, and cohabiting heterosexuals and homosexuals. The proliferation of these different family forms that dominate so many neighborhoods is also reflected in the popular culture. Today, no self-respecting network executive would ever promote a situation comedy of the 1950s variety titled *Father Knows Best.* One can only imagine the huge outcry from women and men alike denouncing the reincarnated program for its blatant sexism. Certainly, that era's programmatic roles for men and women—along with the blatant racial discrimination that was also tolerated—are receding. Most Americans have welcomed the sexual and civil rights revolutions, and they continue to deplore the rigidity that once gave women few choices and discriminated against non-whites. Few want to see these discredited practices restored. Yet, it is also undeniably true that much of the romanticism surrounding the 1950s derives from television's portrayal of the idyllic family that lived in an era of moral certitude. Bob Dole voiced these sentiments when, as the 1996 Republican presidential nominee, he promised a return to a simpler era: "Let me be the bridge to a time of tranquility, faith, and confidence in action. And to those who say it was never so, that America has not been better, I say, you're wrong, and I know, because I was there. And I have seen it. And I remember."10 His evocation of an idealized past prompted Simon Rosenberg of the centrist New Democrat Network to quip: "For a newer, younger America, Bob Dole was always a black and white movie in a color age."11

David Halberstam in his comprehensive book *The Fifties* writes that the family sitcoms of that era "reflected a world of warm-hearted, sensitive, tolerant Americans, a world devoid of anger and meanness of spirit and, of course, failure."12 Today's new family forms create exactly the opposite image, as the values debate that these new families engender creates a spirit of anger and mean-spiritedness that is often heard in the public square. Here's one example: Not long ago after an elementary student returned home from her local public school, her mother, as she usually does, asked how her day went. Without batting an eyelash, the young girl answered, "Good," almost casually adding, "Mr. Gaita told us he was gay." Earlier, it seemed, her first-grade teacher, David Gaita, was discussing biographies of famous people when one pupil asked about his family and if he had a wife. Gaita replied that if he had a partner, "someone you love the way your Mom and Dad love each other," it would be a man. Some parents were pleased with Gaita's candor. Pam Swift, the mother of the child who reported that her teacher was gay, told a large crowd gathered at the local parent-teacher organization meeting that she was "grateful that my child can learn about [homosexuality] in a relaxed manner." But Brian Camenker thought Gaita should be fired, arguing that "a child's psychology isn't put together to handle this stuff."[13]

Undeniably, times have changed. One need look no further than the Central Intelligence Agency, where the prototypical organization man (and woman) held a Gay Pride celebration in June of 2000. Addressing the assembled agents was Massachusetts Democrat Barney Frank, one of two admitted homosexuals in Congress. Frank told the crowd: "People increasingly understand that the prejudice against gay people is silly."[14] But if the traditional two-parent family of the 1950s is no longer the norm, what is? The lack of consensus as to what is "normal" has prompted sociologist Alan Wolfe to observe: "Once upon a time, Americans raised families without being able to know whether their children would turn out to be good or bad. Now they raise children uncertain what good and bad actually are."[15] This profound shift in the expression of our public values underscores two important truisms about American politics: (1) values move voters, and (2) while there is an underlying public consensus about certain values (e.g., the benefits associated with freedom, individualism, and equality of opportunity), there remains much debate as to how these values should be implemented.

Reverberations in the Echo Chamber

It was Ronald Reagan who first demonstrated the power of values politics. Back when he was president, political scientists and pundits alike marveled at his hold on the American electorate, and wondered whether they could patent his formula for success. Colorado Democratic congresswoman Pat Schroeder coined the phrase "the Teflon President" to describe how Reagan mysteriously floated above controversy to win popular acclaim.[16] Certainly, Reagan's ability to charm audiences dated back to his Hollywood days. One of his most popular portrayals was that of Notre Dame football player George Gipp in the movie *Knute Rockne—All American*. Throughout his presidency, Reagan constantly invoked the character of George Gipp. Addressing the graduates of Notre Dame University in 1981, for example, Reagan recalled the young dying Gipp's purported last words to his football coach, Knute Rockne: "Some time, Rock, when the team's up against it, when things are wrong and the breaks are beating the boys—tell them to go in there with all they've got and win just one more for the Gipper. I don't know where I'll be then, Rock. But I'll know about it and I'll be happy."[17] Reagan asked his listeners to "look at the significance of that story":

> Rockne could have used Gipp's dying words to win a game at any time. But eight years went by following the death of George Gipp before Rock revealed those dying words, his deathbed wish. And then he told the story at halftime to a team that was losing and one of the only teams he had ever coached that was torn by dissension and jealousy and factionalism. The seniors on that team were about to close out their football careers without learning or experiencing any of the real values that the game has to impart. None of them had known George Gipp. They were children when he played for Notre Dame. It was to this team that Rockne told the story and so inspired them that they rose above their personal animosities. For someone they had never known, they joined together in a common cause and attained the unattainable.[18]

To Reagan, the moral lesson was clear: "Is there anything wrong with young people having an experience, feeling something so deeply, thinking of someone else to the point they can give so completely of themselves?" Reagan answered his own rhetorical question, saying: "There will come times in the lives of all of us when we'll be faced with causes bigger than ourselves, and they won't be on a playing field."[19]

Reagan's ability to tell riveting stories won him avid followers both in Hollywood and in Washington, D.C. Back in 1959, Vice President Richard M. Nixon wrote a letter telling Reagan to "continue your very effective speeches." Nixon's letter ended with these prophetic words: "You have the ability of putting complicated technical ideas into words everyone can understand. Those of us who have spent a number of years in Washington too often lack the ability to express ourselves in this way."[20]

But the potency of Reagan's storytelling lay not in its simplicity, as Nixon supposed, but in the veteran actor's ability to relate parables in which the values lessons had popular applications to the moment. One of my favorite Reagan stories is about a boy named Billy. One Sunday Billy wanted to play baseball while his father preferred reading the Sunday newspaper. To stall his son for a while, Billy's father gave him the formidable task of reassembling a newspaper map of the world that had been cut into little pieces. Reagan recounted that, after just seven minutes, the young boy had put the map together. Asked how he did it so quickly, Billy replied,

"On the other side of the map there was a picture of the family, and I found that if you put the family together the world took care of itself."[21]

Such homespun tales were part of the Reagan lexicon. Once, he hinted at the secret behind his political success, telling the American Bar Association, "One of my dreams is to help Americans rise above pessimism by renewing their belief in themselves."[22] Certainly, Reagan's gift for storytelling and his television persona contributed to his thick Teflon coating. But what gave the fortieth president such a powerful grasp on public opinion were the *values* conveyed in his parables. He brilliantly summoned the country's nostalgia for the 1950s and in so doing highlighted the consensual values of that bygone era. Also contributing to Reagan's instinctive ability to draw voters to his cause were poll-takers who tested virtually every word of his speeches to see what resonated with the public. Indeed, the search for "reasonators" (values-laden words and symbols that summoned the mystic chords of memory of old verities in the public's consciousness) became an obsession for Republican and Democratic strategists alike long after Reagan exited the Oval Office.

The search for words that resound with voters is an eternal one. Back during the heyday of the New Deal, Franklin Roosevelt found that evocations of class warfare mobilized voters to his cause. During the final days of his 1936 reelection campaign, for example, Roosevelt dramatically appeared on stage at Madison Square Garden and lashed out at the "economic royalists" whom he blamed for the Great Depression: "I should like to have it said of my first Administration that in it the forces of selfishness and of lust for power met their match. I should like to have it said of my second Administration that *in it these forces met their master*."[23] According to Roosevelt biographer James MacGregor Burns, the audience responded to FDR's words with an "almost animal-like roar [that] burst from the crowd, died away, and then rose again in wave after wave."[24] More than six decades later, Al Gore tried to resurrect a similar theme, saying that his campaign was a crusade of "the people versus the powerful." But Gore's populism seemed dated, and even his ticket-mate, Joseph Lieberman, doubted that such declarations of class warfare were the right words for a prosperous time.[25]

There is more to the search for words that move voters than finding the right wordsmith. Behind it is a question that all students of politics must answer: What moves voters? Is it the economy, as Franklin Roosevelt, Bill Clinton, and Al Gore presumed? Is it ideology, as Ronald Reagan or George McGovern might have supposed? Is it a single issue, as both sides on the abortion debate might think? Or are voters just plain ignorant? On one side of the debate is political scientist V.O. Key Jr., whose book *The Responsible Electorate* begins with the simple premise, "Voters are not fools."[26] Key believed Americans operated in an "echo chamber" where their verdicts on parties and candidates "can be no more than a selective reflection from among the alternatives and outlooks presented to them."[27] The other side of the argument was given by Walter Lippmann, whose 1925 book *The Phantom Public* expressed doubt that there was much intelligence behind the balloting: "We call an election an expression of the popular will. But is it? We go into a polling booth and mark a cross on a piece of paper for one of two, or perhaps three or four names. Have we expressed our thoughts on the public policy of the United States? Presumably we have a number of thoughts on this and that with many buts and ifs and ors. Surely the cross on a piece of paper does not express them."[28] Earlier, Woodrow Wilson offered his own twist on Lippmann's argument, saying that while he was a smart voter, those in power could not be trusted: "I, for my part, when I vote at a critical election, should like to be able to vote for a definite line of policy with regard to the great questions of the day—not for platforms, which Heaven knows, mean little enough—but for *men* known and tried in public service; with records open to be scrutinized with reference to these very matters; and pledged to do this or that particular thing; to take [a] definite course of action. As it is, I vote for nobody I can depend upon to do anything—no, not if I were to vote for myself."[29]

The search for the intelligence (or lack thereof) behind the ballots cast in any given election is as old as the political science profession itself, and, over time, the answer to the question, "What moves voters?" has varied. Back in 1928, when Democrat Al Smith, who was the first Roman Catholic to be nominated by a major party for president, the editors of the *Springfield (Massachusetts) Republican* thought they had uncovered the mystery behind people's votes. In an editorial, the paper observed that when Bay State voters discussed politics, they talked in terms of "French, Irish, Pole, and Yankee or Catholic and non-Catholic." The paper concluded, "Votes will undoubtedly be cast on other issues, particularly prohibition and prosperity, but when you get down to the ground there's dirt!"[30] The anti-Catholic slurs were heard in Boston's heavily Catholic wards, where 90 percent of the ballots went to Smith, and in the white Protestant South, where "yellow dog Democrats" in seven states bolted to Republican Herbert Hoover.[31] Thirty-two years later, religion once again seemed to provide the best explanation for the balloting when another Roman Catholic, John F. Kennedy, became the Democratic Party's presidential nominee. According to one study, 78 percent of Catholics supported Kennedy, while 63 percent of white Protestants backed Republican Richard Nixon.[32]

But religion is just one explanation among many offered to explain the motives behind the ballots. Another is racial and ethnic profiling. When Al Smith campaigned in many of the nation's industrial centers in 1928, he could have easily passed by signs posted on business establishments reading "NO IRISH NEED APPLY." Racial profiling continues to be a staple of the politics of "us" versus "them." The influx of blacks into the Democratic Party during the 1960s is one of the principal reasons why southern whites flocked to the GOP. Richard Nixon's so-called Southern Strategy for appealing to white voters below the Mason-Dixon line rested on racial stereotypes of black "welfare queens" receiving government handouts. Reflecting on this era of American politics, veteran political reporter Sander Vanocur noted that race remains "the dirty little secret of American politics."[33] Ethnicity matters once more following the September 11th terrorist attacks. In the aftermath, several reports have circulated of Arabs and Arab-Americans being routinely stopped at airports and closely questioned by authorities. One armed Secret Service agent who was on his way to guard George W. Bush at his Texas ranch during the Christmas holiday was detained when security personnel noticed he was of Arab descent and were troubled by "inconsistencies" in his paper work.[34]

Political scientists have long noted the impact of religious, racial, and ethnic profiling in their studies of voting behavior. Among the first to take sociological factors into account were Bernard R. Berelson and Paul F. Lazarsfeld, who contributed to *The People's Choice* (1940) and *Voting* (1948).[35] In these books, Berelson and Lazarsfeld described how socioeconomic standing (education, income, and class); religion (Catholic, Protestant, or Jewish); and place of residence (rural or urban) formed an "index of political predisposition" that strongly influenced choices made inside the voting booth.[36] How the political parties responded to group interests, the two political scientists reasoned, would determine which one got the most votes. Thus, a well-educated, white, upper-class Protestant from upstate New York would most likely be a Republican; while a black, blue-collar worker from Detroit would tilt toward the Democrats. Joining a political party was not based on the issues per se but instead constituted a declaration about who you were or where you were born. Yet, soon after Berelson's and Lazarsfeld's works were published, scholars began to question their hypothesis. In 1954, Michigan political scientists Angus Campbell, Gerald Gurin, and Warren E. Miller wrote: "Many a political prognosticator has been led into difficulties by the confident assumption that the major population classes will vote in the next election as they have voted in the recent past."[37]

Other scholars believe that voters are more rational-minded and less emotional when entering the polling booths. This view ascribes to the electorate the intelligence to take stock of the candidates' issue positions and react accordingly. Thus, when George H.W. Bush told voters in 1988, "Read my lips, no new taxes," the election returns seemingly gave him an order to keep his word. Speaking to reporters the day after the balloting, Bush declared that "the American people had spoken" and their message was to "hold the line on taxes," adding, "The American people must have understood that when they voted in rather large numbers for my candidacy."[38]

The idea that voters respond to issues alone gained ground back in 1950 when the American Political Science Association issued a report titled *Toward a More Responsible Two-Party System*. In it, the political scientists noted that the "summation of professional knowledge" to that time proved that *issues*, not group in-terests, moved voters to action: *"An effective party system requires, first, that the parties are able to bring forth programs to which they commit themselves and, second, that the parties profess sufficient internal cohesion to carry out these programs."*[39] The report writers blamed poor turnout and party divisions on their inability to pose compelling questions to the voters: *"By and large, alternatives between the parties are defined so badly that it is often difficult to determine what the election has decided even in the broadest terms."*[40]

In the five decades since *Toward a More Responsible Two-Party System* was published, many political scientists continue to believe that issues have a major impact on voter choices. In 1971, Gerald Pomper found a significant increase in the correlation between policy and partisan voting.[41] Likewise, Norman Nie, Sidney Verba, and John Petrocik argued that the Vietnam War and civil rights controversies accentuated partisan differences and that voters could not help but be aware of them.[42] Simply put, despite the sentiment expressed by George Wallace in 1968—that there wasn't "a dime's worth of difference" between Democrats and Republicans—the partisan divide has widened tenfold thanks to the profound policy disagreements the two parties have on a host of hot-button issues. Nonetheless, voter turnout maintains its decline, and worried political scientists continue to take the temperature of an anemic party system.

Others believe that the economy remains the dominant voice in Key's echo chamber. According to this theory, self-interested voters continuously ask candidates, "What have you done for me lately?" Usually, the answers given contain a blizzard of economic statistics. Anthony Downs in his famous 1957 book, *An Economic Theory of Democracy*, stated that economic considerations always prompt citizens to act rationally inside the voting booth: "The most important part of a voter's decision is the size of his *current party differential*, i.e., the difference between the utility income he actually received in period t and the one he would have received if the opposition had been in power."[43] Over the years, Downs's thesis has gained favor among academics. Not surprisingly, the rise in the number of his citations of his book has coincided with the increased number of elections in which the outcome was explained by the country's poor economic health.[44] Back in 1980, for example, Ronald Reagan derided Jimmy Carter's handling of the economy: "Can anyone look at the record of this administration and say, 'Well done'? Can anyone compare the state of our economy when the Carter administration took office with where we are today and say, 'Keep up the good work'?"[45] Later, in a debate with Carter, Reagan supplied the calculus voters needed to make their decision:

> Are you better off than you were four years ago? Is it easier for you to go and buy things in the stores than it was four years ago? Is there more or less unemployment in the country than there was four years ago? And if you answer all of those

questions "yes," why then, I think your choice is very obvious as to whom you will vote for. If you don't agree, if you don't think this course that we've been on for the last four years is what you would like to see us follow for the next four, then I could suggest another choice you have.[46]

A dozen years later Bill Clinton would emulate Reagan's question by using the shorthand sign James Carville posted in his Little Rock headquarters: "It's the economy, stupid!" Exit polls showed just how potent the economy had become as a voting issue: one-third (a plurality) said they were financially "worse off" than they were in 1988, and Clinton won 61 percent of their ballots.[47] The emphasis on the economy reinforced Downs's belief that "each citizen casts his vote for the party he believes will provide him with more benefits than any other."[48] But in 2000, the models of rational voting uniformly predicted an easy victory for Al Gore.[49] The fact that the political scientists were so wildy off the mark made it clear that the perennial question, "What moves voters?" required a new answer.

The emphasis on the economy as the most important variable in determining how people vote conjures an image of the hypothetical voter taking out his or her wallet and using a calculator to figure whether he or she is financially better off than was the case two, four, or eight years earlier. After decades of study, I believe that while race, ethnicity, religion, and the economy remain important concerns to many Americans, values provide the *connective tissue* linking public policy to voter attitudes about contemporary politics. Certainly, during the 1920s Americans had many opinions about the country's immigration or prohibition policies. Likewise, during the 1960s, there was a blitzkrieg of views on civil rights and the sexual revolution. Today, there are lively and contentious debates on many issues. Following the September 11th terrorist attacks, for example, Americans are balancing their security concerns with their traditional respect for constitutionally guaranteed civil liberties. How we decide these issues is influenced by which racial or ethnic group we belong to, as Berelson and Lazarsfeld believed. But also underlying these opinions are core values. How do the values of freedom and equality of opportunity translate into public policy? Which party is acting in ways that make these values more real in the lives of ordinary Americans? It is these controversies that are shaping the new values debate.

The Values Divide

While politicians sometimes give voice to voters' values, what often animates today's politics is a genuine uncertainty as to what constitutes "good values." According to one recent poll, two-thirds of U.S. residents believe the country is "greatly divided when it comes to the most important values."[50] The public's inability to reach a values consensus was evident in a 1998 report issued by the National Commission on Civic Renewal. Co-chairs Sam Nunn and William Bennett—one a Democrat, the other a Republican—saw a nation rife with contradictions and unsettled values:

> We fret about the weakness of our families, but will not make the personal commitments needed to preserve them. We worry about the consequences of out-of-wedlock births, but refuse to condemn them. We deplore the performance of our public schools, but somehow we can't find the time to join parents' associations, attend school board meetings, or even help our children with their homework. We complain about the influence of popular culture on our young people, but as parents we do not try very hard to monitor the programs our children watch and the music they hear. We desert neighborhood associations, and then lament the fraying of community. We elect, and then reelect, leaders for whom we profess mistrust. We say we do not have the time for civic life. But, in fact, we enjoy more leisure than ever before. And too many of us spend it watching television.[51]

These contradictions have resulted in profound disagreements among scholars as to what constitutes good values. In 2001, Alan Wolfe published *Moral Freedom*, a book celebrating the twenty-first century as one where moral freedom will transform civil society just as significantly as the sexual and civil rights revolutions affected the last century.[52] Yet only one year earlier, James Davison Hunter authored *The Death of Character*, which began with the bold claim: "Character is dead. Attempts to revive it will yield little. Its time has passed."[53] Such disagreements among public intellectuals as to the societal implications of the nation's shifting values can enliven and even illuminate our understanding of contemporary politics. In 1998, Andrew Kohut, director of the Pew Research Center for the People and the Press, maintained that ethical concerns "are now weighing down American attitudes as Vietnam, Watergate, double-digit inflation, and unemployment once did."[54] In a year that saw Bill Clinton impeached for lying to a grand jury about his sexual relationship with a White House intern, it was not surprising that debates about public and private morals dominated the rhetoric heard in the public square. What is worth remembering is that Americans have always worried about their values. Back in 1643, a Connecticut Puritan minister preached, "The prosperity and well-being of the Commonwealth doth much depend upon the well government and ordering of particular families."[55] In 1890, the editor of *Youth's Companion* magazine was shocked to see a group of boys aiming their snowballs at some nearby girls. What prompted him to write a stinging editorial condemning the boys was not the offense itself but the fact that it had occurred within sight of the American flag, which symbolized *"fair play, equal chance, protection to the weak, and honor to women."*[56] The editorial writer could only scoff at the goings-on within these families that had produced such abominable behavior. A report to the National Congregational Council issued two years later declared: "Much of the very mechanism of our modern life . . . is very destructive of the family."[57]

Even as the traditional two-parent family was being celebrated in the years immediately after World War II, Americans continued to fret over the country's moral health. In 1965, Lyndon B. Johnson repeated the commonly held assumption that "the family is the cornerstone of our society" and warned that when families are damaged children suffer, and when this happens on a large scale "the community itself is crippled."[58] Three years later, historian Theodore Roszak thought Johnson's fears had come to pass. In his view, the critique of the 1950s-style family had been turned on its head with disastrous results:

> For generations now, radical intellectuals have lambasted the bad habits of bourgeois society: "the bourgeoisie," they have insisted, "is obsessed by greed; its sex life is insipid and prudish; its family patterns are debased; its slavish conformities of dress and cosmetics are degrading; its mercenary routinization of existence is intolerable; its vision of life is drab and joyless, etc., etc." So the kids try this and that, and one by one they discard the vices of their parents, preferring the less structured ways of their own childhood and adolescence—only to discover that many an old-line radical, embarrassed by the brazen sexuality and unwashed feet, glad-rags and playful ways, is taking up the chorus: "No that is not what I meant, that is not what I meant at all."[59]

Roszak coined the term *counter culture* to describe the youthful social experiments: "The counter culture is the embryonic cultural base of New Left politics, the effort to discover new types of community, new family patterns, new sexual mores, new kinds of livelihood, new aesthetic forms, new personal identities on the far side of power politics, the bourgeois home, and the Protestant work ethic."[60] Ironically, even the Students for a Democratic Society, who came to symbolize Roszak's counterculture, agreed that society's values had badly eroded and blamed their parents for the problem: "Making values explicit is an activity that has been devalued and corrupted. . . . Unlike youth in other countries, we are used to moral leadership being exercised and moral dimensions being clarified by our elders."[61]

What makes today's debate about values different is that there is no longer a consensus as to what constitutes "good family values." The values consensus that existed prior to the sexual revolution of the 1960s forbade premarital sex; saw divorce as a horror to be avoided; and never, ever discussed homosexuality in polite company. That general agreement has been shattered. To take but one small example, when the Roper Organization first inquired about premarital sex in 1939, the question asked separately of men and women read: "Do you consider it all right, unfortunate, or wicked when young girls have sexual relations before marriage?"[62] Likewise, one of the first known questions to include homosexuality is also frozen in its own values prism. In 1974, the Roper Organization asked respondents to think ahead twenty or thirty years and list the threats to "life as we know it in the United States." Communism got the most mentions with 50 percent, but homosexuality was cited by 13 percent. Also making the list were sexual permissiveness (25 percent), civil rights (17 percent), and women's liberation (9 percent).[63] In the decades since these polls were taken, survey researchers have asked innumerable questions about sexual matters, and as their inquiries have expanded, new barriers have been broken. In 1994, for instance, pollsters wondered whether there should be legally sanctioned gay marriages. Not surprisingly, 62 percent opposed the idea.[64]

The sexual revolution of the 1960s and 1970s has resulted in a profound rethinking of our values, and the echoes from that era continue to be heard in the political arena.[65] House Speaker Newt Gingrich, for example, once accused President Bill Clinton of advocating "a multi-cultural nihilistic hedonism that is inherently destructive of a healthy society."[66] Democrats retorted that Republicans longed for the "good old days" of the 1950s when women were suppressed, white males reigned supreme, and blacks and gays were relegated to the shadows of life. Given such partisan typecasting, it is not surprising that many of the most important values debates occur far from Washington, D.C. To take but one example, several local jurisdictions have joined with private businesses to give health care benefits to partners of their gay employees. These changes have been controversial. In 1997, for example, the Southern Baptist Convention sponsored a boycott of the Walt Disney Corporation when it decided to extend health care benefits to the live-in partners of its gay employees.

Ironically, the values division has created its own peculiar dualism. While Americans worry that traditional families are a thing of the past and bemoan the cultural decay they see prevalent around them, they also long for a simpler era. Those uncomplicated times are romanticized each night on cable television where 1950s-era programs such as *The Honeymooners* and *I Love Lucy* attract cult followings. For fans of these shows, bus driver Ralph Kramden will forever threaten to send his wife Alice "to the moon," even as he valiantly tries to realize the American dream. And Lucy Ricardo will likewise continue to entertain the children of the twenty-first century with her slapstick antics, just as she delighted their parents.

Into the Mouths of Babes:
The Stories of George W. Bush and Al Gore

This longing for a back-to-the-future existence where life was simpler and values were made clear appeals to baby boomer parents. Many find this ironic, since

George W. Bush

The Bushes' home in Odessa was a two-room apartment, and they shared a bathroom with another family. They were thankful to have a bathroom at all, since most of their neighbors used outhouses. . . . Years later George W. Bush would describe his childhood . . . as "a happy blur," surrounded by love and friends and sports.

. . . .

[B]y 1966, most students at Yale, especially the younger students, were not impressed by fraternities. The mood on many college campuses was for students to question their parents' values. If dad had been a fraternity man, that was reason not to join.

George W. Bush couldn't understand this point of view. His family, his parents, mattered more to him than anything else. . . . George could be wild, but not in any way that challenged "the Establishment." The Establishment was what protesters in the late 1960s called the government, business, parents–anyone in authority. . . . To George, the Establishment was his father—his whole family. He might do things to annoy them, but he would never really rebel against them or question their values. . . . At Yale, the class of 1968 passed around a petition against the war in Vietnam. Most of the class signed it, but not George or his friends.

. . . .

It never occurred to George to try to avoid the military service. Military service was a proud tradition in his family, and his own father was a war hero. He had seen the pictures of his father's rescue by a submarine after he was shot down over the Pacific Ocean. Barbara Bush had glued into a family scrapbook a small piece of the rubber life raft that had kept her husband afloat.

Source: Beatrice Gormley, *President George W. Bush: Our Forty-Third President* (New York: Aladdin Paperbacks, 2000), 5, 26, 54, 58, 59, 60, 62.

these are the same parents who have had to reconcile their rebellious pasts with the values they wish to impart to their children. Two Gallup polls illustrate the change of heart. In 1977, 53 percent believed that possession of small amounts of marijuana should not be treated as a criminal offense; 41 percent disagreed. By 2000, the figures were reversed: 51 percent wanted possession treated as a criminal offense; 47 percent did not.[67]

Al Gore

Albert Gore [Senior] had spent his boyhood on a farm, and he believed that working the land built his character. He wanted his son to have the same experience of working hard, breathing fresh air, and raising crops and livestock. . . . Senator Gore left orders that his son was to get up every morning at six and put in a full day's work, just like the hired hands. "No boy of mine is going to lay up in bed while the sun shines," he declared.

. . . .

Al took no part in any student protests. He was sure that the war in Vietnam was wrong, and he admired his father for speaking out in the Senate against it. But he knew it could hurt his father politically if Al were seen in a demonstration. . . . There was an even stronger reason why Al didn't march on the streets or burn his draft card. He didn't agree with the ideals of the radical Left. Some extremists were saying that America was no better than Nazi Germany and were calling for a revolution. Like his parents, Al believed that government could do great good for its citizens. He was not willing to say, as many students did, that the U.S. government was the enemy. After all, his own father, the man he admired and loved so much, was part of the government. . . . He said that if he found a fancy way of not going [to Vietnam] someone else would have to go in his place. . . .

[T]he violently antiwar students on the Harvard campus didn't know anything about Al's inside. They saw only that he was one of the despised U.S. military. They yelled insults, and they stared at him as if they hated him. Al was astonished and angry—he had gone through such a struggle trying to do the right thing. He was one of only a dozen students in his Harvard class of more than one thousand who would go to Vietnam.

Source: Beatrice Gormley, *President Albert Gore, Jr.: Our Forty-Third President* (unpublished manuscript presented to Aladdin Paperbacks, 2000), 15, 32, 52, 53, 58, 60.

Children's books often provide illuminating insights into our values thinking. In 2000, Beatrice Gormley prepared two biographies of presidential contenders George W. Bush and Al Gore, only one of which was to be published once a winner was determined. Gormley, a gifted writer of dozens of children's books, retold the familiar personal histories of the two candidates for her nine- to fourteen-year-old audience. But the power of both manuscripts lay in the values of faith and family that shaped each candidate's life story. Although both men claimed that vast policy differences separated them, the values each sought to convey were remarkably similar. By evoking a world many Americans wistfully remembered, even if they could no longer return there, Bush and Gore conveyed certain moral truisms that many Americans wanted restored.

As with most children's books, many of the unsavory details in the lives of its subjects are left out. We don't learn, for example, that George W. Bush's father played an instrumental role in making sure his son got a coveted space in the National Guard. Likewise, Bush's alleged drug-taking and alcohol abuse are minimized. In Al Gore's case, the young reader is never told that Gore had some radical views of the military while a college student. Unspoken, for example, is a letter the younger Gore wrote to his father, then a U.S. senator. In it, Gore argued that hatred of communism had bred its own form of national paranoia: "We do have inveterate antipathy for communism—or paranoia as I like to put it. My own belief is that this form of psychological ailment—in this case a national madness—leads the victim to actually create the thing which is feared the most. . . . *For me, the best example is the U.S. Army.*"[68] Years later when shown the letter he had written to his father, Gore was horrified, telling a reporter: "Oh, good Lord! Oh, God! Is that a private letter? Did he share that with you? Good Lord!"[69]

Gore's embarrassment at an enterprising reporter's brandishing a thirty-year-old letter was entirely understandable. Most Baby Boomers prefer not to discuss what they now see as some of the more distasteful aspects of their youth. Many silently agreed with George W. Bush when he dismissed press inquiries about his youthful escapades, saying: "When I was young and irresponsible, I was young and irresponsible."[70] In a way, baby boomers (like many other Americans) have created their own values dualism, wanting the values-based simplicity of the 1950s but not really wanting to return to that time. At the same time, there is a sense that the country is on uncharted territory in its values—a feeling that creates its own fears and apprehensions.

From Reagan to Clinton:
The Insertion of Values into the Public Square

This book describes the values divide that began in the 1960s and accelerated during the Clinton years. This is not my first look at the subject. In 1988, I completed *The New Politics of Old Values*, which studied how Ronald Reagan transformed the presidency by emphasizing the values of "family, work, neighborhood, peace and freedom."[71] Reagan's values politics worked well in his day. But we are now as far removed from Reagan's inauguration as Reagan himself was from John F. Kennedy's swearing-in. In the intervening decades, it is undoubtedly clear that something far more politically significant than the victories of Bill Clinton or George W. Bush has occurred. One incident illustrates the change; back in 1988 when I was completing *The New Politics of Old Values*, Democrat Gary Hart removed himself from the presidential contest when rumors of his purported adultery became the focus of constant media attention. Hart complained that excessive media attention to his personal life had driven the issues he wanted to raise off the front pages: "That link with the voters that lets you listen to their concerns and often your ideas and proposals had been broken."[72] That link broke when a reporter asked if Hart had ever committed adultery. After an awkward silence, the former Colorado senator replied that rumors of his infidelity had nothing to do with his qualifications to be president. By not answering, Hart explicitly refused to endorse the 1960s emblem adopted by civil rights and women's groups that "the personal is political." Hart subsequently exited the race, and Michael Dukakis, whose moral rectitude was never in doubt, was nominated instead.

In contrast, the Clinton presidency was all about the politics of persona. By making the personal so political, Bill Clinton confronted a public that since 1988 had either "matured" in its thinking about its leaders and was more realistic in its expectations, or an electorate whose tolerance of indecency in the Oval Office was the single best indicator that the country's values had gone awry. Clinton's actions—and, indeed, his entire personal history—made clear that the 1960s aphorism that "the personal is political" has come to dominate all aspects of public life. Clinton's own story, first as an Oxford student who avoided the draft and experimented with drugs and later as the married man who conducted numerous extramarital affairs, became a symbol for the loose morality many saw embodied in the 1960s generation that has contributed so mightily to the present values divide. Today, Clinton's wife, Hillary, embodies several of the contradictions many citizens have regarding their own values standards. Supporters see the former Barry Goldwater girl as a role model for independent-minded women who enjoy separate careers apart from their husbands, and they rejoiced when she won a Senate seat from New York. But these same defenders were dismayed when she adopted a Tammy Wynette–like stance (something she once vowed she would never do) and stood by her man during the Monica Lewinsky affair.

Even as powerful and untold a tale as the complicated marriage of Bill and Hillary Clinton, pales in contrast to the values shift that has occurred in everyday family lives of ordinary Americans. How we live, work, and interact with each other, and who we have sex with (and how often), has altered the way we think about each other and ourselves. Not surprisingly, these alterations have animated and transformed present-day politics. For the moment, Americans have been given a respite from the values controversy. George W. Bush is no Bill Clinton, and he is unlikely to challenge the public much when it comes to reconstructing old values to fit present circumstances. Instead of pointing the way to the future, George and Laura Bush are emblematic of the sedate 1950s, a far cry from Bill and Hillary Clinton who seemed to enjoy challenging conventional mores. Yet, even with George and Laura Bush as the present-day incarnation of

Dwight and Mamie Eisenhower, a new values politics continues to echo in the nation's civic life. By making the personal entirely political, it is clear that the values divide, which intensified during Bill Clinton's presidency and marked George W. Bush's election in 2000, is *the* demarcation line for an intensely personal politics as it is practiced at the beginning of the twenty-first century.

The Plan of the Book

The Values Divide beings with the premise that values matter most in understanding contemporary politics. But whose values? This debate is changing long-established rules that govern how voters behave. Chapter 1 tells four contemporary stories, each signifying the transformation in public values. These stories include the ratification in Vermont of civil unions for gay couples; the many values contradictions contained in the legal dispute between Arizona state representative Steve May and the U.S. Army; the surprising public reaction to Bill Clinton's dalliance with Monica Lewinsky; and the virtual tie between George W. Bush and Al Gore. In the first three tales, the public was faced with a series of values conundrums they would have preferred to avoid. During the 2000 campaign, both Bush and Gore were offering the voters a respite from the values divide. Even so, the split between Bush and Gore voters was largely along values lines. Moreover, the ongoing arguments as to how to interpret the enduring American values of freedom, individualism, and equality of opportunity has advanced the values debates to new levels. Chapter 2 describes the controversies caused by these shifting values, and how the country's changing ethnic and familial composition is contributing to the new values divide. The result is a struggle not just for political supremacy by the country's new immigrants and family forms that are challenging what is left of Scammon and Wattenberg's "real majority," but over the idea of just what values the nation stands for and how they should be translated into public policy. Simply put, whose country is it anyway?

The lack of a compelling answer to this question makes assembling a partisan majority an exceptionally difficult task. Chapter 3 describes how the Republican Party came to embody the values of freedom and individualism during the New Deal era. But during the 1990s, adherents of the religious right and a powerful cadre of congressional leaders seriously questioned this long-held Republican faith in the virtue of the citizen to freely make good moral choices. Like its detractors, these morally-minded Republicans came to believe that the once all-powerful Moral Majority was neither. The result has been an internal split between the party's more libertarian-minded thinkers and its moralists that has cost the party vital public backing on the crucial value of tolerance.

But neither have the Democrats been spared their values troubles. As previously noted, Bill Clinton came to embody many of the values contradictions of the 1990s. Although he survived impeachment, when it came to representing values Americans wanted personified in their political leaders, Clinton and his fellow Democrats suffered. While Democrats may have an advantage on the value of tolerance, voters who wish a restoration of traditional family roles turn to the Republicans.

Chapter 5 describes how these partisan values liabilities shaped the 2000 presidential campaign. Each of the major party presidential candidates—Bill Bradley and Al Gore for the Democrats, and George W. Bush and John McCain for the Republicans—sought to cast himself as a restorer of values. Each promised that he could serve as a moral example to the nation's children, and in so doing, he would give the public a respite from the Clinton scandals. Moreover, the eventual nominees, George W. Bush and Al Gore, both achieved some success in reducing their vulnerabilities on values issues. Specifically, Bush sought to overcome his party's weakness on tolerance issues by stressing his belief in a "compassionate conservatism." Gore sought to distance himself from Clinton by emphasizing his preference for traditional families. Both strategies worked just enough to produce the perfect tie that contributed to the Florida fracas.

Chapter 6 tells the story of how George W. Bush coped with the values divide that still gripped the country during the first nine months of his controversial presidency. After some reflection, I decided to leave this chapter relatively unamended following the September 11th terrorist attacks for two reasons: (1) the chapter describes certain aspects of the Bush persona that remain unchanged; (2) the challenges that face government, business, and religious leaders in an era where morality is writ small and deference to authority is no longer a given, linger on in the post–September 11th environment, and (3) the renewed form of four-party politics depicted in the chapter quickly reasserted itself in the hundred days following the terrorist attacks.

Chapter 7 tries to bring the traumatic events of 11 September 2001 into focus. Clearly, the actions of Osama bin Laden united all Americans, and talk of a values divide has disappeared for a while. Yet, while it is true that nearly everyone was taken aback by the brazenness of the strikes, there remained significant differences as to how many Americans perceived the values lessons contained in the stories of the heroes who survived them. Some saw numerous examples of individual bravery, including heroic acts by a homosexual airline passenger who fought with the hijackers and the gay priest who died giving last rites to those on the ground. Others, including Republican evangelists Pat Robertson and Jerry Falwell, believed that the terrorists were God's wrathful instruments designed to inflict harm on a sinful nation. Still others saw the American-turned-Taliban-sympathizer John Walker Lindh either as a young man gone awry, or as the byproduct of a liberal-minded, morally loose Southern California culture. While it is much too early to know the full significance of the September 11th attacks, one aphorism holds true: Expect the unexpected. In this case, the unexpected may mean a rebirth and redefinition of the value of tolerance, the implication of which is likely to alter the values divide in ways unlikely to satisfy activists on either side.

CHAPTER 1

Four Stories for Our Time

Wake up, Tocqueville, they've gone mad.
　　　　　—*Le Figaro*, editorial, 9 January 1999

1. We Are Family

It's dinnertime, and this house, like so many others with young children, is a scene of semi-ordered chaos. Winnie-the-Pooh books lie atop a pile of newspapers. Toys litter the living room. An infant cries. One frazzled parent desperately awaits the arrival of the other to provide a few moments of relief while dinner is prepared. It's a familiar scene, one often replicated in popular television programs like *The Adventures of Ozzie and Harriet, Leave It to Beaver, Father Knows Best,* or *The Cosby Show*. But this picture is dramatically different. Set in bucolic Vermont, this family consists of two gay moms: Stacey Jolles, a working psychologist, and Nina Beck, the "other mom" who gave birth to her infant son, Seth (thanks to artificial insemination), and nurses him.[1] Their family life began in 1992 when both women stood under a *chuppa* (a Jewish wedding canopy), exchanged vows before a rabbi, and signed a *ketuba* (a Jewish wedding contract).[2] After the ceremony, all that remained was for the State of Vermont to issue a marriage license. But when the pair petitioned a local justice of the peace for one, they were promptly denied. Jolles and Beck filed a lawsuit, and the Vermont State Supreme Court enjoined the legislature to pass a "civil union" law permitting these two moms (along with thousands of other gay couples) to obtain some of the legal benefits associated with marriage.[3] Throughout their legal battle, both women maintained that their notion of marriage and family threatened no one. According to Jolles, "All the things I want in my family are the same things all my heterosexual friends want in their lives. I just want to be married and have kids. More than ever in my life, I want to be regular. . . . We believe strongly in family values."[4]

Jolles and Beck are just two faces on the cutting edge of a dramatic transformation in the way Americans live, work, think of themselves, and relate to each other. These changes have produced a values divide that is being fought with virtually every weapon except bullets. When Vermont's governor signed the civil union law, the state became ground zero in the culture wars. Marion Spooner, an antigay activist who runs her own maple syrup roadside stand, says: "It's pitted friends against friends. It's just like the North-and-South war."5 Kathy Racette, a stay-at-home mom who home-schools her children, agrees: "We didn't seek this war. I've never been politically active, but this is a behavioral and religious issue. They want to get our children to accept homosexuality as a normal lifestyle."6 The Catholic bishops of Boston entered the fracas, declaring that support for homosexual unions "attacked centuries of cultural and religious esteem for marriage between a man and a woman and has prepared the way for an attack on the well-being of society itself."7 One Baptist minister posted a message on his website that read, "Vermont is now a leper colony where the unclean dwell."8

Political parties have also been caught in the crossfire. Most Republicans opposed civil unions, but so, too, did some Democrats. Rene Blanchard, a Democratic state representative and former justice of the peace, expressed her reservations: "I just really didn't want Vermont to become the first state to break this barrier. . . . My personal belief is that marriage is between a man and a woman, and I actually think that's the personal belief of most Vermonters. I think we're moving very quickly on this issue. Too quickly."9 Thirteen thousand citizens contacted Governor Howard Dean's office to express their opinions, and hundreds attended town meetings to discuss the proposed law. At one gathering, long-time resident Kenneth Wolvington wondered what all the fuss was about: "Mrs. Wolvington and I have been married for fifty-two years [and] for the life of us, we can't imagine how gay marriage would adversely affect anyone in our family."10 Wolvington was quickly rebuked by Robert Charlesworth who argued: "The government is responsible for protecting minorities. It is not responsible for imposing minority values on the majority."11

Enactment of a civil union law did not quell the protestors—in fact, they grew louder and more strident. As the 2000 election drew closer, five thousand black-and-white "Take Back Vermont" signs littered the landscape from the Massachusetts to the Canadian borders. Hateful bumper stickers, such as "Kill a Queer, Not a Deer," transformed what was a civil debate into an uncivil one.12 "Woodchucks," the popular nickname for native Vermonters, saw their state being corrupted by pro–civil union "flatlanders," the name given to out-of-staters. Leo Valliere, a furniture maker from rural granite town of Barre, was disgusted by the prospect of de facto gay marriages: "We swung way to the left in Vermont. Now we want to swing back."13 Valliere, a Republican, ran for the state legislature on a one-plank platform: repeal the civil union law. He won, thanks to the strong support he received from woodchuck Republicans. In September 2000, five pro–civil union GOP lawmakers (and one Democrat) were defeated in acrimonious primary contests. Two months later, Republicans gained sixteen seats in the Vermont House, giving them control of that body for the first time in a dozen years. In the state senate, Republicans added one seat, narrowing the Democratic majority to a mere two.[14] Craig Scribner, one of the successful Republican candidates, boasted that he defeated a ten-year Democratic representative "without knocking on a single door because of his vote on civil unions."[15] Another woodchuck exalted: "Vermont is ready to come back to its conservative foundation. It took civil unions to wake them up to how liberal we had become."[16]

Democrats reeled from the anti–civil union fallout. During the 2000 campaign, Governor Dean, whose reelection had once been thought to be assured, faced stiffer-than-expected challenges from both the left and the right. Anthony Pollina, the Progressive Party candidate, attacked Dean for being too conservative on the civil union issue. Republican standard-bearer Ruth Dwyer denounced the "homosexual agenda" and warned that since ancient Rome "any society that has fooled around with the basic structure of the nuclear family has come to grief."[17] Despite the obvious weaknesses of Dean's opponents, they held him to just 50 percent of the vote and nearly forced the Vermont House of Representatives to decide the outcome.[18] Exit polls showed the deep divisions created by the civil union controversy: 49 percent described themselves as "enthusiastic" or "supportive" of the new law; an equal number said they were either "angry" or "opposed."[19]

Even the presidential contenders entered the fray. Al Gore favored civil unions, claiming that the rights of domestic partners should be legally protected. George W. Bush professed his tolerance for gay couples but maintained that marriage must be "a sacred institution between a man and a woman."[20] His running mate, Dick Cheney, had a more libertarian view: "People should be free to enter into any kind of relationship they want to enter into," and states may arrive at "different conclusions" as to whether or not same-sex marriages should be recognized.[21] One reason for Cheney's libertarianism was that his own family has been touched by the new values divide. Cheney has a daughter who is in a committed relationship with a female partner. But Cheney's libertarianism did not please every Republican. Gary Bauer, a contender for the party's 2000 presidential nomination, excoriated the Bush-Cheney ticket for its "fuzzy morality," adding, "The last thirty years have been a social disaster largely because people have felt free to enter into—or leave—any relationship they wanted."[22] Not surprisingly, Vermont's Gore and Bush supporters took opposing stances on the civil union issue. Of those who were enthusiastic, 80 percent backed Gore; those who were angry gave 75 percent of their votes to Bush.[23]

The battle over civil unions was part of a conflict that has raged far beyond the confines of the Green Mountain State. Many high schools and colleges across the nation have formed "gay/straight alliance" organizations. Pollster John Zogby finds that 63 percent of high school seniors say they would be comfortable in a class taught by a gay teacher; eight out of ten say homosexuals should be "accepted by society"; two-thirds favor gay marriages; and 71 percent would allow gay men to serve as Boy Scout leaders.[24] In most cases, these opinions are considerably at odds with those of their parents. Nonetheless, many adults are also changing their minds toward gays. By 2000, eleven states and the District of Columbia, along with 124 municipalities, had passed gay rights measures prohibiting discrimination in the workplace.[25] Robert Knight, director of cultural studies for the conservative-based Family Research Council, notes that these new laws have not quelled gay demands for more legal protection: "Just a few years ago they were demanding tolerance. Now they're demanding gay marriages and homosexual curriculums in the schools."[26]

Writing for a 5–4 majority in 1986, Supreme Court Justice Byron White upheld Georgia's sodomy law, noting that it was "based on notions of morality . . . [and] the presumed belief of a majority of the electorate in Georgia that homosexual conduct is immoral and unacceptable."[27] But in the years following this controversial decision, public opinion about homosexuality has undergone a dramatic transformation. Georgia's state courts invalidated its sodomy law in 1998, and only seventeen states currently have sodomy laws on the books.[28] Nationwide, 44 percent favor civil unions—a remarkably high figure.[29] In 2001, the Gallup Organization found a growing public acceptance of homosexuality in all aspects of social and cultural life:

- Agreement that homosexuality is an acceptable alternative lifestyle rose from 38 percent in 1992 to 52 percent.
- Those believing "homosexual relations between consenting adults should be legal" increased from 43 percent in 1977 to 54 percent.
- Equal numbers say homosexuality is genetically caused as opposed to being environmentally caused—the first such tie in twenty-four years.
- Those believing homosexuals should have equal job opportunities rose from 56 percent in 1977 to 85 percent.
- Record numbers believe homosexuals should be considered for prestigious posts, including doctors (78 percent), the president's cabinet (75 percent), the armed forces (72 percent), high school teachers (63 percent), elementary school teachers (56 percent), and clergy (54 percent).[30]

But greater tolerance toward homosexuality does not always translate into acceptance. When asked in 1998 whether homosexuals "share your values," 57 percent said "hardly any" or "none"; only 35 percent said "most" or "some."[31] Still, many believe that the skirmish over gay rights will eventually be resolved in favor of greater tolerance. Looking ahead to the year 2025, 74 percent predict that gay marriages will be commonplace, and 69 percent think such ceremonies will be legal.[32] David Smith, communications director for a national gay rights organization, says, "I think the next decade is basically the decade of the gay family."[33] But the paradoxes remain, and the bitter battles between woodchucks and flatlanders persist in Vermont and elsewhere.

2. "Don't Ask, Don't Tell" Redux

Half a continent away, another drama in the culture wars was being played out, this one starring Steve May, a conservative Republican legislator from Arizona. Born and raised a Mormon (his father was a Mormon bishop), the young May worked in his family's herbal tea and natural food company in Phoenix.[34] After meeting future senator John McCain when he was just twelve years old, May became enamored with both politics and the military.[35] He took an active part in student government (becoming president of his ninth-grade class) and enrolled in the Boy Scouts, eventually rising to the rank of Eagle Scout.[36] The Republicans were May's team of choice: "I believe in the core values of the Republican party: a limited government, a strong national defense, individual liberty, economic freedom. That's the Republican party I belong to . . . the party of Barry Goldwater."[37] Determined to embark upon a political career, May knew that the conservative citizens of Arizona valued military service. Having heard McCain speak about his days as a prisoner of war in North Vietnam, May was inspired by his hero's sense of patriotism and call to duty. He joined the ROTC while in college and after graduation served in the U.S. Army's First Infantry Division. By all accounts, Lieutenant May was an exemplary officer. Receiving a honorable discharge on 31 August 1995, he was placed on the army's Inactive Individual Ready Reserve (IRR), a list the military uses in case of war. On 27 February 1999, Lieutenant May received orders to report to the U.S. Army Reserves following the military conflict in Kosovo, which had created a shortage of available personnel.[38] Serving as second-in-command to the 348th Transportation Company in Phoenix, May donned his uniform and reported for duty. Said May, "I can't refuse orders when the nation's at war."[39] His battalion commander, Major Eileen Norton, was so impressed with May's soldiering that she enthusiastically recommended him for promotion to captain. Others shared Norton's assessment. One army evaluator called him "the finest lieutenant on the battalion staff." Another said, "I have not seen a more intelligent and perceptive officer." A third effused, "A dynamic and personable leader with unlimited potential."[40]

May's political star was also rising. After leaving the military in 1995, he ran for the state legislature and was elected in 1998 by a comfortable majority.[41] Young and handsome, the twenty-six-year-old state representative was viewed by many political observers as a "comer." But all that changed a mere three weeks after he was sworn into office. During a debate over a proposal prohibiting Arizona's cities and towns from using public funds to pay for health benefits for unmarried domestic partners, Representative May became visibly angry. In a speech denouncing the idea, conservative Republican Karen S. Johnson told the legislators that homosexuals were at "the lower end of the behavior spectrum";[42] that rampant homosexuality would inevitably lead to "bestiality, animal sacrifice, and cannibalism";[43] and that "history tells us that good public policy cannot accept varying levels of morality."[44] Listening to Johnson's remarks on his office intercom, an outraged May stormed to the floor and told his colleagues, "When you attack my family and you steal my freedom, I will not sit quietly in my office. This Legislature takes my gay tax dollars, and my gay tax dollars spend the same as your straight tax dollars. If you're not going to treat me fairly, don't take my money."[45] May lashed out at his fellow partisans, claiming that his beloved Arizona Republican Party, whose founding father was the libertarian-minded Barry Goldwater, had been hijacked by a group of "theocratic fascists who want to use government to impose their religious and moral viewpoint on the people of our state."[46]

May's actions prompted a political firestorm. The *Arizona Republic* ran headlines about the two Republican lawmakers battling over the morality of homosexuality.[47] Meanwhile, the U.S. Army moved to discharge May, saying he had violated the "don't ask, don't tell" policy Bill Clinton had reluctantly endorsed in 1993. Major Norton, who had no choice but to commence an "involuntary separation action," urged her superiors to consider May's "past record of service and continued professional demeanor."[48] But the army was unyielding, even when May claimed that his speech was protected since it occurred in the Arizona House chamber. Colonel John R. Hawkins III spoke for the army: "I don't think that the individual has been, shall we say, keeping this under wraps, as to his sexual orientation."[49] May refused to surrender his commission, claiming that the army's "don't ask, don't tell" policy violated his own sense of personal values:

> Honesty, courage, loyalty, and integrity are core Army values. They are in conflict with our policy which asks me to lie. In talking with my soldiers, they were confused initially, as we all were. They had not been confronted by this issue. But now they are universally supportive. They think it's so silly. Those who say "don't ask, don't tell" protects morale, unit cohesion, and readiness are wrong. Keeping homosexuals out of the military endangers military readiness. We lose three to four people every day in the military. You're taking soldiers out of units. No one has argued that an individual homosexual person has hurt unit morale or cohesion.[50]

The army remained unswayed, saying May's speech "created a presumption that he engages in, attempts to engage in, or intends to engage in homosexual acts."[51] Georgia Republican congressman Bob Barr, the thrice-married author of the Defense of Marriage Act, sided with the military, saying, "Homosexuality is incompatible with military service."[52] Former Marine colonel Oliver North told May to "pack your bags, salute smartly, and say thanks for having the opportunity to serve."[53] North and May had the following exchange on CNN's *Larry King Live*:

> NORTH: The reason we give separate bunk spaces to women on Navy ships, the reason we have separate and segregated showers and heads, is so that temptation, the laws of biology, does not become overwhelming and we create even bigger problems than we already have today, given that [the Clinton] administration wants to use the military like a bunch of lab rats in a radical social experiment.
>
> MAY: Sir, are you saying that if you and I shared a bedroom in the barracks that you would succumb to some strange laws of biology?
>
> NORTH: No, I would strangle you, Steve, before you could get away with it.[54]

Religious leaders also voiced their support for the military's antigay stance. Fred Phelps of the Topeka, Kansas, Westboro Baptist Church took his protest to Arizona capitol, telling passers-by that "a burning everlasting hell—a lake with fire and brimstone—awaits homosexuals."[55] Jerry Falwell also admonished May: "As a minister of the gospel of Jesus Christ who believes the Bible to be the word of God, of course, I believe that homosexuality is wrong. It's a moral perversion."[56] Support for May came from Hillary Clinton and Al Gore, who wanted the "don't ask, don't tell" policy repealed. Seeking election to the U.S. Senate from New York the First Lady said: "The policy was the result of a political assessment that it was the best that could be done at the time. . . . It hasn't worked." Gore agreed: "I don't think it has been implemented correctly, because it hasn't reached the stated objective."[57]

In September 2000, a panel of three U.S. Army colonels took the unusual step of recommending that May be given an honorable discharge—an offer May refused. His cause was subsequently taken up by Congressmen Tom Campbell (R-Calif.) and Barney Frank (D-Mass.) who sent a letter to President Clinton, co-signed by 108 members, asking that the case against May be dropped. Throughout the 2000 campaign, Clinton adopted a "hands-off" approach and referred all questions to Secretary of Defense William Cohen, a Republican. But with only days remaining in the Clinton presidency, the army relented and allowed May to serve until 11 May 2001, when his commission was due to expire—the first time the military had ever dropped a "don't ask, don't tell" case.[58] May believed the outcome vindicated his position, but it was not without cost. A scheduled promotion was canceled, and the Mormon Church, which automatically excommunicates gay members, remained eerily silent. (May describes himself as a "recovering Mormon," and has been inactive in the church for several years.)[59]

Throughout the ordeal May's constituents commended him for his honesty, even as they frequently wrote, "I don't approve of your homosexuality, but I hope you win." As May put it, "It's as if they have some need to distance themselves from approving my being gay, but supporting me politically." May was reelected by a comfortable margin in 2000, and his colleagues made him chair of that state's powerful Ways and Means Committee. Nonetheless, the Arizona legislator says he is "tired of reading about my homosexuality in the paper everyday" and remains tormented by his anti-army stance: "I have feelings of guilt. Am I going too far? Is this what I should be doing? On the other hand, I'm just telling my story. I'm not trying to make anyone look bad at all. I'm just telling the truth. If it makes them look bad, it's the politics that is doing that."[60] Meanwhile, the bill that prompted Karen Johnson's ire and May's memorable outburst died in the Arizona legislature. In conservative-minded Arizona, May's political star remains on the rise.

3. The Shaming of the [More Popular] President

During the time Steve May was facing what seemed like certain dismissal from the military service he loved, an executive who led a large enterprise was headed for a very different fate. Accused of having "inappropriate" contact with a female employee nearly half his age, this CEO first denied and later admitted the worst when DNA evidence surfaced that nullified his protestations of innocence. President Bill Clinton's affair with White House intern Monica Lewinsky put the nation to a test it wished it could have avoided, and its eventual denouement astonished pundits and public alike. The controversy culminated in 1998 when Independent Counsel Kenneth Starr released a report accusing Clinton of

- lying under oath in a civil deposition and to the grand jury about his affair with Lewinsky while he was a defendant in Paula Jones's sexual harassment lawsuit;
- attempting to influence the testimony of a potential witness [Lewinsky] who had direct knowledge of facts that would prove his deposition testimony false;
- seeking to obstruct justice by facilitating Lewinsky's plan to refuse to comply with a subpoena;
- obstructing justice by encouraging Lewinsky to file an affidavit he knew to be false and making use of that false affidavit in his own deposition;

- lying to potential grand jury witnesses, knowing they would repeat those lies before the grand jury; and
- engaging in a pattern of conduct inconsistent with his constitutional duty to "take care that the laws be faithfully executed."[61]

Starr's report was instantaneously available over the Internet, the first time a presidential scandal produced documents that could be viewed in real time by anyone who wanted to see them. Congressional sites were overwhelmed with interested readers, among them Chelsea Clinton, then a college student at Stanford University. *The Starr Report* contained so much graphic sexual detail that wire services warned that the contents "may be OFFENSIVE to some readers." The zeal that Starr brought to this case (he once famously said, "There is no room for white lies.")[62] inexorably led to Clinton's impeachment by the Newt Gingrich–led House of Representatives, marking only the second time in history a president has been impeached. As Starr noted in excruciating detail, Clinton had given his enemies plenty of ammunition: first, by denying he had sex with "that woman," and later, by claiming that oral sex did not constitute intimate sexual relations ("It depends on what the meaning of *is* is.").

Clinton's impeachment spiraled into a bitter partisan battle that left many Americans disillusioned with the intense partisanship that had gripped the nation's capitol. When House Judiciary Committee chairman Henry Hyde stepped before television cameras to announce that a bipartisan decision on the ground rules for impeachment had been reached, Democrat Barney Frank interjected, "If this is bipartisanship, the Taliban wins a medal for religious tolerance."[63] The Republicans' single-minded determination to exorcize Clinton from the presidency puzzled most foreign observers. An editorial in the French newspaper *Le Figaro* summoned the ghost of its native son Alexis de Tocqueville to explain what it saw as a reactionary puritanism battling against the forces of progressive tolerance: "Wake up, Tocqueville, they've gone mad. When you look at that distressing spectacle that American democracy is offering, you say to yourself that the man who described it best must not be very comfortable up there in the heavens."[64] A BBC television commentator expressed similar sentiments, wondering aloud on the air, "Have they all gone mad?"[65] Robert Reich, Clinton's former labor secretary, sought to reassure British viewers that it was only the Republicans who had "gone mad." Former White House adviser David Gergen was less reassuring, wryly noting that Americans were simply behaving normally.[66] When asked about the controversy at a joint White House news conference, Czech Republic president Vaclav Havel candidly expressed his puzzlement: "There are some faces of America which I don't understand."[67]

But the greatest surprise was not overseas, but here at home. Defying every known rule of politics, Clinton's job approval ratings climbed throughout the scandal. Exasperated Republicans were particularly perturbed to learn that, on average, more citizens approved of Clinton's overall performance than of that of their hero, Ronald Reagan (Clinton, 55 percent; Reagan, 53 percent).[68] Clinton's popularity ran counter to the conventional wisdom that the public's grant of power to any president rests on his ability to typify fundamental values. In his Farewell Address, George Washington famously observed, "Of all the dispositions and habits which lead to political prosperity, religion and morality are indispensable supports."[69] To that end, Washington maintained that a president must embody morality in order to ensure a vigorous presidency. Reflecting on Washington's character, political scientist Forrest McDonald later wrote, "He embodied all the desirable virtues of a president—morality, strength, integrity, steadfastness, sense of purpose, vision, intelligence, initiative, sensitivity to the nation's love of country, and so on—but there was more. He understood that the presidency is inherently dual in nature, partly executive, but also partly ritualistic and symbolic, and that the latter part is quite as important to the well-being of the nation as the former."[70]

Bill Clinton challenged the conventional wisdom that had prevailed since Washington's era. A Gallup poll found 53 percent saying Clinton's personal life did not matter as long as he did a good job running the country.[71] Many seemed surprised that they had given Clinton such high job approval ratings. When asked about it, 65 percent said they had adopted a more "realistic" view that presidents should be judged on their performance, not on their personal lives.[72] Yet, in another twist, 56 percent said that Clinton's high approval ratings reflected a national decline in personal standards and morality.[73] And, in a supreme irony, pollster Daniel Yankelovich found that if Americans could have chosen between Clinton and George W. Bush, they would have preferred Clinton, 48 percent to 44 percent.[74]

Thus, a riddle. If Bill Clinton "defined public morality down,"[75] as former Reagan education secretary William Bennett contends, then why were most Americans content (and even happy) that he continue his public service? The answer is that moral authority proved less important than the values of security and continuity. In fact, many sided with Clinton for these largely conservative reasons. Only 37 percent said Clinton's affair was "very important" or "fairly important"; 62 percent thought it of little consequence. But, in another apparent contradiction, when asked whether Clinton's lying under oath was important, 74 percent said yes.[76] *Washington Post* reporter Peter Baker wrote that Clinton's impeachment had warped the nation's politics beyond recognition:

> A president could be caught enjoying sexual favors from an intern barely older than his daughter, then lie about it on national television, cover up his misconduct and yet soar to record heights in political popularity polls. A special prose-

cutor could force a young woman to divulge her most intimate secrets, haul her mother into a grand jury, and even compel the Secret Service agents who guard the president to break their code of silence, all without anyone able to tell him to stop. A Speaker of the House [Newt Gingrich] could seek to use the president's wrongdoing to his advantage in an election, only to endure a devastating defeat and find himself forced from power just days later, all the while conducting his own secret, five-year extramarital affair.[77]

Yet the terrain upon which Clinton would fight to keep his job was not unfamiliar territory, but well-trod ground. To Republicans, Clinton's behavior in the Oval Office represented something more sinister than mere personal misdeeds. For them, impeachment was one more battle in the culture wars, a conflict that began in the late 1960s when a generation of college students challenged society's mores on sexual relations and the nature of family, resisted the draft, and questioned the U.S. government's unsuccessful prosecution of the Vietnam War. Their values still resonate with today's MTV-influenced Generation Xers. Twenty-something Paul Hemesath spoke for many when asked about the Clinton-Lewinsky tryst: "I don't think you'd find too many unattached single women who would pass that up. In a similar position, if there was an attractive woman who was the most powerful woman in the world, who knows how I would have reacted?"[78] Moreover, many of the nation's young seemed to share Clinton's distinction between oral sex and sexual intercourse. Republican House whip Tom DeLay thought such thinking brought into sharp relief the conflict between "[moral] relativism versus absolute truth."[79] When the *Wall Street Journal* editorialized in favor of Kenneth Starr, it declared that he was "not just prosecuting Bill Clinton; he was prosecuting the entire culture that gave birth to what Bill Clinton represents."[80] Many Americans seemed to agree. When asked which events in the second half of the twentieth century most represented the country's declining morality, 34 percent named Clinton's affair with Lewinsky; 19 percent said Woodstock and the acceptance of free love and drugs; 13 percent, the Watergate scandal; and 5 percent, John F. Kennedy's marital infidelities.[81] By purging Clinton, Republicans believed they would also expunge the worst excesses of the counterculture.

Yet in the impeachment battle that followed, Clinton turned the tables on the Republicans by making them the target of public ire. Hillary Clinton led the charge, saying that the accusations about her husband were part of a "vast right-wing conspiracy."[82] Only five House Democrats voted for Clinton's impeachment, and not a single Democratic senator supported his conviction and removal from office. Even Democratic vice-presidential nominee Joseph Lieberman, who had denounced Clinton's behavior as "immoral" and "harmful," thought impeachment was "unjust and unwise."[83] The bitter partisan wrangling turned into a shouting match that became fodder for such entertainment-minded programs as *Crossfire* and *The McLaughlin Group*. However enthralling the Clinton spectacle was to political junkies, the mass audience quickly tired of it. According to the Pew Research Center, those closely following Clinton's impeachment were sandwiched between the 33 percent who tracked televangelist Jim Bakker's trial and guilty verdict back in 1989 and the 32 percent who monitored the ups and downs of the stock market in September 1998.[84]

One reason television viewers weren't watching the Clinton saga was that they no longer believed that the morality of individual politicians has much of a role in public life. When one pollster asked whether "other people's morality is very important to me in terms of what I think of them," or, "I don't judge other people's personal morality if it doesn't affect me," 53 percent refused to pass judgment. Likewise, 47 percent thought it more important to show tolerance toward those who are different; only 41 percent thought respect for community standards was more important.[85] When asked about good versus evil, most Americans tend to say, "*Evil* . . . that's a strong word." "Never," says sociologist Alan Wolfe, "have so many people been so free of moral constraint as contemporary Americans."[86] In this let's-not-condemn-anyone milieu, the language of condemnation is frowned upon. Historian Gertrude Himmelfarb observes that liberal Protestant theologians now avoid using words associated with an older morality—including *sin*, *shame*, and *evil*—in favor of less harsh words such as *inappropriate*, *unseemly*, and *improper*.[87]

Alan Wolfe describes this new values structure as a "morality writ small": "There *is* a moral majority in America; it just happens to be unwilling to follow anyone's party line about what morality ought to be."[88] But in this new "morality writ small" climate, each side claims the other "doesn't get it." In Clinton's case, those on both sides of the cultural fault line argued over whether a morally flawed but effective president should remain in office. In a *New York Times* op-ed article, Marshall Blonsky and Edmundo Desnoes made an insightful observation: "Clinton is a post-modern relativist who believes not in Truth, but in many truths. Clinton is a byproduct of the 1960s who lived through the sexual revolution, Vietnam, and the end of the bipolar world."[89] Editors at *The Nation* charged that the Republican attacks on Clinton were "directed at civil libertarians, feminists, and anyone else on the wrong side of the cultural war."[90] In this instance, the values promulgated during the 1960s prevailed. The Newt Gingriches, Rush Limbaughs, Pat Robertsons, Kenneth Starrs, members of the religious right, and other assorted Clinton-haters had proven to be very useful enemies indeed.

But even as most Americans approved of Clinton's job performance, they expressed a profound dislike for him personally; 79 percent disapproved of the way he behaved in his personal life, and a mere *1 percent* listed him as a positive role model for children.[91] Most damning was the fact that 42 percent said Clinton's morals were on a par with those of *an average teenage boy*.[92] Never before had a U.S. president experienced such a gulf between his performance and his persona.

4. The Inverted Election

The last story that illustrates the present-day values contradictions is the 2000 Bush-Gore contest. The election results contain two anomalies: One is George W. Bush's defeat of the incumbent party candidate during a time of unprecedented prosperity. The other is how close the race was, given Bush's popularity among married voters who live in the suburbs and have children living at home. Bush's long lead throughout much of Campaign 2000 surprised most political observers. From May 1998 (when Gallup first tested a Bush-Gore matchup) until June 2000, Bush beat Al Gore in all thirty-one Gallup trial heats (including a 20-point win in a September 1999 survey).[93] So bleak were the Democratic prospects that throughout 1999, Gore's rival, former New Jersey senator Bill Bradley, benefited from the party's private agony about Gore's prospects.

But several mathematical models developed by political scientists came to a conclusion that was diametrically opposed to that held by the party insiders: a near-certain Gore victory ranging from 51 to 60 percent.[94] These models relied heavily on the public's perception of the state of the economy and presidential approval scores. Using these measures as guideposts, 55 percent were satisfied with the overall direction of the country; and 66 percent rated the economy as "excellent" or "good." Moreover, 53 percent were satisfied with their personal finances, a 4-percent increase from 1996 when Bill Clinton easily defeated Bob Dole.[95] Not surprisingly, 68 percent judged the Clinton presidency a success; only 29 percent deemed it a failure.[96] After the election, one of the equation writers declared, "Needless to say, the election outcome left a bit of egg on the faces of the academic forecasters." Another clung to his model, saying the Bush victory was a "stochastic shock," adding: "The Gore outcome is clearly on the fringe of our known world, the world of post–World War Two elections."[97]

Thus, a riddle: why did George W. Bush beat Al Gore (if only barely in the electoral college and not in the popular vote)? Put another way, why did the election of 2000 so closely resemble that of 1876, when a split decision in the popular and electoral votes also led to a contested result? One common answer offered was "Clinton fatigue." According to one poll, 53 percent said, "I'm just plain tired of Bill Clinton."[98] To these weary voters, George W. Bush was a welcome tonic. A poll taken on the eve of Election Day found 38 percent believing the next president should have as his top priority promoting a restoration of moral and family values, while 31 percent thought the chief executive should maintain economic growth.[99] In short, Bush was perceived as an honest, trustworthy, and strong leader who would not rock the boat.

But it was more than the public's perception of Bush as a likeable leader that worked strongly in his favor. When asked to name "the most important problem facing the country today," a plurality cited education, closely followed by ethics and morals.[100] Bush had an education record in Texas of improved test scores and accountability—a tale he loved to tell. Yet, it was his unstained family name, in contrast to Gore's association with the disgraced Clinton, that gave the Republican nominee a lift. Following the shootings at Columbine High School in April 1999, the decline in the nation's values had emerged as a potent political force. Americans are inherently conservative, and many people's first instinct after the shootings was to bemoan the erosion of family life, the rise of divorce, and the absence of God from the classroom. Richard B. Wirthlin, Ronald Reagan's polltaker, found 59 percent saying that family life was either "not very strong" or "weak and losing ground." The top four reasons given for family decay were: (1) a lack of discipline and respect; (2) greater work demands; (3) failure to teach children moral values; and (4) an increase in the divorce rate.[101] After another brutal school killing in Santee, California, one local television station dropped its regular programming and showed a text message urging parents to turn off the TV and talk to their kids.[102] The culture had finally turned against itself.

The decline of family life was a compelling reason for choosing Bush. By the summer of 2000, 79 percent named values as an issue that would influence their presidential vote, and 51 percent said they were pessimistic about the nation's future moral and ethical standards.[103] When pollsters asked those who believed that the country's moral decline was the most important problem, Bush won by a mile: 68 percent to Gore's 16 percent.[104] Thus, while the political scientists had Gore winning comfortably, they failed to take into account the role values play in our politics. The result of this disparity was an *inverted election*—one in which a virtual incumbent running on peace and prosperity lost thanks to the public's consternation about declining values and the role they should play in the nation's life.

Yet, the very closeness of the election is surprising, given Bush's lead among those who were living the American dream. Married voters backed Bush, as did those with children under the age of eighteen living in the household. Whites also gave Bush strong backing. Finally, those who attended religious services frequently were strong Bush backers.[105] So, why was the election close? Gore got the lion's share of support from those who were single or divorced, first-time voters, young people, minorities, homosexuals, and those who seldom or never attend church services.[106] What many saw as the prototypical family of the 1950s and 1960s had been reduced to minority status. In the early 1970s, three-quarters of all American adults were married; thirty years later that percentage had dropped to just 56 percent. Similarly, in 1972, married couples with children constituted 45 percent of all households; by 1998, that figure had fallen to 26 percent.[107]

Divorce, blended families, and the insertion of cultural issues created a new lifestyle voter who was guided by the "morality writ small" dictum of Alan Wolfe. But these new voters were not evenly distributed across the nation. If you lived in the South, the Great Plains and the West (save for the Pacific rim), you were likely to be on one side of the values divide. This was George W. Bush country. However, if you lived in the Northeast or the Pacific rim states, you were likely to be on the other side of the values divide. This was Al Gore country. The cultural divide was so powerful that Gore lost heretofore Democratic states such as Bill Clinton's Arkansas and West Virginia. Even Gore's native Tennessee backed Bush, a powerful testament to the potency of cultural and values issues.[108] If Gore had carried just one of those states, he would have won. In the topsy-turvy world of Campaign 2000, both Gore and Bush could have hung signs at their headquarters reading, "It's values, stupid!"

Values Matter Most

As the foregoing stories suggest, we are living in an era in which the old rules— certainly the old political ones—no longer apply. Change has become the order of the day. Instant Internet access has altered the definition of "first class" mail and revolutionized the way information is obtained. Little more than a decade ago, the Internet connected approximately 600 computers; by 1999, there were 76 million Internet users, with 1 million new customers logging on to the World Wide Web each month.[109] By making so much information available so quickly, the Internet has altered our definition of "real time." So, too, have instant TV dinners, instant coffee, and express or e-mail, which have created their own high-speed, real-time culture with its emphasis on the latest fad. Patience is no longer a virtue in this fast-paced new world.

Change is also the byword in the workplace. Along with the intrusion of computer technology into most offices has come a lack of job security. The idea of a career spent with one employer has become an antiquated concept. One man recently described how the old values of loyalty were no more:

> My father owned a corporation. . . . His advice to me was, "Look, you work like hell. You get the job done, things will happen to you. . . . When you work for a guy, you give him a day's work and more." That certainly isn't the attitude today. The attitude today is that I get this job and I float—the day I get the job I start floating my resume somewhere else, hoping for a better job. . . . Nobody's looking for a gold watch anymore.[110]

One AT&T worker who found herself suddenly without a job expressed her dismay: "When I was hired for the phone company I thought, 'This is it! I'm going to retire with this company.' Now I don't know what's going to happen tomorrow."[111] Clinton's first-term labor secretary, Robert Reich, worried about the impact of these layoffs on the public psyche. "All the old bargains, it seems, have been breached," he said. "The economic bargain was that if you worked hard and your company prospered, you would share the fruits of success. There was a cultural bargain, too, echoing the same themes of responsibility and its rewards: live by the norms of your community—take care of your family, obey the law, treat your neighbors with respect, love your country—and you'll feel secure in the certainty that everyone else would behave that way."[112] Two-thirds say America was a better place when people had a strong attachment to where they lived and didn't move around so much.[113]

Adding to the uncertainty about life in the workplace has come a sense that other places that were once havens of security are no more. Schools top that list. In 2001, 45 percent of parents with children in grades K–12 said they feared for their child's safety at school; in 1977, the figure was a mere 24 percent.[114] After the shootings at Columbine High School in April 1999, there was a widespread feeling that something precious had been lost. One student who had dodged the bullets said, "I'm scared to go back to school. I can't trust people." Her mother added, "I don't feel safe sending any of my kids to school. This is getting out of hand."[115] While there have been several school shootings, both before the Columbine massacre and afterwards, the Columbine tragedy struck especially close to home. The two white boys, Dylan Klebold and Eric Harris, who committed the crime grew up in relatively prosperous middle-class settings. Their homes were physically nicer than most; divorce had not split their families; and they did not lack for any material goods (one of the killers drove a BMW). In a final videotape, Klebold spoke of his "great parents" who taught him "self-awareness [and] self-reliance."[116] But having "great parents" did not prevent the worst school massacre in history—fifteen dead, including Klebold and Harris, and two dozen wounded. In a videotape made prior to the killings, Eric Harris, quoting Shakespeare, said, "Good wombs hath borne bad sons."[117] But Harris's excuse for his misdeeds did little to quell the queasy feeling that "It *can* happen here."[118]

Columbine, not Clinton's impeachment, became the most remembered event of 1999; 68 percent said they followed the tragedy closely, and 72 percent worried that such a thing could happen to either them or someone they love.[119] Voracious readers could not get enough, and many were tantalized with stories of heroism. When one of the killers asked Rachel Scott if she believed in God, she replied, "There is a God and you need to follow along God's path." The shooter responded, "There is no God," and fatally shot her in the head.[120] Others took to Tom Mauser's crusade for stricter gun controls after his son, Daniel, was murdered. Democrats and Republicans argued over what the tragedy meant. To President Clinton, the answer lay in passing "common-sense gun legislation."[121]

House Republican majority whip Tom DeLay thought the exclusion of religious values from public life was to blame.[122]

Both positions found favor with the public, yet the wrangling missed something that was more deeply felt—namely, that while the country was economically prosperous, its values were headed in the wrong direction. When asked which was more important, strengthening families or increasing job opportunities, 64 percent chose strengthening families; just 35 percent wanted more jobs.[123] Not surprisingly, 71 percent answered "agree strongly" that this country would have many fewer problems "if there were more emphasis on traditional family values."[124] Sensing the public disquiet, George W. Bush and Al Gore cast themselves as values restorers. Bush often told receptive audiences, "The success of America has never been proven by cities of gold, but by citizens of character. Men and women work hard, dream big, love their family, serve their neighbor. Values turn a piece of earth into a neighborhood, a community, a chosen nation."[125] Gore expressed similar sentiments: "The issue is not only our standard of living, but our standards in life. The measure is not merely the value of our possessions, but the values we possess."[126]

Whether in the schools with their "character counts" campaigns or out on the campaign trail itself, values are reshaping the nation's politics in ways that create new divisions in our society and test political parties in ways that they have not been tested before. In a 1995 book, political analyst Ben Wattenberg wrote, "I have come to the conclusion that values issues are no longer merely co-equal with economic concerns. *The values issues are now the most important.*"[127] Democratic pollster Geoff Garin agrees, noting that values have become "the connective tissue of politics."[128]

It is in this "connective tissue" that many Americans see a pervasive problem. While most people in the United States characterize themselves as virtuous citizens, they often feel that their compatriots lack good values. In 1998, CBS News posed a series of hypothetical situations that many of us often confront in the realities of day-to-day life. In each case, respondents indicated that while they would often do the right thing, their fellow citizens faced with the same situation would frequently lie, cheat, or steal (see table 1.1, pp. 38–39).

Because values are internalized in the individual and often involve issues and complex situations that do not lend themselves easily to compromise, political leaders are finding it difficult to solve what the public sees as a pervasive problem. Oklahoma state legislators have recently permitted parents to paddle, spank, and switch their children. Indiana legislators have forbidden teenagers from piercing their navels without parental permission. Louisiana requires teenagers to "sir" and "ma'am" their teachers in school. Mississippi legislators require public schools to display the slogan "In God We Trust" in classrooms, cafeterias, and auditoriums.[129]

But new laws can do little to solve what the public perceives to be a serious

TABLE 1.1 THE VIRTUOUS PUBLIC AND THE "VALUE-LESS" NATION

Situation	"Correct" Values Response for Self	"Value-Less" Response for Self	"Correct" Values Response for Others	"Value-Less" Response for Others
You have friends over and play some music CDs (compact discs) you've been enjoying. Your friends also like the music and ask you to tape copies for them. . . . Assuming you would not get caught, would you be more likely to say sure and make copies of the CDs, or would you be more likely to tell your friends you're uncomfortable with that and refuse?	Tell them you're uncomfortable, 41%.	Say sure and make copies, 51%.	Tell them you're uncomfortable, 12%.	Say sure and make copies, 78%.
You've just spent a relaxing weekend at a hotel far away from home. The bath towels in the room were nice and you decide you would like to have a couple as a souvenir. . . . Assuming you would not get caught, would you be more likely to pack the towels in your bag and say nothing at checkout time, or would you be more likely to call the front desk and ask where you could purchase them?	Call the front desk, 72%.	Pack the towels and say nothing, 11%.	Call the front desk, 22%.	Pack the towels and say nothing, 61%.
At an automated teller machine, you put your card in the machine and ask to withdraw $40. When the money comes out, you find that you have been given $240—an extra $200—and your account has not been debited. . . . Assuming you would not get caught and your account would not be debited, would you be more likely to take the money and not report the incident, or would you be more likely to notify the bank of the mistake?	Notify the bank of the mistake, 84%.	Take the cash and not report the incident, 13%.	Notify the bank of the mistake, 33%.	Take the cash and not report the incident, 55%.

Suppose you have a thirteen-year-old son and he is small for his age. You take him to a movie and the theater offers children's tickets at half-price for children age eleven and under. . . . Assuming you would not get caught, would you be more likely to tell your child not to say anything and buy one adult ticket and one child ticket, or would you be more likely to pay the adult price for both tickets?

| Buy the two adult tickets, 69%. | Say nothing and buy one adult and one child ticket, 28%. | Buy two adult tickets, 21%. | Say nothing and buy one adult and one child ticket. 60%. |

You are a supervisor at work and one of your friends works for you there. This friend and employee is on a six-month disability leave recovering from injuries suffered in a car accident. You go visit her at home and when you arrive you find this "injured" person outside doing heavy yard work. . . . Assuming you would not get caught, would you be more likely to finish the visit and say nothing about the "injury," or would you be more likely to file a report at your company?

| File a report at the company, 39%. | Finish the visit and say nothing, 35%. | File a report at the company, 23%. | Finish the visit and say nothing, 55%. |

Your car is broken into on the street. Only the passenger side window is damaged and nothing is missing. Repairing the broken window will cost $250, but your insurance only covers repairs above $500. . . . Assuming you would not get caught, would you be more likely to tell your insurance company that the car window was not only broken but also that the car contained an expensive CD (compact disc) player and 10 CDs all worth more than $500, or would you be more likely to pay out of your own pocket in accordance with your insurance policy?

| Pay out-of-pocket in accordance with the insurance policy, 92%. | Lie to the insurance company, 5%. | Pay out-of-pocket in accordance with the insurance policy, 44%. | Lie to insurance company. 42%. |

Source: CBS News poll, 20–22 April 1998.

values crisis, since so much of it is internal. Changing presidents, as happened in 2001, is unlikely to make the issue go away. In 1976, Jimmy Carter noted that there was a "moral hunger" in the electorate and promised to restore trust in government by the mere presence of his honesty in the White House.[130] George W. Bush, like Carter, is an honest and trustworthy man. But he is likely to find that public worries about a values decline will not subside simply because he may embody the best of its values. Less than one hundred days into the Bush presidency, more school shootings occurred. The incident at Santana High School in Santee, California, whose graduates include the wife of California's governor, left many shaken. Andy Williams, a fifteen-year-old boy, killed two of his classmates and wounded thirteen others. Williams's guidance counselor said after the shootings, "Andy was a typical adolescent boy." [131] Williams, whose parents are divorced, faces life imprisonment thanks to a proposition approved by 62 percent of Californians which mandates that juveniles as young as fourteen be tried as adults for crimes committed with a gun.

But it was what happened in the aftermath of the shooting that was especially chilling. Forty-eight hours after Williams's arrest, sixteen other California students were arrested or detained for making threats or taking guns to school; in Higley, Arizona, an eleven-year-old boy threatened to kill the girl he liked and the boy who kissed her; and a Pennsylvania eighth-grader at a Catholic high school shot the head cheerleader in the cafeteria. "No one thought I would go through with this," she yelled as she fired her .22 pistol.[132] Ten days after the dead were buried in Santee, an eighteen-year-old armed with a handgun and a shotgun opened fire at the Granite Hills High School in El Cajon, California, wounding four before being shot and wounded by the police.

Just as George W. Bush is finding it difficult to assuage voter concerns about values, neither major political party is likely to have much success with the issue. While one segment of voters may be attracted to one party's position, another is just as likely to be alienated. The remainder of this book examines how voters and the parties are coping (or not) with a values divide that has turned the old rules upside down and left Republicans and Democrats alike bereft of easy answers. This is *the* story for our time.

CHAPTER 2

Whose Country?

It's a complex fate, being an American.
—Henry James, novelist and American expatriate, 1872

AFTER TOURING THE UNITED STATES during the third decade of the nineteenth century, the great French writer Alexis de Tocqueville observed, "I know of no country in which there is so little independence of mind and real freedom of discussion as in America."[1] Today, these words seem extraordinarily out-of-date, as twenty-first century Americans celebrate the values of diversity and tolerance. Seven in ten U.S. residents say that "we should be more tolerant of people who choose to live according to their own moral standards, even if we think they are wrong."[2] Clearly, placing a premium on tolerance seems advisable in an era in which the once-traditional nuclear family has given way to all sorts of blended or otherwise "nontraditional" families. That point was underscored in the 1993 film *Mrs. Doubtfire*, in which Robin Williams portrays a divorced father who masquerades as a matronly woman and hosts a successful children's television program. One day Mrs. Doubtfire receives a tormented letter from a Katie McCormick, whose parents have separated. The child wonders if her brother is right when he says they are not a family anymore. Mrs. Doubtfire reassures the little girl, saying, "There are all sorts of different families, Katie. Some families have one Mommy. Some families have one Daddy, or two families, and some children live with their uncle or aunt. And some live with their grandparents. And some children live with foster parents. Some live in separate homes and separate neighborhoods in different areas of the country. And they may not see each other for days, weeks, months, or even years at a time. But if there's love, dear, those are the ties that bind. And you have a family in your heart forever."[3]

Strangers at the White House

These changes inside our homes have been accompanied by enormous transformations outside them. Our once white, male-dominated culture now gives women a seat at the table of power and has become much more racially and religiously diverse in the process. The cabinet selected by George W. Bush in 2001, for instance, consists of just six white males, two blacks, three women, one Mexican American, and two Asian Americans. Most did not even know the Texas governor before joining his administration. The same is true for Bush's subcabinet and White House personnel appointments, where white males have but 55 percent of the top jobs.[4] Today, when the senior White House staff gathers at 7:30 each morning in the Roosevelt Room, eight of the eighteen attendees are women—a record.[5] This is a stark contrast to the cabinet assembled by Bush's father back in 1989, which had ten white males, two Mexican Americans, one female, and one African American, most long-time friends and acquaintances of the Bush family.

The strangers at the White House are the proverbial tip of an iceberg of change. In many corporate boardrooms, barriers once separating men from women and management from employee are rapidly diminishing. In their best-selling book *Blur: The Speed of Change in the Connected Economy*, Stan Davis and Christopher Meyer describe the profound transformations taking place in the workplace:

> [You see] a meltdown of all traditional boundaries. In a blur world, products and services are merging. Buyers sell and sellers buy. Neat value chains are messy economic webs. Homes are offices. No longer is there a clear line between structure and process, owning and using, knowing and learning, real and virtual. Less and less separates employee and employer. In the world of capital—itself as much a liability as an asset—value moves so fast you can't tell stock from flow. On every front, opposites are blurring.[6]

Even the hegemony of white Anglo-Saxon Protestants is rapidly disappearing. This is an enormous change from the post–World War II era. In 1961, the *Charleston News and Courier* editorialized, "To understand the United States today, it is necessary to know something about the Establishment. Most citizens don't realize it exists. Yet the Establishment makes its influence felt from the President's Cabinet to the professional life of a young college teacher who wants a foundation grant."[7] Writer Richard Rovere noted that the Establishment held effective control over the executive and judicial branches of government, most educational institutions and the intellectuals who inhabited them, organized religion (Fundamentalists and Roman Catholics excepted), and philanthropic foundations. According to Rovere, the Establishment has "very nearly unchallenged power in deciding what is and what is not respectable opinion in this country."[8] The major political parties were often guided by Establishment opinion, frequently pairing an Establishment candidate for president with a non-member on their national tickets. Consider that Franklin D. Roosevelt (Establishment) teamed with Harry S. Truman (non-Establishment); Dwight D.

Eisenhower (Establishment) was conjoined with Richard M. Nixon (non-Establishment); and John F. Kennedy (Establishment) allied himself with Lyndon B. Johnson (non-Establishment) in the infamous Boston Austin axis.[9]

The Death of the Establishment

Not everyone celebrated the Establishment's hegemony. In 1957, the theologian Paul Tillich preached to college audiences, "We hope for nonconformists among you, for your sake, for the sake of the nation, and for the sake of humanity."[10] A decade later, Tillich's prayer had been undeniably answered. Beginning in the 1960s, the hegemony of the Establishment was broken, thanks to an unpopular war in Vietnam and restless baby boomers who questioned the unconditional acceptance of authority along with other Establishment values. The academic year 1969–70 saw 1,800 college demonstrations, with 7,500 arrests, 462 injuries, 247 arsons, and 8 deaths linked to them. During the height of the Vietnam War, President Richard M. Nixon told a cheering crowd at the Pentagon, "You see these bums, you know, blowing up the campuses. Listen, the boys that are on the college campuses today are the luckiest people in the world, going to the greatest universities, and here they are burning up the books, storming around about this issue."[11] Vice President Spiro T. Agnew was equally appalled at the anti-Establishment behavior, denouncing the Students for a Democratic Society as "supercilious sophisticates," adding, "I would swap the whole damn zoo for a single platoon of the kind of young Americans I saw in Vietnam."[12] In a report to Nixon on the causes of the 1970 campus unrest, which resulted in the killing of four students at Kent State, the Scranton Commission (headed by Pennsylvania governor William Scranton, a pillar of the Establishment) described the emergence of a "new youth culture" that rejected "the work ethic, materialism, and conventional social norms and pieties. *Indeed, it rejected all institutional disciplines externally imposed upon the individual, and this set it at odds with much of American society.*"[13]

What the youth culture opposed was the Establishment, whose unquestioned ability to control the social and political discourse was being challenged by the nation's burgeoning college population. Former Beatle Paul McCartney claims that his group's influence extended far beyond the music they created: "I think we set free a lot of people who were blinkered, who were perhaps starting to live life along their parents' authoritarian lines."[14] By the end of the 1960s, the Establishment's unquestioned political preeminence ended with the election of two non-Establishmentarians, Richard Nixon and Spiro Agnew, as president and vice president.[15] Nixon not only railed against those who opposed the Vietnam War, he directed his venom against the Establishment itself, confiding to aides about a growing "rot" within the nation's elites and complaining that the leadership class was "failing the country."[16]

Today, the Protestant Establishment that once had such a powerful impact on George W. Bush's father and grandfather, George H.W. Bush and Prescott Bush, has been reduced to a series of black-and-white photographs that are rapidly gathering dust. Everywhere one looks, the Establishment is under siege. Conservatives, for example, decry the waning WASP presence in secondary school history texts, while works by women, blacks, and Native Americans gain greater prominence. WASPs had long maintained that they were heirs to the European culture. "Have John learn Greek," were the dying instructions given by John J. McCloy, a key foreign policy adviser to the Roosevelt, Truman, and Kennedy administrations, regarding his son's education plans.[17] Today, this sense of cultural inheritance is seriously questioned. During the academic year 1964–65, William Shakespeare, John Milton, Geoffrey Chaucer, John Dryden, Alexander Pope, T.S. Eliot, Samuel Johnson, Matthew Arnold, Jonathan Swift, and John Donne received the greatest number of citations in college catalogues at twenty-five liberal arts colleges. A 1997–98 survey of the same college catalogues found the list had changed: gone were Pope, Eliot, Johnson, Arnold, and Swift.[18] In 1987, conservative scholar Allan Bloom published *The Closing of the American Mind*, a book that deplored a lack of Western values in college classrooms.[19] According to a recent study of seventy universities, only twenty-three require English majors to take a course in Shakespeare. Following the trend, Georgetown University announced in 1996 that courses in Chaucer, Milton, and Shakespeare—once required of all English majors—would henceforth become electives. The American Council of Trustees and Alumni issued a report on the inclination to snub the great books of Western literature, which declared: "It matters to us all if Shakespeare and other great authors are allowed to languish. This country cannot expect a generation raised on gangster films and sex studies to maintain its leadership in the world."[20]

The receding of the once-dominant WASP culture has produced a powerful political backlash. As the number of white Anglo-Saxon Protestants has declined along with their influence, the migration of non-whites to the United States has emerged as a contentious political issue. According to a 2000 Gallup poll, 43 percent of Americans said they would support a law that would stop almost all *legal* immigration to the United States; 55 percent said they were dissatisfied with present immigration levels; and nearly four in ten had a negative view of immigrants.[21] One year later a survey of California residents by John Zogby found that seven years after approving Proposition 187—a measure that banned all state spending on illegal immigrants and required police to report suspected illegals to the state Department of Justice and the U.S. Immigration Service—a plurality believe that there should be a three-year moratorium on legal migration to the state.[22] Pat Buchanan was among the first to recognize the potency of the immigration issue. In his best-selling book, *The Death of the West*, Buchanan warns that "uncontrolled immigration threatens to deconstruct the nation we grew up in and convert America into a conglomeration of peoples with almost nothing in common—not history, heroes, language, culture, faith, or ancestors." According to the former presidential candidate, "Balkanization beckons."[23] The issue remains potent. In 1998, Steve Womack, a lieutenant colonel in the Army National Guard was elected mayor of Rogers, Arkansas. During the 1990s, the town had experienced a 20 percent increase in its Latino population, and with it came a large number of illegal Hispanic immigrants. Womack pledged to get tough on the illegals, telling voters, "If you're coming to America illegally, you don't want to come to Rogers."[24] Two years later officials in Siler City, North Carolina, saw controversy erupt when they invited former Ku Klux Klan leader David Duke to address how they could curb the wave of Mexican immigrants who had moved into their town.[25]

A related issue is a proposal to make English the "official language" of the United States. In 1990, Alabama voters approved by a 7-to-1 margin a proposition making English that state's official language. Under the new law, state officials were required to take "all steps necessary to ensure that the role of English as the common language of the state of Alabama is preserved and enhanced." Twenty-five other states have approved similar laws, buoyed by sentiments like those expressed by one Californian: "We even have to go to the bank, and its says do you want this in English or Spanish? Well, phooey. This is America, you want to live here, you speak the language."[26] In 1995, Republican presidential candidate Bob Dole told a gathering of American Legionnaires: "We must stop the practice of multilingual education as a means of instilling ethnic pride, or as a therapy for low self-esteem, or out of elitist guilt over a culture built on the traditions of the West."[27] But just six years after this speech, a Republican would become the first president to utter a few Spanish words before a joint session of Congress. Pleading for support for his domestic programs, George W. Bush told the lawmakers: "Juntos podemos. [Together we can.]"[28] A few months later, Bush paid tribute to the Mexican holiday, Cinco de Mayo, by becoming the first president to broadcast his weekly radio address in Spanish.[29] In August 2001, the White House website was modified to include Spanish translations of the administration's press briefings, biographies of the president and First Lady, and Bush's radio addresses. As Bush wrote in his campaign autobiography, *A Charge to Keep:* "Those who advocate 'English-only' poke a stick in the eye of people of Hispanic heritage. 'English-only' says me, not you. It says I count, but you do not. This is not the message of America."[30] As Bush implicitly acknowledged, a new multilingual, multicultural country was being born ahead of schedule.

The Future Arrives Ahead of Schedule

In 1990, Martha Sandoval, a Mexican immigrant, failed the Alabama driver's test. She sued, claiming the English examination violated Title VI of the 1964 Civil

Rights Act, which bars discrimination based on race, ethnicity, or national origin. Sandoval claimed that she would have passed the test if it had been given in Spanish, which was forbidden by Alabama's English-only law. The State of Alabama countered by saying that in addition to violating state law, public safety was at issue since road signs are written in English. The case reached the U.S. Supreme Court, and in a controversial 5-to-4 decision written by Justice Antonin Scalia, the Court maintained that private individuals, like Sandoval, could not sue to enforce antidiscrimination provisions contained in the Civil Rights Act. As Scalia wrote, "Having sworn off the habit of venturing beyond Congress's intent, we will not accept respondent's invitation to have one last drink."[31]

The *Sandoval* case is likely to be one of many the Supreme Court will be asked to consider involving the rights of immigrants in the years ahead. Birth figures show that nonwhites are writing a new and significant chapter in the American story. According to the 2000 census, the Hispanic population grew 58 percent from 1990 to 35.3 million.[32] In some places, the demographic shifts are enormous. During the decade from 1990 to 2000, Texas gained 3.8 million residents, 2.3 million of whom were Hispanic. During that same period, Florida saw one million more Hispanics migrate there—a surge that caused the state's Hispanics to outnumber blacks for the first time. Elsewhere, the demographic changes are nothing short of fantastic. In Arizona, for example, the Hispanic population grew by an astounding 80 percent during the past decade.[33] At this rate, former president Bill Clinton will be proved right in his prediction that by 2050, there will be no majority race in America.[34]

Golfer Tiger Woods, whose father is black and mother is Thai, is a noteworthy symbol of the changing times. In 1997, Woods became simultaneously the first African American and the first Asian American to win the Masters tournament. He is not the only American of mixed race to tear down old racial barriers. In 2000, Angela Perez Baraquino, who was the reigning Miss Hawaii, finished ahead of a black woman from Louisiana, a Vietnamese-American contestant from California, and two white women from Mississippi and Kentucky, to be crowned Miss America 2001. In the Bush family, George P. Bush, the son of Florida governor Jeb Bush and his Mexican-born wife, Columba, symbolized the increase of the "little brown ones"—as George H.W. Bush referred to his grandchildren during his 1988 presidential campaign.[35] Addressing the delegates at the 2000 Republican National Convention, George P. extolled his uncle, George W., as "un hombre con grandes sentimientos . . . who really cares about those he was elected to serve, including those of us whose faces look different."[36]

These stories are portents of things to come. In 1998 alone, there were 1.3 million intermarriages among whites, Asians, and Hispanics. Pollster John Zogby describes the advent of what he calls the "Tiger Woods Effect." Back in 1860, Zogby notes, the U.S. Census contained only three racial categories: black, white, and *quadroon*—a term that described someone of mixed heritage who was at least one-fourth black.[37] Virginia's governors started the practice of identifying persons as black who met the "one drop" test.[38] Prejudice was not limited to blacks alone. In 1917, Congress passed a law barring all Asians from entering the United States. Six years later, the U.S. Supreme Court interpreted *white* as meaning a person of European origin. One consequence of this decision was to strip forty-five naturalized Asian Indians of their U.S. citizenship.[39]

By the twenty-first century, things have dramatically changed, thanks to more relaxed immigration laws and new attitudes. In the 2000 census there are nineteen racial categories to choose from—including White, Black, African-American or Negro, American Indian or Alaska Native, Mexican, Mexican-American, Chicano, Puerto Rican, Cuban, Other Spanish/Hispanic/Latino, Asian-Indian, Chinese, Filipino, Japanese, Korean, Vietnamese, Other Asian, Native Hawaiian, Guamanian or Chamorro, Samoan, and Other Pacific Islander. These categories reflect the melding of different racial cultures. Nationwide, 2.4 percent categorized themselves as multiracial, and among children under the age of eighteen, 4.2 percent listed themselves as of mixed race. One respondent, Levonne Gaddy of Tuscon, Arizona, checked the boxes labeled White, African-American, and American Indian on her census form. When asked about her choices, she remarked: "When I see the word 'race,' I cringe, because I don't see there is much connected to the word."[40] In a concession to the blurring of racial and color lines, the San Diego city council adopted a measure in 2001 that bans the word *minority* from all city documents and discussions. Citing the city's divergent racial composition, the council declared that the word *minority* is disparaging.[41]

This new twenty-first-century American nation is much more diverse—and much less white—than its twentieth-century ancestor. The 2000 census found that the number of whites fell from 80.3 percent in 1990 to 75.1 percent. Moreover, the influx of Vietnamese, Cambodian, and other Asian immigrants after the disastrous end to the Vietnam War in 1975, along with the continued increase in Hispanic immigrants in the same quarter-century, means that in the twenty-first century the predominant racial color is going to be neither white nor black, but some form of beige. In 2001, the future arrived ahead of schedule. For the first time since George Washington asked Thomas Jefferson to conduct the first census in 1790, whites are a minority in the Old Colony mecca of Boston. According to Cheng Imm Tann, director of the Mayor's Office of New Bostonians: "In the beginning here, the people of color—the Native Americans—were in the majority. Now the people of color are again the majority. The diversity is amazing."[42] Indeed it is. According to the 2000 census, 297,580 Bostonians listed themselves as minority or multiracial—many hailing from such places as the Caribbean, Asia, or Africa—whereas 291,561 Bostonians defined themselves as white.[43]

Elsewhere the picture is much the same. Whites are the majority in just fifty-two of the nation's one hundred largest cities—down from seventy in 1990. Overall, the nation's largest cities lost more than 2 million whites between 1990 and 2000. But in the twenty fastest-growing cities, the number of blacks rose 23 percent; Asians, 69 percent; and Hispanics, 72 percent.[44] The number of Asian Americans living in the towns dotting the New Jersey Turnpike grew by 93 percent to become that state's fastest growing racial minority.[45] Farther down Interstate 95, in Fairfax County, Virginia, Asian Americans outnumber African Americans.[46] The rise of Hispanics is just as astonishing. Between 1990 and 2000, the U.S. Hispanic population rose 58 percent to 35.3 million—equal to that of blacks for the first time in history.[47] Moreover, the nation's largest cities gained 3.8 million Hispanic residents, a 43 percent increase.[48] For example, the Hispanic population of New Jersey increased 51 percent; in Loudon County, Virginia, one of many suburbs that ring Washington, D.C., the increase was an astounding 368 percent; Chicago gained 208,000 Hispanics; and in Milwaukee County, Wisconsin, the number rose by 84 percent.[49]

The increased Hispanic numbers are reflected in the popular culture. Spanish singers—especially Ricky Martin (Puerto Rican), Gloria Estefan (Cuban), the late Selena (Mexican), and Julio Iglesias (Mexican)—have enjoyed an unprecedented string of hits in the United States. Martin sold 5 million copies of his album, *Livin' La Vida Loca,* to eager audiences of young teenagers. Thanks to Martin—and a host of new Latin artists including Marc Anthony, Enrique Iglesias, and Jennifer Lopez—Latin music sales rose 6.5 million units (an increase of 18 percent) in 1998–99.[50] The success enjoyed by these young music stars is due to the relative youth of the Hispanic population (a median age of 25.9 years compared to 35.3 years for all Americans),[51] and the racially mixed audiences that buy their records.

The consequences of these changing demographics is readily apparent. Unlike those in Alabama, California driver's licenses can be obtained by passing one of thirty tests given in different languages.[52] Across the country, Spanish ballots are increasingly commonplace. In Florida and New York, two states that use bilingual ballots, Spanish is the most frequently spoken language after English, thanks to an influx of Cuban Americans, Puerto Ricans, and immigrants from Central and South America. In New York City, ballots are printed in both Spanish and Chinese, and an influx of Korean immigrants may mean that Korean ballots will be available in time for the 2004 presidential election. And in 2002 there was another first: two Hispanic Democrats competing for their party's gubernatorial nomination in Texas conducted their debates in Spanish.

But what is on the ballots is even more important than the language in which they are printed. For example, 60 percent of Alabama voters who went to the polls in 2000 repealed that portion of their state constitution forbidding interracial marriages—a stunning development in this bastion of the Old Confederacy. Nationwide, 75 percent say marriage between blacks and whites is acceptable; among teenagers, the figure is an all-time high of 91 percent. Four in ten Americans report dating someone of another race, and three in ten say these were "serious relationships."[53] Three-quarters of blacks and two-thirds of Asians and Latinos say it makes no difference which race they marry. Among whites, 53 percent say it makes no difference who someone marries; 46 percent say people should marry someone of their own race.[54] These figures represent a remarkable change of heart. As late as 1948, California legislators made it a criminal offense for blacks and whites to marry. In 1967, Virginia defended its miscegenation law before the U.S. Supreme Court, saying that it had a duty to "preserve the racial integrity of its citizens" and prevent "the corruption of the blood," "a mongrel breed of citizens," and "the obliteration of racial pride." A unanimous Court rejected Virginia's arguments and overturned laws in sixteen states banning interracial marriage.[55]

Still, old attitudes died hard. In 1959, Mildred and Richard Loving violated Virginia's ban on interracial marriage and were sentenced to a year in prison. The trial judge suspended their sentence on the condition that the black-white couple not return to the Old Dominion for twenty-five years. Issuing his judgment, the judge declared: "Almighty God created the races white, black, yellow, malay, and red, and He placed them on separate continents. And but for the interference with his arrangement there would be no cause for such marriages."[56] Most Americans agreed with the sentiments expressed by the Virginia judge. A 1958 Gallup poll found 94 percent disapproving of marriages between whites and "colored people."[57] Ten years later, 53 percent thought there should still be laws against miscegenation.[58] In 1967, the daughter of Secretary of State Dean Rusk, who was once described by Richard Rovere as the "chairman of the Establishment,"[59] was featured on the cover of *Time* magazine because she had defied conventional mores by marrying a black man. The wedding sparked an enormous controversy. White southerners, who supported Rusk's hawkish Vietnam policy, wondered how a native of Cherokee County, Georgia, and the grandson of two Confederate soldiers could have given his only daughter's hand in marriage to a black man. As Rusk's cousin Ernest Stone said, "I think he should've done something about it, not let it get this far. He should've prevented it." One grande dame at the Orlando Country Club in Florida gloated, "It will serve the old goat right to have nigger grandbabies." Black Power activist Lincoln Lynch saw a more sinister motive: "I wonder to what lengths Dean Rusk has to go in order to gain support for his and Johnson's war in Vietnam." Speculation had it that Rusk tendered his resignation when he informed Lyndon Johnson of his daughter's wedding plans. Only Martin Luther King Jr. seemed to view the nuptials as a personal affair. "Individuals marry," said King, "not races."[60] Today the wedding would merit a mere mention on the society pages of the *New York Times* and

Washington Post, and, as David Brooks points out, the emphasis would be on the couple's college degrees and respective career paths.[61]

Changes in skin tone have been accompanied by the growth of new and often non-Christian religious communities, chief among them Muslims, Hindis, and Buddhists. Islam is the eighth largest denomination in the United States—bigger than the Episcopal Church, the Presbyterian Church U.S.A., the United Church of Christ, or the Assemblies of God.[62] Today there are between 1.5 million and 3.4 million Muslims in the United States.[63] Thanks to an influx of immigrants from Iran, Pakistan, Yemen, Lebanon, and Afghanistan, Muslims are quickly assimilating into American life.[64] One recent survey found 78 percent of American Muslims were foreign-born. Their presence has literally changed the landscape, as two thousand mosques and numerous Islamic schools have been built in the past two decades. Moreover, there are an estimated 1,200 interest groups, publishers, and radio stations that cater to largely Muslim audiences.[65] The effect has been to make the Muslim community an increasingly potent force in the cultural and political life of the nation, especially in states rich in electoral votes, such as Michigan.

The presence of so many Muslims raises important social and cultural questions. Recently, a Woodbridge, Virginia, high school student, Theheerah Ahmad, decided to follow her mother's example and cover her hair with a scarf (called a *hijab*) during the Muslim holy month of Ramadan. After consulting with the Islamic Center in Washington, D.C., the school principal decided that Ahmad had violated the dress code, which forbade the wearing of hats or head coverings indoors. Ahmad risked an after-school suspension for each day she wore the scarf. Her case was only one of many to cross the principal's desk—with a student population of 2,700 and dozens of cultures and languages represented, avoiding examinations on holy days, discussing whether international students should pledge allegiance to the U.S. flag, and providing special lunch menus are commonplace cultural concerns. After a flurry of letters between school officials and the girl's parents, Ahmad was allowed to wear her *hijab*. Later, she explained the moral lesson the experience had taught her: "My father just told me to believe in your faith, believe in what is right. I knew from the start how I'm supposed to be wearing my scarf. I know I wasn't wrong. I know my religion."[66]

Like the Muslims, the number of Asian-Indian immigrants has also risen dramatically. The first wave began in the 1960s when thousands of students and professionals emigrated from India to the United States. A decade later they were joined by other, less well-educated family members who took jobs as taxi drivers, clerks, small business operators, and factory workers. During the 1990s there was another boom of Indian immigrants—particularly among students and professionals who had previously studied at the prestigious India Institute of Technology founded by Prime Minister Jawaharlal Nehru in the 1950s. From 1990 to 2000, the number of Asian-Indian immigrants rose from 800,000 to more than

1.6 million. Many of these college-trained immigrants found high-paying jobs in the high-technology industries. Among the most successful are Vinod Khosla, who cofounded Sun Microsystems, and Sabeer Bhatia, who started Hotmail.[67]

In the Information Age towns that dot Southern California, the presence of so many Indians has dramatically changed the landscape. Fremont—once known as a lily-white, blue-collar bedroom community that made Chevrolets and Toyotas—is now home to a variety of Sikhs, Hindus, and other Asians who have taken jobs in the high-technology industry. That change was evident at a recent public meeting, when Hillside Drive was renamed Gurdwara Road in honor of a temple built by the town's Sikh residents, many of whom had previously fled the horrors of Afghanistan's Taliban regime. The name change was not without controversy. One resident protested, saying he could not pronounce Gurdwara; a Sikh countered by saying he could not pronounce Paseo Padre, another major town thoroughfare.[68]

The increase in the Indian population throughout the United States is reflected in many other ways both large and small. During the 1990s, there was a phenomenal rise in the number of Indian-based interest groups, including the American Association of Physicians from India (AAPI) (whose 1995 convention was addressed by President Clinton), the Association of Indians in America (AIA), the Federation of Indian Associations (FIA), the National Federation of Indian American Associations (NFIA), and the National Association of Americans of Asian Indian Descent (NAAAID).[69] More important, perhaps, is the widespread presence of Indian culture. Indian restaurants are popular, and even Hindu temples are much more prevalent than they used to be. Twenty-nine-year-old Rajesh Kempasagara, who arrived in the United States in 1996 and works as a software consultant for EDS Corporation in Virginia, rejoices that he can buy Indian spices at stores near his home. Best of all, he can even find movies in Kannada, his native language.[70]

The number of Buddhists has also sharply increased. Today, there are more than seventy-five forms of Buddhism and 5 million Buddhists scattered across the United States, thanks to increased immigration from Japan, China, and Vietnam.[71] Kathy Jaekles, a twenty-five-year practitioner, says things have changed since her mother converted to Buddhism when she was a teenager: "People are more accepting and tolerant of Buddhists. I feel freer to tell people I'm Buddhist."[72] She is not alone. A 1997 survey of 750 human resource professionals found 68 percent offering flexible schedules for religious observances.[73] The proliferation of non-Christian religions prompted one member of the Colorado State Board of Education to *disagree* with the idea of encouraging public schools to display the motto "In God We Trust" following the Columbine massacre: "We are a much more pluralistic nation than we were at the founding of our nation. In this pluralistic society, we must question the proclamation of one belief to the exclusion of another."[74]

This is not the first time that the United States has faced a profound shift in its demographic, ethnic, and religious composition. From 1841 to 1850, three-quarters of a million Irish Catholics immigrated to the United States following an especially dire potato famine. This was the first real breach in the WASP hegemony. Returning to Hartford in 1869 after eight years of service in Washington, D.C., as secretary of the navy, Gideon Welles found his native city "greatly altered. . . . A new and different people seem to move in the streets. Few, comparatively, are known to me."[75] The Industrial Revolution, which became firmly entrenched following the Civil War, only accelerated the influx of newcomers looking for work. From 1890 to 1930, more than 15 million people left central, eastern, and southern Europe to land on American shores, roughly the same number who had immigrated to the United States from *all* countries from 1820 to 1890.[76] One New England writer spoke of the "conquest of the immigrant," as Catholic and Jewish immigrants challenged that region's dominant Protestant culture.[77] By the second decade of the twentieth century, more Americans, many of them first- or second-generation immigrants, lived in the cities than in the countryside. The transformation of the United States from a homogenous enclave of white Anglo-Saxon Protestants to an ethnic polyglot culture was complete. With it came a profound shift in the way Americans lived, worked, and interacted with one another.

At the beginning of the twenty-first century, a similar transformation is underway. The old industrial order is being rapidly replaced by the Information Age. One sign of the changing times is found in the decline of American labor unions, which were the organizational behemoths of the Industrial Age. In 2000, just 13.5 percent of U.S. workers were union members, the lowest figure since the 1930s.[78] Today, the union label has given way to the nonaffiliated independent entrepreneur. According to pollster Peter D. Hart, 59 percent of Americans report having access to the Internet either at home or at work, and 64 percent say they use the Internet every day.[79]

This new Internet-inspired "death of distance"[80] has altered how Americans work and interact with one another. E-mail has replaced first-class mail as a preferred means of communication. During the Senate impeachment trial of President Clinton, the flood of e-mails sent to Congress rose to as many as *one million* per day.[81] The Information Age, with its plethora of Internet resources and wired computers, has arrived almost like a thief in the night. So dramatic is its expansion that it is almost impossible to track its influence.

The New American Dream

Despite the transformations of the nation's populace, economy, and culture, the behaviors and predispositions of Americans remain remarkably constant. Americans still love their country and believe that they can accomplish almost anything. A recent poll found 91 percent who agreed with the statement, "Being an American is a big part of who I am."[82] Only 11 percent said they would like to emigrate elsewhere, a sharp contrast with one-third of Britons and Germans, and one-fifth of Frenchmen and Canadians, who would prefer living somewhere else.[83] Frenchman Clotaire Rapaille captured this unique aspect of American patriotism: "The inner life of America is not a place—Canada is a place. Maybe the best place in the world. But if you are Canadian and you have a dream, you leave. Why? Because America is not a place. It is a dream."[84]

That dream contains three elements: (1) a celebration of freedom, (2) the enthronement of the individual, and (3) a firm belief in equality of opportunity. Taken together, these values comprise an ideology often referred to as classical liberalism. After visiting the United States in the 1920s, G.K. Chesterton concluded, "America is the only nation in the world that is founded on a creed."[85] At the heart of the American creed is a belief that the individual can shape the future. Throughout history, politicians have paid homage to this uniquely American ideal. As Ronald Reagan once told a television audience, "Think for a moment how special it is to be an American. Can we doubt that only a Divine Providence placed this land, this land of freedom, here as a refuge for all those people in the world who yearn to breathe free?"[86] Bill Clinton echoed similar sentiments: "America is far more than a place. It is an idea, the most powerful idea in the history of nations."[87] Minnesota governor Jesse Ventura, an independent, expanded on the idea of unlimited opportunity in the advice he once gave to a hypothetical college student longing to enter politics:

> I would say to that kid to believe in himself, and—because ultimately, that's who he's going to answer to in the end is himself. And I would tell him to be focused and to believe that this still is truly the United States of America where anything can happen if you have that belief. And I would tell him not to ever quit. Sure, you're not going to win everything, but ultimately, never quit in your desire to be as great as you can possibly be, and to try each and every thing you possibly can in this life.[88]

This uniquely American belief in the Protestant ethic of hard work and the success that derives from it forms an integral part of our national identity. Evangelical Protestant ministers such as Norman Vincent Peale and Robert H. Schuller preach the gospel of "positive thinking" to their faithful flocks.[89] Their messages eerily parody a 1782 essay by Jean de Crevecoeur titled "What Is An American?" In it, Crevecoeur captured sentiments that have been repeated for more than two centuries: "Here the rewards of his industry follow with equal steps the progress of his labour; his labour is founded on the basis of *self-interest*;

can it want a stronger allurement? Wives and children, who before in vain demanded of him a morsel of bread, now, fat and frolicsome, gladly help their father to clear those fields whence exuberant crops are to arise to feed and clothe them all; without any part being claimed by a despotic prince, a rich abbot, or a mighty lord."[90] While Americans have left the farms of the eighteenth century for the World Wide Web of the twenty-first, their penchant for hard work remains undiminished: 77 percent believe that the United States is unique among countries because it offers the opportunity for a poor person to get ahead by working hard, and 76 percent say they are satisfied with their opportunities to get ahead by means of hard work.[91]

Not surprisingly, more Americans are working longer and harder than ever before. A study by the International Labour Organization found that Americans work more than 2,000 hours a year, more than the citizens of any other industrialized country.[92] Upon a recent visit to Princeton University, writer David Brooks was surprised to receive e-mails sent at 1:15 A.M., 2:59 A.M., and 3:23 A.M. When Brooks asked the students when they slept, one senior replied that she went to bed at 2 A.M. only to awaken five hours later. The students were so overworked with classes, study groups, club activities, and exercise that many had to schedule appointments just to chat with their friends. As one said, "I just had an appointment with my best friend at seven this morning."[93]

Things aren't much better for their parents. A report issued by President Clinton's Council of Economic Advisers found a substantial increase in the number of hours parents were employed, thanks to more women working outside the home. The expansion in mothers' paid work, combined with the increase in single-parent households, meant parents had twenty-two fewer hours each week to spend with their children.[94] Henry Pearson, a San Diego risk management specialist, maintains that children are being ignored in this competitive work environment: "I'm gonna get in trouble for [saying] this, but families work when there's a way to make sure that children, particularly until they're ten or eleven or twelve years old, are well cared for, are well directed, and are the prime focus of the family as a social unit. That doesn't happen when both parents work sixty-five hours a week."[95] A few years ago an incident in my personal life illustrated how profound this transformation of family life had become. My late mother was visiting my wife and daughter at our Maryland home. When the clock struck five, Mom wondered where I was. After all, my father had always punctually arrived home by 5 P.M., and dinner was on the table no later than 5:30.[96] When I arrived home a little after seven, she was appalled. Today, 69 percent place a lot of importance in having dinner with their families, but only half claim to have dinner with them almost every night.[97]

Thanks to the introduction of the home computer, cellular phone, and fax machine, more Americans than ever before no longer have the luxury of escaping work. Now their work follows them home where the tools exist to continue being on the job. In 1997, 3.6 million households purchased fax machines, 14 million bought notebook computers, and a whopping 31 million paid for personal computers. A 1998 study found that two-thirds of all households had cell phones and half had pagers. Not all of these purchases were job-related, of course, but many were. One survey found that an estimated 7 million working Americans regularly monitored their business e-mails outside the office.[98] Pollster Peter D. Hart finds 52 percent saying that fax machines, cell phones, and the Internet have given them less free time.[99] One woman describes traveling on a commuter train from her New York City job to her Scarsdale home, all the while using her cell phone to answer business calls. She usually arrives home sometime after 6:15 P.M. Having dinner with the family is no problem, but once the clock strikes 7:30, the dishwasher is started and the children are sent off to bed. Then she retreats to a spare bedroom that doubles as a home office, where she talks on the telephone, sends faxes, and answers e-mails.[100] In her case, as with so many others, the boundaries between home life and work have all but disappeared.

Hard work and the success that often accompanies it have reinforced the American devotion to classical liberalism. Political scientist Louis Hartz once noted that this ideology was particularly well-suited to a prosperous and confident middle class.[101] Indeed, the American devotion to liberalism is so strong that it pervades our language and the way we speak about things that are inherently political. Phrases such as "the American dream" and "the American way of life" are freely used in everyday conversations with hardly any explanation given. The term *American dream* was first coined by historian James Truslow Adams, who was writing about the presidency of John Quincy Adams. The historian noted that the sixth president believed his country stood for opportunity, as "the chance to grow into something bigger and finer, as bigger and finer appealed to him."[102] With the turn of the centuries, little has changed. Growing up in rural Midland, Texas, George W. Bush became familiar with the city's motto posted on a billboard at the edge of town: "The sky's the limit."[103] The sense of having unlimited possibilities is common to most Americans; nearly two-thirds say they have been able to live the American dream, and 71 percent believe it is possible for anyone to achieve it.[104] In 1998, Henry Johnson, a successful middle-class black man from DeKalb County, Georgia, gave a powerful testimonial to the endurance of the American dream: "I think the American dream is alive and well, and I think I could sell the American dream to my kids through myself. This stuff about working hard and being morally sound and the more you give, the more you receive and things will come to you—I think those are all things that are not fantasies. Those things can happen and, through my own experiences, those things have happened. . . . Like I said, I believe in the American dream, I do." Sitting nearby, Johnson's wife told the interviewer, "Wow, that was good; quote him on that."[105]

Today, when people are asked to define the American dream, the most frequent responses involve having a good family life and taking care of one's family (25 percent); the freedom to choose (20 percent); having financial stability and making a good living (19 percent); achieving success and reaching one's goals (16 percent); enjoying life and achieving happiness (16 percent); home ownership (11 percent); and having a good job and being happy with one's work (10 percent).[106] Certainly, having financial wealth is an important part of the American dream, and in the "dot-com" Information Age, Bill Gates is its best-known symbol. Gates has become a modern-day Horatio Alger figure who is almost universally admired for his ingenuity and dedication to hard work.[107] With an estimated net worth of $90 billion, Gates consistently appears on Gallup's "most admired man" list. Two-thirds view Gates favorably, and many see him as the premier business leader of the twentieth century, with an astounding one-third naming him as the greatest business figure of the past thousand years.[108]

As these numbers indicate, Gates's success is generally celebrated, despite the recent attempts by the U.S. government to break up Microsoft. This, too, has much in common with the past. A 1940 *Fortune* magazine survey found that 74 percent rejected the idea that there "should be a law limiting the amount of money an individual is allowed to earn in a year."[109] Throughout history, the American dream has served as a reference point for achieving financial security. During the "me decade" of the 1980s, for example, most saw the American dream in these terms: 61 percent said it meant doing better than one's parents; 79 percent spoke of home ownership; 58 percent said it was starting one's own business; 52 percent said it was rising from being a clerk to company president.[110]

But in the 1990s, there was a shift away from an American dream centered in materialism toward one founded on spiritual and family values, including finding love and attaching a broader meaning to one's existence. A recent survey among young people aged twenty to thirty-nine found two-thirds saying their Number 1 goal in life was to do whatever they wanted. One-fifth hoped to work on behalf of society, and only 6 percent said they wanted to get rich.[111] Jeffrey Meyer, a thirty-year-old software engineer, is one of many Generation Xers who had a premature midlife crisis:

> I'd always grown up knowing that math and sciences were this thing that would provide reason in life, and the idea of humanities and service to the community were absurd. Then I left college and realized there's a lot of materialism that comes along with the engineering field and there has to be a place for emotion.[112]

Determined to find greater meaning to his life, Meyer joined a youth ministry at his local church four years ago and began doing other volunteer work. He currently leads Bible-study classes for high school students and takes them to soup kitchens to volunteer. Now, he says, "I have an extremely rich life in terms of the money I'm making. But there has to be more than those material aspects. A feeling of belonging."[113]

Aware of this redefinition of the American dream, Madison Avenue's Citibank recently dropped its "Why Aren't You a Millionaire Yet?" television slogan in favor of an advertisement celebrating life's simpler pleasures. Advising prospective clients that the surest way to "get rich quick" is to play with your kids, the world's most powerful financial institution now uses the tag line, "There's more to life than money." Likewise, the memorable 1999 Discover brokerage commercial featuring a scruffy tow-truck driver whose day-trading talents earned him enough money to buy his own island is banished from the airwaves. Former labor secretary Robert Reich writes that in the 1990s financial institutions enticed customers by saying, "Come with us and make a bundle." "Now," he says, "people are thinking about saving a little bit more, slowing down, getting a life." Marge Magner, head of Citigroup's consumer businesses, agrees: "Our target customer is not the person who thinks they're going to become a millionaire with the next IPO."[114] And even the well-to-do stockbrokers are asking, "Is this all there is?"

In asking and answering this question, more Americans are making significant lifestyle changes. Richard B. Wirthlin finds that a decade ago the dominant employee value was having a job with good pay and benefits. Today, says the former Reagan pollster, there is an emerging group of workers who see salary and the perks that accompany it as a means to achieve a better balance of work and family life.[115] Since 1995, one-fifth of the workforce has left a stress-filled job for a less stressful one. This often means earning less money but having more time to spend with family. As one woman said, "I'm more discreet [in my spending habits] now, but I really enjoy it."[116] Other companies have decided to avoid losing their employees by creating more spiritually fulfilling work environments. Armed with mottoes such as "Bring Your Soul to Work" and "God is My CEO," several of the nation's most successful businesses believe that they must not only pay their employees well but also give their jobs new meaning. At the Container Store, for example, morale is built through a daily ritual knows as "the huddle." In each of the company's twenty-two stores, employees convene prior to the opening bell and discuss how best to implement a "solutions-based" approach to selling products such as closet organizers and kitchen accessories. The Timberland Company, an outdoor firm based in Stratham, New Hampshire, takes a somewhat different approach: it gives its employees forty paid hours yearly to work in after-school mentoring programs, soup kitchens, or other nonprofit causes. Jeffrey B. Swartz, the company's chief executive officer, explains, "We can be partners with God in the act of creating something from nothing. The marketplace is a marvelous place for advocating ideas. It's not just 'Show me the money.'"[117]

Another sign of the new less materialistic and more family-centered American dream is the phenomenon builders term "co-housing." Co-housers cooperatively manage (and often develop and build) their own small neighborhoods, owning their individual housing units and sharing ownership of a common house where they make decisions by consensus and enjoy neighborhood dinners several nights a week. Today, more than 3,000 people live in fifty co-housing communities, as opposed to none a decade ago.[118]

In their search for community, many Americans yearn for the innocence of their baby boomer childhoods, realizing, of course, that they cannot quite return to that idyllic version of the American dream. Sixty-one percent say finding "true love" in today's hectic society is getting harder to achieve than in the past.[119] While most acknowledge that it may be necessary for mothers to work because the family needs money, 80 percent think families would be better off if Mom could stay home and take care of the house and children.[120] Not surprisingly, there are a few new television programs that seek to recreate the Nelsons and Cleavers for receptive audiences. In the popular comedy *My Wife and Kids*, for example, the husband played by Damon Wayans wants his wife, who works as a stockbroker, to stay home and tend to their children. "*Wife*: You want me barefoot and pregnant? *Husband*: No, you can wear shoes. In fact, the pumps will help you get pregnant." The result is a friendly clash of values in which the ever-reasonable wife laments that all she wants is what her husband already has, a fulfilling career, while the bumbling-but-lovable Dad is reduced to saying, "You're trying to trick me with common sense." The result is a compromise in which the husband stays home and is forced to deal with his children's problems, so that when one child tries to sneak off to school wearing a halter top, hot pants, and high heels, Dad advises, "Put on some flatter shoes and longer pants—and a veil."[121]

Warm-hearted comedies (often called "warmedies") like *My Wife and Kids*, which attempt to update the traditional values of the 1950s for twenty-first century audiences, are a reflection of something more substantial, recasting the American dream from one focused on materialism to one that is more spiritually grounded. While Americans are more prosperous than ever before, most agree that prosperity does not bring them happiness (many think they are happier than Bill Gates, for example). [122] Thus, they are willing to question prosperity's value in an age that seems lacking in spiritual values. Put another way, the table is full, but there remains a feeling of emptiness after the meal.

Redefining the American dream is qualitatively different from frontally challenging it. Ever since the nation's founding, Americans have seldom questioned the idea that life for the next generation will be better than it was for their own. In the late 1950s, researchers Lloyd Free and Hadley Cantril discovered that when respondents were given a picture of a ladder with eleven rungs numbered zero to 10, with 10 representing the best possible life and zero the worst, people often placed themselves toward the lower end of the scale five years earlier and saw themselves headed for its upper reaches five years hence.[123] Americans seem almost genetically optimistic, even during hard times. Once during a period of high unemployment in the 1980s, singer-songwriter Bruce Springsteen asked in a tune entitled "The River," "Is a dream a lie if it don't come true? Or is it something worse . . . ?" But most refuse, both then and now, to confront Springsteen's haunting question, preferring to blame themselves for having failed to live up to expectations. As one 1960s-era mechanic who judged himself a failure said, "I could have been a lot better off but through my own foolishness, I'm not. What causes poverty? Foolishness. When I came out of the service, my wife had saved a few dollars and I had a few bucks. I wanted to have a good time, I'm throwing money away like water. Believe me, had I used my head right, I could have had a house. I don't feel sorry for myself—what happened, happened, you know. Of course you pay for it."[124]

Not surprisingly, devout believers in the "can-do" ideology of American liberalism can all too easily wander into the world of fanaticism. Seeking entrance to the United States during the Red Scare in 1920, Englishman G.K. Chesterton was amused to find himself being asked at the American consulate, "Are you an anarchist?" and "Are you in favor of subverting the government of the United States by force?" To these queries, Chesterton was tempted to answer, "What the devil has that to do with you?" and "I prefer to answer that question at the end of my tour and not the beginning."[125] This tendency to turn ideological devotion into fanaticism is nothing new. As longshoreman-turned-philosopher Eric Hoffer wrote in his book, *The True Believer:* "All mass movements . . . breed fanaticism, enthusiasm, fervent hope, hatred, and intolerance; all of them are capable of releasing a powerful flow of activity in certain departments of life; all of them demand blind faith and single-hearted allegiance."[126] During the Cold War, the term *McCarthyism* was coined to describe the American meandering into the fanatical world of anticommunism. Hundreds of citizens were summoned before Congress to profess their faith in the American ideology and to name names of those who supposedly did not. In 1978, Garry Wills wrote that in the United States one must adopt the American dream "wholeheartedly, proclaim it, prove one's devotion to it."[127]

Wills clearly had in mind the House Committee on Un-American Activities, which existed before World War II and was formally established following the worldwide concern about communist expansionism at the end of the war. For three decades the committee inquired into the public and private lives of suspected communists. Most notable among the committee's many investigations was one led by Congressman Richard M. Nixon in 1948. Nixon doggedly pursued Alger Hiss, a high-level State Department employee and secretary-general of the conference that organized the United Nations in 1945. Hiss had been accused by *Time* magazine writer Whittaker Chambers of being a member of the U.S.

Communist Party. Hiss's denials eventually resulted in his indictment and conviction for perjury. With Hiss in jail, Nixon's career skyrocketed, and by age thirty-nine he had been elected vice president of the United States. But the committee's injudicious blacklisting of other witnesses cast an indelible stain on both. In 1975, the Committee on Un-American Activities was abolished on the grounds that it, too, was un-American.[128]

The Committee on Un-American Activities illustrates the country's rigid enforcement of its political orthodoxy. Daniel Boorstin rhetorically asks, "Who would think of using the word 'un-Italian' or 'un-French' as we use the word un-American?"[129] But the American penchant for conformity stems in part from our ideological hegemony. During the height of the Vietnam War, for instance, nearly one in ten labeled the war's hawkish supporters *or* its dovish detractors "un-American."[130] Long after the Cold War ended, classical liberalism remains credited with toppling communism and spreading democracy on the other side of the Iron Curtain and into the heart of the former Soviet Union itself. As Louis Hartz once observed, "When one's ultimate values are accepted wherever one turns, the absolute language of self-evidence comes easily enough."[131] Indeed, our evangelical advancement of the "American Way of Life" has taken on missionary proportions. In 1630, John Winthrop, the British colonial governor of the Massachusetts Bay Colony, described that Puritan-dominated settlement as "a city on a hill." In the nineteenth century, Herman Melville compared Americans to the biblical tribes of Israel, calling them "the peculiar chosen people, the Israel of our time."[132] Today, the phrase "American exceptionalism" is used to refer to this idea of a nation set apart from all others.[133]

Whose Country?

Over the centuries, Americans have been highly pluralistic, yet their ideological zealotry often places limits on speech. Back in 1938, 97 percent told the Gallup Organization that they believed in "freedom of speech," but only 38 percent said they believed in it to the extent of allowing communists to hold meetings and express their views in their communities.[134] When asked during the 1950s what should be done with members of the U.S. Communist Party in the event of a war with Russia, 22 percent said "put them in internment camps"; 18 percent said "imprison them"; 15 percent wanted to "send them out of the United States, exile them"; 13 percent said "send them to Russia"; another 13 percent wanted to "shoot them, hang them"; 4 percent answered "watch them, make them register"; and a mere 1 percent said, "do nothing, everyone is entitled to freedom of thought."[135] In 1968, Sacvan Bercovitch, a Canadian national who arrived in the United States for an extended stay, was struck by the ideological rigidity he encountered from all ends of the political spectrum:

My first encounter with American consensus was in the late sixties, when I crossed the border into the United States and found myself inside the myth of America. Not of North America, for the myth stopped short of the Canadian and Mexican borders, but of a country that despite its bewildering mix of race and creed, could believe in something called the True America, and could vest that patent fiction with all the moral and emotional appeal of a religious symbol. . . . Here was the Jewish anarchist Paul Goodman berating the Midwest for abandoning the promise; here, the descendant of American slaves, Martin Luther King, denouncing injustice as a violation of the American way; here, an endless debate about national destiny . . . conservatives scavenging for un-Americans, New Left historians recalling the country to its sacred mission.

Nothing in my Canadian background had prepared me for that spectacle. . . . It gave me something of an anthropologist's sense of wonder at the symbol of the tribe. . . . To a Canadian skeptic, a gentile in God's country . . . [here was] a pluralistic, pragmatic people bound together by an ideological consensus.[136]

Despite classical liberalism's emphasis on individualism, conformity has always been part of our culture. In a 1791 report to President George Washington, Treasury secretary Alexander Hamilton proclaimed, "Ideas of a contrariety of interests between the Northern and Southern regions of the Union, are in the main as unfounded as they are *mischievous*."[137] Hamilton's belief that special interests should be muted remains a popular notion. Addressing the Republican National Convention in 1956, Dwight Eisenhower asserted that the Republican Party was "a one-interest party; and that one interest is the interest of every man, woman, and child in America!"[138] Eisenhower won a landslide victory over the hapless Adlai Stevenson. Writing in *The Affluent Society*, John Kenneth Galbraith declared, "In the Communist countries stability of ideas and social purpose is achieved by formal adherence to an officially proclaimed doctrine. In our society a similar stability is enforced far more informally by the conventional wisdom."[139] Even now, when the stakes do not involve nation-building or the country's survival during the Cold War, the desire for conformity and the conventional wisdom that conformity creates still reign. To take but one small example, in the business world powerful men are expected to don a red power tie and gray or black suit. One notable deviation occurred when Al Gore wore a blue tie, instead of the obligatory red one, during the second presidential debate in 2000. Women, too, are expected to be conservative in both dress and appearance. Virtually everyone says that their spouse, friends, and what the people at work wear are the strongest influences on how they dress.[140]

But it is in the expression of our values that the desire for hegemony is greatest. Eight decades ago a conference on immigrant education maintained that the nation's schools bore a heavy responsibility for ensuring the longevity of the

American creed: "We believe in an Americanization which has for its end the making of good American citizens by developing in the mind of everyone who inhabits American soil an appreciation of the principles and practices of good American citizenship."[141] In 1987, the American Federation of Teachers reaffirmed this view, urging educators to abandon a "morally neutral" approach to teaching and assert that "democracy is the worthiest form of human government ever conceived."[142] Most Americans agree. A 1996 National Opinion Research Center (NORC) poll found majorities wanting classroom history lessons to include the following themes:

- "With hard work and perseverance, anyone can succeed in America." (83 percent)
- "American democracy is only as strong as the virtue of its citizens." (83 percent)
- "America's contribution is one of expanding freedom for more and more people." (71 percent)
- "From its start, America had a destiny to set an example for other nations." (65 percent)
- "Our nation was founded on Biblical principles." (58 percent)
- "America has a special place in God's plan for history." (50 percent)[143]

Even as our values have remained constant, Americans continuously seek to broaden the meaning of Thomas Jefferson's memorable phrase in the Declaration of Independence that government has a solemn obligation to protect an individual's inherent right to "life, liberty, and the pursuit of happiness." The Civil War redefined Jefferson's words, as the Thirteenth, Fourteenth, and Fifteenth Amendments were ratified ending slavery, extending the Bill of Rights to the states, and giving blacks political franchise. Today, the changing nature of family and the broadening of the American ideology to include its many forms has sparked an intense debate. Two-thirds of respondents to a 1992 poll said that "a decline in people's moral values" severely threatens the American dream, and 54 percent cited a change in the traditional family structure as a direct threat to their conception of that dream.[144] During the height of the Clinton-Lewinsky scandal, 69 percent said that their fellow countrymen had become "too tolerant and accepting of behaviors that in the past were considered immoral or wrong," and 55 percent maintained that groups holding similar values to theirs were losing influence.[145] As he began his term of office, 40 percent thought it was more important for George W. Bush to concentrate on restoring moral and family values; just 37 percent thought maintaining economic growth should be a priority.[146] Richard Easton Jr., a twenty-eight-year-old shipping clerk in Turner's Falls, Massachusetts, expresses the sentiments of many: "Our values are in very, very poor shape and society is dropping at a dramatic rate."[147]

Signs of a values shift are all around us. In 1999, the Miss America Pageant changed its rules to allow contestants who had been previously married or had an abortion.[148] This reversed the pageant's fifty-year-old tradition, which equated beauty with virginity. Officials declared that the change was necessary to prevent a discrimination lawsuit. Nonetheless, a major controversy ensued. Libby Taylor, president of the National Association of Miss America State Pageants, declared, "Miss America has a long history of high moral standards, and I'm opposed to anything that changes that." Leonard Horn, a former general counsel and chief executive officer of the Miss America Pageant, argued that the new rule would "ultimately lead to the destruction of the Miss America program." According to Horn, premarital sex, abortion, and divorce are "acceptable in today's society, but no one could argue that an unwanted pregnancy or an abortion is an ideal. A failed marriage is not an ideal. It's acceptable, and it happens, but it's not an ideal."[149] Leanza Cornett, Miss America 1993, agreed: "There are still little girls out there who have held Miss America and others like her up on a pedestal. When you're sitting around the dinner table with your daughter or your little niece, it'll bring up so many questions." The controversy subsided when the pageant's executive director was dismissed and the governing board agreed to explore "possible alternatives that ensure we are compliant with applicable law and consistent with the traditional values associated with Miss America."[150]

Yet, when Bert Parks's replacement sings the old standard, "There she is, Miss America; there she is, your ideal," the notion of what is ideal is no longer a universally acknowledged truth. Even as the Miss America Pageant tries to remain faithful to its past, premarital sex, births to single mothers, abortion, and divorce are no longer taboo. Nearly two out of three Americans believe that sex before marriage is acceptable; back in 1969, only one in five thought so.[151] Moreover, 52 percent find it morally acceptable for an unmarried man and woman to live together; 57 percent say out-of-wedlock childbearing is permissible;[152] 51 percent find abortion okay;[153] and 59 percent say a divorce is morally acceptable.[154] Of course, some sexual situations remain "not-sa-postas": 72 percent think that a married person having an affair is intolerable, and 53 percent say the same about homosexual relations.[155]

Nowhere are changing sexual attitudes more apparent than when it comes to the institution of marriage. According to the 2000 census, for the first time in U.S. history the number of Americans living alone surpassed that of those who were married with children.[156] Moreover, the number of households with married couples having children eighteen years of age or younger dropped from 45 percent in 1960 to 23.5 percent in 2000, a record low.[157] One reason for this precipitous decline is that during the 1990s one-third of all babies were born to unmarried women, compared to just 3.8 percent in 1940.[158] Also noteworthy is the doubling of unmarried partners from 3.2 million in 1990 to 5.4 million in 2000.[159] The 2000 census also found a 700-percent increase in the number of gay households.[160]

According to Andrew J. Cherlin, a Johns Hopkins University sociology professor: "Americans at all adult ages prefer to live alone. They like to be near their families, but not with them. It expresses American individualism."[161]

While television's mythical Nelsons, Cleavers, and Huxtables are no longer a majority, among the remaining married couples traditional notions about marriage are rapidly diminishing. Today only 51 percent believe marriage will be desirable for future couples; 43 percent say it will be less desirable. While older Americans are more enthusiastic about marriage (56 percent say the institution will be more desirable in the future), younger Americans are decidedly less so; among those aged eighteen to twenty-nine, 62 percent said that marriage will be less desirable in the future.[162] This generation gap reflects a values gap. Older Americans are profoundly influenced by the traditional values transmitted by their parents and represented in television programs such as *The Adventures of Ozzie and Harriet*, *Leave It to Beaver*, and *The Miss America Pageant*. But younger Americans have grown up in an era in which divorce is the norm, single parenthood is not something to be ashamed of, and couples living together without the benefit of marriage are commonplace. Forty-seven percent of those aged twenty to thirty-nine find having a child before marriage to be perfectly acceptable.[163] The television program *Three's Company*, which formed part of their childhood, featured John Ritter sharing an apartment with two women. The *Ozzie and Harriet* and *Leave It to Beaver* worlds of the 1950s and 1960s have been relegated to cable's Nickelodeon channel, while some of today's television stars, including Rosie O'Donnell and Calista Flockhart, glamorize unwed motherhood. Louis Hartz's 1955 assertion that the United States is a land of ideological and cultural homogeneity now seems quaint indeed.

Changing sexual attitudes have prompted numerous controversies over how classical liberal values should be applied in today's society. Southern Baptists, for example, recently lost one of their most high-profile members, Jimmy Carter, over just this issue. Carter cut his ties with the organization after struggling with what he called the "increasingly rigid" creed of the nation's largest Protestant denomination. Baptists are told that wives should "submit graciously" to their husbands, and homosexuality remains a sin in the eyes of the church. Carter disagreed with these pronouncements, saying: "I personally feel the Bible says all people are equal in the eyes of God. I personally feel that women should play an absolutely equal role in the service of Christ in the church." Leaving was not without pain and loss, as Carter explained: "For me, being a Southern Baptist has always been like being an American. I just never thought of making a change. My father and his father were deacons and Sunday school teachers. It's something that's just like breathing for us." But the president of the Southern Baptist Convention bid Carter good riddance: "With all due respect to the president, he is a theological moderate. We are not a theologically moderate convention."[164] Evangelist Pat Robertson sides with the conservative Baptists: "Either we will return to the moral integrity and original dreams of the founders of this nation . . . or we will give ourselves over more and more to hedonism, to all forms of destructive anti-social behavior, to political apathy, and ultimately to the forces of anarchy and disintegration that have throughout history gripped great empires and nations in their tragic and declining years."[165]

Defining what it means to be an American is subject to considerable and varied interpretation. Just as Jimmy Carter linked his religious beliefs with Americanism, a California video store owner who was prosecuted for violating that state's pornography laws connected his Americanism to liberty: "I feel like I'm fighting for our rights as Americans." Each side in the culture wars is fighting a battle that gives very different answers to the question, "What does it mean to be an American?" One faction emphasizes duty and morality; another stresses individual rights and self-fulfillment. The result is a values divide. As one activist put it, "This is a war of ideology, it's a war of ideas, it's a war about our way of life. And it has to be fought with the same intensity, I think, and dedication as you would fight a shooting war."[166]

The values divide has created its own political lexicon. Liberals routinely label their orthodox counterparts "right-wing zealots," "religious nuts," "fanatics," "extremists," "moral zealots," "fear brokers," "militants," "demagogues," "homophobes," "latter-day Cotton Mathers," or "patriots of paranoia." They maintain that their opponents are "anti-intellectual and simplistic," with a message that is "vicious," "cynical," "narrow," "divisive," and "irrational." While serving as president of Yale University, the late A. Bartlett Giamatti once told the freshman class that the religious right is "angry at change, rigid in the application of chauvinistic slogans, absolutist in morality, [and threatens] through political pressure or public denunciation whoever dares to disagree with their authoritarian positions."[167] Giamatti felt certain that his Yale freshmen would find a more enlightened answer to the question, "What does it mean to be an American?"

Newly formed liberal organizations have sought to promote their interpretation of freedom, individualism, and equality of opportunity. The National Organization for Women (NOW) advocates greater economic and cultural freedoms for women: "We believe that a true partnership between the sexes *demands a different concept of marriage*, an equitable sharing of the responsibilities of home and children and of the economic burdens of their support."[168] The People for the American Way likewise sees itself as promoting an authentic Americanism: "In Congress and state capitals, in classrooms and in libraries, in courthouses and houses of worship, on the airwaves and on the printed page, on sidewalks and in cyberspace, we work to promote full citizen participation in our democracy and safeguard the principles of our Constitution from those who threaten the American dream. Join us in defending the values our country was founded on: pluralism, individuality, and freedom of thought, expression, and religion."[169]

Those who belong to the NOW and People for the American Way, like many others who espouse liberal causes, extol the new freedoms individuals have to make choices in their personal lives. When asked by pollster John Zogby whether there are "absolute moral truths that govern our lives," those who classified themselves as "progressives" or "very liberal" were evenly divided: 48 percent agreed, 46 percent disagreed. Those who were "very conservative" were much more emphatic: 74 percent said there are absolute truths; only 25 percent disagreed.[170]

As these poll numbers indicate, the values divide between liberals and conservatives over lifestyle issues has become a chasm. Jen Morgan, a conservative Christian from San Diego, worried that the messages conveyed by the popular culture represent a wholesale attack on the biblical truism that two-parent families work best: "Society wants us to think that two women are just as qualified to raise children, or two men are just as qualified to raise children. All of the . . . wrong morals that go along with that sort of a lifestyle and . . . because of that, the whole definition of the family is changing. . . . It all is breaking the family down, because God wanted it to be man and woman raising a family. He must have had a reason for that."[171]

Back in 1992, Dan Quayle drew attention to this issue by criticizing the fictional "Murphy Brown." In the television program of that name, Brown, a television newscaster played by the forty-something Candice Bergen, has an out-of-wedlock baby. Quayle claimed the program mocked "the importance of fathers by bearing a child alone and calling it just another lifestyle choice."[172] Liberals saw Quayle's speech as a diversionary tactic, given the straitened economic circumstances and the race riots in Los Angeles plaguing the Bush-Quayle reelection effort. Rather than criticizing Brown, they believed the television character was preaching a lesson about tolerance in a postmodern age. Like *Murphy Brown*, many of today's most-watched television programs—including *Seinfeld*, *Friends*, *Will and Grace*, *Ally McBeal*, and *Temptation Island*—share an underlying assumption that the human intimacy usually associated with the standard heterosexual married couple is no longer possible.[173] Roland Jaffe, director of MTV's popular program *Undressed*, describes his show's premise: "I wanted to create a forum where people had a sort of unrestricted access to the politics of desire. A world where no aspect of sexuality would be approached as either immoral or frightening."[174]

The ratings success of *Survivor* is especially revealing. The first installment of the program, in which the contestants competed and voted one another off the show, garnered an audience of 75 million. But there was a Grand Canyon–like generation gap in its demographics: 47 percent of those aged eighteen to twenty-nine saw the show, as compared to 40 percent of those aged thirty to forty-nine; 35 percent of fifty to sixty-four year-olds; and 21 percent of those sixty-five or older who also watched it.[175] The predominance of younger viewers may be indicative of a general acceptance of the tentative and momentary relationships that are reshaping American life in the twenty-first century.

In attacking *Murphy Brown*, Dan Quayle promised to renew the Republican Party's commitment to "our Judeo-Christian values," including "family, hard work, integrity, and personal responsibility."[176] But the ferocity of the opposition to Quayle and his conservative allies made it sound as though Quayle's opponents were against love, marriage, and traditional families. Sociologist Alan Wolfe writes that many liberals see "traditional neighborhoods as hostile to excluded racial minorities, traditional religiosity as intolerant of non-believers, and traditional families as oppressive to women and homosexuals."[177] Clearly, the rigid conformity of the mythical Nelsons, Andersons, Cleavers, and Huxtables is stifling to them, even as they preach conformity to their interpretation of classical liberal values. Television programs such as *The Adventures of Ozzie and Harriet, Father Knows Best, Leave It to Beaver, The Cosby Show*, and others of the same genre are viewed by many Americans as an unreal, hypocritical, and unrecognizable depiction of how children and adults relate. The images of women staying at home, of children unquestioningly obeying their parents, and the relative prosperity of these suburban neighborhoods are unrecognizable in an era when women work, children question parents, and families of all types live next door. Conservatives, on the other hand, wax nostalgic about a time when families stayed together, children obeyed their parents, and everyone believed in God.

The conservative backlash has become institutionalized in groups such as Christian Voice, the Moral Majority, the Coalition for Traditional Values, Americans United for Life, Focus on the Family, and the Family Research Council. Members of these interest groups often believe that those who disagree with them are against Christianity, morality, traditional values, and even life itself. One fundamentalist publication declares, "'Tolerance,' as the word is commonly used (or abused) today, usually means that we should 'tolerate' evil, 'tolerate' sin, 'tolerate' apostasy, 'tolerate' treason. . . . Under the cloak of 'TOLERANCE' and 'DEMOCRACY,' anti-Christian and anti-American propagandists are undermining the very foundation upon which this great republic was built." In his book *Slouching Towards Gomorrah*, Robert Bork describes a popular culture in a "free-fall with the bottom not yet in sight."[178] According to the conservative jurist, "What America increasingly produces and distributes is now propaganda for every perversion and obscenity imaginable. If many of us accept the assumptions on which that is based, and apparently many do, then we are well on our way to an obscene culture. This is what the liberal view of human nature has brought us to."[179] In 1996, Bob Dole likened liberals to the post–Cold War equivalent of political subversives: "It's as though our government, our institutions, and our culture have been hijacked by liberals and are careening dangerously off course."[180] James Dobson, head of Focus on the Family, agrees: "We are in a civil war of values and the prize to the victim is the next generation—our children and grand-children."[181]

These arguments have struck a chord. *Slouching Towards Gomorrah* was a *New York Times* best-seller when it was published in 1996. Bork's thesis won him even more followers during the Clinton-Lewinsky affair: 66 percent said they worried that the United States "will become too tolerant of behaviors that are bad for society."[182] Alice May Pugh, the Democratic mayor of Dillonville, Ohio, saw the Clinton scandals as part of a larger societal problem: "So many young people seem to have no values. And a lot of the people who are leading have no morals. I'm more or less disgusted with the whole political situation and I'm very dis-gusted with all the media attention to the wrong issues." Patrice Weston, a schoolteacher from Hudson, North Carolina, agreed: "I feel that nowadays no one stands up for things they would have stood up for twenty years ago. You will be berated if you do."[183]

Nowhere are the cultural differences greater than they are between those who attend church frequently (whatever their denomination) and those who go less regularly or not at all. This gap between the "churched" and the "less churched" has contributed to the passions behind the debate about the country's values. Without a doubt, the United States is a very religious country. More than 90 per-cent believe in God; 85 percent view the Bible as the actual or inspired word of God; and 52 percent have an unfavorable view of atheists.[184] Back in 1958, 83 per-cent told the Gallup Organization that the "ideal president of the United States" would be someone who attended church regularly.[185] And most Americans con-tinue to pay homage to religion: 72 percent believe that religious groups should be permitted to use public school grounds to hold their after-school meetings; 66 percent favor daily prayer in public classrooms; and 80 percent want prayers said at high school commencements.[186] Running for the U.S. Senate in 1998, Arkansas Democrat Blanche Lincoln touted her "personal relationship with Jesus Christ," which began in college when she became a member of Billy Graham's Campus Crusade for Christ. At a church gathering, Lincoln addressed her "brothers and sisters in Christ," saying, "When I talk to Him, it's pretty informal. I just lay it all out there, say it like it is."[187] Lincoln won easily, with 55 percent of the vote. Two years later, George W. Bush roused audiences by proposing a greater gov-ernment role in assisting faith-based social programs, and 72 percent said that the discussion of religion and God in the presidential campaign had been good for the country.[188]

But since the 1960s there has been a substantial increase in those who do not attend church. In 1963, 49 percent told the Gallup Organization they attended church regularly; 27 percent were occasional churchgoers; 4 percent seldom at-tended; and 19 percent did not go to a church at all.[189] According to the latest Gallup data, 42 percent claim to attend church "at least once a week" or "almost every week," while 57 percent say they go to religious services "about once a month," "seldom," or "never,"[190] The result has been a diminution of the moral authority religious institutions once wielded. In 1988, three-quarters believed that a person can be a good Christian or Jew *without* attending a church or synagogue.[191] Twelve years later an astonishing 58 percent agreed with the statement: "It is *not* necessary to believe in God in order to be moral and have good values."[192] Finally, 53 percent believe it is possible to improve the nation's moral values without placing more emphasis on religion.[193]

As the number of churchgoers decreases, those who remain in their pews are even more devoted to their religious beliefs. Jen Morgan, the fundamentalist San Diego Christian, is angry that those who are less religious have such influence in educational and cultural institutions. Speaking of atheists, Morgan says, "They are winning. We don't say 'Merry Christmas' anymore in the public school. We say 'Happy Holiday' because Christmas denotes God, denotes Jesus. There are a lot of Roman Catholics in the schools. There are a lot of Protestants. They still believe in God. . . . But here comes along people who are atheists and who are only a certain portion of the population, and they are the ones being heard." Across the other side of the values divide, Patricia Bates of DeKalb County, Georgia, counters: "The Scripture says 'Only my Father can judge which is heaven.' All of you are playing God here. Get a mirror. Are you that great? If everybody would step back and look at themselves, take a mirrored look at themselves and then ask, 'What is my purpose? Where do I fit [in] this puzzle?,' then we'd be much better off."[194]

Unlike the early twentieth century, when many Americans battled against an influx of members of other religious groups (especially newly arrived Catholic and Jewish immigrants), today's religious controversies are with the religious institutions themselves. Those who belong to an organized religion often find answers to today's problems in God's revealed truth. The less-churched question God and seek answers from within themselves. Today there are more Americans than ever before who do *not* find answers to life's difficulties in the practice of any religious faith. The Gallup Organization has compiled an index of leading religious indicators, which measures the importance Americans place on religion, weekly church or synagogue attendance, confidence in religious institutions, and belief in God. In 1941, the index stood at 730; today it reads 673.[195] The result is a growing values gap between those who are "churched" and the increasing number of "less-churched" Americans. According to a survey conducted by the *Washington Post* and the Henry J. Kaiser Family Foundation, of those who agreed that the federal government should take steps to protect the nation's religious heritage, 64 percent said religion was very important in their life. Likewise, of those who agreed with the proposition that there should be a high degree of separation between church and state, 84 percent said religion was not important at all to them.[196]

TABLE 2.1 THE GENERATION GAP REVISITED (IN PERCENTAGES)

Age Group	Statement A: Governed by Strict Code of Morality	Statement B: Governed by Common Sense
Under 35 years	40	45
36–55 years	52	38
56–65 years	54	32
Over 65	54	32

Source: Dick Morris, *Vote.com* (New York: Renaissance Books, 1999), 78–79.

A similar division occurs between those who are highly educated and those who lack college exposure. When Americans are asked if they pray in the hope of receiving some reward, 44 percent of high school graduates (a plurality) said yes; 52 percent of college graduates disagreed.[197] College graduates and the ever-larger numbers of those obtaining graduate degrees subscribe to what sociologist Daniel Bell once called "the antinomian self," that is, the belief that individuals, not institutions, are the ultimate source of moral judgment. This phenomenon has been aided by the fact that academic institutions have historically been critical of society. As Joseph Schumpeter once noted, academicians revel in criticism, particularly "criticism that stings."[198] In the Information Age, the adversary culture of academia has become a powerful force simply because there are more ivory towers.

A generation gap is also present, with seniors more likely to be churchgoers and believers in moralistic truths, while younger voters are likely to be less religious and adopt a "live and let live" attitude toward life. Former Clinton pollster Dick Morris once asked respondents to choose between two propositions: Statement A said, "I believe in a strict code of morality and right and wrong which comes from God's word and the Bible. I try to live by it. Drugs and illicit sex are wrong, so I don't engage in them. To do so would violate my personal, moral, and religious beliefs." Statement B presented a very different values construct: "My conduct is governed more by common sense and practicality than by abstract morality. It is more factors like the dangers of AIDS, the possibility of pregnancy, and the importance of a good marriage than morality or religion that stops me from illicit sex. The bad experiences people have had with drugs and the way I have seen it mess up lives is the reason I abstain from them, not some moral judgment that drugs are wrong." When Morris asked, "Which statement comes closest to your view?" a generation gap appeared (see table 2.1).

In a country that is increasingly diverse and tolerant, there is a also a greater sense of discomfiture as different lifestyles, and the individual outlooks that prompt them, gain greater acceptance. The question that plagues virtually all contemporary political debate, "Whose country is it anyway?" divides Americans by their religious beliefs, age, race, ethnicity, and region. It is a debate destined to transform American politics.

The Private Public

Some years ago the novelist Henry James exclaimed, "It's a complex fate, being an American."[199] Today, the complexities of citizenship have become magnified, as issues once considered private are transformed into legal and political ones. As society becomes more multiracial, Americans must answer questions about marriage and family, placing their responses in the context, "What does it mean to be an American?" Heather Tarleton, the twenty-one-year-old daughter of a racially mixed couple, was asked many years ago by a young playmate, "If your mother is black and your father is white, is this a legitimate family?" Heather's mother says the answer has become clear: "Now that we're seeing that there are more interracial families and more people with multiracial heritage, I think it's going to be reflected in some of the institutions we have."[200] Heather's mom has it exactly right. Just as the question of miscegenation so troubled Americans at the time of Dean Rusk's daughter's wedding and forced society to confront Martin Luther King's plea that the American way is to judge people on their character rather than their color, the proliferation of so many different family forms forces institutions and individuals to answer a centuries-old question, "What does it mean to be an American?"

The answers are not always easily found. Connecticut Supreme Court chief justice Robert J. Callahan describes how changing societal conceptions of what constitutes a family have racked both his courtroom and his conscience:

> One of the things that will be a big issue, certainly within the next twenty years is the question, "What is a family?" What will be the definition of a nuclear family? Family issues involving homosexuals will certainly involve complicated legal issues in the years ahead. Also, there will be legal complications involving new methods of conception. There are now surrogate mothers. This can contribute to legal complications. We had a case of a couple who employed a surrogate mother. After fourteen years of marriage the couple decided to divorce. The father claimed it was his child, and not his wife's because a surrogate mother gave birth to the child. What do you do in an instance like this? Nobody ever thought of these issues and their legal aspects, but there will be more of them in the future.[201]

In this new and complicated environment, defining what it means to be an American, and reclaiming the country in its name, is both an intensely personal and a deeply political concern. During the 1960s, a popular phrase often heard was "the personal is political." Back then, women's rights advocates and civil rights leaders maintained that gender and race were not merely private affairs. Deciding when to marry and when not to, when to have sex and when not, when to work and when to be a stay-at-home mom, and whether blacks could enter the nation's prestigious universities or its voting booths were political controversies that were eventually resolved by politicians. As questions about race and sex became public, the federal government vastly expanded its reach. In 1961, John F. Kennedy signed an executive order creating the President's Commission on the Status of Women.[202] Days before his death, Kennedy attached his name to another order establishing an Interdepartmental Committee on the Status of Women that would "further the effort to achieve the full participation of women in American life."[203] After Kennedy's assassination, Lyndon B. Johnson moved aggressively to enact his Great Society programs. According to Johnson, the Great Society was more than a matter of mere economics: "[In the Great Society] the demands of morality and the needs of the spirit can be realized in the life of the nation."[204] To uplift the nation's morality and spirit, Johnson sought passage of the Civil Rights Act of 1964 and the Voting Rights Act of 1965, which forbade racial and gender bias and allowed blacks access to the polls. Johnson's program of moral and spiritual renewal had strong public backing until the Vietnam War ruined his presidency.

As baby boomers adopted the slogan "Question Authority" and experimented with drugs and sex, conventional notions of liberalism and conservatism were revamped. Instead of using traditional economic formulations, a new values construct equated liberalism with moral permissiveness and conservatism with traditional family values. Not surprisingly, most Americans preferred the conservative construct. In 1968, Richard M. Nixon and George C. Wallace exploited the theme of "law and order" with considerable success. Nixon won the presidency, reversing the Johnson landslide of 1964. Running as a third-party candidate, Wallace received 13.5 percent of the vote, thanks in part to his taunting of the anti-Establishment youth: "You young people seem to know a lot of four-letter words. But I have two four-letter words you don't know: S-O-A-P and W-O-R-K."[205]

The successes of Nixon and Wallace notwithstanding, the extension of political discussion into areas once deemed off-limits has expanded the range of political conflict rather than limited it. It is an alarming trend. In *The Semi-Sovereign People*, E.E. Schattschneider wrote, "The best point at which to manage conflict is before it starts."[206] Political scientists like Schattschneider often put a premium on conflict management and exalted political parties for their ability to define and restrain it. Today, the rules of political warfare have been both expanded and upended. Jean Bethke Elshtain describes an emerging "politics of displacement," which, in her words, has "two trajectories": "In the first, everything private—from one's sexual practices to blaming one's parents for a lack of 'self-esteem' becomes grist for the public mill. In the second, everything public—from the grounds on which politicians are judged to health policies to gun regulations—is itself privatized, the playing out of a psychodrama on a grand scale. That is, we fret as much about a politician's affairs as his foreign policy."[207]

Such an expansion of the scope of conflict comes at a time when those who remain politically active see their involvement as a series of political crusades. During the fifty-year history of the Cold War, the United States was placed on a constant state of war-readiness that transformed our political dialogue. In 1952, during a particularly ominous moment in U.S.–Soviet relations, Republican Dwight D. Eisenhower declared that his campaign would transcend traditional politics and be a "*a great crusade*—for freedom in America and freedom in the world."[208] Today, the search for new enemies following the successful conclusion of the Cold War has resulted in new political crusades. Neoconservative intellectual Irving Kristol is one of the crusaders:

> There is no "after the Cold War" for me. So far from having ended, my cold war has increased in intensity, as sector after sector of American life has been ruthlessly corrupted by the liberal ethos. It is an ethos that aims simultaneously at political and social collectivism on the one hand, and moral anarchy on the other. . . . Now that the other "Cold War" is over, the real cold war has begun. We are far less prepared for this cold war, far more vulnerable to our enemy, than was the case with our victorious war against a global communist threat. We are, I sometimes feel, starting from ground zero, and it is a conflict I shall be passing on to my children and grandchildren. But it is a far more interesting cold war— intellectually interesting, spiritually interesting—than the cold war we have recently won, and I rather envy those young enough for the opportunities they will have to participate in it.[209]

The initial response to the culture wars has been to recoil from changes that challenge conventional thinking. By a 3-to-1 margin, Americans describe themselves as having "traditional, old-fashioned values" as opposed to "modern values."[210] A 1998 survey conducted by the *Washington Post* and the Henry J. Kaiser Family Foundation found plenty of values divisions but a public predisposed to conservative responses when asked about cultural matters (see table 2.2, p. 74).

The conservative responses to this poll, coming as they did in the midst of Bill Clinton's impeachment, suggest a country profoundly uncomfortable with the values divide that besets it. Though Americans profess to be tolerant, they frequently prefer conformity in the expression of conventional values and mores. As the personal becomes political, politics becomes an object of hatred because what was essentially private is no more. This does not mean Americans are uncaring. They may not espouse the gay rights cause, for example, but they have lots of compassion for Matthew Shepard (the gay man who was beaten to death in Wyoming) and for the friend or next-door neighbor who is gay. Congressman

TABLE 2.2   A CONSERVATIVE NATION

Text of question: "Now here are some values that everyone agrees are important. But sometimes we have to choose between each of the following two values. Which is more important to you, personally?"

Values Choice	Conservative Response	Liberal Response
"Being tough on criminals, or protesting the rights of those accused of crime?"	Tough on criminals, 76%	Rights of accused, 17%
"Guaranteeing law and order in society, or guaranteeing individual freedom?"	Law and order, 56%	Individual freedom, 34%
"Working for the rights of women, or preserving traditional family values?"	Traditional family values, 60%	Working for women's rights, 31%
"Defending the community's standards of right and wrong, or protecting the rights of individuals to live by their own moral standards?"	Defend community standards, 55%	Protect individual rights, 39%
"Encouraging a belief in God, or encouraging a modern scientific outlook?"	Belief in God, 76%	Scientific outlook, 5%

Source: Washington Post/Henry J. Kaiser Family Foundation poll, 10–27 August 1998.

Barney Frank, who is openly homosexual, says George W. Bush is unlikely to rescind Bill Clinton's "don't ask, don't tell" executive order covering gays in the military or propose additional hate-crimes legislation. (In fact, he has done neither.) But, says Frank, Republicans are faced with a growing dilemma because "so many people have acknowledged being gay and lesbian to their families." According to Frank, the values shift means that "You're not just beating up on gays and lesbian kids, you're beating up on all their relatives. That's why there has been a real change of opinion."[211]

Alexis de Tocqueville once hypothesized that "as the circle of public society is extended, it may be anticipated that the sphere of private intercourse will be contracted."[212] The early twenty-first century has proven the wisdom of Tocqueville's remark. The threads that bind people together seem tenuous and in danger of fraying. What happens to society at large seems of little concern. In such a climate, Wilson Carey McWilliams argues that George W. Bush's compassionate conservatism may wish everyone well, but it contains no great imperative to help those who need it.[213] Todd Gitlin writes that most Americans live in a "twilight of common dreams," thereby creating an overwhelming need to reconstruct the frayed linkages between private and public lives.[214] Such a reconstruction is unlikely to happen anytime soon. In 1998, Czech president Vaclav Havel described two faces of life that enervated Czech society. His words are equally applicable to the U.S. situation:

> The first face consists of the things people do: they go to work, with varying degrees of success, they engage in business, they marry or they divorce, they have children or remain childless, they associate in various ways, they go on holidays abroad, they read books or watch television and, if they're younger than most of us, they go dancing in discotheques. All things considered, I think our everyday life is incomparably better and richer now than it was in times when almost everyone was afraid to say aloud what he or she really thought.
>
> The life of our society, however, has another face, which we might describe as the relationship of citizens to their state, to the social system, to the climate of public life, to politics. It is our primary responsibility to concern ourselves with this second face, to try to understand why it is so gloomy, and to think about ways to brighten it up—at least a little.[215]

In the brightest face of American life—people's personal lives—most Americans have found some measure of happiness. In 1998, 86 percent told the Gallup Organization that they were satisfied with the way things were going in their personal life.[216] This number was remarkably consistent among all age groups, races, regions, sexes, and income levels. In fact, since Gallup first began asking the question in 1979, three-quarters have consistently responded that they like the way things are going in their personal lives.[217] This figure has remained steady, even when Americans have been profoundly dissatisfied with their government. Recall that in 1979 inflation and unemployment were high, hostages were being held in Iran, and Jimmy Carter was widely regarded as one in a series of presidential failures.

The discontent with politics also remains constant, even though Americans rate two of Carter's successors, Ronald Reagan and Bill Clinton, as success stories. Today, when pollsters probe about facets of life beyond the home front, many say they are less than satisfied. Richard B. Wirthlin finds that while 67 percent are "very committed" to their employers, only 38 percent say the employer returns the same feeling in kind.[218] Likewise, when asked about politics and government, the gap between home life and politics widens into a chasm. This is especially evident in a series of polls conducted by Louis Harris. As tables 2.3 and 2.4 (pp. 76–77) indicate, Havel's two faces of life are juxtaposed in the alienation of citizens from their government versus the positive feelings they have about themselves, with the lone and notable exception of the negative assessment of the values held by other Americans. Although alienation from government has decreased and warm fuzzy feelings about one's self have increased since 1997, the dichotomy between these two faces remains highly visible.

TABLE 2.3   THE HARRIS ALIENATION INDEX, 1997–2000 (IN PERCENTAGES)

Issue	2000	1999	1998	1997
"The rich get richer and the poor get poorer."	69	74	72	78
"What you think doesn't count very much any more."	56	68	60	63
"Most people with power try to take advantage of people like yourself."	59	60	58	69
"The people running the country don't really care what happens to you."	53	62	54	57
"You're left out of things going on around you."	39	46	33	43
Harris Alienation Index*	55	62	56	62

TABLE 2.4   THE HARRIS FEEL GOOD INDEX, 1997–2000 (IN PERCENTAGES)

Issue	2000	1999	1998	1997
"Do you feel good about your relations with your family or not?"	95	96	97	95
"Do you feel good about your home or not?"	93	92	93	92
"Do you feel good about the quality of your life overall or not?"	91	94	95	91
"Do you feel good about your health or not?"	88	90	89	88
"Do you feel good about your social life or not?"	86	86	87	86
"Do you feel good about your standard of living or not?"	85	87	90	83
"Do you feel good about the city, town, or county in which you live or not?"	82	85	82	79

TABLE 2.4 (CONTINUED)

Issue	2000	1999	1998	1997
"Do you feel good about the morals and values of people in your community or not?"	69	70	70	65
"Do you feel good about the quality of the air, water, and environment where you live and work or not?"	69	69	68	61
"Do you feel good about the nation's economy or not?"	68	68	64	40
"Do you feel good about your financial security for the future or not?"	65	61	67	55
"Do you feel good about your children's future or not?"	63	60	65	48
"Do you feel good about your job, if you have one, or not?"	63	65	67	60
"Do you feel good about your marriage, if you are married, or not?"	60	64	60	60
"Do you feel good about the state of the nation or not?"	58	63	59	52
"Do you feel good about the values of Americans in general or not?"	39	36	42	34
Harris Feel Good Index*	73	74	75	68

Source: *The Polling Report,* 11 March 2001.
*Mean of affirmative responses to the questions listed above.

One reason for this bifurcation is the emergence of values issues that have created a new "politics of rights." In her book, *Rights Talk*, Mary Ann Glendon describes how this rights politics has led to an impoverishment of political discourse: "Discourse about rights has become the principal language that we use in public settings to discuss weighty questions of right and wrong, but time and again it proves inadequate, or leads to a standoff of one right against another."[219] By transforming values politics into rights politics, America has become a nation that is both tolerant of new family lifestyles and uncomfortable with adapting old values to these new circumstances. One reason for the distinction between the personal value of tolerance and an inability to apply the same value to public problems derives from the fact that how values are taught is a highly individualistic enterprise. Listen to Peter Hamilton of Brookline, Massachusetts: "I've never believed that one can explicitly teach values. Values are something you learn through induction. It's more that you absorb them as you go along by observing others and how they react to situations and what's the right thing to do."[220] But as a values-based politics become an ever-larger part of the national discourse, the result has been, as Tocqueville reminds us, to contract the circle of private life and expand the public circle. As the next chapters illustrate, this expansion of the public circle has been fraught with problems for Republicans and Democrats alike.

CHAPTER 3

Republicans and
the Politics of Virtue

This is the death of libertarianism.
　　　　　　　　　　—Marshall Wittman, former
Christian Coalition Director of Legislative Affairs, 2001

IN HIS 1888 BOOK entitled *The American Commonwealth*, James Bryce devoted more than two hundred pages to the subject of American political parties. His treatment of them was unusually laudatory: "Parties are inevitable. No free large country has been without them. No one has shown how representative government could be worked without them. They bring order out of chaos to a multitude of voters."[1] As the newly created discipline of political science matured during the twentieth century, party scholars became staunch defenders of the two-party system. In 1950, the American Political Science Association published a report from its own Committee on Political Parties that declared, "Throughout this report political parties are treated as indispensable instruments of government."[2] In the fifty years that followed publication of *Toward a More Responsible Two-Party System*, most political scientists unfailingly agreed with the assumption that party success and governing achievements went hand-in-hand.[3] The Committee for Party Renewal, a bipartisan organization founded by the indefatigable political scientist and historian James MacGregor Burns in 1976, likewise declared, "Without parties there can be no organized and coherent politics. When politics lacks coherence, there can be no accountable democracy."[4]

But what is often left out of these pro-party discussions is that the two major parties have endured because they advocate different values that are equally dear to all citizens. Democrats frequently preach from the gospels of *equality* and a public longing for *community*, and they unfailingly find receptive audiences. Among those who went to the polls in 2000, 78 percent said they would be more likely to support a presidential candidate who said, "I believe in an America that offers opportunity for all, demands responsibility from all, and fosters a community of all, with a government that equips all Americans with the tools they need for economic success."[5] Alexis de Tocqueville once declared that if given the choice between freedom and equality of opportunity, most would choose the latter. The reason, Tocqueville believed, was that freedom can always be taken away, but equality was a permanent condition.[6] Though Tocqueville wrote about nineteenth-century Americans, his words still have resonance. G.K. Chesterton noted that what separated the United States from England was the American commitment to a democratic theory based on the idea of equality: "It is the pure classic conception that no man must aspire to be anything more than a citizen, and that no man should endure anything less." The ideal citizen, said Chesterton, was someone who believed in "an absolute of morals by which all men have a value invariable and indestructible and a dignity as intangible as death."[7]

A decade after Chesterton's departure from the United States, Franklin D. Roosevelt became the first in a string of Democratic presidents who were forceful champions for equal opportunity and the greater sense of community that resulted from it. In 1936, Roosevelt proposed amending the Constitution to allow the federal government to act in the best interests of "the family and the home."[8] Five years later in his "Four Freedoms" speech, Roosevelt maintained that in a world beset by aggression and tyranny, "this is no time for any of us to stop thinking about the social and economic problems which are the root cause of the social revolution which is today a supreme factor in the world." The foundations for a healthy and strong democracy, Roosevelt argued, were "equality of opportunity for youth and for others; jobs for those who can work; security for those who need it; the ending of special privilege for the few; the preservation of civil liberties for all; [and] the enjoyment of the fruits of scientific progress in a wider and constantly rising standard of living."[9] Twenty-four years later, Lyndon B. Johnson told graduates at Howard University, "Freedom is the right to share, share fully and equally, in American society—to vote, to hold a job, to enter a public place, to go to school. It is the right to be treated in every part of our national life as a person equal in dignity and promise to all others."[10] Taken together, Democratic presidents from Roosevelt to Clinton helped expand the concept of equality of opportunity to include more Americans than ever before, even the descendants of slaves. Seeking the presidency in 1964, Johnson told attendants at a Louisiana fundraiser that he would fight for equality and community and would not, as so many other southern Democrats had before him, bait audiences with cries of "Negro, Negro, Negro!"[11] Raising his huge arms, Johnson pleaded for civil rights, and his campaign rally was transformed into a revival meeting when one large black man leapt to his feet and shouted, "Knock yourself out, L-B Baby! Knock yourself out!"[12]

In making their case, Democrats have frequently compared the United States to a large family, with each region, race, and citizen bound to the others by fraternal ties. At the 1996 Democratic National Convention, Hillary Rodham Clinton maintained that "we are all part of one family, the American family, and each one of us has value."[13] In her best-selling book, *It Takes A Village*, the First Lady declared that each citizen is "responsible for deciding whether our children are raised in a nation that doesn't just espouse family values but values families and children."[14] This declaration implied that there was plenty of room for federal action designed to protect the national family. For her part, Clinton named teachers, clergy, business people, community leaders, doctors, police officers, *and the president* as essential actors in raising a "happy, healthy, and hopeful child."[15] The First Lady believed that the best presidents were activist village-builders like her husband, Bill Clinton. Historian Arthur M. Schlesinger Jr. maintains that there are cycles to American history when public longing for equality and community paves the way for such activist presidents.[16] In the twentieth century, that often meant Democrats. By eloquently espousing the values of equal opportunity and community, the Democratic Party became fully ingratiated with the American psyche, and its longevity, whatever electoral setbacks may await it in the future, is undoubtedly assured.

Like the Democrats, Republicans espouse values of freedom and self-reliance, which are also deeply cherished by nearly all citizens. Eulogizing Henry Clay, Abraham Lincoln pronounced him a patriot who "loved his country partly because it was his own country, but mostly because it was a free country."[17] But it was in the aftermath of the New Deal that Republicans became vigorous proponents of the virtues of freedom, individualism, and self-reliance. Campaigning for the presidency in 1936, Alf Landon assailed the "folly" of Franklin Roosevelt's New Deal and denounced the "vast multitude of new offices" and the "centralized bureaucracy" from which "swarms of inspectors" swooped over the countryside "to harass our people." Landon's tone was urgent, since he believed Roosevelt's New Deal posed a clear and present danger to liberty: "America is in peril. The welfare of American men and women and the future of our youth are at stake. We dedicate ourselves to the preservation of their political liberty, their individual opportunity, and their character as free citizens, which for the first time are threatened by government itself."[18] Using language conservatives would often later emulate, Landon attacked the centerpiece of the New Deal, Social Security, with these words: "Imagine the vast army of clerks which will be necessary to keep these records. Another army of field investigators will be necessary to check up on the people whose records are not clear, or regarding whom current information is not coming in. And so bureaucracy will grow and grow, and Federal snooping will flourish."[19]

As he campaigned, Landon's bill of particulars grew to include presidential usurpation of the powers of Congress, Roosevelt's flaunting of the integrity and authority of the Supreme Court, and his high-handed reinterpretation of the Constitution by appropriating rights heretofore reserved to the states and the people under the Tenth Amendment.[20] Landon promised that his own restrained and prudent management of the federal bureaucracy would result in an outpouring of freedom by a simple adherence to the following dictum: "I want the Secretary of the Treasury to be obliged to say to committees of Congress every time a new appropriation is proposed, 'Gentlemen, you will have to provide some new taxes if you do this.'"[21]

Seeking the presidency sixty years later, Landon's fellow Kansan, Bob Dole, preached from the same gospel of self-reliance. Introducing himself to the electorate, Dole alluded to his service in World War II, in which a crippling injury left his right arm useless. Dole's story of being wounded in Italy featured many heroes: the soldier who saved him from certain death; the two medics who died trying to reach him; the small Kansas town that rallied to his side and raised money to help with his medical care; and Dole himself, in the starring role as the determined veteran who endured punishing exercises in a futile attempt to make his arm whole. Although he would never fully recover, Dole literally willed himself back to life, even learning to write with his left hand.[22] The moral lessons drawn from the values of individual self-reliance, faith in small-town virtues, and a belief in the inherent goodness in each person also marked Dole's service in Congress: as a congressman, Dole was one of twelve House members to oppose Medicare, while in the Senate, he voted against the Family and Medical Leave Act (once previously vetoed by George H.W. Bush) and the Clinton health care plan (which many Republicans likened to socialism). In each instance, Dole thought these bills were needless government intrusions that conflicted with sacred Republican values.

Evoking Landon, Dole campaigned for the presidency in 1996 by promising to restore the Tenth Amendment: "Where possible, I want to give power back to the states and back to the people."[23] In keeping with the spirit of the Tenth Amendment, the Republican nominee vowed to eliminate the departments of Housing and Urban Development, Commerce, Education, and Energy, and to "de-fund" other federal agencies, including the National Endowment for the Humanities, the Corporation for Public Broadcasting, and the Legal Services Corporation. Deficits bothered Dole, and like Landon he believed that shrinking government was not only sound fiscal policy but also would have the salutary effect of restoring the values of individualism and self-reliance to their rightful places in American life.[24] Dole especially took issue with Hillary Rodham Clinton's assertion that community efforts, rather than individual enterprise alone, were needed to raise successful families:

After the virtual devastation of the American family, the rock upon which this country was founded, we are told that it takes a village, that is, the collective, and thus, the state, to raise a child. The state is now more involved than it has ever been in the raising of children, and children are now more neglected, abused, and more mistreated than they have been in our time. This is not a coincidence. And, with all due respect, I am here to tell you, it does not take a village to raise a child. It takes a *family* to raise a child."[25]

Landon and Dole's warnings of an encroaching federal establishment have deep roots in the public psyche. Long before Landon and Dole entered politics, many Americans feared that an all-too-intrusive federal government could take away their freedoms. During the debates over the ratification of the U.S. Constitution, the Anti-Federalists exploited fears that in a large republic the people "will have no confidence in their legislature, suspect them of ambitious views, be jealous of every measure they adopt, and will not support the laws they pass."[26] Historian Ralph Ketcham captured the essence of the Anti-Federalist sentiments: "Anti-Federalists saw mild, grassroots, small-scale government in sharp contrast to the splendid edifice and overweening ambitions implicit in the new Constitution. . . . The first left citizens free to live their own lives and to cultivate the virtue (private and public) vital to republicanism, while the second soon entailed taxes and drafts and offices and wars damaging to human dignity and thus fatal to self-government."[27]

The 1936 Republican platform, drafted by the Landon forces, had much in common with the Anti-Federalists. In making their pitch for a weak federal establishment, Republicans expressed their "inalterable conviction that, in the future as in the past, the fate of the nation will depend, not so much on the wisdom and power of government, as on the character and virtue, self-reliance, industry, and thrift of the people and on their willingness to meet the responsibilities essential to the preservation of a free society."[28] In painting this vision of a virtuous small-town America, Landon embraced Thomas Jefferson as progenitor of the Republican Party's determination "to establish the rights and institutions of free men upon this continent."[29] Ronald Reagan had a similar vision, seeing the United States as a series of diverse communities, each one different and independent. His 1984 "Morning in America" television commercial was a paean to small-town values. In it, a bride hugged her mother while an elderly man and a police officer hoisted an American flag as a group of bright-eyed youngsters pledged allegiance to it. Seeking the presidency in 1988, George H.W. Bush evoked a similar picture of small-town life by likening the United States to "a brilliant diversity spread like stars; like a thousand points of light in a broad and peaceful sky."[30] As president, Bush established the nonprofit Points of Light Foundation, which encouraged individuals and communities to redouble their volunteer efforts.

Individualism and self-reliance have deep roots in the United States. In 1832, Alexis de Tocqueville observed that most Americans had "acquired or retained sufficient education and fortune to satisfy their own wants." According to Tocqueville, these Americans "owe nothing to any man, they expect nothing from any man, they acquire the habit of always considering themselves as *standing alone*, and they are apt to imagine that their whole destiny is in their own hands."[31] Nearly a century later, Supreme Court justice Louis Brandeis asserted that the U.S. Constitution conferred upon each citizen "the right to be let alone—the most comprehensive of rights and the right most valued by civilized men."[32] Seeking the presidency in 1980, Ronald Reagan evoked Brandeis by promising to take "government off the backs of the great people of this country" and turning its citizens "loose again to do those things that I know you can do so well."[33]

For Republicans, the ancient Roman concept of *civitas* means that each citizen, as opposed to government, is responsible for improving civic life. Ronald Reagan found his *civitas* in the "thousands answering Peace Corps appeals to help boost food production in Africa, to millions volunteering time, to corporations adopting schools, and communities pulling together to help the neediest at home." George W. Bush's notion of *civitas* is intertwined with his Christian faith, as his faith-based initiative seeks individuals with strong religious commitments (a testament to their character) who want to help others. While each of these Republican presidents' notion of *civitas* has a somewhat different emphasis, individualism and self-reliance are at the core of the concept for all of them. These values appeal to party loyalists. In 1992, Republican identifiers were asked to explain why they rooted for the GOP: 33 percent mentioned cutting government spending and lowering taxes; 25 percent said it was their party's commitment to private enterprise rather than big government to solve people's problems; 21 percent cited its promotion of conservative moral values; and 13 percent said it was the Republicans' historic Cold War commitment to a strong national defense.[34]

The combined 58 percent who acknowledged their party's belief in smaller government and individual enterprise as reasons for backing Republican candidates is a reflection of important values that are cherished by virtually all citizens regardless of their party affiliation. The same can be said of the Democratic Party's espousal of equality of opportunity and community. These twin values were at work in the space race declared by President John F. Kennedy in 1961. Democrats prized the sense of community the race to the moon offered, as scientists gathered under government auspices to tackle the unique problems posed by such a challenge. The National Aeronautics and Space Administration (NASA) became the primary government agency engaged in solving these problems and, in the process, created a spirit of teamwork. For their part, Republicans lauded the heroism and individual enterprise of the astronauts. Both of these values were emphasized in the movie *Apollo 13*, a film that recounted that flight's ill-fated mission and the heroism and teamwork required to ensure a safe return of the crew. Americans liked the movie in part because they could applaud both of these complimentary values at work. But at other times, Americans are asked to choose between individualism and equality, and in such moments they find the choice difficult. For example, when asked in 1999 whether society should encourage self-reliance or more emphasis should be placed on those in need, the public was closely divided: 41 percent chose self-reliance; 44 percent, those in need.[35]

This evenly divided populace reflects the close competition that presently exists between a Republican Party that espouses self-reliance and a Democratic Party that stresses equality of opportunity. If the Republican Party were suddenly to disappear, it would have to be reinvented because the values of individualism and self-reliance are so deeply ingrained in the public psyche. Such a reinvention may yet have to take place, as key elements of the post–Reagan era Republican Party seem hell-bent on destroying the party's libertarian antecedents in the name of values.

The Death of Libertarianism?

In stressing the values of individualism and self-reliance, the Republican Party has, since its inception, espoused its belief in the virtuous citizen. In 1936, Alf Landon saluted the Republican delegates who nominated him as "living proof that there are men and women able enough and brave enough to see the facts of our national problems *and to meet them in the American way.*"[36] Former *New York Times* columnist Tom Wicker's interesting take on Richard M. Nixon is that he became "one of us," as Americans saw in him "their own sentimental patriotism and confidence in national virtue, their professed love of God and family, their theological belief that hard work would pay off, their desire to get ahead and live well, their preference for action over reflection, . . . and their vocal if not always practiced devotion to freedom and democracy."[37]

But it was Ronald Reagan who elevated the practice of referring to the virtuous citizenry into an art form. Delivering his annual State of the Union addresses before Congress, Reagan began the tradition of naming heroes who had been strategically placed in the House gallery. In 1982, for example, the Great Communicator hailed Lenny Skutnik, the government employee who had rescued several drowning passengers from an airplane that had crashed into the Potomac River. Two years later he lauded Sergeant Stephen Trujillo, an Army medic who had risked his life saving the wounded in Grenada. In 1985, Reagan praised Jean Nguyen, a Vietnamese refugee who had graduated with honors from West Point, and Mother Hale, a Harlem resident who cared for drug-addicted infants.[38] To Reagan, their stories were parables with a common theme: "For us, faith, work, family, neighborhood, freedom, and peace are not just words; they're expressions of what America means, definitions of what makes us a good and loving people."[39] Such evocations of homespun values proved so successful that Bill Clinton emulated Reagan's technique, pointing to his own heroes sitting in the House gallery during State of the Union addresses.

Closely related to the idea of the virtuous citizen is the notion of a virtuous party that nominates candidates of outstanding individual character. Alexander Hamilton once argued that the intricate design of the electoral college would insure that future presidents would be known for their "ability and virtue."[40] Though Hamilton's objective of establishing a civic-minded presidency was thwarted by the development of political parties, his idea that character counts in choosing presidents was preeminent during the dark days of the Cold War. In 1964, Lyndon Johnson's supporters insinuated that Barry Goldwater had psychiatric problems. Among the many groups supporting Johnson's candidacy was one called Psychiatrists for Johnson.[41] Johnson asked a worried electorate whether they wanted Goldwater's seemingly itchy finger on the nuclear trigger. My parents, both of whom were ardent Democrats, had instinctively opposed other Republican presidential candidates, but they were truly frightened of Goldwater. Their fear was heightened by the famous "daisy spot" commercial, which showed a little girl picking a daisy as a nuclear bomb exploded. At the end of the thirty-second spot, Johnson's disembodied voice says: "These are the stakes. To make a world in which all of God's children can live—or to go into the dark. We must either love each other, or we must die." This advertisement became the most remembered political commercial in history. Goldwater himself said he had been so demonized by the Democrats that he would have voted for Johnson had he not known the opposing candidate so well.[42]

Barry Goldwater's supporters countered by extolling their candidate's virtue as a representative of the larger citizenry. In 1964, political scientist Aaron Wildavsky wrote that Goldwater's nomination had awakened moralistic strains long dormant in American political life. Interviewing Goldwater delegates at the 1964 Republican National Convention, Wildavsky was overwhelmed by their passion and their willingness to sacrifice victory for their single-minded adherence to conservative principles. One delegate, asked if the primary qualification of a candidate should be an ability to win votes, replied: "No; principles are more important. I would rather be one against 20,000 and believe I was right. That's what I admire about Goldwater. He's like that."[43] Wildavsky claimed that the Goldwaterites' devout anticommunism and their hatred of big government (with the noteworthy exception of the Defense Department) created a new moralism within the Grand Old Party.[44]

The political successes Republicans have enjoyed since Goldwater's 1964 defeat—especially the collapse of communism—have enhanced the moral absolutism that currently threatens to tear the party apart. Throughout the Cold War, Republicans were able to stick together thanks to the willingness of the party's elites to tolerate the new moralists by conceding the *words* of politics to them while the elites controlled the *policy*. Now that bargain is in danger of being breached, as GOP moralists desire a greater voice in shaping policies that reflect their own values and will, they believe, help alleviate the poverty of values they see all around them. Their moral absolutism dates back to the emphasis the Anti-Federalists and their Republican successors placed on the gospel of self-reliance. In extolling the individual, all Republicans attach great importance to local civic virtue. Individuals, because they are of sound character, can do the work Democrats often ascribe to government, or so the GOP argument goes. Such appeals to a virtuous republic continue to be a staple of the party's rhetoric.

But by the late 1980s, the Republican view of the virtuous citizen began to wane. Seeking the presidency in 1988, televangelist Pat Robertson decried the "secular humanism" that was rapidly corrupting the nation's moral climate. Instead of speaking optimistically about human nature, Robertson saw Satan rampant. Unlike Ronald Reagan's happy world of suburban communities populated by upright citizens, Robertson's world was more sinister and turbulent. The Christian evangelist believed that it was twilight in America, evoking in apocalyptic language the "unmistakable scent of the Antichrist spirit . . . [which] spreads like a disease." In this sin-filled America, "honor, decency, honesty, self-control, sexual restraint, family values, and sacrifice are replaced by gluttony, sensuality, bizarre sex, cruelty, profligacy, dishonesty, fraud, waste, debauched currency, rampant inflation, delinquency, drunkenness, and drug-induced euphoria."[45]

Over time, a view developed among Republican evangelicals that politics was a battle between good and evil. Ralph Reed, executive director of the Christian Coalition, threatened to withdraw his support for the Republican ticket in 1996 unless its presidential and vice-presidential candidates opposed abortion. The Texas delegation signed a pledge promising to support an antiabortion plank and oppose any prospective vice-presidential candidate who was not pro-life. Those who refused to sign were sent home by the state party. One of the prospective delegates who packed his bags said of the pro-lifers, "These people don't understand and don't care about traditional politics."[46] Meanwhile, Bob Dole argued in vain for a plank in the Republican platform that preached tolerance on the abortion issue. Dole's staff found an innocuous line in the 1980 Republican platform that read, "We recognize that members of our party have deeply held and sometimes differing views on issues of personal conscience." Dole believed that his party could hardly reject the insertion of a plank Ronald Reagan himself had once approved. He was wrong. Right-to-Lifers maintained that abortion could not be "tolerated." GOP platform chairman and ardent pro-life activist Henry Hyde threatened to quit. Dole acknowledged defeat, and his faith in virtuous citizens to make sound decisions on abortion was rejected by Republican delegates who handed him a stinging rebuke on the eve of his nomination. Fed up, Dole claimed that he did not have time to read the platform and that, in any event, he did not feel honor bound by it.[47]

Four years later, John McCain lambasted Pat Robertson, Jerry Falwell, and the Christian Coalition for having "lost confidence in the Republican message." Speaking in Pat Robertson's hometown of Virginia Beach, McCain urged his fellow Republicans to return to their traditional conservative beliefs, including "our belief in personal freedom and personal responsibility; our belief in a strong national defense and vigorous and capable world leadership; our belief in small, but effective government and in fiscal conservatism." Seeking to become the 2000 Republican standard-bearer, McCain described himself as a "proud conservative" in the tradition of party hero Ronald Reagan:

> Throughout my presidential campaign I have remained true to our conservative principles. It is conservative to pay down the national debt; to save Social Security and Medicare. It is conservative to insist on local control of our children's education. It is conservative to expose the pork barrel spending practices of both political parties. It is conservative to seek to improve the lives of our servicemen and women, and the means with which we ask them to defend us. And it is conservative to demand that America keep its promises to our veterans.[48]

McCain's self-described "principled message that trusts in the people to guide our nation" contradicted the conservatism preached by evangelists Pat Robertson and Jerry Falwell. In a bold move, McCain attacked both men for advocating a type of "political intolerance" that did not honor his party's conservative tradition and was an ineffective strategy for winning elections: "They are corrupting influences on religion and politics and those who practice them in the name of religion, or in the name of the Republican party, or in the name of America shame our faith, our party, and our country."[49] McCain's plea for a Republican Party that would reclaim its historic view of the noble citizen and rebuke the sin-filled world view held by Robertson and Falwell fell mostly on deaf ears. Virginia Republicans insisted that voters in its presidential primary sign a "loyalty oath" pledging to support the party and its presidential candidate in November regardless of who the nominee was. The "loyalty oath," a clear sign of distrust, diminished turnout, especially among McCain supporters. Realizing the negative impact the Christian Right was having on his chances of winning the GOP nomination, McCain sharpened his denunciations of Robertson and Falwell, telling reporters, "You're supposed to tolerate evil in your party in the name of party unity?"[50]

McCain's message won him more public attention and supporters, especially among independents in states where they could participate in Republican primaries. In flinty, conservative-minded, and Yankee-dominated New Hampshire, for example, McCain walloped Bush, 49 percent to 30 percent. This, of course, was prior to McCain's attack on evangelical conservatives, but his attacks would have found a receptive audience, since New Hampshire Republicans have long been hostile to evangelicals. Pat Robertson, for example, received just 9 percent of the vote in that state's 1988 Republican presidential primary.

Stung after his New Hampshire defeat, Bush retreated to South Carolina and addressed students at fundamentalist Bob Jones University, where he described Jesus's teachings as the "foundation for how I live my life."[51] Evangelicals rallied to the Bush cause. James Dobson, head of Focus on the Family, a powerful Christian Right organization, declared that McCain's divorce, along with his admitted past adultery and tolerance toward gays, made him unacceptable no matter how conservative he was on other issues. The National Right-to-Life Committee also entered the fray, spending more than $500,000—an amount that was more than half of what the organization spent in 1998 for *all* its pro-life candidates—on phone calls to prospective Republican primary voters urging them to defeat McCain. In its telephone messages, the pro-life group depicted McCain as a stealth supporter of abortion rights and pleaded, "For the children's sake, please vote for George Bush."[52] At McCain rallies some Bush supporters circulated fliers saying that McCain was "the fag candidate" who would appoint homosexuals to his administration. McCain countered by saying that Bush "twists the truth like Clinton"—as low a blow as any Republican could throw against a fellow party member.[53]

As the Christian Right spread the word about its opposition to McCain, it all but assured Bush's nomination (see table 3.1, p. 90). Buoyed by Christian Right supporters, Republicans were much more likely to name a decline in moral values as the most important problem facing the country, and these voters were profoundly more disposed to support Bush (see table 3.2, p. 90). This view is consistent with a belief that the world is going to hell and that all means necessary, including political ones, should be used to prevent Armageddon (which may be unavoidable anyway).

Bush is not the first Republican to recognize the power of the Christian Right. In an abortive attempt to gain the GOP presidential nomination in 2000, Missouri senator John Ashcroft (later to become George W. Bush's attorney general), addressed students at Bob Jones University. In his speech, Ashcroft likened politics to Armageddon, as two nations—one Christian-dominated, the other not—battled for power: "[One] culture that has no king but Caesar, no standard but the civil authority, [versus another] culture that has no king but Jesus, no standard but the eternal authority. . . . When you have no king but Caesar, you release Barabas—criminality, destruction, thievery, the lowest and the least. When you have no king but Jesus, you release the eternal, you release the highest and the best."[54]

Ashcroft is not alone in seeing a values divide where one side represents virtue and the other its antithesis. Addressing the Christian Coalition in October 2000, House majority whip Tom DeLay called the Bush-Gore contest a "battle for

TABLE 3.1   RELIGIOUS RIGHT AND NON–RELIGIOUS RIGHT PREFERENCES IN BUSH-
MCCAIN CONTEST, SELECTED STATES, 2000 (IN PERCENTAGES)

	New Hampshire	South Carolina	Michigan	Virginia	New York
Religious right voters	16	34	27	19	15
Non–religious right voters	80	61	67	77	80
Religious right preferences: Bush-McCain	36–26	68–24	66–25	80–14	62–28
Non–religious right preferences: Bush-McCain	28–54	46–52	36–60	45–52	47–47

Source: Derived from Mark J. Rozell, "The Christian Right in the 2000 GOP Presidential Campaign," in *Religion and Liberal Democracy: An American Perspective*, ed. Mary Segers (Lanham, Md.: Rowman and Littlefield, 2001).

TABLE 3.2   REPUBLICAN PRIMARY VOTERS WHO NAMED VALUES AS THE COUNTRY'S
MOST IMPORTANT PROBLEM AND VOTED FOR GEORGE W. BUSH OR
JOHN MCCAIN, 2000 (IN PERCENTAGES)

State	Cited Moral Values as the Most Important Issue	Voted for George W. Bush	Voted for John McCain
Arizona	29	39	53
California	35	56	33
Colorado	32	71	16
Connecticut	29	44	47
Delaware	27	58	23
Georgia	37	70	23
Maine	36	56	36
Maryland	36	58	30
Massachusetts	30	29	68
Michigan	29	51	40
Missouri	34	65	24
New Hampshire	28	32	47
New York	26	56	37
Ohio	34	63	29
Rhode Island	30	37	58
South Carolina	37	55	36
Vermont	31	40	54
Virginia	33	61	34

Source: Voter News Service, Republican primary exit polls, 2000.

souls," adding: "Will this country accept the world views of humanism, materialism, sexism, naturalism, post-modernism, or any of the other -isms? Or will we march forward with a biblical world view, a world view that says God is our creator, that man is a sinner, and that we will save this country by changing the hearts and minds of Americans? . . . We have the House and the Senate. All we need is the presidency!" In DeLay's view, the task ahead was a difficult one, not because the Republicans' message was wrong, but because too many Americans lacked virtue: "Our entire system is built on the Judeo-Christian ethic, but it fell apart when we started denying God. If you stand up today and acknowledge God, they [Democrats and liberals] will try to destroy you." DeLay sees his God-given purpose in politics as bringing "us back to the Constitution and to Absolute Truth that has been manipulated and destroyed by a liberal world view."[55]

Many of DeLay's colleagues, especially southern Republicans, share his view of politics as a religious exercise. In 1978, Senator Jesse Helms advised his fellow North Carolina Republicans, "Southerners are good basic people. They believe in the Bible. They follow the teachings of God. Most of them strive to be like Jesus. And as long as the Republican Party attempts to work within the scope of His teachings, it will win."[56] Years later, Robert Aderholt, a Republican congressman from Alabama, espoused a similar prescription for his party's success:

I firmly believe that for a democracy as we know it to survive that we need religion and morality to be part of it. There is a moral crisis, and the roots of our problems stem from the weakening of our moral foundation. . . . Republicans, as a general rule, put a higher priority on these issues [than Democrats do] and think that there is a moral foundation in our government's foundation that obliges them to do that. . . . I always felt it was important for government leaders to stand for those issues that had a moral side to them.[57]

Many Republicans agree. Addressing a group of gay Orlando high school students, Florida Republican state legislator Allen Trovillion thundered, "God destroyed Sodom and Gomorrah, and he is going to destroy you and a lot of others."[58] Guided by their passions, these social conservatives have taken control of key power centers away from the more dispassionate country-club Republicans who believe religion should remain a private matter. A 1994 survey undertaken by *Campaigns and Elections* magazine found that the Christian Right dominated the Republican Party in seventeen states and exerted substantial influence in another thirteen.[59] In May 2001, Ralph Reed, the former executive director of the Christian Coalition, became chairman of the Georgia Republican Party. His Democratic counterpart, David Worley, was ecstatic: "We assumed from the beginning that he would win. And I just thought, great! One, fundraising—we've already done a direct mail piece on him. Two, it clearly shows that their party has been captured by the extremists. I think that Ralph Reed helps us."[60] At the presidential level, no candidate can be nominated without the active support of the Christian Coalition. Likewise, when the religious right opposes a candidate, his or her nomination is doomed.

The movement of the Republican Party away from its traditional libertarian, praise-the-citizen past had a large exclamation point placed next to it when James Jeffords, a lifelong Republican from an old Vermont family, became an independent and terminated the short-lived experiment with Republican-controlled government following the 2000 elections. In a statement that left many in the congressional corridors thunderstruck, Senator Jeffords declared, "I became a Republican not because I was born into the party, but because of the kind of fundamental principles that these and many Republicans stood for: moderation; tolerance; fiscal responsibility." Citing native Vermont Republicans, among them former president Calvin Coolidge, Jeffords charged that his party was no longer moderate, tolerant, or fiscally prudent. Specifically, Jeffords foresaw a host of upcoming differences with George W. Bush on "the issues of choice [abortion], the direction of the judiciary, tax and spending decisions, missile defense, energy and the environment, and a host of other issues large and small."[61]

Jeffords's announcement left Vermont without a single Republican in its congressional delegation for the first time since the party's founding in 1854. But he was not the first Vermonter to defect. Richard Mallary, a former Speaker of the Vermont House, became an independent in 2000, saying Republicans were "departing from [the] principles" of Lincoln, including "justice and opportunity for all, individual initiative, and responsibility."[62] Vermont's movement away from the Republican Party is itself astounding, since it was one of two states (Maine was the other) to side with Alf Landon against Franklin D. Roosevelt in 1936. After that election, a Burlington newspaper ran the headline, "Vermont Stands Firm While Rest of Nation Follows Strange Gods."[63] Besides Jeffords, Vermont's congressional delegation includes Bernard Sanders, a socialist who, like Jeffords, often votes with the Democrats. Not surprisingly, Jeffords's leave-taking proved popular, as two-thirds of Vermonters voiced their approval.[64] One of them was Republican David Boyden, whose family has farmed the black soil of the Lamoille River Valley for a century. After Jeffords's defection, Boyden told a reporter: "Who cares what party Jeffords belongs to? We're super lucky to have him."[65]

Jeffords's heresy earned him the enmity of conservative Republicans, but it won him plaudits throughout the Northeast. Across the region over the past quarter century, many Republican moderates have abandoned the party, have been defeated in its primaries, or have withdrawn from public life altogether, including Jacob Javits, Clifford Case, Lowell Weicker, William Scranton, and Nelson Rockefeller. Weicker, who cast the GOP aside to form his own independent party in Connecticut and carried it to victory in his 1994 gubernatorial campaign, says:

"Let's dispel the idea—whether it's Jeffords or Weicker or anyone else—that we left the party. The party's changed radically. They left us." Angus King, who like Weicker won election in 1994 as the independent governor of Maine, believes that New England's roots lie in "independent professions" such as farmers, loggers, and fishermen and that "there's something in the [New England] culture that values that [independence and self-reliance]." King adds: "If truth be known, a person who's a fiscal conservative and a social moderate, which describes about 60 percent of the American people, there just isn't a party that speaks to that."[66] Michael Forbes, a Long Island Republican congressman who became a Democrat in 1999, writes that today's Republican Party "has become a narrow-minded, intolerant and uncaring majority, tone deaf to the concerns of most northeasterners and most Americans."[67] John McCain agrees: "Tolerance of dissent is the hallmark of a mature party, and it is well past time for the Republican party to grow up."[68]

The results have been catastrophic for Republicans in a region that at the turn of the twentieth century they reliably called their own. In 1924, Republicans held twenty-eight of thirty-two congressional seats from New England; in 2001 they have just five of twenty-three. The remaining Republican moderates in Congress, including Maine's Olympia Snowe and Susan Collins, Pennsylvania's Arlen Spector, and Rhode Island's Lincoln Chafee, are a long way from taking over the party machinery, or even asserting much influence in Republican affairs outside the Senate. Today's new brand of conservatives got their start in the intellectual ferment that stirred in think tanks such as the Heritage Foundation and the American Enterprise Institute in the late 1970s and 1980s. Today, all of the intellectual muscle within the Republican Party remains securely fastened on the right. Indeed, many Republican intellectuals actively seek to bolster the party's religious conservatives. Michael S. Greve, director of the Federalism Project at the conservative American Enterprise Institute, argues that the best bet for morally minded Republicans is to pursue what he calls a strategy of "cultural federalism." Greve likens the Democrats to cultural nationalists, since their constituencies in the Northeast and on the West Coast adhere to a federalist perspective that forbids states from wandering into social and cultural concerns:

> Democratic nationalism comes with so much sweet talk that we tend to overlook its tyrannical nature. Advocates for "choice" will not let a single state legislature choose to express its respect for life, let alone enact laws that would encourage women to think before having an abortion. Having demolished traditional sexual morality (which was enforced, by and large, gently and informally), liberalism has erected in its stead a rigid national regime of laws, regulations, agencies, and lawsuits to enforce its new morality against sexual harassment. When Democrats enthuse about diversity, they mean that every single college must be racially balanced; when they shout "tolerance," they are getting ready to shut

down the Boy Scouts. Democratic nationalism may occasionally, for tactical reasons, fight in state or local areas. But it must in the end be *nationalism*, for it must close off the exits where half the country is headed.[69]

In Greve's view, "cultural federalism" allows the thirty pro–George W. Bush states to act on their own values agendas without much federal interference. Undoubtedly, these state legislators would bow to their constituents' desires and enact laws that would insulate them from the values prescribed by the Democratic nationalists.

Greve's advocacy of "cultural federalism" is based on the premise that a growing number of Americans believe that the federal budget deficit matters less than the growing deficit in the nation's moral and spiritual ledger books. This view of a less-than-virtuous citizenry is shared by many Americans whatever their partisan stripe: A 1995 survey found that 63 percent agreed with the statement "You can't be too careful in dealing with people"; 48 percent believed people "would take advantage of you if they got a chance"; and an equal number thought their fellow citizens were "mostly just looking out for themselves."[70] Simply put, it wasn't just notable Christian Right leaders such as Pat Robertson or Jerry Falwell, but a near-majority of Americans who thought their fellow citizens lacked virtue. A popular bumper sticker during the 1980s read "The Moral Majority Is Neither." Now, many Republicans (and others not affiliated with the party) agree with at least one part of that statement: the moral majority is no longer quite the majority it once was. The longstanding Republican view of a relatively virtuous electorate, a belief that had characterized Republican thinking since the party's founding, *has been turned on its head.*

To many Republicans, the culture wars that have replaced the Cold War are the direct result of a virtue deficit and must be fought with the same zeal with which the party's Cold Warriors attacked communism. While politics is one venue for those wars, many Republicans became discouraged with traditional politics when pragmatists within their own party—whose Iron Law of Politics is that to govern you must first win—eschewed the desires of social and cultural conservatives for a renewed emphasis on moral values. During the 1980s, Barry Goldwater, a libertarian who had always believed in the virtue of the private citizen, declared that Moral Majority leader Jerry Falwell and his ilk deserved "a swift kick in the ass."[71] Goldwater rebuked "fellows like Pat Robertson," saying they were "trying to take the Republican party away from the Republican party, and make a religious organization out of it." "If that ever happens," Goldwater warned, "kiss politics goodbye."[72] In a 1994 interview with the *Los Angeles Times*, the former Arizona senator attacked his fellow Republicans for maligning the word *conservative*: "A lot of so-called conservatives today don't know what the word means. They think I've turned liberal because I believe a woman has a right to an abortion. That's a decision that's up to the pregnant woman, not up to the pope or some do-gooders or the religious right. It's not a conservative issue at all."[73] Goldwater's resentment of the new political moralism was partially based on his own family's life experiences. His first wife helped found Planned Parenthood in Arizona, a daughter had an illegal abortion in the mid-1950s, and a grandson is gay and HIV-positive. At age eighty-five, Goldwater lent his name to gay rights activities and spoke out on behalf of gays in the military. Later, he backed a Democrat for Congress (once a heresy for the very partisan Goldwater) against a Christian conservative.

But Goldwater's displeasure with his party at the time of his death in 1998 largely stemmed from its deemphasizing of the libertarian principles he cherished. Addressing the Western Republican Conference in 1959, Goldwater gave the faithful the boilerplate libertarian thinking that had always characterized the conservative movement: "For twenty-five years the apostles of the welfare state have been busy transforming that stern old gentleman in a top hat, cut-away coat and red, white and blue trousers from a symbol of dignity and freedom and justice for all men into a national wet nurse, dispensing a cockeyed kind of patent medicine labeled 'something for nothing'—passing out soothing syrup and rattles and pacifiers in return for grateful votes on Election Day." Even in the area of civil rights, Goldwater opposed the 1954 Supreme Court decision in *Brown v. Board of Education* on libertarian grounds: "I believe it is both wise and just for Negro children to attend the same school as whites, that to deny them this opportunity carries with it strong implications of inferiority. I am not prepared, however, to impose that judgment of mine on the people of Mississippi or South Carolina or tell them what methods should be adopted and what pace should be kept in striving toward that goal."[74]

Goldwater later cast a "no" vote against the 1964 Civil Rights Act, citing similar concerns. Taking note of Goldwater's evocation of libertarianism, Marshall Wittman, himself a former Christian Coalition official, speaks of "the death of libertarianism" and says that the activist government policies pursued by those Republicans who seek to instill virtue in a virtue-deprived public represent "a major turning point from what Ronald Reagan and Barry Goldwater talked about."[75]

Libertarianism certainly has not died altogether within the GOP. The last three Republican presidents have shied away from the religious right when it suited their purposes. Social conservatives were dismayed when Ronald Reagan preferred to address antiabortion rallies by telephone instead of in person. George H.W. Bush was a severe disappointment to cultural conservatives, not much of a surprise given that his New England upbringing and cultural temperament made him inherently uncomfortable with the evangelicals. Even George W. Bush has provoked their displeasure. During his first hundred days in office, Bush named Scott H. Evertz, a gay Republican and fundraising executive, as his candidate to head the White House Office of National AIDS Policy. Evertz's nomination aroused the enmity of several organizations associated with the religious right. Reverend Louis P. Sheldon, chairman of the Traditional Values Coalition, declared, "We are very concerned about the fact that [Evertz] is an activist, that he opposes the Boy Scouts, supports homosexual marriage—all the homosexual agenda."[76] Richard Lessner, executive director of American Renewal, an arm of the Family Research Council, agreed: "This is another case of Republicans trying to ingratiate themselves with natural opponents, and a thumb in the eye of supporters." Steve Gunderson, a former Wisconsin congressman who is gay, countered, "We ought to cut to the chase: Is the real reason they are opposed is that they don't want anyone who is openly gay serving in a Republican administration?"[77] Subsequently, Bush appointed a gay man to serve as the U.S. ambassador to Romania, appointed gay activist Donald A. Cappoccia to head the U.S. Commission on Fine Arts, and decided to keep in place executive orders Bill Clinton signed to ensure equal treatment for gays in the federal workforce.[78] Robert Knight, executive director of the Culture and Family Institute, described the Bush record on values issues as "shockingly bad," adding, "You'd almost think they were Democrats trying to infiltrate what makes the Republican party distinctive."[79]

Later, Bush incurred the wrath of the religious right when he and Senator Edward M. Kennedy (the devil incarnate to many evangelicals) cooperated on an education bill that lacked vouchers for private schools, a long-sought-after goal of the religious right. The Family Research Council denounced Bush for "ripping the conservative heart out" of the bill. James Dobson, Phyllis Schlafly, Robert Novak, Paul Weyrich, Bill Bennett, and many other conservatives expressed similar views.[80]

But it was Bush's controversial decision on stem-cell research that really rankled social conservatives. By trying to straddle the issue and allow sixty existing stem-cell lines to be used for government-funded research without any further embryos being destroyed, Bush won broad public support by casting himself as a thoughtful, "compassionate conservative" who would protect life, yet allow scientific research to proceed on a limited basis. Pro-life activists were dismayed, saying that by allowing research to proceed on the destroyed embryos, Bush had violated his pro-life principles. Kenneth Connor, head of the Family Research Council, said, "The president has introduced the camel's nose into the tent, and inevitably we'll have the whole beast in there. Moral principles are not divisible." Bishop Joseph A. Fiorenza, president of the U.S. Catholic Conference of Bishops, agreed: "The trade-off he has announced is morally unacceptable. We hope and pray that President Bush will return to a principled stand against treating some human lives as nothing more than objects to be manipulated and destroyed for research purposes."[81] House majority whip Tom DeLay described himself as "disappointed" in Bush, noting that "the technique used to create the stem-cell lines did not respect the sanctity of life."[82]

Religious right leaders, including Ralph Reed and James Dobson, often view Republican officeholders as seeking cover under what political scientist Clinton

Rossiter once described as the "vast, gaudy, and friendly umbrellas" of two-party politics.[83] To them, there is nothing friendly about being lumped together with people who are so amoral that they will do anything to win. Paul M. Weyrich, head of the Free Congress Foundation, faulted his fellow conservatives for "identifying with a politics that says it really doesn't matter what happens to the community as long as those who can survive get theirs."[84] Christian conservative Chuck Colson writes in a similar vein that a country that countenances abortion cannot count on the support or loyalty of its Christians. He asks the Christian Right to consider whether this "flawed republic" is really "their country."[85] Moderate Republicans, such as Maryland congresswoman Constance Morella, find such talk appalling: "I find it incongruous that those who appear to be so religious can be intolerant to the point where they cannot listen, compromise, or work it out. . . . It's the 'rule or ruin' syndrome."[86] To many social conservatives, the centrist rhetoric of Republicans like Morella is itself *value-less*. In the face of what they see as a win-at-all-costs mentality that often guides Republican national and statewide officeholders, conservative activist Paul Weyrich took the unusual step of advising social conservatives in 1999 to withdraw from politics altogether:

> The culture we are living in becomes an ever-wider sewer. In truth, I think we are caught up in a cultural collapse of historic proportions, a collapse so great that it simply overwhelms politics. . . . I believe that we probably have lost the culture war. That doesn't mean the war is not going to continue, and that it isn't going to be fought on other fronts. But in terms of society in general, we have lost. This is why, even when we win in politics, our victories fail to translate into the kind of policies we believe are important.[87]

The fact that a conservative activist would urge his supporters to withdraw from the political arena is remarkable. Moreover, Weyrich was not the only one advocating such a course of action. Cal Thomas, a former vice president for communications of the Moral Majority, and Ed Dobson, also formerly associated with the Moral Majority and pastor of Calvary Church in Grand Rapids, Michigan, wrote that the Moral Majority and Christian Coalition had failed because their central message had been obscured as they were "seduced by the siren song of temporal political power." According to Thomas and Dobson, "It is always the church that suffers, because the kingdom of no compromise that the church is supposed to represent becomes involved in a political kingdom that is all about compromise and almost always is seduced by the world and follows its appeals and agendas, rather than leading the world to the only agenda that can change a life: Jesus Christ."[88]

That a significant faction of the Republican Party would urge its followers to leave politics behind represents a profound change. During the Cold War,

Republicans did not withdraw from politics; on the contrary, they summoned the passions of the party faithful to wage a life-or-death struggle against communism. In so doing, the disparate elements of the party came together as one. Dwight Eisenhower, Richard Nixon, Barry Goldwater, and Ronald Reagan could rally their flocks as they battled against the Soviet-controlled "evil empire." Reagan, in particular, gathered his fellow Republicans around him by fusing his anti-communism with a belief in the Divine. Addressing a prayer breakfast at the 1984 Republican Convention in Dallas, Reagan declared:

> The truth is, politics and morality are inseparable. And as morality's foundation is religion, religion and politics are necessarily related. . . . Without God there is no virtue, because there's no prompting of the conscience. Without God, we're mired in the material, that flat world that tells us only what the senses perceive. Without God, there is a coarsening of the society. And without God, democracy will not and cannot long endure. If we ever forget that we're one nation under God, then we will be a nation gone under.[89]

Reagan reminded his audience of the values each listener shared with him. Religious faith, especially when contrasted with "godless communism," could support substantial sacrifices, including the appropriation of huge sums of money to the Pentagon. To Reagan and his fellow Republicans, such commitments illustrated an abundance of civic virtue that would eventually ensure victory in the Cold War. Yet, it was Bill Clinton who saw Reagan's appeals to the Almighty as a political weakness. Addressing a small Democratic gathering in Charlotte, North Carolina, in 1981, Clinton said, "Reagan is pandering to the people who want to tell the rest of us how to live. The Republican party is trying to tell the rest of us whether we are moral or not. We will never make Heaven on Earth; that is what Heaven's for."[90]

By emphasizing virtue, Republicans have embarked on a course in which the self becomes paramount. If one has virtue and a fellow citizen does not, one can "rehabilitate" that person through one-to-one evangelization. But on a larger scale, if most citizens lack virtue, the tendency is to withdraw from the public sphere altogether. This is exactly what Paul Weyrich advised social conservatives to do in a 1999 letter:

> The radicals of the 1960s had three slogans: turn on, tune in, drop out. I suggest that we adopt a modified version. First, turn off. Turn off the television and video games and some of the garbage that's on the computers. Turn off the means by which you and your family are being infected with cultural decadence.
> Tune out. Create a little stillness. I was struck by the fact that when I traveled to the former Soviet Union, I couldn't go to a restaurant or any place else

without hearing this incessant Western rock music pounding away. There was no escape from it. No wonder some Russians are anti-American. When they think of the United States, they think of the culture that we exported to them.

Finally, we need to drop out of this culture, and find places, even if it is where we physically are right now, where we can live godly, righteous, and sober lives.[91]

But as Republicans prepared in January 2001 to take over both Congress and the presidency for the first time since 1953, there was a renewed sense of political engagement. Suddenly, Weyrich and his followers were not about to abandon politics in the face of a hard-fought victory.

The New Republican "Theocrats" and the Politics of Virtue

Arizona state legislator Steve May, the gay Republican whose dust-up with the U.S. Army was recounted in chapter 1, believes the Republican Party is struggling with its core values of freedom and self-reliance: "The idea of America is freedom—individual freedom. Yet, we have people who think the idea of America is a Christian nation and that they should impose their particular interpretation of Christianity on everyone else. They have very little respect for individual liberty. In order to have individual liberty, we have to respect diversity. That diversity includes who we are as a people and how we choose to live as families."[92]

The intolerance May detects has led him to describe those Republicans motivated solely by moral issues as "theocrats [who] want to use government to impose their religious and moral viewpoint." Constance Morella shares May's disdain for the Republican Party's dalliance with the religious right:

Many issues have no place in Congress for us to be voting on. They're not in our purview. These are always emotional issues. You can call them values issues. I don't. They are not issues of values. They are publicity-getting issues. . . . The abortion issue is one—especially late-term abortion. We've already voted on it once. Why do we keep voting on it again and again? There are a number of other areas that we vote on [that have no place in our politics]. For example, a day of remembrance where everybody should pray to Christ. . . . The Defense of Marriage Act is another issue that should have *never* come before us on the floor. It was offered by someone [Republican Bob Barr] who had been divorced three times![93]

Alabama's Robert Aderholt responded to Morella's complaints about her colleagues in an interview:

There are certain moral issues out there that as a Republican I think supercede the individual or states' rights and that there has to be a federal response. . . . I think people outside of Washington, D.C., feel there has been a moral decline. The Supreme Court rulings [on abortion and school prayer] have treaded on these issues. Congress has, too. But the bottom line is many people in America do feel there is a "values disconnect" in Washington, D.C. They want to see those issues protected. Certainly, those people from the district I represent do. Now, you may go to a different district and find something else. Connie Morella's district may be different.[94]

Aderholt has a point. In 2000, Republican Roy Moore easily won election as chief justice of the Alabama State Supreme Court. Moore became known as the "Ten Commandments Judge" for his fight to display the Old Testament laws in his Etowah County circuit courtroom. Moore, a West Point graduate and Vietnam veteran, had been ordered to remove the Ten Commandments and cease opening court sessions with a Christian prayer. (A state court later dismissed the case against him on a technicality.) In Moore's view, the United States was rapidly becoming a "moral slum," and he looked to redeem it by seeking the highest position on the State Supreme Court. At campaign rallies, Moore told Alabama voters that judges should "maintain the honor and integrity of the court system . . . [and] preserve the moral foundation of our law."[95] Moore believed that the moral foundation of the law is inherently religious: "There is an Absolute Truth, and the truth is in the Bible. It represents the truth upon which this nation was founded and is the basis of the laws of our nation."[96] Spurred by Moore's easy win, Republicans captured an 8–to–1 majority on the Alabama State Supreme Court.

Republican theocrats like Aderholt and Moore, who remain engaged in politics while distancing themselves from more traditionally individualistic and independent-minded Republicans like Morella, adhere to four basic tenets:

- They are motivated by their conviction that moral values trump economics as important political issues.
- They believe that the popular culture has been degraded to the point that a majority no longer subscribes to their view of morality. The unwillingness of a majority to remove Bill Clinton from office following the Monica Lewinsky affair was proof-positive of the failure of politics and left the Republican theocrats more disillusioned and cynical than ever before.
- Like the Goldwaterites, theocrats do not extol the art of political compromise. Instead, it is seen as a negative tactic often used by "traditional politicians" who are all too willing to compromise *moral* principles and, therefore, contribute to the ongoing cultural degradation.

- Unlike Landon and Dole, theocrats are much more willing to use the power of government to enforce their moral views, seeing it as a necessity in the face of a losing political struggle with the secular humanists.

The earliest manifestations of a new "virtue politics" occurred in the 1970s when voter concerns about violent crime prompted many Republicans to support laws restricting judicial discretion by requiring judges to impose mandatory jail sentences. This form of values politics was perfected in the 1990s when the governors of several states, including California's Pete Wilson and New Jersey's Christine Todd Whitman, signed versions of a "three-strikes-and-you're-out" law. These statutes mandated that judges institute a life sentence for any violent criminal who received a third conviction. Another attack on crime came when several Republican governors reinstated capital punishment, among them New York's George Pataki in 1995. Democratic holdouts, like Pataki's predecessor, Mario Cuomo, were defeated at the polls. Even Bill Clinton imposed the death penalty on a mentally impaired inmate while seeking the presidency in 1992. Bob Dole tried to transform crime into a values issue in 1996, telling cheering Republican delegates, "As our many and voracious criminals go to bed tonight, at, say six in the morning, they had better pray that I lose the election. Because if I win, the lives of violent criminals are going to be hell."[97]

Four years later George W. Bush boasted of killing more death-row inmates than any previous Texas governor, among them Karla Faye Tucker, the first woman executed in Texas in more than a century. In an interview published in *Talk* magazine, Bush parodied Tucker pleading for her life on CNN's *Larry King Live*: "Please," Bush whimpered, "don't kill me."[98] Bush's pro–death penalty views captured the growing public sentiment for retribution rather than redemption. When asked in 1999 whether society should show forgiveness toward those who do wrong or whether it should punish wrongdoers, 53 percent of respondents chose punishment to just 28 percent in favor of forgiveness.[99] Republicans believed that the politics of virtue commanded widespread popular support. Megan's Law, the Flag Protection Amendment, and the Ten Commandments Defense Act Amendment seemed to have proved them right.

Megan's Law

One especially striking example of virtue politics in action was the congressional rush to judgment in passing Megan's Law in 1996. The law was prompted by the slaying of Megan Kanka in the prosperous, white, middle-class town of Hamilton Township, New Jersey, in July 1994. Kanka, a seven-year-old, had been lured by an offer from her thirty-two-year-old neighbor, Jesse Timmendequas, to show her a puppy. Timmendequas, who strangled the child and raped her as she lay dying, had been convicted for committing child sex offenses twice before and was living with two other sex offenders in a house across the street. Megan's Law required child molesters to register with the state and have their names and addresses made public. Republicans (and many Democrats) viewed this heinous crime as an example of the moral degeneration that had gripped the nation. On 7 May 1996, Megan's Law won approval in the House of Representatives by a vote of 418–0. Two days later, the Senate unanimously passed Megan's Law by a voice vote, and eight days after that President Clinton signed the measure into law.

Despite the rare congressional unity, there were Democratic voices that repeated the more libertarian-minded Republican arguments of a bygone era. John Conyers wondered whether the registration requirement represented an unfunded mandate to the states, since it imposed a penalty for noncompliance. Mel Watt questioned the wisdom of not allowing states "to make their own decisions about whether they want a Megan's Law or do not want a Megan's Law." Echoing Alf Landon, Watt criticized "Big Brother Government" for trying to force state compliance with something that is not necessarily a federal issue.[100] But given the overwhelming public sympathy for the Kanka family, and undoubtedly fearing the television advertisements that would inevitably depict them as being "soft on crime," both Conyers and Watt cast their doubts aside and voted for the measure.

The Flag Protection Amendment

Another example of virtue politics is the Flag Protection Act. In 1984, at the Republican National Convention in Dallas, Gregory Lee Johnson staged a "die-in" to protest the proliferation of nuclear weapons. Shouting slogans that included "Ronald Reagan, killer of the hour, perfect example of U.S. power" and "red, white, and blue, we spit on you, you stand for plunder, you will go under," Johnson burned the American flag. Prosecuted under a Texas law that prohibited the flag's desecration, the case eventually reached the U.S. Supreme Court. By a 5–4 decision, the Court invalidated laws in forty-eight states and maintained that flag burning was a form of expression protected by the First Amendment: "We do not consecrate the flag by punishing its desecration, for in doing so we dilute the freedom this cherished emblem represents." This position won support from some of the court's more libertarian-minded conservatives, including Anthony M. Kennedy and Antonin Scalia. Chief Justice William Rehnquist issued a stinging dissent, noting that "flag burning is the equivalent of an inarticulate grunt or roar that, it seems fair to say, is most likely to be indulged in not to express any particular idea, but to antagonize others."[101]

Initially, most Americans overwhelmingly agreed with Rehnquist. According to an ABC News/*Washington Post* poll taken immediately after the decision was issued, 78 percent disagreed with the court majority, and another 73 percent wanted immediate congressional action.[102] Moreover, 58 percent said the issue would be "very important" in deciding how they would vote in the upcoming congressional elections.[103]

Republicans sensed an opportunity. Burning the flag is an action many Americans find abhorrent. In 1988, the Dukakis campaign was hurt by unfounded rumors that Kitty Dukakis had once burned an American flag while protesting the Vietnam War. This, in addition to Governor Dukakis's refusal to make recitation of the Pledge of Allegiance mandatory in public schools, made it easy for Republicans to caricature Democrats as unworthy values caretakers. Today, many continue to believe that potential presidents (and their wives) must pay homage to the flag. Asked in 1996 whether they could support a presidential candidate who had burned a U.S. flag at a student antiwar demonstration, 36 percent said they could overlook such an incident; 58 percent could not.[104] Spurred by morally minded Republican legislators, Congress passed the Flag Protection Act of 1989. The new law criminalized the conduct of anyone who "knowingly mutilates, defaces, physically defiles, burns, maintains on the floor or ground, or tramples upon" a U.S. flag. The issue was a good one for Republicans: 50 percent named them as doing a better job on this issue; only 37 percent picked the Democrats.[105]

But soon after George H.W. Bush signed the bill banning flag burning, protestors burned several flags on the Capitol steps. Prosecutions commenced, and the matter became entangled in the courts. A federal district judge declared the new law unconstitutional, and the Supreme Court affirmed the decision by another 5–4 vote. These court rulings prompted intense efforts to amend the U.S. Constitution and place flag-burning outside the First Amendment's realm of protected speech. In 1995, 1997, 1999, 2000, and 2001, the House mustered the two-thirds majority needed to pass a flag protection amendment that would restrain conduct but not expression. Although the language has slightly differed, the proposed amendment reads as follows: "The Congress shall have power to prohibit the physical desecration of the flag of the United States." Support for the amendment was especially strong among World War II veterans, who remembered the awe-inspiring raising of the flag after the victory over the Japanese at Iwo Jima. Retired Major General Patrick Brady, chairman of the Citizen Flag Alliance, declared:

> This is a values issue, and the entire debate over values is centered on what we teach our children. Flag burning is wrong, but what it teaches is worse. It teaches our children disrespect. It teaches that the hateful conduct of a minority is more important than the will of the majority. It teaches that our laws need not reflect our values, and that the courts, not the people, own the Constitution.[106]

Opponents evoked a libertarian argument, noting that the amendment would infringe on the individual right of self-expression, which included not only flag burning but also displaying the flag on clothes or other commercial products that are highly sought after by the younger generation. Carole Shields, president of People for the American Way, maintained that safeguarding free speech helped distinguish the United States from the rest of the world: "We have to be able to allow political protest. Otherwise, we are Cuba, and we are Iran."[107]

While three-quarters of Americans continue to view flag burning as an inappropriate form of political expression, they have become increasingly leery about amending the U.S. Constitution to remedy the situation. In 1999, General Colin Powell issued a statement saying he would not be in favor of amending "that great shield of democracy to hammer a few miscreants."[108] According to a survey sponsored by the Freedom Forum in April 2000, 51 percent thought the Constitution should *not* be amended to prohibit flag burning or its desecration; 46 percent favored such an amendment.[109]

Most congressional Republicans dismissed the libertarian arguments made by the Supreme Court and the Democrats who liked to cite it. Each time the Republican-controlled Congress considered a flag-burning amendment, they gave it their unqualified backing. A report issued by the Senate Judiciary Committee, chaired by Utah Republican Orrin Hatch, provided the following rationale for amending what conservatives heretofore considered a sacred document:

> Protecting the flag from physical desecration preserves the values of liberty, equality, and personal responsibility that Americans have passionately defended and debated throughout our history and which the flag uniquely embodies. It is commonly accepted today that the traditional values upon which our Nation was founded, and which find tangible expression in our respect for the flag, are essential to the smooth functioning of a free society. Flag protection highlights and enhances these values and thus helps to preserve freedom and democratic government. Without these values, our children will not be able to distinguish good from bad or right from wrong. By replacing what the Supreme Court has stripped away, the proposed amendment will be a step toward reestablishing the values that made this country great.[110]

The majority-controlled Republican Congresses since 1994 have come close to making protection of the flag the Twenty-eighth Amendment to the U.S. Constitution. In 2001, 207 Republican House members supported the amendment; just 11 voted against it. Democrats were more evenly split, with 90 in favor and 113 against. The measure is likely to become stymied in the Senate, as it has on previous occasions. In 2000, for example, Republicans in the Senate fell four votes short of the two-thirds required. Fifty-two Republican senators lent their backing to the amendment (and only four were against), while Democrats were opposed by a better than three-to-one margin, with just ten senators in favor and thirty-three against.

The Ten Commandments Defense Act Amendment

In 1999, the values divide between the two parties widened following the Columbine High School massacre, which took the lives of twelve students, one teacher, and the two assailants. Democrats wanted stricter gun-control laws, and they held the National Rifle Association responsible for Congress's failure to pass new legislation. After Congress killed gun-control legislation in June 1999, Bill Clinton took on the NRA directly: "One more time, the Congress of the United States said, 'We don't care what's necessary to protect our children. We can't possibly bear to make anyone in the NRA mad.'"[111] Republicans ignored Clinton and blamed Hollywood for the shooting rampages, citing violent films such as *Natural Born Killers* as having a particularly negative influence on teenagers. Missouri Republican representative Jo Ann Emerson offered a "sense of the Congress resolution," calling upon Hollywood to "do everything in its power to stop these portrayals of pointless acts of brutality by immediately eliminating gratuitous violence in movies, television, music and video games." It passed by a vote of 355 to 68. According to Emerson, the entertainment industry must recognize "the power and influence it has over this nation's youth."[112]

But time did not heal the wounds of Columbine; rather, the debate between Republicans and Democrats became even more furious. Republicans sought a federal ratings system for monitoring violence in movies, videos, and computer games. Congressman Zack Wamp of Tennessee was a principal proponent: "Our kids are being killed in the head, poisoned. Mass media products are clearly having an effect on our children, because children do not kill children."[113] John Conyers, a Michigan Democrat, disagreed, saying Wamp's bill would "create a Politburo [and] move much of the entertainment industry to Washington, D.C.," ominously adding, "We ought to stop and think about what we're doing."[114]

Amid this partisan rancor, Representative Robert B. Aderholt attached an amendment to the juvenile justice bill allowing the Ten Commandments to be displayed on property owned or administered by the states, including the public schools. According to the Alabama congressman, displaying the Ten Commandments "is an important step to promote morality and end children killing children."[115] He maintained that the laws of Moses teach the values of "forbearance, respect and temperance" often found lacking in the public schools.[116] Moreover, Aderholt believed that his Ten Commandments Defense Act Amendment was in keeping with the U.S. Constitution, since the Tenth Amendment permits states to display the Ten Commandments, and the First and Fourteenth Amendments guarantee freedom of religious expression. Harkening to the Cold War era when the Republican Party was perceived as superior to the Democrats on defense issues, Aderholt inserted the word "defense" into the title of his amendment. In his words, it was perfectly justified: "The Ten Commandments Defense Act Amendment will work to restore our religious liberties, allowing the faithful to express our beliefs in the public square. For too long, the federal government has attempted to eliminate expression of religion. Discrimination against religion under the guise of separation of church and state needs to end."[117]

Aderholt's passion for and entry into politics stemmed in part from his desire to use the powers of government to change the nation's moral climate. Elected to the House in 1996, he became the first Republican to win in northern Alabama since Barry Goldwater's sweep there in 1964. His platform for moral revision included a constitutional ban on abortion (the only exception being to save the life of the woman), voluntary school prayer, and opposition to same-sex marriages and gun control. As he often told friendly audiences, "We want to go to Washington to deliver a message, and that is, don't mess with our traditional family values."[118]

In the post-Columbine era, Aderholt's passion for changing the nation's morals gained momentum. One poll found two-thirds of the respondents believing that the nation's moral standards had gotten worse in recent years.[119] One response to this sentiment was the emergence of a grassroots movement with the catchy title "Hang Ten," which sought to build public support for the Ten Commandments Defense Act Amendment. Its efforts were largely successful: 74 percent favored posting the Ten Commandments in public schools, and 64 percent wanted to go even further by having religious-based instruction on morals and values in the public schools.[120] When asked to choose between promoting greater respect for traditional social and moral values or encouraging greater tolerance of people with different lifestyles and backgrounds, 60 percent opted for "traditional values," while 29 percent said "tolerance" was more important.[121]

With public opinion on his side, Aderholt sought backers for his proposal both inside and outside Congress. One of them was Dr. Laura Schlesinger, the conservative talk radio host. About her, the Alabama Republican said, "Let me say that Dr. Laura talks a lot about these issues. She has been very supportive of the Ten Commandments. Of course, she has been attacked very viciously as well. And she's Jewish. It is very important in all of this discussion that this nation was founded on Christian principles. The Founding Fathers widely used Scripture."[122]

Leading the opposition were the Americans United for the Separation of Church and State and the American Civil Liberties Union (ACLU). Barry Lynn, president of Americans United for the Separation of Church and State, said, "The Ten Commandments have done pretty well for themselves for centuries; they don't need help from politicians."[123] Martin McCaffery, president of the ACLU's Alabama chapter, agreed: "The Founders intended and the Supreme Court has held, that the duty of the state toward religion is strict neutrality. Neutrality does not exist where the state displays the Ten Commandments in a prominent place, unadorned by any other secular or historical artifacts."[124]

But these opponents were relatively lonely voices, and Aderholt's amendment easily passed the House on a vote of 248 ayes to 180 nays. Pat Robertson hailed the measure as a "tremendous victory for faith."[125] Yet, as in so many other votes on cultural issues in the 106th Congress, the gap between the two parties was wide: Republicans cast 203 yeas for the Aderholt-sponsored amendment; 164 Democrats were opposed. Virginia Democrat Robert C. Scott made the libertarian argument: "Rather than trying to honor and promote that tradition of religious diversity by focusing on the Ten Commandments, this amendment seeks to elevate one particular religion over all others. This singling out of one religion is contrary to the American ideal of religious tolerance and is blatantly unconstitutional."[126] Aderholt disagreed, citing the religious beliefs of the Founding Fathers:

> This country was established on moral principles, and even on principles that are in the Bible. If you read the writings of the Founding Fathers, that is very clear. They felt that this nation, in a democracy as we know it, would best survive with having moral leadership and the principles that are actually found in the Bible. Does that mean they were trying to presume that everyone who lived here should follow these principles? I don't think so. But they felt it was very important that this nation and democracy as a whole had to be built on a religious foundation. Religion and morality went hand-in-hand.[127]

Constance Morella was one of the few Republican dissenters. In an interview, she explained her position:

> When it comes to posting the Ten Commandments [in public schools], I voted against that. I believe in the Ten Commandments. These are the basic tenets of all religions. Yet, I don't think that we should be mandating the allowance of the Ten Commandments to be posted in a public facility. I feel we have to factor the First Amendment into our decision. The First Amendment is important, and I think our Founding Fathers believed in the separation of church and state. It's part of our freedom and independence. . . . I think Congress by and large has been involved much too much with mandating personal values that I think the Constitution's framers would look upon differently.[128]

But Morella's more libertarian-minded position was becoming a minority view within the House GOP. As time passes, the forsaking of libertarian thinking has created its own political backlash, which poses a new set of difficulties for the Republican Party.

The Backlash

So long as the Republican-led politics of virtue was targeted against assorted rapists, criminals, and those who burned the American flag, Americans approved. Over time, the GOP became entrusted to safeguard the traditional sanctuaries of hearth and home. Democrats were challenged to explain why they should be entrusted with the authority to govern, given their propensity to defend the rights of the accused. This form of "wedge politics" reached its zenith in 1988 when George H.W. Bush accused Michael Dukakis of being a "card-carrying" member of the ACLU. One Democratic operative deplored the Bush campaign's emphasis on faith, family, flags, and furloughs, saying, "It was deplorable, despicable, degrading, and *effective*."129

During the Clinton years, however, the politics of virtue began to take its toll on the GOP. First came the attacks on illegal immigrants. For some time, resentment had been building among established whites in vote-rich states that experienced a surge of both legal and illegal immigrants, including California, Florida, New Jersey, Texas, Illinois, and New York. In a country that often views politics as "us versus them," it was all too easy to depict illegal immigrants as a threat to citizens' livelihood and symbolic of a values decline. A nation that looked less white—and less like the mythical Nelsons and Cleavers of television fame—gave Republicans a ready-made wedge issue, the virtue deficit. After all, their targets were *illegal* immigrants who had violated state and federal laws and whose honesty and veracity were in question. Moreover, since their outrage was directed at illegal immigrants, rather than those who had entered the country legally, Republicans believed they had neutralized any serious political opposition.

At first, they were proved right. In 1994, California governor Pete Wilson backed Proposition 187, which banned all state spending on illegal immigrants and required the police to report any suspected illegals to the California Department of Justice and the U.S. Immigration Service. Wilson's television campaign featured spots showing dozens of illegal Mexicans swarming across the border as an announcer intoned, "They just keep coming." Despite the opposition of Republicans Jack Kemp and William Bennett, who argued that Proposition 187 was "politically unwise and fundamentally at odds with the best tradition and spirit of our party," Wilson and Proposition 187 went on to easy victories.130

Proposition 187 marked the first time since 1988 that the values politics of "us versus them" went awry for the GOP. Legal immigrants, whose numbers are especially large in vote-rich states, saw the Republican Party as targeting them for expulsion. In fact, the Republican-controlled Congress passed legislation in 1996 doubling the number of U.S. Border Patrol agents to 10,000 and hastening the deportation of immigrants who used false documents. Moreover, Republicans attached an amendment to the welfare reform bill denying benefits to the illegals.

Suddenly, there was a rush of legal immigrants lining up to become naturalized citizens. Alfredo Alvarez was one. He told the *Washington Post*, "I love this country, but I feel unwanted. I feel like unless I am a true American, the government could one day knock on my door and tell me, 'Alfredo, go back to Honduras!'"[131]

Their harsh stance on immigration issues hurt Republicans with Hispanic voters. In 1996, support for Bill Clinton among this strategically placed group rose 11 percent from four years earlier. Two years later, Democrat Gray Davis became California's new governor, thanks to the 78 percent backing he received from Hispanics. Moreover, Cruz Bustamante won the lieutenant governorship (a separate race in California), becoming the first Latino elected to statewide office there since 1871. Jesse Henriquez, an El Salvadoran immigrant, captured the sentiments of many California's Hispanics: "The only way we can tell the people that we are working hard and that Latinos should not be blamed for all the country's problems is to register and vote. . . . Little by little, we are telling people, 'No more Proposition 187s.'"[132] For the first time since the three Franklin D. Roosevelt and Harry S. Truman victories in the Golden State (1940, 1944, and 1948), Bill Clinton and Al Gore have scored three decisive presidential wins in a row: 1992, 1996, and 2000. Gore's win was particularly impressive, having beat George W. Bush by more than one million votes. Nationwide, Bush received 35 percent of the Hispanic vote, and just 29 percent in California. These smaller-than-expected percentages came despite much ballyhoo that Bush would draw more Hispanic support for the party, given his strong showing in the 1998 Texas gubernatorial election and his repeated calls for the GOP to become more inclusive. Besides California, Bush narrowly lost New Mexico, another state with a large Hispanic population, and he had more decisive losses in Illinois and New York thanks in part to Gore's crucial Hispanic majorities. Only in Florida did Bush eke out a win among Hispanics (49 percent to 48 percent), thanks to lingering Cuban resentment over the Clinton administration's handling of the Elián González case.[133]

Undeterred in their belief that the United States has a large virtue deficit, Republicans have repeatedly gone after other tempting targets. One is homosexuals. In 1996, Bob Dole returned a $1,000 check from a gay Republican group, saying he did not want to create "the perception that we were buying into some special rights for any group, whether it is gays or anyone else."[134] For some time, Republicans argued that gays should not be given "special treatment" when it comes to protecting their rights to job security, health care, or housing. But sensing an opportunity to score political points, Republicans abandoned their "we're all equal" stance in 1996 by passing the Defense of Marriage Act. Proposed by Georgia congressman Bob Barr, the legislation forbade any state from recognizing a marriage ceremony involving couples of the same sex. At the time, Hawaii was on the verge of recognizing same-sex marriages, meaning that all states would have to acknowledge the validity of any marriage performed there, as required under the Full Faith and Credit

Clause of the U.S. Constitution. For federal purposes, Barr defined marriage as the legal union of one man and one woman.

The legislation stirred emotions on both sides. Barr saw himself a hero in the culture wars, telling his colleagues, "The flames of hedonism, the flames of narcissism, the flames of self-centered morality are licking at the very foundation of our society, the family unit."[135] Even some Republicans who might have otherwise opposed the law, supported it. One was Arizona congressman Jim Kolbe, who voted for the Defense of Marriage Act even though he is gay. Another was the late Sonny Bono, a former singer and partner of Cher, who had a gay daughter by her. Explaining his no vote to Massachusetts Democrat Barney Frank (a self-professed homosexual), Bono said: "I simply can't handle it yet, Barney. I wish I was ready, but I can't tell my son it's OK."[136]

Democrats saw the legislation as gay-baiting. Barney Frank declared, "I find it implausible that two men who decide to commit themselves to each other threaten the marriage of people who live two blocks away."[137] Illinois senator Carol Moseley-Braun said the bill was "really about the politics of fear and division."[138] Ted Kennedy tried unsuccessfully to attach a provision prohibiting job discrimination against gays, losing by a single vote of 49 to 50. Democrats voted 41 to 5 for the Kennedy amendment; but Republicans solidly opposed it with just 8 in favor and 45 against. The Defense of Marriage Act subsequently won Senate approval by a vote of 85 to 14. The House had earlier passed the legislation by a 342–67 margin. Presidential spokesman Michael McCurry condemned the legislation as a "classic use of wedge politics designed to provoke anxieties and fears."[139] But McCurry's boss knew that 57 percent of Americans believed that gay marriages should not be legally sanctioned.[140] Fearing that he would be on the wrong side of the culture wars if he vetoed the bill, and not willing to risk his re-election on the issue, Bill Clinton signed the Defense of Marriage Act into law at the unusual hour of 12:50 A.M. on an otherwise quiet September night at the White House.

Abortion is another example of the dangers posed by the politics of virtue. During the Clinton years, Republicans twice sought to outlaw partial-birth abortions, only to be rebuffed with a presidential veto. Debate on this controversial procedure has been particularly vehement. Illinois congressman Henry Hyde deplored the "abortion culture," which he believed Bill Clinton condoned: "Our beloved America is becoming 'The Killing Fields,'" a reference to the horrific movie depicting the slaughter of Cambodians after the communist takeover in 1975. Seeing partial-birth abortions as indicative of a larger virtue deficit, House Republicans twice mustered the two-thirds majority needed to override Clinton's vetoes. In 1997, 219 House Republicans supported overriding Clinton; just 8 were opposed. The Senate upheld Clinton's vetoes, but only by the barest of margins. This action ran counter to public opinion: 73 percent supported a ban on late-term abortions, and 51 percent said they were less likely to vote for a candidate who held a contrary viewpoint.[141] Sensing a winning issue, the Republican National Committee in 1998 considered terminating campaign support for those candidates who did not support a partial-birth abortion ban. Despite strong public opposition to partial-birth abortions, the move met with strong resistance from the party's rank and file: 49 percent opposed the ban; 43 percent supported it.[142] In the face of such intraparty opposition, members of the national committee were forced to abandon their quest for ideological purity.

Nonetheless, the Republican-led effort to ban partial-birth abortions was only one of many legislative initiatives designed to limit abortions. Republicans have lobbied to restore Reagan-era prohibitions against federal funding for family-planning organizations promoting overseas abortions. They sought to impose an abortion ban in all U.S. military hospitals. Roger Wicker, a Mississippi House Republican who was elected president of the 1994 freshman class, sponsored legislation outlawing fetal tissue research. In 1999, House Republicans overwhelmingly voted to restrict teenage abortions by making it a federal crime for an adult to take a minor to another state for an abortion that would have bypassed a parental notification law in the girl's home state. Violators would be subject to one year in jail and a $100,000 fine. Tom DeLay was a strong supporter of the new restrictions: "Schools must obtain parental permission for field trips. But for a dangerous and sometimes fatal procedure a child . . . can be transported across state lines without a simple notification of their parent."[143] Democrats heaped scorn on DeLay's argument. Wisconsin representative Tammy Baldwin maintained that "there are times when a pregnant teenager cannot go to her parents."[144] New York representative Nita Lowey wondered whether police would set up "granny checkpoints [to] catch grandmothers helping their granddaughters? Will we have dogs and searchlights at state borders to lock up aunts and uncles?"[145] Despite Lowey's vociferous objections, the measure passed the House on a vote of 270 yeas to 159 nays. Republicans voted 206 to 14 in favor; Democrats were more divided, with 64 yeas (enough for a comfortable majority) and 144 noes.

Each of these antiabortion measures met with Bill Clinton's strong disapproval. At a White House ceremony featuring women who had partial-birth abortions because their malformed fetuses would have made them barren, Clinton deplored the fact that these parents had become "political pawns."[146] Clinton supported a partial-birth abortion ban if the Republicans had included language protecting the life of the mother (which they did) and an "appropriate exception" for health (which they did not). While Clinton's pro-choice positions riled many Republican activists, it was his behavior with White House intern Monica Lewinsky that proved to them once and for all that the virtue deficit had become a virtue crisis.

The Clinton-Lewinsky Scandal and the Republican Theocrats

The Republican Party's dalliance with the politics of virtue was in full public view during the House impeachment and Senate trial of President Clinton. Clinton's affair with Monica Lewinsky, and his clumsy attempts to hide his extramarital relationship from Paula Jones's lawyers, provided Republicans with a vivid example of the virtue deficit in the Oval Office. Wisconsin congressman James Sensenbrenner, one of the impeachment managers, likened the scandal to a "cancer on the body politic" and declared it was the duty of the House to excise it.[147] Charles Canady, a member of the House Judiciary Committee, saw in the scandal a story as old as the Book of Genesis, concluding that in Clinton's case, like Adam and Eve or Cain and Abel before him, "the president's sins led him to commit crimes."[148]

Clinton's moral lapse resulted in the first impeachment since the Republican-led Congress exacted its retribution on Andrew Johnson in 1868. Although they never came close to mustering the two-thirds vote needed to remove Clinton from office, most Senate Republicans were persuaded; forty-six voted guilty on the perjury charge and fifty said Clinton had obstructed justice. In each instance, the Senate GOP defectors were 1960s-style "me-too" northeastern moderates (including Jim Jeffords) who saw themselves as faithful to their party's individualistic and freedom-loving traditions and were disturbed at Independent Counsel Kenneth Starr's overreach. Party voting also dominated in the House. The Judiciary Committee approved three of four articles of impeachment on a straight party-line vote of 21–16. In the full House, 98 percent of Republicans supported Article One (accusing Clinton of lying before a federal grand jury); 88 percent passed Article Two (which claimed that Clinton gave false testimony in his Paula Jones deposition); 95 percent approved Article Three (which charged Clinton with obstruction of justice); and 64 percent backed Article Four (which stated that Clinton had abused his office). In his closing argument before the U.S. Senate advocating Clinton's impeachment, Henry Hyde declared: "Equal justice is what moves me and animates me and consumes me. And I'm willing to lose my seat any day in the week rather than sell out on those issues. Despite all the polls and the hostile editorials, America is hungry for people who believe in something. You may disagree with us, but we believe in something."[149]

What is especially striking about Clinton's impeachment is the uniformity of the impeachment managers on the other proposed bills previously cited in this chapter where the politics of virtue was paramount. This unanimity, and Clinton's desire to undercut the Republicans by stealing their most popular issues, served to increase the vehemence of the congressional Republicans. Presidential press secretary Mike McCurry warned Clinton in 1996 that if he adopted Republican policies, then the GOP "can only win by doing the single most dangerous thing [to] Clinton which is to totally destroy him as a human being."[150] By reluctantly endorsing measures like the Defense of Marriage Act, Clinton aroused the ire of the virtue-minded Republicans who hated him just as passionately as the Republican recalcitrants of the 1930s loathed Franklin D. Roosevelt. Many of the House impeachment managers were leaders in this new politics of virtue. Bob Barr wrote the Defense of Marriage Act, in which he was joined by James Sensenbrenner and Charles Canady as cosponsors. Henry Hyde had written many antiabortion laws. As table 3.3 makes clear, the House impeachment managers were reliable yeas when it came to voting for laws that would impose their values on the larger body politic.

While the Republicans were successful in impeaching Clinton, their victory came at a price. A 1998 Gallup poll found an eleven-point Republican deficit in the party's favorability ratings compared to the Democrats, exactly the same deficit the party faced during George H.W. Bush's reelection campaign in 1992.[151] In 1999, pollster John Zogby asked whether the GOP had become a party "that does not respect privacy and spends too much time moralizing and investigating political opponents." According to the results, 54 percent agreed and 43 percent disagreed.[152] Two years later a Gallup poll found 50 percent saying the Republican Party had become "too conservative" under President George W. Bush.[153]

However history may ultimately judge the Clinton impeachment, it is clear that the less libertarian, more moralistic House managers were part of a much larger movement that had pulled the Republican Party some distance from its historic roots. Conservative commentator Andrew Sullivan believes that Kenneth Starr helped create "a conservatism [that has] become puritan—a scolding, moralizing conservatism, [and] a conservatism that has lost sight of the principles of privacy and restraint, modesty and constitutionalism, which used to be its hallmarks."[154] But to the conservative moralists who were the objects of Sullivan's barbs, the inability of Congress to convict Clinton and remove him from office represented a larger failure. In a letter to his supporters, James Dobson wrote, "What has alarmed me throughout this episode has been the willingness of my fellow citizens to rationalize the President's behavior even as they suspected, and later knew, that he was lying. I am left to conclude that our greatest problem is not in the Oval Office. It is with the people of this land."[155] To Andrea Shelton, the willingness of so many Americans to keep Clinton in office signified the emergence of a "post-Christian culture": "People say they go to church, they pray. But simultaneously they live in a culture of 'live and let live,' 'do whatever feels good' attitude."[156]

Authoritative or Authoritarian?

Concern for high moral standards and piety continues to garner strong public backing, especially following the Clinton scandals. In a 1999 poll conducted in

TABLE 3.3 HOUSE IMPEACHMENT MANAGERS AND THE POLITICS OF VIRTUE

Impeachment Manager	Megan's Law (1996)	Curbing Illegal Immigration (1996)	Defense of Marriage Act (1996)	Partial-Birth Abortion Override (1997)	Flag Protection Amendment (1999)	Ten Commandments Defense Amendment (1999)
Bob Barr	Yea	Yea	Yea	Yea	Yea	Yea
Ed Bryant	Yea	Yea	Yea	Yea	Yea	Yea
Steve Buyer	Yea	Yea	Yea	Yea	Yea	Yea
Charles Canady	Yea	Yea	Yea	Yea	Yea	Yea
Christopher Cannon	Not in Congress	Not in Congress	Not in Congress	Yea	Yea	Yea
Steve Chabot	Yea	Yea	Yea	Yea	Yea	Yea
George Gekas	Yea	Yea	Yea	Yea	Yea	Yea
Lindsay Graham	Yea	Yea	Yea	Yea	Yea	Yea
Asa Hutchinson	Yea	Yea	Yea	Yea	Yea	Yea
Henry Hyde	Yea	Yea	Yea	Yea	Yea	Yea
Bill McCollum	Yea	Yea	Yea	Yea	Yea	Yea
James Rogan	Not in Congress	Not in Congress	Not in Congress	Yea	Yea	Yea
James Sensenbrenner	Yea	Yea	Yea	Yea	Yea	Yea

Source: Congressional roll calls, various years.

the midst of the Clinton-Lewinsky affair, 54 percent said there are absolute standards of right and wrong for everyone.[157] Yet while a majority of Americans believe in absolute truths, they also hold the somewhat contrary view that morality can be arrived at by individual mediation rather than adherence to any particular religious doctrine. For example, when asked to decide whether people are inherently good and will behave morally unless they are taught bad values, or whether they are naturally sinful and will behave immorally unless they are taught good values, 60 percent said people are naturally good; just 35 percent opted for the doctrine of original sin.[158]

Republicans rapidly lose popular support when they summon the doctrine of original sin and believe that it is government's responsibility to correct the values of its citizens. Fifty-one percent believe the GOP has been too pessimistic about moral standards.[159] Moreover, when asked, "Which party is more tolerant of different kinds of people and different points of view?" Democrats are viewed as the more tolerant party by nearly a 3-to-1 margin.[160] But the Republican theocrats are undeterred by these poll results, and they continue to favor an activist government when it comes to making social policy. Such thinking runs counter to the values historically associated with the Republican Party—individualism and self-reliance.

An active role for government in making social policy also runs counter to public sentiment, which cherishes the values of individualism, self-reliance, and tolerance. For example, when asked which institution has the most potential to improve the nation's social and moral values, 65 percent named families, 11 percent cited religious institutions, 9 percent mentioned the media, 8 percent said schools, and just *2 percent* named the government.[161] During the height of the debate over the Defense of Marriage Act, 73 percent said there were other more important issues that demanded Congress's attention.[162] Even when queried about the emotionally charged issue of homosexuality, an overwhelming 69 percent believe government should not get involved with this issue.[163] Clearly, many want the bedroom removed from politics, even as many in public life want to transform lifestyle choices into political issues. On this point, most Americans share the libertarian skepticism of government's ability to reshape the nation's moral climate in any significant way.

Ironically, libertarianism may have more of a home in the Democratic Party, at least on social issues. Steve May, the gay Arizona legislator, believes Republicans must return to their roots of individualism and freedom: "I hope that the people who believe in the core values of the Republican Party will regain control of it as opposed to the extremists who have hijacked our party. That's really the problem. The core values of our party haven't changed, but the people who are controlling it have. I wish they would form a third party. I wish more of them would find a home somewhere else."[164] May's desire is an unlikely one, as the theocrats still call the GOP home. Republicans face an ongoing struggle, with a desire to be authoritative in expressing their ideas for improving the nation's moral climate while, at the same time, not appearing to be authoritarian to a public that likes its morality writ small. Reflecting on his term as Speaker of the House, Newt Gingrich says the Clinton impeachment provided an important lesson: "I realized that I was out of sync with the culture. This is a culture that is much more open, and has gone through many more experiences, than a person of my age and my background understood."[165] Sociologist Alan Wolfe argues that conservatives like Gingrich are discovering that most Americans do not want to surrender the moral freedoms they have acquired.[166] Republican pollster Bill McInturff says his party must change course: "Rightly or wrongly, the phrase 'family values' has taken on a political meaning that has a downside that no one ever intended. For some people, it doesn't leave room for divorced Moms, single parents, or people of color."[167]

The Republican Party's inability to draw fine distinctions between authoritative and authoritarian modes of thinking presents several opportunities for Democrats to exploit the GOP weakness on this subject. Clearly, the conservative social and foreign policy thinking that began with Richard Nixon's election in 1968 in the midst of the Vietnam War is a spent force. Issues that once prevented Americans from choosing the Democrats, including the twin charges that Democrats were "soft on crime" and "soft on communism," no longer carry the same resonance. Yet Democrats face their own values dilemma. Their inability to bridge the values divide is explored in the next chapter.

CHAPTER 4

Democrats and the Lingering Legacy of Bill Clinton

Out, damned spot! Out, I say!
—Lady Macbeth, *Macbeth*

IN MAY 1997, Bill Clinton had much to smile about. Seven months earlier, he had defied the pundits, who all but wrote him off for dead after the Republican rout of 1994, and easily dispatched Bob Dole off to retirement. Clinton's 1996 victory marked the first time a Democrat had won two terms since Franklin D. Roosevelt accomplished the same feat sixty years earlier. On May 2, Roosevelt was foremost in Clinton's thoughts as he joined the surviving members of the Hyde Park clan to dedicate the FDR Memorial, a stately expanse set across the Tidal Basin from Thomas Jefferson's stunningly beautiful monument. Clinton had always aspired to be as memorable and beloved a president as Roosevelt, whom he referred to in his dedication speech as "a master politician and a magnificent Commander-in-Chief."[1]

While Clinton did not have the momentous challenges FDR faced during his twelve years in office (few presidents are confronted with such dire circumstances), Clinton, like FDR, sought to wrest the Democratic Party from a decayed philosophical past and transform its thinking in ways that promised greater electoral success. For Clinton, that meant reaching a balanced budget agreement with House Speaker Newt Gingrich and the Republican-controlled Congress. While balancing the federal ledgers may not seem like a Democratic achievement, especially in light of FDR's extravagant spending to cure the Great Depression and wage a world war, it proved to be an unfettered triumph. The compact Clinton achieved boosted education spending dramatically, cut taxes for community-college tuition, remedied most of the flaws Clinton reluctantly accepted in the 1996 welfare reform bill, expanded heath-care coverage for poor children, and cut taxes. Now Clinton boasted of becoming the first president since Lyndon Johnson to submit a balanced budget to Congress, and of having fewer federal employees since John F. Kennedy's administration. As a cheery Clinton told reporters gathered in the sunny Rose Garden to hear the news, "The sun is rising on America."[2]

Ever the politician, Clinton was already looking forward to the 2000 elections. Wanting to apply the same strategy he had successfully used in the budget negotiations, the president met with his closest confidants after the FDR Memorial dedication and told them, "Strategically, I want to remove all divisive issues for a conservative [Republican presidential] candidate, so all the issues are on progressive terrain." At the meeting, Clinton sat poised to outline the objectives for his remaining thousand days in office in an address to be delivered at American University. As copies of a speech draft circulated, Vice President Al Gore squirmed. Thinking about Clinton's stated desire to eliminate any contentious issues Republicans might want to use in the upcoming presidential election, Gore cleared his throat and took aim at Clinton's speechwriters: "One word that doesn't jump at me in these documents is 'values.' And if you were in a room full of Republicans doing the same thing, that would be number one on their list."[3] Gore urged Clinton to make his proposals on the economy, changing the tone of the popular culture, and endorsing campaign finance reform consonant with enduring American values.

Clinton immediately grasped Gore's point. Ever since he had shaken John F. Kennedy's hand as a teenager, Clinton longed to be president. His chief biographer, David Maraniss, wrote that Clinton's desire to sit in the Oval Office "was always there, not a matter of predestination but of expectation and will, and it had built up year by year, decade by decade."[4] After leaving the Rose Garden on that hot summer's day in July 1963, Clinton was determined to learn everything he could about politics, and as his knowledge grew he relished even the most minute details. In 1992, candidate Clinton frequently acted as his own campaign manager. During the final days leading up to the vote, Clinton instructed his staff to run television advertisements in the key Paducah, Kentucky, media market. (Clinton won Kentucky.) Eight years later, Clinton had the best political job he could have wished for—aside from being the candidate, which he always preferred—and that was to act as the de facto manager for his wife Hillary's Senate race.

While studying the art of politics, Clinton came to admire those who were skilled practitioners regardless of their party affiliation. One of those he sought to emulate was Ronald Reagan who, like Clinton, was only the second man since Dwight D. Eisenhower to serve two full terms as president. Clinton studied Reagan intently. Once, in an endeavor to improve his presidential salute, Clinton watched old television outtakes of Reagan saluting awaiting soldiers while departing Marine One. Clinton admired how Reagan filled the presidential role.

Reagan himself attributed his strong acting skills for his success, confiding to David Brinkley just days before his departure, "There have been times in this office when I've wondered how you can do this job if you hadn't been an actor."[5]

The Gipper and the Comeback Kid

Ronald Reagan's stellar performance gave him something Bill Clinton craved, popularity. As noted in the introduction, Reagan was much beloved by the public, and many Americans, regardless of party affiliation, instinctively rooted for him to succeed. On the eve of the 1980 election, Reagan was asked by a reporter what he thought people saw in him. His response was revealing: "Would you laugh if I told you that I think, maybe, they see themselves and that I'm one of them? I've never been able to detach myself or think that I, somehow, am apart from them."[6] Such was Reagan's strong identification with his audience that he possessed an uncanny ability to arouse what William Shakespeare once called "the spirits of the vasty deep." This is a quality all leaders desire and the most-remembered presidents, like Reagan, have in spades. The point was made by John F. Kennedy only a few days before his tragic assassination. In a letter thanking political scientist Clinton Rossiter for his book on the American presidency, Kennedy offered a mild criticism. Rossiter believed the essence of the presidency lay in the enormous burdens the public placed on its custodians. Thus, he began *The American Presidency* with an epigraph from Shakespeare's *Macbeth*: "Methought I heard a voice cry, 'Sleep no more.'" Kennedy disagreed with Rossiter's choice and thought other Shakespearean lines were "more appropriate." In particular, he mentioned *King Henry IV, Part One*, in which one character says, "I can call spirits from the vasty deep," to which the reply is given "Why, so can I, or so can any man;/But will they come when you do call for them?"[7]

In Reagan's case, summoning spirits from the vasty deep meant serving as civil priest for the values embedded in classical liberalism. From the humble log cabin origins of nineteenth-century presidents, to the more prosperous suburban enclaves of twentieth-century chief executives, all presidents have embraced the values of individualism and equality of opportunity found in these communities which make classical liberalism such a powerful force in a successful, middle-class country. By talking about their hometown values so often, many presidents, including Reagan, have immersed themselves in American mythology. Upon achieving national notoriety, for example, Abraham Lincoln told admirers that he was just a poor boy made good: "It is a great piece of folly to attempt to make anything out of my early life. It can all be condensed into a single sentence and that sentence you will find in Gray's *Elegy*—'the short and simple annals of the poor.'"[8] Patrick Buchanan saw the value in frequent recitations of heroic efforts made by poor men to achieve greatness, telling Richard Nixon in a 1972 memo,

"My strong belief is that one of the functions of the President is the celebration—through the use of powers and honors at his disposal—of traditional American values and their exponents and defenders."[9] Nixon, who lost no opportunity to identify himself with the conservative values of his middle-class Silent Majority, did as Buchanan requested.

For Ronald Reagan, honoring traditional values meant paying close attention to what he said. According to Peggy Noonan, Reagan's principal speechwriter, Reagan understood that one of the president's jobs was to edit speech drafts with a sharpened pencil and, if that proved unsatisfactory, to rewrite them himself—a practice Reagan employed long before he entered the White House and had extraordinarily gifted speechwriters to help him.[10] Noonan writes that speech writing was "the center of gravity in that administration where ideas and principles still counted."[11] In fact, many of Reagan's biographers claim he was much more attentive to words than to deeds (a charge that never adhered to Clinton, the "policy wonk"). As former House Speaker Tip O'Neill once memorably said of Reagan, "He wouldn't have made much of a prime minister, but he would have made a hell of a king."[12]

Seeking the presidency in 1980, Reagan perfected his stagecraft by evoking a values mantra of "family, work, neighborhood, peace, and freedom" that he repeated over and over again at campaign rallies.[13] The image Reagan created with his recitation of these old-fashioned values was that of small-town America populated by hardworking, middle-class families who were besieged with serious, though not insurmountable, economic difficulties. Underlying Reagan's message were other values, including self-esteem, patriotism, self-realization, and religiosity. This values strategy worked wonders. Reagan beat Jimmy Carter handily, winning 51.6 percent of the vote and carrying forty-four states, making Carter's showing the worst of any Democratic president seeking reelection in U.S. history.

The same values strategy Reagan used in 1980 would be employed throughout his presidency. Pollster Richard B. Wirthlin advised the incoming Reagan team, "The values [of family, work, neighborhood, peace, and freedom] the President-Elect described in his Detroit acceptance speech should now begin to be rearticulated [*sic*] as operational components of a new sense of civic duty for all Americans."[14] Reagan acted on the premise that the essence of the American polity is less about the structures of government than a romantic preference for shared values. Values would henceforth be an important component in Reagan's renegotiation of the compact between the federal government and its citizens. In particular, he sought to refurbish family, work, neighborhood, peace, and freedom by pursuing conservative economic and social policies that would make these values greater realities. Midway through the Reagan-Carter contest, Daniel Patrick Moynihan, a Democrat with a keen political antenna, picked up some disturbing signals for his party: "There is a movement to turn Republicans into

Populists, a party of the people arrayed against the Democratic party of the state. Of a sudden, the GOP has become a party of ideas."[15] In articulating his new ideas, words like *family, work, neighborhood, peace,* and *freedom* were not mere platitudes; as Wirthlin explained, "In being the person who establishes a tone, a president has influence on every American—be it a young person entering the job market, an individual on the margin of deciding whether to study or whether to work, an entrepreneur trying to determine whether to invest in his own business or go to work for someone else."[16]

Reagan's success was remarkable. Combining the results of the 1980 and 1984 elections, Reagan won 93 states (out of 100) and 1,014 electoral votes (out of 1,076). In 1988, Reagan could not constitutionally seek reelection, but his popularity and power were sufficient to turn the reigns of government over to George H.W. Bush, who became the first vice president to be elected in his own right since Martin Van Buren followed the wildly popular Andrew Jackson into the White House back in 1836. From the beginning of his administration to its denouement, Reagan cloaked his speeches with values talk. Bidding farewell to the delegates at the 1988 Republican National Convention, Reagan told of a letter he had received from a young boy that read, in part, "I love America because you can join the Cub Scouts if you want to. You have a right to worship as you please. If you have the ability, you can try to be anything you want to be. I also like America because we have about two-hundred flavors of ice cream."[17] Such schmaltzy remarks led former Democratic presidential candidate Gary Hart to exclaim, "I don't want to be president of a country that thinks like Ronald Reagan."[18]

But Reagan's values strategy did not help his party. An examination of the handful of party-related values questions asked before 1988 shows that Democrats maintained a strong advantage when asked which party would do the better job of protecting traditional family values. No doubt the lingering memories of the New Deal, along with the Watergate scandals and the taint of the Nixon presidency, contributed to the Republican Party's values plight. Remarkably, however, the Democratic values advantage persisted through the Reagan years. Thus, Reagan's values strategy gave him political successes that enured only to him, not his party (see table 4.1).

In many ways, George H.W. Bush succeeded where Reagan could not. Seeking the presidency in 1988, Bush painted Democrat Michael Dukakis as an unrepresentative and unworthy steward of traditional family values. In so doing, Bush muted Dukakis's preferred storyline that stressed his Greek immigrant roots and notorious frugality. By campaign's end, the Bush team had transformed the Massachusetts governor into a 1960s-style liberal caricature who had little respect for family values. Their strategy crystalized when Bush operatives invited two dozen residents of Paramus, New Jersey, to a local hotel to discuss the candidates

TABLE 4.1   PARTIES AND VALUES, 1974–86 (IN PERCENTAGES)

Year	Question	Democrats	Republicans
1974	Do you feel that the Democratic Party or the Republican Party more closely represents your views and values, or don't you feel either one really does?	47	15
1984	Which party is the party of traditional family values?	40	29
1986	Do you think the Republican Party or the Democratic Party is the party of traditional family values?	45	33

Sources: 1974: Yankelovich, Skelly and White poll, March 1974. 1984: CBS News/*New York Times* poll, 5–9 August 1984. 1986: CBS News/*New York Times* poll, 28 September–1 October 1986.

and issues. Most of the blue-collar, Roman Catholic workers present had twice before backed Reagan but were currently supporting Dukakis. When the moderator asked, "What if I told you that Dukakis vetoed a bill that required schoolchildren to say the Pledge of Allegiance? Or that he was against the death penalty? Or that he gave weekend furloughs to first-degree murderers?" one of those present exclaimed, "He's a liberal!" Another retorted, "If those are really his positions, I'd have a hard time supporting him." Forty percent in one group and sixty percent in another switched allegiances on the spot.[19] By mid-October, Bush amassed an almost two-to-one lead over Dukakis as the candidate who would do a better job of protecting traditional American values.[20]

As historian Garry Wills wrote, "It was a brilliant stroke to run the incumbent Vice-President, who was boasting of his own Administration's success, as the candidate of *grievance*—of affronts localized in a liberalism that is soft on crime and defense, exotic as a Harvard boutique, yet stealthy enough to win an election by misrepresenting itself to the American people."[21] Tom Hayden, himself a former student radical turned politician, also recognized the effectiveness of the Reagan-Bush values strategies: "Having thus lost God, the flag, national defense, tax relief, personal safety and traditional family values to the conservatives, it became more than a little difficult for these liberals to explain why they should be entrusted with the authority to govern."[22] A poll conducted late in the campaign emphasized Hayden's point. Asked to describe whether Michael Dukakis was "a liberal in the tradition of Franklin D. Roosevelt, Harry S. Truman, and John F. Kennedy," or whether he was "a liberal in the tradition of George McGovern and Walter Mondale," only 21 percent saw the Massachusetts governor in the Roosevelt-Truman-Kennedy liberal mold; 35 percent cast him in the more damning McGovern-Mondale mold.[23]

Thus, the Democratic Party that Bill Clinton inherited in 1992 was a dispirited one. Democrats had lost four of the five preceding presidential elections since

1968, winning only in 1976 after the Watergate scandal and Nixon's resignation, and barely at that. In 1987, Democratic strategist Robert Shrum warned, "The Democratic party has lived off the legacy of John F. Kennedy for twenty-eight years. The torch will go out unless it finally passes to a new generation. We need to invent a new legacy."[24] Many Democrats, including Shrum, despaired of winning the presidency ever again. In June 1992, as he was about the capture his party's nomination, Clinton told the *New York Times* that since Hubert H. Humphrey's defeat in 1968, "the Democrats have had a lot of trouble," adding,

> What I have tried to do during this campaign, and before that during my work with the Democratic Leadership Council, is to articulate a new approach for the Democrats that goes beyond where both parties have been, one that emphasizes a commitment to strong economic growth and opportunity, one that assumes more responsibility in certain critical areas, moving from welfare to work, strong child-care enforcement, changes in the nature of the American workplace and the nature of American schools. Changes in the behavior of our corporate executives, up and down the line. And one that was unabashedly pro-growth and for rebuilding in America a sense of American strength based on mainstream values.[25]

By making continuous references to opportunity, community, and responsibility, Clinton learned, as his speechwriter David Kusnet memorably phrased it, how to "speak American."[26] According to Clinton campaign pollster Stanley B. Greenberg, the challenge his candidate faced was to dispel the 1960s-era view of the Democratic Party as socially permissive and culturally liberal: "Democrats were seen not to understand the values that were important to mainstream middle-class families."[27] To counter this, Clinton empathized with those who "work hard and play by the rules." In so doing, he was immeasurably helped by George H.W. Bush's inability to provide for a strong economy and transform the values strategy he had used so effectively against Dukakis into a plan for governance. Kansas farmer Orville Mitchell neatly described Bush's values gap: "You can talk about family values and military service and all that stuff. But when its gets down to the bottom line, it's how the economy is going. The economy is in trouble. We had a heck of a time getting Bush to even admit it was in trouble. Now he knows it's in trouble because he's in trouble."[28]

By mid-1992, most Americans had decided to fire Bush. The problem was finding a worthy successor. To enhance his appeal, Bill Clinton skillfully employed Reagan-era values and phrases and made them his own. Accepting the Democratic nomination, Clinton exhorted his television audience, saying: "We offer our people a new choice based on old values. We offer opportunity. And we demand responsibility. The choice we offer is not conservative or liberal, Democratic or Republican. It is different. It is new. And it will work." "Opportunity, community, and responsibility" became the values mantra that Clinton would use both as a candidate and as president. Clinton reveled in telling stories that exemplified the lasting truths contained in these old verities, and his ability to tell stories rivaled Reagan's. In his 1992 acceptance speech, for example, Clinton introduced himself by relating how his father had died before he was born; how his mother went to work as a nurse; how with manic determination he was awarded entry into the nation's most prestigious universities; and how as governor of Arkansas he used the values of opportunity, community, and responsibility to make his constituents' lives better. Born in the small town of Hope, Arkansas, Clinton ended his peroration with the words, "I still believe in a place called Hope."[29]

Republicans were beside themselves, accusing Clinton of stealing their values code words. Besides making speeches that emphasized opportunity, community, and responsibility, Clinton spoke with a self-confidence and smile that contrasted strongly with Jimmy Carter, Walter Mondale, and Michael Dukakis, who in their losing campaigns often had a dour mein. This helped make Clinton a different kind of Democrat. Like his role model Ronald Reagan, Clinton espoused a new form of partisan thinking that matched his values rhetoric. Being as far removed from the New Deal as Franklin Roosevelt was from the Civil War, the time for updating Democratic Party dogma had long passed. Consecutive presidential losses only deepened the Democrats' despair. Instead of relying on big New Deal–era federal government programs and the bureaucracies required to implement them, Clinton began to speak of a "Third Way" whereby government would be a catalyst, but not the primary means, to induce fundamental change. Making the case for a smaller government, Democrats said, "Government's job should be to give people the tools they need to make the most of their lives."[30] The 1992 party platform elaborated the party's new thinking:

> We offer a new social contract based neither on callous, do-nothing Republican neglect, nor an outdated faith in programs as the solution to every problem. We favor a third way beyond the old approaches—to put government back on the side of citizens who play by the rules. We believe that by what it says and how it conducts its business, government must once again make responsibility an instrument of national purpose. Our future as a nation depends upon the daily assumption of personal responsibility by millions of Americans from all walks of life—for the religious faiths they follow, the ethics they practice, the values they instill, and the pride they take in their work.[31]

For Clinton Democrats, personal responsibility, not government, "is the most powerful force we have to meet our challenges and shape the future we want for ourselves, for our children, and for America."[32]

But as the first of the 1960s-era "flower children" to secure a major party nomination for president, Clinton was subjected to a series of questions that dogged him throughout his presidency and created persistent doubts about his capacity to serve. In an interview with *60 Minutes*, he tacitly admitted that he had not always been faithful to his wife. Later, he acknowledged experimenting "a time or two" with marijuana, although he "didn't inhale." The press discovered that Clinton had avoided military service during the Vietnam War by winning a student deferment and that he had undertaken a number of contorted efforts to obtain it. Not surprisingly, two-thirds thought Clinton lied about inhaling marijuana; half thought he was dishonest in not admitting an affair with Gennifer Flowers; and many were divided about whether he misrepresented his draft status during the Vietnam War.[33]

Compounding the personal doubts about Clinton's character was his complicated relationship with his wife Hillary, which was not a traditional 1950s-era marriage but more of an equal personal and political partnership. When Clinton was first elected governor of Arkansas in 1978, Hillary Clinton kept her maiden name, Rodham, as so many women of her generation did. Only after her husband was defeated for reelection two years later did she begin to use her married name in an attempt to ingratiate herself with traditional Arkansas values. When Bill Clinton sought the presidency in 1992, his wife was referred to as "Hillary Clinton." But as the campaign began and Hillary Clinton's financial dealings while serving as a lawyer in private practice became subject to press scrutiny, the future First Lady replied, "I suppose I could have stayed home and baked cookies and had teas. But what I decided to do was pursue my profession, which I entered before my husband was in public life." During the infamous *60 Minutes* interview, Clinton emphatically declared that she as not "some little woman standing by my man like Tammy Wynette." Only after her husband's victory was secured did she start referring to herself as "Hillary Rodham Clinton." For his part, Bill Clinton hinted during the campaign of a more powerful role for his wife. He often told campaign rallies that if he won, voters would get "two for the price of one"—meaning that Mrs. Clinton would become a full partner in making public policy. Americans were evenly divided at the prospect of such a powerful first lady: 40 percent thought Hillary Clinton came closer to representing their values and lifestyles than previous first ladies; an equal number disagreed.[34]

Sensing that both Clintons were vulnerable on values issues, Patrick J. Buchanan, in a fiery speech at the 1992 Republican National Convention, sought to turn public doubts about the Clintons into a GOP asset. Buchanan argued that the nation was in the throes of a culture war, whose latest protagonists were the duo of "Clinton & Clinton":

The agenda Clinton & Clinton would impose on America—abortion on demand, a litmus test for the Supreme Court, homosexual rights, discrimination against religious schools, women in combat—that's change, all right. But it is not the change America wants. It is not the kind of change America needs. And it is not the kind of change we can tolerate in a nation that we still call God's country. . . . There is a religious war going on in our country for the soul of America. It is a cultural war, as critical to the kind of nation we will one day be as was the Cold War itself. And in that struggle for the soul of America, Clinton & Clinton are on the other side, and George Bush is on our side.[35]

But Bill Clinton's emphasis on the economic dislocations caused by the end of the Cold War gave him an enhanced credibility whenever he discussed values. According to one poll, 51 percent said that when Clinton spoke about family values he was referring to their families.[36] Another survey found 54 percent believing that Clinton shared the moral values most Americans try to live by.[37] By early October, Clinton had a slender four-point lead over George H.W. Bush as the candidate who would do the best job of dealing with family values.[38] Remarkably, the Democratic Party had regained its Reagan-era values advantage: 34 percent said Democrats would do a better job of "upholding traditional family values"; 32 percent thought the Republicans were better at this task.[39] To paraphrase the old Virginia Slims cigarette commercial, Democrats had "come a long way baby." The party of George McGovern, once caricatured by Richard Nixon's supporters as favoring "amnesty, acid, and abortion,"[40] suddenly found itself being listened to by Nixon's Silent Majority. Democrats were euphoric. In the words of Joe Lyons, a Chicago Democratic precinct captain, "There is a God: A Democrat can be president again."[41] Shortly after Clinton's win, even Ronald Reagan paid him homage. The two men met briefly at Clinton's request in the ex-president's California office, whereupon Reagan offered his beaming successor a jar of his favorite brand of jelly beans.[42]

But in the flush of victory, considerable public tentativeness about Clinton lingered. Leaving the polls on Election Day, 58 percent said they were "concerned" or "scared" at the prospect of a Clinton presidency.[43] Nick Niederlander, a librarian in Richmond Heights, Missouri, captured the fragility of Clinton's support: "I want to like Clinton more than I like him."[44] For his part, Clinton seemed to have forgotten the lessons Reagan taught and found it nearly impossible to make the transition from candidate to president. Clinton seemed uncomfortable with his new-found role, and reports circulated that the president and first lady were ill at ease under the watchful eyes of the Secret Service. Clinton's inability to envision himself as president became evident during an MTV appearance when he was asked by a seventeen-year-old, "The world is dying to know: Is it boxers or briefs?" Clinton replied, "Briefs, usually," wistfully adding, "I can't believe I said that."[45] After that inadvertent disclosure, Clinton's advisers constantly urged him to be "more presidential." Irritated at the incessant refrain, Clinton asked one just what he meant. The answer: "Less than papal, but more gubernatorial."[46] As Clinton's discomfort grew, so did his lack of self-confidence. In a deposition filed in the Paula Jones case, Clinton described how the bruises of the 1992 campaign lingered long after he entered the White House: "After I went through a presidential campaign in which the far right tried to convince the American people I had committed murder, run drugs, slept in my mother's bed with four prostitutes, and done numerous other things, I had a high level of paranoia."[47]

Compounding Clinton's troubles was a poor start in which he seemed to govern more like a 1960s liberal instead of the New Democrat he promised to be. Rather than emphasizing "reinventing government," which promised a downsized bureaucracy and a balanced budget—both central "Third Way" campaign themes—Clinton became enmeshed in controversy. He advocated a "don't ask, don't tell" policy that allowed gays to serve in the military. One 1993 poll taken in the wake of the gays-in-the-military fiasco found 68 percent saying Clinton believed homosexuality should be accepted by society.[48] In addition, he signed legislation named after former Reagan press secretary James Brady (who was grievously wounded in the 1981 assassination attempt) that established a ten-day waiting period for purchasing a handgun. This set Clinton at odds with attitudes in his native South, especially among white men. After the 2000 campaign, Congressman Barney Frank maintains that one "not-sa-posta" of presidential politics is for prospective Democratic candidates to emulate Clinton's support of gun-control measures.[49] Finally, both Clintons proposed a health care reform bill that was portrayed on the "Harry and Louise" television advertisements as the epitome of big government. The bill proved so unpopular that not even the Democratic-controlled Congress brought it to a final vote. Gays-in-the-military, the Brady Bill, and the failed health care proposal reminded voters why they disliked Democrats in the first place. Many began to suspect they had elected George McGovern rather than Bill Clinton.

"I Want My Presidency Back"

The 1994 midterm elections were a watershed for both the Republican Party and Bill Clinton. For the first time since 1952, Congress came under new management. Bob Dole and Newt Gingrich suddenly found themselves in charge of both houses of Congress, and it seemed only a matter of time before their dream of Republican control of all three branches of the federal government fell into their grasp. For Clinton, too, the midterm election debacle was a kind of caesura. Just after the ballots had been counted, Clinton told his political advisers, "I want my presidency back."[50] At the time, the likelihood that Clinton's wish could be granted seemed bleak. At an April 1995 news conference, a forlorn president told reporters that he remained "relevant" to the goings-on in Washington: "The Constitution gives me relevance. The power of our ideas gives me relevance."[51] Clinton's assertion that House Speaker Newt Gingrich would eventually have to deal with him seemed like wishful thinking. But the next day, Clinton's political resurrection materialized when a truck bomb exploded inside the Murrah Federal Office Building in Oklahoma City. Emulating Reagan, Clinton took center stage as mourner-in-chief, consoling victims' families and healing a grieving nation. The bomb's detonation and Clinton's soothing voice left Republicans speechless.[52] After the Oklahoma City bombing, Clinton press secretary Michael McCurry said, "The debate in America is shifting out of economic policy and to moral values and what kind of society we are. The Republicans have had strong, resonant statements on that and the Democrats have fallen short. This gives Clinton an opportunity to talk about civil discourse and social values. Oklahoma has been a great opportunity to do that. Clinton is struck by the power of these themes."[53] Connecticut Democratic senator and then–national party chair Christopher Dodd noticed a perceptible change in Clinton's demeanor: "He sort of filled out. . . . The [presidential] suit finally fit."[54]

Now fully engaged, Clinton used the bully pulpit to become the nation's storyteller-in-chief. By repeating tales of individual heroism, Clinton amplified his values themes of opportunity, community, and responsibility and gave them added resonance. Like Reagan, he used his State of the Union addresses not merely to outline a legislative laundry list but to tell heroic stories. In his 1995 speech, for example, Clinton told not one story, but *six*. There was Lynn Woolsey, a single mother from California who found her way off welfare to become a member of Congress. Then came Cindy Perry, a mother of four who passed her high school equivalency exam and teaches second-graders to read in rural Kentucky. Next, was Steven Bishop, the police chief of Kansas City, Missouri, an AmeriCorps volunteer, and an innovator in community policing. Then, Corporal Gregory Depestre, a Haitian American who was part of the U.S. force that landed in Haiti, was asked to stand. His commander-in-chief took note: "We must be the only country in the world that could have gone to Haiti and taken Haitian Americans there who could speak the language and talk to the people, and he was one of them, and we're proud of him."[55]

Clinton was hardly finished. He praised the Reverends John and Diana Cherry, noting that the church they formed in the 1980s had grown to 17,000 members and expanded into the high-crime and drug-infested neighborhoods of Washington, D.C. Finally, Clinton recognized Jack Lucas, a World War II veteran from Hattiesburg, Mississippi. Lucas was badly wounded at Iwo Jima after he threw himself on two grenades and saved the lives of three of his fellow soldiers. Only seventeen, Lucas miraculously survived and became the youngest citizen to win the Congressional Medal of Honor. For Clinton, the moral lesson contained in each of these stories was clear: "We all gain when we give and we reap what we sow." He then connected the dots between these stories and his cherished New Covenant of opportunity, community, and responsibility:

> That's at the heart of this New Covenant: responsibility, opportunity, and citizenship. More than stale chapters in some remote civics book, they are still the virtues by which we can fulfill ourselves and reach our God-given potential and be like them, and also to fulfill the eternal promise of this country, the enduring dream from that first and most sacred covenant. I believe every person in this country still believes that we are created equal, and given by our Creator the right to life, liberty, and the pursuit of happiness.[56]

At last, Clinton had learned how to apply Reagan's values lessons successfully. By 1996, this skilled politician had become one of America's premier storytellers, and he encouraged others to echo his themes. At the Democratic Convention that renominated him, Clinton turned the podium over to paralyzed actor Christopher Reeve and gunshot victim James Brady so that they, too, could tell their stories of hope and courage—and, by inference, add their biographies to Clinton's own. Indeed, one Clinton television advertisement featured the wheelchair-bound Brady saying of Clinton, "When I hear people question the president's character, I say look at what he's done. Look at the lives the Brady Bill will save."[57]

By having convention speakers stick to values rather than substantive policy discussions, the Democratic conclave became a kind of "Oprahland," a cathartic talk show for the viewing television audience. This reflected Clinton's belief that his reelection involved more than just defending a successful economy, it was about values. In an October 1995 memo, Clinton pollsters Mark Penn and Doug Schoen explained how the president could link his "opportunity, community, and responsibility" mantra to governing in a second term:

1. *Standing up for America.* Every time our actions and words are interpreted as standing up for America, our support grows. . . . This is not a value we say we are doing, it is one that comes through a series of strong, definite actions that have us standing up to threats in the world from a very U.S. point of view.
2. *Providing opportunities for all Americans.* This is clearly what our defense and expansion of education are all about—giving people the opportunity to make the best of their own lives. Despite all the frustration with government, people are NOT frustrated with their own abilities as long as they and their children are given a chance to get ahead.

3. *Doing what's right even when it is unpopular.* Standing up to the to-
    bacco companies and supporting the assault weapons ban are examples
    not just of doing what's right, but doing it despite what are perceived
    as heavy political costs. There is no benefit to a values-based strategy if
    people say the president is taking the easy way out. Only when they
    see a cost can they come to admire the actions as extraordinary.

4. *Preserving and promoting families* (helping parents protect kids from the
    bad in society). In every poll we have taken, this is the top-scoring
    issue. It is made doubly important by the fact that we are so far behind
    with the votes of people with families. We have to change the percep-
    tion we have of promoting the single-parent family over the conven-
    tional, two-parent family by grouping as many of our programs under
    a banner of "putting families first." This means that the Family Leave
    Bill is just a small part of a program that helps kids with their educa-
    tional opportunities, young people with the new minimum wage, par-
    ents with a middle-class tax cut, and our aging parents with their
    health care. This is an administration helping families at all levels. And
    parents will be getting some of the help they need to raise their kids
    with the anti-smoking initiative and the V-chip.[58]

The poll takers urged that every jot and tittle of Clinton's speeches describe
"a view of the world [of] what is happening in values terms, not just economics;
[place] our accomplishments in values terms, not just economic ones; [place] our
new programs in the same terms; [and conclude] that taking this approach is the
real way we can find a common ground and get this country moving."[59] Mark
Penn, in particular, believed that Clinton had turned the values debate in his
favor by avoiding divisive issues such as abortion, gay rights, and school prayer
and contrasting his values to those of the Republican-controlled Congress: "We
said if you're for families, you should be doing things for Medicare and education, the kinds of things that help children and their families."[60]

Clinton followed his pollsters' advice to the letter, and the result was a re-
versal of his own values misfortunes and those of the Democratic Party. Although Bob Dole enjoyed a ten-point lead over Clinton as the candidate providing the best moral example,[61] Clinton was seen as the more effective moral
leader. In addition, Clinton had a slender three-point lead as the man best able
to deal with the country's moral problems,[62] and 51 percent described him as a
moral person.[63] To further emphasize his commitment to opportunity, community, and responsibility, Clinton issued a 1996 campaign book with each values
theme serving as a chapter.[64] The Democratic Party's standing on moral and values issues also improved: 52 percent thought the Democrats better represented
their values; just 39 percent chose the Republicans.[65] Moreover, the GOP lead as

TABLE 4.2 PARTY VALUE PREFERENCES, 1996 (IN PERCENTAGES)

Value	Democrats	Republicans
Fairness	45	29
Community	46	33
Hope	45	35
Opportunity	43	40
Work	42	39
Ethics and Honesty	30	30
Personal Responsibility	33	43

Source: The Tarrance Group and Mellman, Lazarus and Lake poll, 27–29 January 1996.

the party that best represents family values shrank to just 4 points.[66] And on a host of other values characteristics, Democrats enjoyed a substantial lead or were tied with the Republicans. Only when asked which party best represented the value of personal responsibility did the Republicans have a significant advantage (see table 4.2).

A rollicking economy, along with adroit practicing of the new politics of old values, produced a decisive Clinton victory. Twenty-nine states and the District of Columbia—with a total of 379 electoral votes—backed Clinton, nineteen of them (including D.C.) by decisive majorities. Even Whiteside County, Illinois, which contains Ronald Reagan's hometown of Tampico, twice supported Clinton, the first time a Democrat won back-to-back victories there since the founding of the Republican Party in 1854. Moreover, the election gave Clinton one more chance to use his strategy of values and remake the Democratic Party in his own image. In a November 1997 interview, Clinton cast his vision for the country in values terms: "I had a vision [in 1992] for what I wanted America to look like when I left office. I wanted this to be a country where there was opportunity for every person responsible enough to work for it, where our country was still the leading nation for people and freedom and prosperity, and where with all these differences we've got, we're still coming together as one America. That's my vision. I hope someday some scholar will say it was my legacy."[67]

The Shaming of the President

Clinton's legacy, however, suffered irreparable damage in the wake of the Monica Lewinsky scandal. In January 1998, press reports surfaced about a sex scandal involving Clinton and a twenty-something White House intern named Monica Lewinsky, who intimated in secretly tape-recorded conversations made by her close friend Linda Tripp that Clinton lied under oath about their relationship and conspired with *his* close friend Vernon Jordan to find Lewinsky a job in order to procure her silence. The sordid affair, replete with graphic nightly news soundbites saying that Clinton had engaged in oral sex with Lewinsky, led many to believe that the Clinton years had come to an abrupt, fatal end. Columnist George Will wrote that the Clinton presidency was "deader than Woodrow Wilson's was after he had a stroke."[68] One Montana newspaper editorialized, "Whatever happens in the end, Clinton will be remembered as a president lucky enough to have served during prosperous economic times, a president whose progressive policies were increasingly undermined as much by his move to the center and beyond as by his declining credibility, and a president who shamed his wife and daughter and his party and the people of the United States by his mind-bendingly [sic] reckless inability to keep it in his pants."[69]

Talk of impeachment filled the air, and a handful of House Republicans led by Georgia's Bob Barr introduced impeachment resolutions. On the first day the allegations became public, an astounding 82 percent told pollsters they had heard the tale.[70] Those who lingered in the congressional cloakrooms could talk of nothing else. In the wake of the scandal, a series of polls uncovered a set of facts that seemed devastating on their face: 67 percent believed Clinton had sexual relations of some kind with Lewinsky; 62 percent thought he lied under oath about having an affair;[71] 50 percent thought his comments about Lewinsky ("I did not have sexual relations with that woman, Ms. Lewinsky.") were untruthful;[72] and 52 percent thought he had engaged in a pattern of sexual misconduct while president.[73] Not surprisingly, 56 percent said Clinton did *not* share their values; an equal percentage thought he showed poor judgment; and 62 percent did not think that Clinton was either honest or trustworthy.[74] Most damning, 45 percent said that if they had a daughter in her late teens or early twenties, they would not feel safe leaving her alone with Clinton.[75]

Such public condemnations did not occur out of the blue. When Clinton was accused in 1992 of being a less-than-perfect role model, voters diagnosed several character flaws in the man they would soon elect as their forty-second president. Two years later, Paula Jones reignited those doubts by accusing Clinton of exposing himself in an Arkansas hotel room while he was governor and she was a lowly state file clerk. Jones brought her complaint of sexual harassment against Clinton (with the blessing of the Republican-dominated U.S. Supreme Court), and the case went to trial in 1998. In her lawsuit, Jones claimed that Clinton had not only acted inappropriately, but had discriminated against her after she refused to satisfy his sexual urges. In making this argument, Jones's attorneys uncovered evidence that Clinton repeated his unsavory sexual behavior while serving as president. Kathleen Willey, wife of a prominent Richmond lawyer and an unpaid White House volunteer, testified that she visited with Clinton in the Oval Office on 29 November 1993, to ask for a job. Willey claimed that Clinton kissed her, fondled her breasts, and placed her hand on his genital area, saying, "I've always wanted to do that."[76] Testifying before the grand jury on the Lewinsky matter,

Clinton admitted, "I did what people do when they do the wrong thing. I tried to do it where nobody else was looking at it."[77]

In his 1998 State of the Union address, which came just as news of the Lewinsky scandal broke, Clinton ignored the sordid allegations and made an implicit, but unstated, distinction between private morality and public values. Once more, Clinton returned to the values mantra of opportunity, community, and responsibility that had served him so well in the past. Addressing a record 75 million television viewers, Clinton told stories that connected his public policies to his values themes. He recalled how Elaine Kinslow of Indianapolis had been on and off welfare for thirteen years. But after Clinton and the Republican-controlled Congress had agreed on a welfare reform package in 1996, Clinton happily reported, Kinslow had found a job as a dispatcher with a van company. Clinton introduced Kinslow, seated in the First Lady's box, to the television audience, noting with pride that "she's saved enough money to move her family into a good neighborhood, and she's helping other welfare recipients go to work." Next, Clinton told the story of how U.S. Army sergeant Michael Tolbert bravely led an infantry unit that stopped a mob from taking over a radio station in Bosnia after Clinton had dispatched NATO forces there. Finally, Clinton praised Ohio senator John Glenn for his courage in returning to space thirty-seven years after his 1961 space flight, recalling the words used when Glenn was first hurled into orbit, "Godspeed, John Glenn." To Clinton, the moral was clear: "John, you will carry with you America's hopes. And on your uniform, once again, you will carry America's flag, marking the unbroken connection between the deeds of America's past and the daring of America's future."[78] Clinton's poll ratings skyrocketed: 79 percent liked what he said; two-thirds said Clinton had held their attention; an equal number approved of the way Clinton was handling his job, a figure that matched Ronald Reagan at his zenith.[79] *Newsweek's* Jonathan Alter wrote that "when the history of the latter part of this century is written, these two authentic actors [Ronald Reagan and Bill Clinton] will be the only ones living large in the theater of our public imagination."[80]

Clinton's storytelling, with all of its implicit moral lessons, proved to be a powerful rhetorical device. More than two-thirds wanted Clinton to remain at the helm, and 62 percent expressed confidence that he was up to the job.[81] Republicans privately marveled at Clinton's ability to resurrect himself in the face of adversity, even as they publicly condemned his private morality. Missouri senator John Ashcroft thundered, "I think there's a values deficit in Washington."[82] Former Tennessee governor and two-time presidential candidate Lamar Alexander said of Clinton, "If he were the head of a large company, he'd be fired. If he were a Cabinet officer, he'd be indicted. If he were a military commander, he'd be court-marshaled." Former vice president Dan Quayle quipped, "My friends, I'm proud to announce that I have a very tough anti-crime proposal for our party. And here's the centerpiece of our anti-crime plan: Three interns and you're out!"

At a GOP gathering in Biloxi, Mississippi (held, ironically, at a gambling casino), Republicans sported buttons reading, "It Takes a Village Idiot to Believe Clinton," "Lose One for the Zipper, Vote Republican," and "Jail to the Chief!"—the latter a revengeful twist on a bumper sticker denouncing Richard Nixon during his last days as president.[83]

Republican pollster Frank Luntz once described Clinton as the greatest communicator since Franklin D. Roosevelt—better, even, than Ronald Reagan: "Reagan was likeable. People don't like Bill Clinton, and yet they follow him."[84] One reason voters were willing to follow Clinton was that he was lucky in who his enemies were. Fifty-two percent believed that Kenneth Starr, the special prosecutor investigating the Monica Lewinsky case, should desist; 64 percent thought Starr had inappropriately called Lewinsky's mother before the grand jury to testify against her daughter; and 53 percent said the Secret Service should not attest to events that may have transpired while they were guarding Clinton.[85] Patricia Schroeder, head of the Association of American Publishers, strongly criticized Starr after he obtained records of Lewinsky's purchases at a Washington-area bookstore: "This is a scenario that belongs in Baghdad or Tehran. I don't think the American people could find anything more alien to our way of life or more repugnant to the Bill of Rights than government intrusion into what we think or read."[86]

As the Clinton-Lewinsky investigation intensified, the rhetoric of the Clinton-haters became more strident. To them, Clinton represented the worst excesses of the 1960s. Dan Burton, chairman of the House Government Reform and Oversight Committee, called Clinton a "scumbag," adding, "That's why I'm out to get him."[87] Mark Corallo, a senior aide to House Speaker-designate Bob Livingston, urged the Republican leadership to remain vigilant, telling Livingston, "Boss, we have a *rapist* in the White House," a reference to an accusation that Clinton had raped an Arkansas woman two decades before.[88] Clinton strategist James Carville delighted in such name-calling, once saying of Kenneth Starr: "How could you have a better guy there? You've got a guy investigating you that two-thirds of the country hates. How could you be better?"[89] According to a *Los Angeles Times* survey, 59 percent believed congressional Republicans were pursuing impeachment because they wanted to hurt Clinton politically.[90] Clinton was not a beloved president, as Reagan and Kennedy had been; rather, he was loved for the enemies he made.

Another useful enemy was the media. For decades, Americans harbored resentments against the press, viewing them as too powerful, mostly biased (especially in favor of the Democrats), and culturally liberal in their outlook. A 2001 Harris poll showed 77 percent think the news media has too much power in Washington,[91] while another study found media elites held uniformly liberal attitudes on social and cultural issues: 90 percent thought a woman should have a right to an abortion; 24 percent said homosexuality is wrong; and only 15 percent would prohibit gays from teaching.[92] Former vice president Spiro Agnew once denounced the network anchormen as an "elite corps of impudent snobs who characterize themselves as intellectuals."[93] When the Clinton-Lewinsky scandal broke, a media "feeding frenzy" occurred. Nightly cable newscasts showed a beleaguered Clinton with a bullseye imposed over his face and a graphic that read, "The President Under Fire." But the barrage backfired; 55 percent said the media acted irresponsibly, with 77 percent saying the press preferred to be first with the latest allegations rather than get the story right. One-third thought most correspondents actually enjoyed talking about Clinton's difficulties.[94] David Brock, the reporter who originally broke the Paula Jones story, offered an abject apology to Clinton and admitted, "A virulent scandal culture was spawned that eventually drew in not only [Clinton's] conservative critics but also the mainstream press."[95] The line between entertainment shows like *Access Hollywood* and *Entertainment Tonight* and the networks' evening news programs became increasingly blurred.

Private Values, Public Morality, and the Plight of the Democratic Party

Hillary Clinton blamed a "vast right wing conspiracy"[96] for her husband's troubles and predicted, "When the truth comes out, this, like all the other accusations that have been made against us for so many years, will fade into oblivion, and the work the President has done will stand the test of time."[97] For his part, Bill Clinton redoubled his efforts to "reclaim my family life for my family," adding, "It's nobody's business but ours." Clinton argued that the country needed to "move on," and that citizens should redraw the boundaries between the public lives of their leaders and their personal lives: "Even presidents have private lives. It is time to stop the pursuit of personal destruction and the prying into private lives and get on with our national life."[98]

But political scientist Jean Bethke Elshtain, who previously decried the interweaving of personal lives with political issues, made an important distinction in Bill Clinton's case:

> In one of my essays on the Clinton mess I argued that if one creates a wall of separation between ethics and politics, one effects an "amoral Machiavellianism" of the sort that corrupts democratic politics over time. Democracy relies heavily on trustworthiness and legitimacy. If people doubt every word a leader says and have concluded that "his word cannot be trusted" (because he is a person of "low moral character" who has demonstrated his untrustworthiness), then he "cannot do his job effectively."[99]

Donna Shalala, Clinton's Health and Human Services secretary, made the same argument at a cabinet meeting: "I can't believe this is what you're telling us, that is what you believe, that you don't have an obligation to provide moral leadership. I don't care about the lying, but I'm appalled at the behavior." Clinton told Shalala that his enlightened "Third Way" policies could compensate for a moral failure to lead. Besides, he added, if Shalala's logic had prevailed in 1960, Richard M. Nixon would have beaten John F. Kennedy.[100]

Americans were closely divided as to how much and what kind of moral leadership contemporary presidents should provide: 49 percent likened the president to the head of any other business organization; while 48 percent thought the president had a greater responsibility than business leaders to set a moral example.[101] When pressed further, the harm Clinton had done to himself became even clearer: 59 percent said he had damaged the moral authority needed to lead the nation, and 57 percent thought he had injured the nation's moral fabric generally.[102] A few months earlier when Clinton urged the government of Pakistan to "take the high moral ground" after neighboring India exploded a nuclear device, 58 percent said it was difficult to take Clinton seriously when he talks about morality.[103] But when asked what constituted moral authority in a president, the public was closely divided: 43 percent said being ethical, telling the truth, or being faithful to one's spouse were the best indicators of whether an individual has the character to be president; 40 percent thought being tough and decisive, caring about people, or working hard mattered most.[104] Naturally, Clinton strove to stress the latter qualities with some success. While Clinton was viewed as hardworking and compassionate, those were not the criteria most Americans used for keeping him in office. Instead, most believed that overturning the 1996 election would undermine security and continuity in the presidency, and those values overrode all other considerations.

Nonetheless, Clinton's character flaws were a serious detriment to an effective performance. Half thought Clinton's moral standards were lower than most other U.S. presidents.[105] Jimmy Carter implicitly agreed, telling a group of reporters that he both "deplored" and was "deeply embarrassed" by Clinton's relationship with Lewinsky.[106] In a survey comparing Clinton's character with Roosevelt, Kennedy, Nixon, Carter, and Reagan, Clinton ranked fifth—just ahead of the disgraced Nixon. Carter ranked first, continuing a postpresidential rehabilitation that has seen his standing as an ex-president gain even more public approval than his presidential years did (see table 4.3).

Even more devastating than the damage to Clinton's persona was the loss of the mystique that all presidents while they are in office. This is more than a patina of dignity or legitimacy; rather, the essence of the presidential mystique is a moral idealism, imbued in the traditional values of hard work, equality of opportunity, and individualism, that sets presidents above politics. In his classic book, *The*

TABLE 4.3   PRESIDENTS AND CHARACTER COMPARED, 1998 (IN PERCENTAGES)

President	Very High/High Character	Average/Low/Very Low Character
Jimmy Carter	66	32
Franklin D. Roosevelt	58	29
Ronald Reagan	57	42
John F. Kennedy	45	52
Bill Clinton	30	69
Richard Nixon	15	82

Source: NBC News/*Wall Street Journal* poll, 26 February–1 March 1998.

American Commonwealth, James Bryce described the presidency as "this greatest office, the greatest in the world, unless we except the Papacy, to which any man can rise by his own merits."[107] When the presidency no longer symbolizes traditional values and lacks the moral idealism associated with them, it is just another elective office occupied by mere mortals.

When most Americans were forced to peer behind the curtains of the Oval Office in Clinton's case, they were surprised at what they found. Immediately, their assessments of both the president and the presidency were downgraded: 79 percent disapproved of the way Bill Clinton behaved in his personal life;[108] 77 percent said he did not have high personal moral and ethical standards;[109] 68 percent saw him as a weak moral leader;[110] 63 percent said he did not share the moral values most Americans try to live by;[111] 54 percent thought he generally showed poor judgment;[112] and 52 percent said they did not respect him.[113] When pollster Peter D. Hart asked survey respondents, "Which of the following people, if any, do you think most symbolizes what is wrong with the country's moral values: Bill Clinton, Jerry Springer, Linda Tripp, Larry Flynt, Mike Tyson, or Heidi Fleiss," Clinton had the dubious distinction of placing first with 30 percent, followed by talk-show host Jerry Springer, 27 percent; Monica Lewinsky's former confidante Linda Tripp, 12 percent; pornographer Larry Flynt, 9 percent; boxer and wife-beater Mike Tyson, 8 percent; and Hollywood madam Heidi Fleiss, 2 percent.[114] Not surprisingly, 61 percent thought the scandal would result in children having less respect for the presidency, and 62 percent did not want their child to look up to Clinton as a role model.[115] As one schoolteacher put it, "Look at the presidency now. Is this what [the children] want to be like?"[116]

Even more troubling, Clinton's lack of credibility on values issues seriously undermined the moral authority of his fellow Democrats. After Clinton's confession that he had had a relationship with Monica Lewinsky that was "not appropriate,"[117] Americans were asked a series of values questions, each requiring them to name which political party would do a better job of upholding the value in question. On

TABLE 4.4   THE DEMOCRATS' VALUES DISADVANTAGE, 1998–99 (IN PERCENTAGES)

Value	Democrats Preferred	Republicans Preferred
1. Encourages high moral standards and values	32	50
2. Upholds traditional family values	30	49
3. Promotes morality and personal responsibility	27	45
4. Has the best ideas for improving morality in the country	29	37
5. Shares your values	35	40
6. Knows right from wrong	28	35
7. Associated with the term *discipline*	16	49
8. Shows compassion toward the disadvantaged	52	21
9. Promotes self-reliance	33	40

Sources: #1: ABC News/*Washington Post* poll, 25–28 September 1998. #2: CBS News/*New York Times* poll, 4–7 November 1999. #3: Princeton Survey Research Associates poll, 27 August–8 September 1998. #4: Pew Research Center poll, January 1999. #5–7: Greenberg Quinlan Research poll, 29 November–1 December 1999. #8–9: *Washington Post*/Kaiser Family Foundation/Harvard University poll, 10–27 August 1998.

a host of issues—ranging from the party that best promotes traditional family values to the one that knows the difference between right and wrong—Republicans had sizeable leads. Only when asked which party best showed compassion toward the disadvantaged did the Democrats maintain their historic advantage. The squandering of the gains Democrats made on the values issues in 1992 and 1996 can only be attributed to Bill Clinton's dalliance with Monica Lewinsky (see table 4.4).

A Tattered Legacy

Addressing the Massachusetts legislature days before his swearing-in as the nation's thirty-fifth president, John F. Kennedy said, "When at some future date the high court of history sits in judgment on each one of us—recording whether in our brief span of service we fulfilled our responsibilities to the state—our success or failure, in whatever office we may hold, will be measured by the answers to four questions. Were we truly men of courage? . . . Were we truly men of judgment? . . . Were we truly men of integrity? . . . Were we truly men of dedication?"[118] In Kennedy's case, one answer came in 2000 when the Hasbro Toy Company, maker of G.I. Joe, decided to produced a John F. Kennedy PT-109 doll. According to a Hasbro spokeswoman, "The JFK figure is representative of everything that the G.I. brand stands for. Heroism, bravery, honor, and the important achievements of American military history."[119]

Kennedy's criteria for judging politicians and presidents seem pertinent when thinking about Bill Clinton and his legacy to the Democratic Party. From his first days in politics, Clinton's admirers sought to connect him to Kennedy. Addressing the delegates to the 1996 Democratic Convention, Edward M. Kennedy pointed to the photograph of a seventeen-year-old Clinton shaking hands with JFK and said, "Thirty-three years ago this summer, a young man from Boys Nation stood in the Rose Garden and shook the hand of a young President. That day, Bill Clinton took my brother's hand, and now he is the young President who has taken up the fallen standard: the belief that America can do better. And we will do better with William Jefferson Clinton leading us into the next American century."[120]

But neither Clinton nor his fellow Democrats have done better. Two-thirds believe that the ex-president will be remembered for his involvement in personal scandal rather than his accomplishments.[121] By the end of the Clinton era, the presidency had been morally diminished. At every level of power, the Democratic Party is in a weaker position since Clinton left office in 2001 than it was when he entered the presidency eight years earlier. In the House of Representatives, Democrats have lost 48 seats (or 19 percent) since 1992. Even in the Senate, where Democrats currently have a one-vote plurality, they had a comfortable six-seat majority when Clinton assumed the presidency. Democrats also went from thirty governors following the 1992 elections to twenty-one by the close of 2001.[122] Governors are a significant leadership cadre for any political party, and their diminution within the Democratic ranks is likely to hurt in a post–Cold War era when future presidents are more likely to come from the statehouses than from Congress.

Most important, Clinton's presidency hurt the Democratic Party on the all-important values issue. Anna Greenberg, an assistant professor of public policy at the John F. Kennedy School at Harvard University, and former Clinton pollster Stanley B. Greenberg write that after two Clinton terms, Democrats lost ground in the battle over values: "People respect the Democrats for their openness to new ideas, their commitment to community, and their defense of tolerance and individual rights. But . . . voters are more impressed with the Republicans' insistence on personal responsibility, discipline, and teaching children about right and wrong. Voters want young people to learn norms and limits. And Democrats are more commonly seen to be permissive about such things."[123]

The Democratic Party's values vulnerability was on full display in 1998 when Gary Mueller, a Democrat challenging Illinois Republican congressman Jerry Weller, signed "an affidavit of integrity" asserting that he had never committed adultery, engaged in homosexual activity, experimented with illegal drugs, or been charged with a felony. When asked why he had taken this unusual action, Mueller responded: "I only brought it up because of the environment we find ourselves in. I'm just saying that if you send me to Washington, you are not going to have to worry about situations like the President is suffering through." Weller replied, "An honest man doesn't need to sign a piece of paper to prove his integrity."[124] Weller needn't have worried—he won his district with a comfortable 59 percent of the vote.

Other candidates also saw the national hunger for persons of integrity and attempted to sell themselves accordingly. Ohio Republican congressional candidate Nancy Hollister sold herself as representative of "Ohio values." Jim Bunning, a Republican senatorial contender from Kentucky, proclaimed his allegiance to "Kentucky values and courage." Farther south, Texas Democratic congressman Charles Stenholm proclaimed his fealty to "Texas values." Meanwhile, across the West, Colorado Republican senator Ben Nighthorse Campbell's television advertisements lauded his "values, independence, and courage."[125] Gary Bauer, president of the Family Research Council, sponsored a television advertisement accusing Bill Clinton of having "taught our children that lying is OK, that fidelity is old-fashioned, and that character doesn't count."[126] The Clinton stain on the Democratic Party's values reputation had become so omnipresent that most Democrats sought to claim credit for Clinton's policy successes, even as they distanced themselves from him personally. Like Lady Macbeth, by 2000 most Democrats—including Vice President Al Gore—seemed ready to say of Clinton, "Out, damned spot! Out, I say!"

Clinton's legacy extends beyond the hurt he has caused Democrats on values issues. Seeking the presidency in 1992, Clinton noted that the problems he would face as president were not of the magnitude of the Great Depression or the two World Wars; rather, they were of a more spiritual nature: "What is killing us is people no longer believe that they're part of a larger community where they matter, and where they can make a difference."[127] Unfortunately, the Clinton presidency did little to ease the pervasive sense of disappointment and disillusionment. During his eight years in office, cynicism toward those in public life deepened. Clinton alluded to this penchant for self-doubt during his speech at the FDR Memorial dedication: "At this time, when the pinnacle that Roosevelt hoped America would achieve in our influence and power has come to pass, we still, strangely, fight battles with doubts."[128] Speaking before a group of young women in Tanzania, Clinton's daughter, Chelsea, described how a sense of "hopelessness and cynicism" had taken hold among some American youths.[129] Her comments were echoed in a conversation Jean Bethke Elshtain had with another Generation Xer: "If you have a thought that doesn't seem cynical, you have to get cynical about your own non-cynicism, so you can be safely cynical again and not seem like a dweeb or optimist of some sort."[130] Harvard sociologist Robert D. Putnam finds that the number attending a public meeting on town or school affairs fell from 22 percent in 1973 to 13 percent twenty years later. In Putnam's view, a nation of joiners has become a nation of loners. To emphasize the point, Putnam notes that memberships in bowling leagues plummeted, while the number of solo bowlers increased 10 percent from 1980 to 1993. Americans are, says Putnam, "bowling alone."[131]

One effect of the Clinton scandals has been a coarsening of the civic dialogue. A similar occurrence happened during the dark days of Senator Joseph McCarthy's railings against suspected communists in government. Back in 1954, army special counsel Joseph Welch, his patience exhausted, asked the Wisconsin Republican: "Have you no sense of decency, sir, at long last? Have you left no sense of decency?"[132] Suzanne Garment of the American Enterprise Institute writes that in place of a civil dialogue a "self-enforcing scandal machine" has emerged: "Prosecutors use journalists to publicize criminal cases [involving members of the administration] while journalists, through their news stories, put pressure on prosecutors for still more action."[133] Indeed, the overall effect of the Clinton scandals may be to empty the public square rather than fill it, as civility recedes in the wake of bitter partisan wrangling that shows no signs of abating. Long-time members of the Washington establishment—including Howard Baker, Bob Dole, Mike Mansfield, and Sam Nunn—claim that the most important change in the capital is the erosion of comity that once permitted political opponents to form long-lasting friendships. Bob Dole, for example, introduced legislation to name the Health and Human Services Building for the late Hubert H. Humphrey and lauded Ted Kennedy and George McGovern in his farewell address to the U.S. Senate. Lyndon Johnson and Everett Dirksen likewise put their differences aside at the end of the day over drinks in the Senate boardrooms and, later, at the White House. Ronald Reagan and Tip O'Neill had a longstanding rule that they would not talk politics after 6 P.M. Reagan often began his telephone conversations with O'Neill by saying, "Hello, Tip, is it after six o'clock?" And O'Neill would respond, "Absolutely, Mr. President."[134]

Now both sides are busily declaring "war" on each other, often using cultural issues as a wedge. In the summer of 2000, Democrats complained that they were being denied an opportunity to introduce amendments promoting gun safety. This led to an acrimonious exchange between the Senate leaders Trent Lott and Tom Daschle:

> LOTT: I feel personally maligned [dramatic pause for emphasis] and I do not appreciate it. I am not going to be threatened and intimidated by the minority in trying to get our work done. If you want to go through this approach, if you want to shut down everything, then everybody loses in the process.
>
> DASCHLE: The way the Senate is being run is wrong. . . . This is getting be be more and more like a second House of Representatives. This is getting to be more and more a gagged body. This has nothing to do with the traditions of the Senate that I admired when I became a Senator.[135]

One year later, after surrendering his post as majority leader following Jim Jeffords's defection, Lott urged his colleagues to "wage war" on Daschle and the

Democrats as soon as they took command.[136] Clinton's various "war rooms," a preemptive strike against all incoming attacks, were skillfully assembled and generally effective. But they may prove to be his most enduring, and dangerous, legacy.

When one thinks of the Clinton presidency, one is left with an overwhelming sense not of accomplishment, but of disappointment and exhaustion. Disappointment that a man so skilled in the craft of politics could survive impeachment but leave his party in worse shape than when his presidency began. During the 2000 campaign, Al Gore, a decent man steeped in traditional family values and deeply offended by Clinton's conduct, would find the values legacy left by Clinton to be a millstone around his own neck. Clinton further tarnished his standing by issuing a series of pardons upon exiting the White House that not even his most fierce partisans could defend. Exhaustion was the other prevailing emotion at the end of the Clinton years. Less than a month after leaving the White House, 55 percent said they were glad Clinton was gone; only 38 percent said they would miss him.[137] Going into the 2000 elections, the prevailing hope most voters had about Clinton's successor was that he would be, unlike Clinton, no trouble. Seventy-two percent said that after the Clinton experience they would consider a candidate's character an important factor in determining their vote.[138] With both Al Gore and George W. Bush presenting themselves as paragons of virtue, the 2000 elections looked to be a dull affair. As the next chapter describes, the election was far from boring primarily because the values divisions in the country—divisions exacerbated during the Clinton years—became *the* determining factor in the outcome.

CHAPTER 5

Campaign 2000:
One Nation, Divisible

We must occupy the land with character.
— George W. Bush, 3 August 2000

We can't allow broken values any more than we allow broken windows.
— Al Gore, 22 May 1999

THE 2000 PRESIDENTIAL CAMPAIGN will be forever remembered not for what the candidates said or did, but for how it ended. Not since the disputed Rutherford B. Hayes–Samuel J. Tilden contest of 1876 had there been so much drama, confusion, and excitement on election night. The trouble began when the broadcast network projections gave the state of Florida to Al Gore, then to George W. Bush, and then to no one. It got worse when the same networks called the presidency for Bush, only to take back their declaration in the wee hours the morning. And it ended only when, for the first time in history, the U.S. Supreme Court determined the winner of the election. But that body's certification of George W. Bush as the nation's forty-third president was not a triumph for our democracy or its institutions; instead, it happened only because Al Gore and the Democrats reluctantly surrendered.

Accepting the Supreme Court's verdict, George W. Bush declared, "Our nation must rise against a house divided."[1] But the country was seriously split during Campaign 2000, and its divisions were vividly on display in the vituperative opinions expressed by the Supreme Court justices in *Bush v. Gore*. By a 7–2 margin, the Court held that the differing standards for reviewing ballots in Florida's sixty-seven counties violated Bush's claim to equal protection under the Fourteenth Amendment. In the blizzard of legal papers, the frequent use of the terms "dimpled chad," "hanging chad," and "pregnant chad" attested to the inherent difficulties in recounting the punch-card ballots. Still, four justices were willing to try. In other cases when the Court was asked to settle difficult political issues—including *Brown v. Board of Education*, the Pentagon Papers case, and *U.S. v. Nixon*— it was able to speak with an authoritative, decisive, and nearly unanimous voice. This time things were different. Justices William Rehnquist, Antonin Scalia, and Clarence Thomas blamed voters for not following instructions to punch their ballots clearly and cleanly. By chastising the voters and protecting Bush, the judicial conservatives turned "strict constructionism" on its head. John J. DiIulio Jr., who was briefly to head Bush's White House Office of Faith-Based and Community Initiatives, maintained that the court's decision crippled "the principled conservative case for limited government, legislative supremacy, and universal civic deference to legitimate, duly constituted state and local public authority." DiIulio noted that prior to the passions aroused by the Bush-Gore drama, "conservatives would have lost a close, hotly contested presidential election, even against a person and a party from whom many feared the worst, than advance judicial imperialism, diminish respect for federalism, or pander to mass misunderstanding and mistrust of duly elected legislative leaders."[2]

It was left to the Court's liberal wing to speak for more conservative restraint. Ruth Bader Ginsburg wrote, "I might join the Chief Justice were it my commission to interpret Florida law." John Paul Stevens was especially acerbic: "Although we may never know with complete certainty the winner of this year's Presidential election, the identity of the loser is perfectly clear. It is the Nation's confidence in the judge as an impartial guardian of the rule of law." Stephen Breyer agreed, noting that confidence in the Court "is a public treasure [that] has been built slowly over many years, some of which were marked by a Civil War and the tragedy of segregation."[3]

The justices were right to worry about the blow the Supreme Court suffered in the arena of public opinion. Surveys taken immediately following its per curiam decision found 48 percent saying that the Court had become *too political*; just 43 percent said it had maintained an "objective balance."[4] Philip Stephens, a columnist for the British newspaper *Financial Times*, wrote that *Bush v. Gore* placed an "indelible stain on the court's always half-illusory reputation as an honest guardian of the Constitution."[5] Indeed, the bitterness expressed by the individual justices was mirrored in the vitriolic rhetoric partisan spokespersons directed at each other throughout the long, bitter postelection contest.[6] Bob Dole called for a boycott of any Gore inauguration, insinuating that if the Democrat won Florida, he would have stolen the presidency from Bush.[7] J.C. Watts, conference chairman for the House Republican leadership, assailed Gore as "a candidate who will not win or lose honorably, but will try to do so through cutthroat tactics that eight years under President Clinton have taught him."[8]

Democrats were equally vituperative. New York congressman Jerrold Nadler told a press conference that the "whiff of fascism is in the air" following a raucous

Republican-sponsored demonstration outside the Miami-Dade canvassing board.[9] Party chairman Terence McAuliffe charged that Bush and his brother, Florida governor Jeb Bush, blocked minority access to the polls: "George Bush says he's for election reform. Reform this! I say, park the state police cars, take down the roadblocks, stop asking people of color for multiple forms of ID, print readable ballots, open the polling places, count all the votes, and start practicing democracy in America again."[10] Brookings Institution scholar Thomas Mann maintained that the accusations made by both parties against each other had escalated to a form of "McCarthyism with accusations of traitorous behavior."[11]

While any discussion of Election 2000 must begin with the Supreme Court's decision in *Bush v. Gore*, the more intriguing question is How did the country become so evenly divided that the contest resulted in a perfect tie?[12] And what a perfect tie it was. Gore won 539,898 more votes than Bush and got more votes than any presidential candidate in history, with the sole exception of Ronald Reagan in 1984.[13] Bush, meanwhile, held a slender one-vote majority in the electoral college (thanks to Florida), thus earning the third consecutive minority presidential victory since 1992. Not since the late nineteenth century (1884, 1888, and 1892) had there been three presidential elections with the winner receiving less than 50 percent of the vote. The electorate's indecision was evident in several state counts. In Florida, Bush's certified 537-vote victory represented a 0.009005-percent difference out of 5,963,110 votes cast. New Mexico saw the difference reduced to a mere fistful of votes, 366, out of nearly 600,000 ballots cast. A few thousand ballots (less than 1 percent) separated the two men in Oregon, Iowa, New Hampshire, and Wisconsin.[14] Nationwide, fifteen states had a margin of difference of 5 percent or less.[15]

At other levels of government, the 2000 election also produced an inconclusive result. Elections left the Senate with a 50–50 split. On the other side of the Capitol, Democrats gained two more House seats, to remain virtually at parity with the Republicans. Yet, these numbers are not the most important result. The real story behind the Bush-Gore contest is the values divide that split the country in two. No party could shape the future until it could provide a clear and compelling answer to the question, "What does it mean to be an American?" While there was plenty of jousting during the campaign, nothing the candidates said or did really mattered much. What really mattered, and what Campaign 2000 failed to bridge, was the values rift that began in the 1960s and has since transformed the meaning of American citizenship. In short, the Bush-Gore contest was not about either man; rather, it was about us.

The Values Candidates

One commonality the Bush-Gore race had with its predecessors was that it was not a contest about the future so much as it was about the past. In 1992, for example, Bill Clinton portrayed himself as an empathetic candidate who "feels your pain." This set Clinton apart from George H.W. Bush, whom Democrats effectively portrayed as being more interested in foreign affairs than in the economic problems afflicting so many Americans at home. Even Bush's impressive résumé— which listed service as congressman, U.N. ambassador, Republican national chairman, liaison to the People's Republic of China, C.I.A. chief, vice president, and president—had become a liability. A Cold War president without the Cold War, Bush compounded his difficulties by allowing himself to be photographed during a factory tour in front of a department-store scanner, seemingly unaware of how the machine worked. Not surprisingly, Clinton won because he presented himself as the opposite of George Bush.

But after two terms in office, Bill Clinton had become the antithesis of what most Americans wanted to see in their next president. While 57 percent said they had approved of the job Clinton had done, only 36 percent had a favorable view of him.[16] Simply put, voters thought Clinton was a successful president, but they did not want to install another Clinton in the White House. The major party presidential contenders understood this, and each one sought to cast himself as a person of sterling character. This is exactly what the voters wanted to hear, since most were not paying as much attention to issue positions as they were to the candidate's values. Sixty percent agreed with the statement that having someone who "shares your moral values" would be a very important factor in deciding for whom to vote.[17] Another survey found one-third citing honesty as the quality they most desired in their next president.[18] As in the election of 1976, when Jimmy Carter's born-again persona appealed to many voters following Watergate, voters judged issue positions in Campaign 2000 in the context of what they revealed about a candidate's character. So paramount was the public's hunger for values that one-quarter of the electorate were reclassified as "values voters," who were determined to mark their ballots based on a candidate's personal morals rather than issues, ideology, or experience.[19] Shaula Clark, a New Hampshire high-school student, was one of these new values voters, and she explained her reasoning:

> A president can't automatically get all his policies because they have to pass through Congress. But the reason the presidency was created was so everyone could have a figurehead—not like a king or queen—but somebody that everyone can look to for direction, almost a morale-booster, someone that everyone can identify with. Kind of a role model, who influences people's attitudes."[20]

The paramount importance voters attached to honesty and integrity resulted in a substantial rewriting of recent presidential history. Back in 1992, most voters viewed George H.W. Bush's stewardship as a dismal failure: 58 percent said they personally were "worse off" than four years before, and 69 percent thought the country was too, thanks to Bush's economic policies.[21] Seven years later an astounding 71 percent said they approved of the way the elder Bush handled his job, and 42 percent ranked him as a "great" or "near great" president, a remarkable turnaround that can only be attributed to Bill Clinton's moral shortcomings.[22] This was a boon to his son, George W. Bush, who capitalized on his family's reputation for public service and moral rectitude. Addressing the delegates at the 2000 Republican National Convention, Bush equated his family's restoration to the presidency with the goal set by the country's founders: "We must occupy the land with character."[23] While Bush pointed with pride to his family's reputation, he was not alone in presenting himself as a someone of upright stature. Each of the four major-party presidential contenders, Bill Bradley and Al Gore for the Democrats and John McCain and George W. Bush for the Republicans, sought to cast himself as a man of character.

Bill Bradley: Basketball and Small-Town Virtues

For Bill Bradley, winning his party's presidential nomination would prove to be an uphill battle. With the Democratic Party establishment and its core constituencies, including labor unions and African-American voters, solidly behind Vice President Al Gore, Bradley attempted to market himself as a values-based candidate who personified small-town virtues. For some time, Bradley had been concerned about the loss of old-fashioned values. After leaving the U.S. Senate in 1996, Bradley authored a memoir titled *Time Present, Time Past* in which he wrote, "We need firm standards, yet daily there are reminders that our standards have slipped or never were." Bradley rhetorically asked: "What happened to the commonsense notion that two parents are better than one? What happened to making the effort and taking pride in a job well done? What happened to the widespread belief that volunteering for the PTA, the Red Cross, or the Boy Scouts is one way not only of helping others, but of finding one's own self-fulfillment? What happened to employer loyalty and employee conscientiousness?"[24]

Bradley's self-portrait of a man longing for old virtues was enhanced by the fact that most voters grew up knowing him not as a politician but as a 1960s basketball star for the New York Knicks. Bradley recalled his basketball days in a book titled *Values of the Game*, noting that it was not his award-winning performances on the court but the values the game represented that mattered most to him. Bradley observed that sports could transform outdated notions about what constitutes acceptable behavior, noting that the desegregation of baseball and basketball in the 1940s and 1950s prompted young fans to question old taboos.[25] Bradley praised black sports heroes for their courage, and pointed out that congressional passage of Title IX of the 1964 Civil Rights Act, which required high schools and colleges to provide women with access to athletic facilities equal to that enjoyed by men, also helped make revolutionary changes. By the 1990s, the Women's National Basketball Association attracted a large following, and players such as Rebecca Lobo, Lisa Leslie, and Cynthia Cooper became media stars by appearing in television commercials pitching shoes, cars, and credit cards.

Announcing his presidential candidacy in his hometown of Crystal City, Missouri, Bradley recalled the countless hours spent practicing on his local high school basketball court and the lessons learned from a penchant for perfectionism:

> It was just behind where I am standing now, on the hardwood floor of Crystal City High School gymnasium, that I found my first great love—the feel of the ball, the leather ball in your hand (Laughter) . . . the squeak of your sneakers on the floor, the swish of the net. I loved everything about the game of basketball. I wasn't the most talented player in the world, but I had three strengths: I had a sense of where I was on the court; I had quick, sure hands; and I could outwork anyone. I loved the fact that on that gleaming wooden floor, hard work paid off and dreams became reality. It was also there that I absorbed the idea that a team is not just about winning; it's about shared sacrifice, it's about giving up something small for yourself in order to gain something large for everybody. And you know, it's the same for our country.[26]

By emphasizing the values of hard work, responsibility, and teamwork, Bradley implicitly contrasted himself with several prominent sports celebrities who eschew the idea of serving as role models for their young fans. Chief among the new antiheroes was former Chicago Bull Dennis Rodman. His 1996 book, *Bad as I Wanna Be*, featured a nude Rodman on the jacket cover, while inside the basketball star detailed his numerous sexual adventures, including his penchant for crossdressing and his "if it feels good, do it" credo.[27] As if in response to Rodman's antics, Bradley liked to quote from a character in Bertolt Brecht's *Galileo*: "Pity the nation that has no heroes."[28]

By offering himself as a contrast to the modern-day Rodmans, Bradley sought to personify individual enterprise and the success that resulted from it. In Reaganesque terms, he told his hometown audience that the value of hard work was a lesson learned: "I was raised here in Crystal City—I'm a small-town boy. I had a paper route, and every afternoon I delivered copies of the *Daily News Democrat* to the doorsteps of my neighbors. I could tell the time of day or night by the trains that passed near our home." In an indirect reference to Al Gore and George W. Bush, Bradley observed that despite the lack of "a famous family name or great wealth, I was given the encouragement and love and the opportunity that enabled me to forge a path on my own."[29] Bradley thus cast himself as a real-life Horatio Alger figure who, unlike the two frontrunners, had worked hard, alongside his hometown's ethnically diverse families, to achieve his version of the American dream.

Yet all was not idyllic in Bradley's childhood. His father suffered from calcified arthritis of the lower spine, which left him barely able to walk and unable to drive a car or dress himself. Bradley described in painful detail how he and his mother would help his father dress in the morning, tie his shoes, and retrieve the morning newspaper before sending him off to work at the local bank. His father's never-say-die attitude impressed the young boy, as did the values conveyed by his mother, a schoolteacher: "Teaching for her was not about transmitting knowledge, but imparting values. Every day she began her class with a lesson about some character trait such as honesty, courage, integrity, or trust."[30]

Bradley's message resonated with Democratic voters. An October 1999 survey of Bradley supporters found 76 percent saying the former New Jersey senator was of "strong moral character."[31] Moreover, 70 percent cited Bradley's character as an important reason for choosing him over Al Gore.[32] But Bradley's values strategy could not overcome the many advantages Gore brought to the campaign. As the incumbent vice president, Gore was poised to make the Democratic primaries a referendum not on his own candidacy but on Bill Clinton's job performance. While this would not be a successful general election ploy, Democratic voters were unlikely to reject Bill Clinton's vice president, since such a rebuke would be unmistakably viewed as a rejection of Clinton himself. Bradley realized this and did not mention Clinton once in announcing his presidential candidacy. Instead, he went out of his way to distance himself from the poll-obsessed Clinton: "As president, you must listen and consult, study and examine, pray and plan. But in the end, you must be guided by the compass of your own convictions, and do what is right as you are given to see the right, and trust that the people will understand." Bradley hoped that by Election Day voters would choose "between two people we esteem, not the candidate we can still tolerate."[33]

Bradley's dream of being his party's nominee proved to be wishful thinking. Gore won every primary, including Bradley's adopted state of New Jersey and his native Missouri. The stage was set in New Hampshire, where Bradley came within four percentage points of beating Gore. Although 55 percent of the Granite State primary voters had an unfavorable opinion of Clinton as a person and 60 percent of that group backed Bradley, *81 percent* approved of Clinton's job performance and 56 percent of those backed Gore.[34] The insurmountable problem for Bradley was that public dislike of Clinton was not enough to sustain a campaign in a race determined largely by votes cast by partisan Democrats. Determined to soldier on after his New Hampshire loss, Bradley's cause was doomed, and five weeks after his defeat he left the race.

John McCain: Patriotic Hero

One truism in politics is that successful presidential candidates match the moment. Back in 1952, Dwight Eisenhower was a man of his time, as his résumé and vast foreign policy experience were well suited to solving the foreign policy crises presented by the Cold War. Much the same could be said of John McCain. In McCain's case, many Americans admired his heroism as a prisoner of war in North Vietnam in an age when there are few heroes left in politics. Colin Powell, for one, is respected for his successful stint as chairman of the Joint Chiefs of Staff during the Persian Gulf War. But in 1996, Powell chose to abstain from politics and concentrated his public activities by founding America's Promise, an organization dedicated to having volunteers mentor disadvantaged youth. Ronald Reagan, too, remains a hero to many, but Alzheimer's disease has robbed him of any public role. Other political heroes often mentioned by voters—such as John F. Kennedy, Robert F. Kennedy, and Martin Luther King Jr.—are long dead.

Given the paucity of living heroes, by 2000 most Americans hoped they could have a president their children could admire. Arizona senator John McCain fit that bill perfectly. Writing about the late Barry Goldwater in 1998, McCain said of his predecessor, "There are some people in public life who speak their minds candidly, whose honesty and passion for the truth, as God has given them light to see the truth, contrasts starkly with the sail-trimming and obfuscation so common in political speech today."[35] McCain's tribute to Goldwater could have easily applied to himself. In a perfectly timed 1999 book titled *Faith of My Fathers*, McCain described how, through faith in God and with the help of his fellow servicemen, he endured a harrowing prisoner-of-war experience in Hanoi, which included torture, broken bones, malnourishment, and numerous other deprivations. McCain wrote that his mistreatment by his North Vietnamese captors only served to reinforce the navy values his father and grandfather had taught him:

An officer must not lie, steal, or cheat—ever. He keeps his word, whatever the cost. He must not shirk his duties no matter how difficult or dangerous they are. His life is ransomed to his duty. An officer must trust his fellow officers, and expect their trust in return. He must not expect others to bear what he will not.

An officer accepts the consequences of his actions. He must not hide his mistakes, nor transfer blame to others that is rightfully his. He admits his mistakes openly and accepts whatever is imposed upon him without complaint.

For the obedience he is owed by his subordinates, an officer accepts certain solemn obligations to them in return, and an officer's obligations to enlisted men are the most solemn of all. An officer must not confer his responsibilities on the men under his command. They are his alone. He does not put his men in jeopardy for any purpose that their country has not required they serve. He does not risk their lives and welfare for his sake, but only to answer the shared duty they are called to answer. He will not harm their reputations by his conduct or cause them to suffer shame or any penalty that only he deserves.[36]

John McCain began his campaign believing that the navy values code he lived by was something Republican and independent-minded voters wanted to hear. Sounding much like Jimmy Carter, McCain told citizens at a New Hampshire town meeting, "I promise you as president of the United States, based on my life, the principles, and the caution of my old dear friends, I will always tell you the truth no matter what."[37] McCain dubbed his cause the New Patriotic Challenge: "I run for president because I want the next generation of Americans to know the sense of pride and purpose of serving a cause greater than themselves."[38] That cause was not to be found in position papers or even in McCain's own longstanding commitment to campaign finance reform. In fact, whenever campaign finance reform was discussed, McCain's sponsorship was seen by his supporters not on the merits of the bill itself, but as an indicator of his sterling character. Arizona legislator Steve May, a fervent McCain supporter, explained:

> The thing that attracted me to McCain since I was twelve years old is that he is a man of great character. He and I disagree from time to time on various issues. But he is fighting for what he thinks is right. I don't like his campaign finance reform plan. I think it's ridiculous. But he is a man who fights for principle. And that is the person I want in public office, as opposed to guys like Bill Clinton or George W. Bush.[39]

McCain believed that his character and military experience would help end an age of cynicism that he attributed to Bill Clinton. Addressing the cadets at the U.S. Naval Academy, McCain declared: "Something has gone terribly wrong when parents no longer want their children to grow up to be President. That shames me. And I want to do something about it." That "something" was to "fight against the pervasive cynicism that is debilitating our democracy, that cheapens our public debates, that threatens our public institutions, our culture and, ultimately, our private happiness. It is a fight to take our government back from the power-brokers and special interests, and return it to the people, and the noble cause of freedom it was created to serve."[40] His message struck a chord. One large sign at a McCain rally said it all: "REPLACE A BUM WITH A REAL AMERICAN HERO."[41] In addition to New Hampshire, McCain won primaries in Michigan, Arizona, Connecticut, Rhode Island, Massachusetts, Vermont, and Washington. Over time, George W. Bush was able to out-muscle McCain, thanks to the near-unanimous support of the Republican Party establishment and the record $91.1 million its members put into his primary campaign.[42] But Bush understood the power of McCain's message and sought to attach it to himself by incorporating a values message that sounded eerily like Bill Clinton's, but without any of the incumbent's character flaws.

George W. Bush: Gimme that Old-Time (Clinton) Religion

Running for reelection as Texas governor in 1998, George W. Bush outlined his themes for a second term in a television advertisement: "Whether for government or individuals, I believe in accountability and responsibility. For too long, we've encouraged a culture that says if it feels good, do it, and blame somebody else if you've got a problem. We've got to change our culture to one based on responsibility."[43] As he crisscrossed the Lone Star State, buses on the Bush caravan were plastered with signs reading "Opportunity and Responsibility."[44] Just as Republicans accused Bill Clinton in 1992 of stealing their values slogans, George W. Bush was shamelessly pilfering from Bill Clinton's poll-tested mantra of "opportunity, community, and responsibility." But Bush did more than mouth the words. As governor, he attempted to translate the values of opportunity and responsibility into policies that gave these words greater meaning. He initiated a Lone Star Leaders Program, which, in Bush's words, was designed to "help young people make the right choices about drugs and alcohol, tobacco, sex, crime, civic involvement and school."[45] Its centerpiece was an aggressive abstinence campaign supported by numerous public-service television messages that encouraged young people to save sexual intercourse for marriage.

One important element of George W. Bush's values agenda was his emphasis on religion. As governor, he established the InnerChange Freedom Initiative, which allowed prison inmates, in partnership with former Watergate convict Chuck Colson's Prison Fellowship organization, to voluntarily participate in a program of Bible study, worship, and physical fitness.[46] Bush even proclaimed 10 June 2000 as "Jesus Day" in Texas.[47] Earlier, during an Iowa GOP presidential debate, when asked to name his favorite philosopher, Bush took his opponents and questioners aback when he replied, "Christ, because he changed my heart."[48]

This was not the only time Bush defied the customs of his Yankee ancestors and wore his religion on his sleeve. In 1986, at a time when he was drinking heavily and wandering aimlessly through life, Bush had a born-again experience and accepted Jesus Christ as his personal savior. He often publicly alluded to his religious awakening, telling a 4 July 2001 celebration in Philadelphia: "Without churches and charities, many of our citizens who have lost hope would be left to their own struggles and their own fate. And as I well know, they are not the only ones whose lives can be changed and uplifted by the influence of faith in God."[49]

But Bush did more than merely assure evangelicals that he was one of them. As governor, he tirelessly sought alliances with religious institutions that tied their faith to social good works. He publicly praised religious charities whose programs helped pregnant teens, illiterate adults, and jailed convicts. According to Marvin Olasky, an influential Republican thinker who coined the phrase "compassionate conservatism," "The thing Governor Bush has going for him is that he's able to make statements about the importance of religion and do it in a way that is nonthreatening. It's not just the words, but the melody too."[50] Texas voters liked both, and in 1998, they gave Bush 69 percent of their votes, including 65 percent of women, 49 percent of Hispanics, 27 percent of African Americans, and 73 percent of independents. Bush became the first Texas governor to retain the seat in twenty-five years and the first Republican ever to be reelected to the post. Moreover, all of Bush's seventeen Republican ticket-mates were swept into office. Immediately after his smashing victory, he became the odds-on favorite to challenge Vice President Al Gore for the presidency. The polls gave Bush even more added momentum; while Democrats were making historic congressional gains in the 1998 off-year elections, Bush was beating Gore in the exit polls by a whopping sixteen percentage points.[51]

Thanks to his family's longstanding political ties and an insurmountable lead in the polls, Bush raised truckloads of cash for his presidential quest. But what propelled Bush to prominence was not the strong institutional backing he received from members of the Republican establishment who thought another Bush deserved a turn at being their party's standard-bearer but his character, which was shaped by a three-generation family commitment to public service. Bush's grandfather, Prescott Bush, had been a U.S. senator from Connecticut, and the family patriarch instilled in his offspring a Yankee sense of noblesse oblige. Both George Bushes attended Andover Academy and Yale University, where the value of civic duty that inspired Prescott Bush to public service was reinforced. Mingling with tourists at the Jefferson Memorial in July 2001, George W. Bush used lines that his father and grandfather could have easily repeated when asked about the many public offices they held: "It's an unimaginable honor to be the president during the Fourth of July of this country."[52]

The Bush record of probity certainly made for good press copy in the wake of the Clinton scandals. Campaigning across the country, Bush did not mention his famous father by name, but he often cited his fidelity to old-fashioned values and his family's commitment to distinguished public service. In a campaign autobiography titled *A Charge to Keep*, Bush lauded the small-town values he learned growing up in Midland, Texas: "We learned to respect our elders, to do what they said, and to be good neighbors. We went to church. Families spent time together, outside, the grown-ups talking with neighbors while the kids played ball or with marbles and yo-yos. Our homework and schoolwork were important. The town's leading citizens worked hard to attract the best teachers to our schools. No one locked their doors, because you could trust your friends and neighbors."[53]

As a presidential candidate, Bush promised a restoration of these old-fashioned values by fostering a wholesale change in the popular culture: "We need to say that each of us needs to be responsible for what we do. And people in the highest office of the land must be responsible for decisions they make in life."[54] Bush suggested that his election would be a crucial first step toward renewing the culture and ensuring an era of responsibility: "When I put my hand on the Bible, I will swear to not only uphold the laws of our land, I will swear to uphold the honor and dignity of the office to which I have been elected, so help me God."[55] These lines inevitably earned Bush standing ovations wherever he went.

Underscoring Bush's upbeat persona and family heritage was a pervasive public feeling that while the country had prospered during the Clinton years, it was morally adrift. Accepting his party's nomination, Bush noted that prosperity had become "a drug in our system—dulling our sense of urgency, of empathy, of duty," and he saw Clinton as the country's foremost symbol of moral decay: "Our current president embodied the potential of a generation. So many talents. So much charm. Such great skill. But, in the end, to what end? So much promise, to no great purpose."[56] Certainly, the feeling of moral rootlessness was reinforced by the shootings at Columbine High School and the violence at several other schools that preceded and followed the Colorado tragedy. Instead of preaching responsibility, many concluded that the popular culture had mutated the value of tolerance into a new form of sexual license that was corrupting the nation's youth. In 1995, Colin Powell called for a restoration of shame based on moral values.[57] Powell's plea was echoed three years later by the National Commission on Civic Renewal, co-chaired by former Democratic senator Sam Nunn and former Reagan education secretary William Bennett. According to the commission's final report:

> Compared with previous generations, Americans today place less value on what we owe others as a matter of moral obligation and common citizenship; less value on personal sacrifice as a moral good; less value on the social importance of respectability and observing the rules; less value on restraint in matters of pleasure and sexuality; and correspondingly greater value on self-expression, self-realization, and personal choice. . . . We must ask ourselves some hard questions about this new understanding of individual liberty. Dare we continue to place adult self-gratification above the well-being of our children? Can we relentlessly pursue individual choice at the expense of mutual obligation without corroding vital social bonds? Will we remain secure in the enjoyment of our individual rights if we fail to accept and discharge our responsibilities? Is there a civic invisible hand that will preserve our democratic institutions in the absence of informed and engaged citizens?[58]

George W. Bush sought to make the commission's concerns the raison d'etre of his campaign. In so doing, he evoked the spirit of Democratic presidents John F. Kennedy, who summoned the nation to greatness, and Jimmy Carter, whose moral piety was a welcome tonic after Watergate. As Bush told appreciative audiences: "The measure of our nation's greatness has never been affluence or influence—rising stocks or advancing armies. It has always been found in citizens of character and compassion. And so many of our problems as a nation—from drugs, to deadly diseases, to crime—are not the result of chance, but of choice. They will only be solved by a transformation of the heart and will."⁵⁹ His media spokeswoman and confidante Karen Hughes candidly described how Bush intended to make values "a huge theme" of his campaign, "The whole need to change to a culture of responsibility and teach children to accept responsibility in life will be a major part of the governor's message."⁶⁰

The emphasis on teaching children responsibility began in New Hampshire with Bush's maiden speech of the campaign. Unlike other conservative Republicans who wanted to eliminate any federal responsibility for public education, Bush promised to enhance the scope of the U.S. Department of Education and triple funding for a values-based curriculum that promoted character formation. He also called for more Internet filters to be installed at schools and public libraries and proposed more after-school money for faith-based programs. But the Texas governor candidly told listeners that more federal dollars would not solve the nation's values crisis. From his vantage point, the sexual license of the go-go Kennedy-Johnson 1960s needed to be replaced with the traditional family values often associated with the sedate 1950s era of Dwight Eisenhower:

> The real problem comes, not when children challenge the rules, but when adults won't defend the rules. And for about three decades, many American schools surrendered this role. Values were "clarified," not taught. Students were given moral puzzles, not moral guidance. But morality is not a cafeteria of personal choices— with every choice equally right and equally arbitrary, like picking a flavor of ice cream. We do not shape our own morality. It is morality that shapes our lives.⁶¹

Bush often cited his own life story of redemption and the values he learned from previous mistakes as a guide for making the changes he thought the country needed. Speaking to a New Hampshire audience during the primary season, Bush observed that while winning the presidency would be an extraordinary honor, it would not be his most important accomplishment in life: "After power vanishes and pride passes, this is what remains: The promises we kept. The oath we fulfilled. The example we set. The honor we earned. . . . We are united in a common task: to give our children a spirit of moral courage."⁶² *Washington Post* columnist E.J. Dionne Jr. wrote that Bush's words resonated with a growing number of Americans who were troubled by the nation's moral course: "If you hate the 1960s, you love this stuff."⁶³ By explicitly rejecting the sexual freedom espoused during the "Make Love, Not War" days of the 1960s, Bush offered himself as a father-figure, someone who, unlike Clinton, would set a moral example that would complement his values rhetoric. Accordingly, Bush promised to "return the highest standards of honor to the highest office in the land."⁶⁴ Bush liked to quote Franklin Roosevelt, who saw the presidency as "a place of moral leadership." This was, he often added, "a charge I plan to keep."[65]

But in his desire to roll back the moral freedoms of the 1960s, Bush was an imperfect messenger. As a college student at Yale, he had experimented with drugs; one rumor even had it that he had tried cocaine on more than one occasion.[66] Like many of his peers, Bush had avoided combat in Vietnam by serving as an Air Force reserve officer in the National Guard. As an adult, he had lived a life of privilege without much purpose, running unsuccessfully for Congress in 1978 and later serving as an executive for a failed oil company. These setbacks caused Bush to drink to excess, and, following a wild fortieth birthday party in 1986, his wife Laura gave him an ultimatum: "It's either me or Jim Beam."[67] Faced with a potential divorce, Bush foreswore alcohol and became a strong advocate for twelve-step programs such as Alcoholics Anonymous. But Bush's past continued to haunt him. A few days before Americans went to the polls, the news came out that he had been arrested in 1976 for driving under the influence at his father's vacation compound in Kennebunkport, Maine. This revelation caused many to have renewed doubts about the Texas governor and contributed to a flurry of late-deciders for Vice President Gore.

Nonetheless, Bush continued to translate his youthful excesses of the past into moral lessons for the present. Describing himself in the 1960s as "young and irresponsible,"[68] Bush advised fellow baby boomers to tell their children, "I've made mistakes in the past, and I've learned from my mistakes." He avoided reporters' questions as to whether he had used cocaine: "I have told the American people all I'm going to tell them. . . . I don't want to send a signal to children that whatever I may have done is O.K."[69] Instead of focusing on his youthful indiscretions, Bush advised everyone to learn from his experiences and "understand the consequences of their behavior."[70] Once again, he drew larger moral lessons from the 1960s, lessons that baby boomer parents needed to reinforce with each other and their children: "At times we lost our way; but we are coming home. So many of us have held our first child, and saw a better self reflected in her eyes. And in that family love, many have found the sign and symbol of an even greater love, and have been touched by faith. We have discovered that who we are is more important than what we have. And we know we must renew our values to restore our country."[71]

Bush's message resonated with the public. Three-quarters said the Texas governor had high personal and moral standards, and 70 percent thought he shared the moral values that most citizens tried to live by.[72] By a five-to-one margin, Bush was viewed as having higher moral standards than Bill Clinton, and an astounding 81 percent of Republicans cited his strong moral character as a "very important" reason for backing him.[73] Moreover, by 53 percent to 29 percent, Republicans thought Bush had the personal character and moral values they were seeking in a potential president, as opposed to John McCain.[74] Finally, 43 percent of all voters said they would be more likely to vote for Bush because he would bring morality and ethics back to the White House.[75]

TABLE 5.1   GEORGE W. BUSH AND AL GORE VALUES CHARACTERISTICS
            COMPARED (IN PERCENTAGES)

Value Characteristic	Bush	Gore
Shares your values	44	36
Personal responsibility	42	34
Community	40	35
Ethics and honesty	41	36
Respect	43	34
Faith in God	36	31
Knowing right from wrong	38	32
Standing up to special interests	39	32
Protecting our senior citizens	37	40
Strengthening our families	39	35
Giving children the right start	35	39
Representing middle-class values	38	41

Source: The Tarrance Group and Lake, Snell, Perry, and Associates poll, 3–5 January 2000.

These numbers spelled trouble for Al Gore. Fifty-three percent thought that the Clinton-Gore administration had lowered the nation's moral and ethical values.[76] Moreover, ethical questions surrounding the vice president's conduct harmed him. In 1996, he visited a California Buddhist temple in what was billed as a community outreach event but, in fact, was a fundraiser. In addition, he used White House telephones to help raise the large sums of money needed to put the Democratic message on television. At a White House press conference, Gore claimed that there was "no controlling legal authority" that prevented him from making the questionable calls. With the press focused on Gore's ethical troubles, Bush obtained an even more decisive values advantage. During the spring and summer, Bush had an eight-point advantage on moral leadership, an eleven-point edge when it came to having the proper moral character to be president, and a ten-point lead as the candidate more likely to improve the country's moral climate.[77] Especially disturbing to the inner councils of the Gore campaign was an earlier January 2000 survey that found Bush beating the vice president on several key values characteristics (see table 5.1). Only on three values dimensions did Gore have a slight edge: protecting senior citizens, giving children the right start, and representing middle-class values. As the fall campaign got underway, Gore had a serious values deficit to overcome.

Al Gore: "We've Got to Get God Back"

Beginning once more his lifelong quest for the presidency in 1999, Al Gore was in an enviable position.[78] Announcing his candidacy at his hometown in Carthage, Tennessee, the vice president pointed with pride to the fact that the budget deficits he and Bill Clinton had inherited from the Reagan-Bush administrations had been transformed into record surpluses. The bulging federal ledgers resulted in low interest rates and fueled an economic boom that saw stock prices triple, not to mention the creation of 22 million new jobs and 4 million new businesses. The robust economy, with its unprecedented 3.9 percent unemployment rate, was a stark contrast to the recession that framed the 1992 campaign. Seeking to capitalize on the economic good times, Gore offered himself as Clinton's logical successor: "I want to keep our prosperity going—and I know how to do it. I want to do it the right way—not by letting people fend for themselves, or hoping for crumbs of compassion—but by giving people the skills and knowledge to succeed in their own right for the next century."[79]

The last time a president's party lost the White House in such prosperous economic times was in 1920. Back then, the wartime boom had created prosperity but left voters hungering for a "return to normalcy." In 2000, for the first time in eighty years, the conventional wisdom, which held that a sound economy would propel Gore into the presidency, was upended. Instead of, "It's the economy, stupid!" both Gore and Bush could have posted signs at their headquarters reading, "It's values, stupid!" At times, Gore mimicked Bush, once telling supporters: "[T]he issue is not only our standard of living, but our standards in life. The measure is not merely the value of our possessions, but the values we possess." As Gore readily admitted, economic deficits had been replaced by several values deficits, including "the time deficit in family life, the decency deficit in our common culture, [and] the care deficit for our little ones and our elderly parents." The picture that resulted from this values shortage was not a pretty one as painted by Gore in his announcement speech: "Dinner tables that sit empty, when working parents do not have time to share a meal with their children. . . . Entertainment that glorifies aggression and indecency, with lessons more vivid and overpowering than those in the classroom. . . . Schools where discipline is eroding—and the school hallways were guns and fear are becoming too common."[80]

Gore, who like other vice presidents seeking the presidency automatically inherited the title "the status-quo candidate," had to forfeit this crown and become an advocate for change. As Gore himself stated, "I am not satisfied. Indeed, I am restless. I believe we can do better. I believe we must . . . make our values the strongest compass for our future, and the strongest force on Earth."[81] As the campaign progressed, Gore became even more forceful in addressing the nation's values deficit. He proclaimed his friendship for Bill Clinton but after his announcement speech backpedaled from his postimpeachment statement that Clinton was "one of our greatest presidents" and denounced his affair with Monica Lewinsky: "I felt what the president did, especially as a parent, was inexcusable."[82] In Gore's view, the Clinton-Lewinsky affair, along with the school violence at Columbine, was symptomatic of a new values poverty: "There is a theory of crime prevention called 'broken windows.' It says that if there is a community with broken windows, and litter on the street, and graffiti on the walls, that sends a powerful message: if you want to commit a crime, then you've come to the right place. We tolerate disorder here. As a nation, we can't allow broken values any more than we allow broken windows."[83]

In an attempt to alleviate this poverty of values, Gore took a page out of George W. Bush's rhetorical playbook and incorporated religion into his values message: "If you elect me President, the voices of faith-based organizations will be integral to the policies set forth in my administration." Addressing the graduates at the University of New Hampshire, the vice president boldly introduced God into the political dialogue: "I believe in serving God and trying to understand and obey God's will for our lives."[84] As a devout, self-described "born again" Southern Baptist,[85] Gore liked to introduce himself to religious audiences as "a child of the kingdom."[86] Mixing religion with politics was nothing new for Gore. In his 1992 book, *Earth in the Balance*, Gore equated restoring the environment with a public hunger for spiritual values: "The resurgence of fundamentalism in every world religion, from Islam to Judaism to Hinduism to Christianity; the proliferation of new spiritual movements, ideologies, and cults of all shapes and descriptions; the popularity of New Age doctrines and the current fascination with exploratory myths and stories from cultures the world over—all serve as evidence for the conclusion that there is a spiritual crisis in modern civilization that seems to be based on an emptiness at the center and the absence of a larger spiritual purpose."[87] Eight years later Gore promised to create a "New Partnership" between government and faith-based institutions by expanding the "charitable choice" provision of the 1996 welfare reform law, which allowed states to enlist faith-based organizations to move people from welfare to work. The reasoning behind Gore's emphasis on religion and faith was clear; as one Gore adviser explained, "We've got to get God back."[88]

On the surface, Gore was well positioned to "get God back." Faithfully married for thirty years, Gore had four children and, as he liked to remind audiences, one grandson who was born on the Fourth of July. Gore celebrated family life, beginning with his parents who were married sixty-one years before his father, former Tennessee senator Albert Gore Sr., died in 1998. Accepting the Democratic presidential nomination, Gore eulogized his parents: "My parents taught me that the real values in life aren't material but spiritual. They include faith and family, duty and honor, and trying to make the world a better place." As a young man, Gore had volunteered for military service during the Vietnam War and often spoke of how "proud" he was to wear the army uniform.[89] During his Senate career, wife Tipper Gore became a prominent spokeswoman for a moral reawakening. In 1985, she teamed up with Susan Baker, wife of Treasury secretary James Baker, to form the Parents Music Resource Center, which lobbied the record industry to adopt a ratings system warning parents about violent or sexu-ally explicit music lyrics. In 1987, Tipper Gore published a book titled *Raising PG Kids in an X-Rated Society* in which she wrote: "There is a responsible, non-fanatical, growing concern over pornography that can't be pinned on outdated images of prudish misfits attempting to Lysol the world. As parents we have a spe-cial duty to establish a moral imperative for our children."[90]

Her husband also saw connections between moral values and politics, espe-cially when it pertained to the environment: "By experiencing nature in its fullest—our own and that of all creation—with our senses and with our spiritual imagination, we can glimpse, 'bright shining as the sun,' an infinite image of God."[91] During his vice presidency, Gore continued to link morality with public policy and became a powerful advocate for placing V-chips on television sets, which would allow parents to block inappropriate programming for children. In addition, he advocated a ratings system for television programming that warned parents about excessive violence, sex, and foul language. As Gore told campaign crowds, "Parents now feel like you have to compete with the mass culture in order to raise your kids with the values that you want them to have."[92] Finally, both Al and Tipper Gore participated in yearly White House conferences to monitor the state of the American family.

By emphasizing the family, Gore drew attention to the fact that throughout his life, he had developed a strong reputation for virtue when it came to family mat-ters. In 1992, he abstained from running for president after his son, Albert III, was seriously hurt in a 1989 automobile accident. Gore later reflected: "I had just turned forty years old. I was, in a sense, vulnerable to the change that sought me out in the middle of my life and gave me a new sense of urgency about those things I value most."[93] Gore's penchant for self-reflection and his constant search for life's mean-ing made him and Tipper culturally different from Bill and Hillary Clinton. Un-like Hillary Clinton, for example, Tipper Gore was unpretentious and had no prob-lem adapting to the role of a typical politician's wife.[94] Adding to the differences was the fact that both Gores came from privileged backgrounds, while Bill Clinton had grown up dirt-poor in Arkansas. These cultural differences were reflected in the wariness with which the two men viewed each other. Back in 1988, Gore's mother, Pauline, told her son that Clinton had a bad moral character, and warned, "Bill Clinton is not a nice person. Don't associate too closely with him."[95]

Gore's desire to separate himself from Clinton and enhance his own values message was immeasurably strengthened by his selection of Connecticut senator Joseph I. Lieberman to be his vice-presidential running mate. Lieberman was the first person of the Jewish faith to be placed on a major-party ticket. While Demo-crats repeatedly drew attention to the fact that Lieberman's nomination gave greater meaning to the American dream—as Lieberman put it, "Only in Amer-ica"[96]—that was not the core of the party's values message. Instead, it was Lieberman's religious fidelity and his abhorrence of Bill Clinton's sexual adventures that were emphasized. Throughout his public career, Lieberman had been a faithful Orthodox Jew. He took the Sabbath seriously, even refusing to attend Connecticut State Democratic Conventions, which for years were held on Saturdays, because it would violate his religious tenets. Lieberman continued to observe the Sabbath, and absented himself from the presidential campaign trail on Saturdays. Americans liked what they saw: by a four-to-one margin they thought Lieberman added value to the Democratic ticket.[97] They liked him even more when his 1998 Senate speech denouncing Clinton's moral leadership was replayed on television over and over again. In it, Lieberman became the first Senate Democrat to denounce Clinton for failing to act as a steward for American values:

> In this case, the president apparently had extramarital relations with an employee half his age, and did so in the workplace in the vicinity of the Oval Office. Such behavior is not just inappropriate. It is immoral. And it is harmful, for it sends a message of what is acceptable behavior to the larger American family—particularly to our children—which is as influential as the negative messages communicated by the entertainment culture. . . . I believe that the harm the president's actions have caused extend beyond the political arena. I am afraid that the misconduct the president has admitted may be reinforcing one of the worst messages being delivered by our popular culture, which is that values are fungible. And I am concerned that his misconduct may help blur some of the bright lines between right and wrong in our society.[98]

Lieberman had long been active in condemning a popular culture "where sexual promiscuity is often treated as just another lifestyle choice with little risk of adverse consequences."[99] Long before Clinton's dalliance with Lewinsky, he and Republican William Bennett joined forces to lead a "revolt of the revolted" to remove the "trash" from daytime television talk shows: "A growing number of Americans are sickened by the morass of sex, vulgarity, and violence that increasingly dominates our electronic media; and they are disgusted by what they see as the entertainment industry's abandonment of basic standards of decency, as if anything goes. The result is an increasingly debased culture that rejects, rather than reflects, the basic values that most Americans share."[100] During the presidential campaign, Lieberman repeatedly decried the country's "values vacuum"[101] and offered his own personal story of religious faith as an illustration of how public morality could be restored: "Without the connection to a higher law, we have made it more and more difficult for people to answer the question why it is wrong to lie, cheat, or steal; to settle conflicts with violence, to be unfaithful to one's spouse, or to exploit children; to despoil the environment, to defraud a customer, or to demean any employee."[102] Clearly, by choosing Lieberman, Gore made a dramatic break with Clinton and sought to redefine himself as the values candidate.

It nearly worked. By a 49-to-41-percent margin, Americans said the Gore-Lieberman ticket made them feel that Gore himself was a man of faith and strong moral values.[103] Nearly three-quarters said Gore had high moral and ethical standards, and 58 percent thought he would do a better job than Clinton in providing moral leadership for the country.[104] More importantly, Gore's emphasis on values at the Democratic Convention—including his nomination by daughter Karenna, the prolonged kiss and embrace of Mrs. Gore after he entered the hall to accept the nomination, a film emphasizing Gore's family life, and the Lieberman nomination—resulted in a values dead heat. An ABC News/*Washington Post* poll found Gore and Bush tied at 44 percent when respondents were asked which one would encourage high moral standards and values.[105] (Bush had previously held a ten-point lead on this issue.)[106] A Fox News survey produced another stalemate when voters were asked to select which candidate would do the most to improve the moral climate of the country.[107] A Gallup poll found Gore holding a slim three-point lead as the candidate who shares your values.[108] Given the fact that both candidates were offering themselves as moral men, it is not surprising that a CBS News/*New York Times* poll found 63 percent saying they were satisfied with their presidential choices.[109]

Despite gaining in the polls, Gore was severely disadvantaged by the Democratic Party's relatively poor positioning on similar values issues. Republicans held a 23-point advantage over the Democrats as the party that better upholds traditional family values; a 15-point edge as the party more closely associated with the value of knowing right from wrong; and a 9-point lead when it came to protecting religious values.[110] But it was a poll conducted by NBC News and the *Wall Street Journal* that found the most startling juxtaposition between the two parties. When asked whether the Republicans stood for strong moral values, 66 percent answered that this "tends to be the case"; just 25 percent said no. But when the same question was posed concerning the Democrats, voters were evenly divided: 44 percent, yes; 46 percent, no.[111] Only when asked about the value of tolerance did the Democrats hold a significant 54-percent to 23-percent advantage.[112] But even this proved to be a double-edged sword, since tolerance often signified acceptance of new lifestyles. No matter how hard Gore tried, he could not break through to enough voters—many of them in heretofore solidly Democratic states—who wanted a president who would extol traditional family values. Gore's inability to transform his life story into an overarching values message helped create an election result that essentially divided the country into two separate nations—one where traditional morality was cherished and the 1950s fondly remembered, the other where morality was a matter of individual choice and the 1960s social and cultural revolution, which increased those choices, was similarly honored.

The Two Nations

While Bush and Gore pledged allegiance to family values and sought to monop-olize the center of American politics, those who in fact did occupy what historian Arthur M. Schlesinger Jr. once called the "vital center" were a very different species than, say, the 1970s.[113] The image often conjured of centrist Americans is that of a suburban married couple with underage children living at home and an income in the $25,000–$50,000 range. But in 2000, Middle America was a more divided, less "centrist," and a less homogeneous place. Changing demographics have meant that the fictional Ozzie and Harriet Nelsons of the 1950s, Ward and June Cleavers of the 1960s, and Heathcliff and Claire Huxtables of the 1980s no longer depict what can be described as the "normal" suburban family. Even tele-vision programming, which in the 1950s and 1960s extolled traditional families, has significantly altered its content. *Friends*, the popular NBC television show, depicts six characters in and out of various sexual relationships. *Will and Grace*, another NBC sitcom, is not about a happily married couple; instead, Will is an openly gay character who has a platonic relationship with his live-in roommate Grace. Other prime-time shows also feature actors in gay roles. *Ellen*, the first net-work series to depict a real-life gay character playing the lead, attracted 36 million viewers to her 1997 "coming-out" episode—almost as many as watched the final Bush-Gore debate.[114]

This demographic shift as reflected in the popular culture has produced an electoral divide as sharp as the old North-South Civil War split. If a voter lived in the South (including the Bible Belt), the Great Plains, or the West (save the Pacific Rim), she was likely to be on one side of the cultural divide, where traditional fam-ilies were valued and belief in religious institutions (and the absolute truths they convey) was prevalent. This was George W. Bush country. Nine of his top ten states were in this L-shaped formation that extended from the Dakotas down through Texas and across to the Georgia coast.[115] But if a voter lived in the Northeast or along the Pacific Rim she was in Gore country. All of Gore's top ten states were in the Northeast, with the exceptions of California and Hawaii.[116] Overall, those who lived in the Northeast cast 56 percent of their ballots for Gore; southerners gave Bush 55 percent of their ballots.[117] As one Gore supporter from Chicago said of George W. Bush, Texas was "in the United States, but not part of it."[118]

The cultural divide was so powerful that Gore lost his native Tennessee, in-cluding his old congressional district.[119] In addition, Gore lost other traditional De-mocratic states, most notably West Virginia. Following Franklin Roosevelt's New Deal and Lyndon Johnson's War on Poverty, which had Appalachia as its focus, West Virginia has been a Democratic bastion. It occasionally supported Republican presidential candidates in landslide years—notably Dwight Eisenhower in 1956, Richard Nixon in 1972, and Ronald Reagan in 1984. But that has not always been the case; in 1980, West Virginia was just one of six states to back Jimmy Carter's re-election bid, and eight years later the state was one of the few in Michael Dukakis's column. But Gore's environmental stands and his position on guns alienated many West Virginians who depended on coal for their livelihoods and were culturally apart from the new Democratic base Gore represented. Besides West Virginia, Gore lost Arkansas and Louisiana, states with long pro-Democratic histories that Bill Clinton had carried twice. If Gore had been able to win just one of these states, the country would have been spared the Florida wrangling.

This cultural divide created its own moral federalism. Simply put, if you were gay, you were more likely to live in Vermont; if you wanted the Ten Command-ments posted in the courts, you liked living in Alabama; if you were antigun, you had lots of company in Massachusetts; but if you were pro-gun, you were not alone in Wyoming. The result was an increased partisanship thanks to the cultural divide separating Democrats and Republicans on most moral issues: 91 percent of all Re-publicans supported Bush; 86 percent of Democrats backed Gore. But the party gap was only one of many. The gender gap returned with a vengeance: 54 percent of women supported Gore, and 53 percent of men voted for Bush. Other gaps in-cluded married versus single; churched versus less churched; the religious right ver-sus those who were not "born again"; whites versus blacks versus Latinos; working women versus stay-at-home moms; union members versus non–union members; working class versus the prosperous middle versus the brie-and-chablis set; liberals versus conservatives; gays versus straights; gun owners versus those who didn't have guns in their homes; rural versus urban America; and in Vermont, those who were enthusiastic about civil unions versus those angry at the idea (see table 5.2).

The gaps created by this new moral federalism were especially present in how voters viewed the country's moral direction. Overall, 39 percent said that the moral climate was headed in the right direction, whereas 57 percent said things were on the wrong track. Not surprisingly, Bush voters saw the nation's morals askew, with 62 percent answering "wrong track." Gore voters were considerably happier with the status quo: 70 percent of them thought that the country's morals were going in the right direction. The state of the country's moral values became a prism through which voters saw politics. Blacks, liberals, and Democrats, for example, thought the country's morals were just fine. Whites, conservatives, and Republicans disagreed. How one viewed the country's moral condition also colored perceptions of the pres-idency, of life for the next generation, of Bill Clinton's legacy, whether the country needed a fresh start or should stay on course, whether the military had become too weak, and whether they could trust the candidates (see table 5.3, p. 166).

Church attendance proved to be a major cultural divide in the 2000 vote. Those who went to church frequently were apt to be Bush supporters; those who went less often or never were more likely to back Gore. This was true even within religious denominations. A postelection survey conducted by political scientists

TABLE 5.2   THE TWO NATIONS (IN PERCENTAGES)

Demographic/Issue	Bush	Gore
Democrats	11	86
Republicans	91	8
Men	53	42
Women	43	54
Whites	54	42
Blacks	8	90
Hispanic	31	67
Those married with children	56	41
Those single/divorced	38	57
Those who attend religious services more than weekly	63	36
Those who never attend religious services	32	61
Those who consider themselves members of the religious right (whites only)	80	18
Those who don't consider themselves members of the religious right (whites only)	42	54
Working women	39	58
Stay-at-home moms	52	44
Union members	34	62
Non–union members	52	44
Working class	46	51
Upper-middle class	54	43
Upper class	39	56
Liberals	13	80
Conservatives	81	17
Gays/Lesbians	25	70
Straight	50	47
Gun owners	61	36
Non–gun owners	39	58
Those who say abortion should be legal in all cases	25	70
Those who say abortion should be illegal in all cases	74	22
Those from cities with a population of more than 500,000	26	71
Those from rural areas	59	37
Those enthusiastic about same-sex civil unions[a]	8	80
Those angry about same-sex civil unions[a]	75	23

Source: Voter News Service exit poll, 7 November 2000.
a. Vermont only.

John C. Green, James L. Guth, Lyman A. Kellstedt, and Corwin B. Smidt found that more observant white evangelical Protestants gave Bush 84 percent of their support, while only 55 percent of the less observant evangelicals backed Bush. Among white mainstream Protestants there was a similar split: 66 percent of the more observant backed Bush, while 57 percent of those who were less observant

TABLE 5.3 MORAL DIRECTION OF THE COUNTRY AND POLITICAL OUTLOOK, ELECTION DAY 2000 (IN PERCENTAGES)

	Right Direction	*Wrong Track*
By vote		
Bush	27	62
Gore	70	33
By race		
White	37	60
Black	54	41
Hispanic	43	51
By party		
Democratic	56	40
Republican	24	74
Independent/Other	34	63
By political philosophy		
Liberal	55	40
Moderate	43	54
Conservative	24	76
By expectation for the next generation		
Life will be better	47	50
Life will be worse	23	74
Life will be about the same	38	58
Is Al Gore honest and trustworthy?		
Yes	55	41
No	22	75
Is George Bush honest and trustworthy?		
Yes	30	67
No	51	44
Which is more important in a president, his ability to manage the government or his ability to provide moral leadership?		
Manage government	49	47
Provide moral leadership	25	73
Which do you agree with more: the country needs a fresh start, or the country needs to stay on course?		
Fresh start	21	76
Stay on course	53	43
In the past eight years, do you think the U.S. military has become stronger, weaker, or stayed the same?		
Stronger	57	39
Weaker	23	75
Stayed the same	54	42
Do you think history will remember Bill Clinton more for his leadership or more for his scandals?		
Leadership	64	32
Scandals	29	68

Source: Voter News Service exit poll, 7 November 2000.

supported him. Among observant and less observant Roman Catholics, there was a partisan divide of significant proportions: more observant Catholics gave Bush 57 percent of their votes to Gore's 43 percent, while less observant Catholics supported Gore by a comfortable margin of 59 percent to 41 percent.[120]

The coming of the Information Age also contributed to the new values divide. As noted earlier in the book, those most plugged into the Internet tend to have college or postgraduate degrees and are more attuned to sociologist Alan Wolfe's concept of "morality writ small."[121] Many live in so-called Latte Towns—including Burlington, Vermont; Madison, Wisconsin; and Boulder, Colorado[122]—and were much more likely to support Al Gore who, like them, preferred his morality writ small. In an interview with the *New York Times*, Gore said, "I have a defined set of beliefs, but I also believe the eternal truths are difficult if not impossible to capture."[123] Gore's own moral outlook, and that of his Democratic Party, coincided with that held by so-called New Economy voters. Of the top twenty states having the greatest number of college and postgraduate degree-holders and research dollars, Gore won thirteen while Bush captured only seven.[124]

The situation in California illustrates the Republican Party's values problem in several of these New Economy states. After winning the Democratic presidential nomination in Los Angeles, Gore never spent one dime on television commercials in the state. The reason was simple; thanks to most Californians' belief in a morality writ small, the state was not even contested (although George W. Bush made a feint at doing so). In conservative Orange County, once a bastion of Reaganism, Republican registration has fallen below 50 percent. One group of disgruntled California Republicans explained their party's problems this way: "It's the platform, stupid!" After the state Republicans elected a conservative, pro-life party chair, the victor thanked his supporters "for standing up for our values," to which a party dissident responded, "What values are those? As long as we keep talking about abortion and keep showing our ugly side, we are going to keep losing and keep losing until we reach the point of complete irrelevance."[125]

California was only one example of an electorate turned upside down from the New Economy era. While Gore carried those without a high school diploma (a traditional Democratic group) by a 59-to-39-percent margin, he also won majority backing from those with postgraduate degrees, 52 percent to 44 percent. Several former Republican strongholds, including Oakland County, Michigan—once home to Henry Ford—also voted Democratic. In fact, Gore won ten of the sixteen states Thomas E. Dewey carried against Harry S. Truman in 1948.[126] Dewey, who was popular in the Northeast, swept the region with the sole exceptions of Massachusetts and Rhode Island; Gore, as noted, did just as well. Abortion was one reason, as suburban women did not want *Roe v. Wade* overturned. The environment is also an important issue to well-educated New Economy voters who desire its preservation and see it as a values issue (see table 5.4).

But cultural issues and outlooks also mattered. As David Brooks points out in his incisive book, *Bobos in Paradise*, suburban counties like Oakland have seen a cultural homogenization (witness the prevalence of Starbucks coffee shops). Even more importantly, they are brokers to a profound cultural compromise: wealth is not bad, and neither are the values of the 1960s. According to Brooks, the 1960s generation that inspired the sexual revolution has been transformed into "bourgeois bohemians," prosperous and celebrating its good fortune but also wanting more moral choices and having the power to make them without interference from outside institutions like religion or government.[127]

While Gore won broad support from Latte Towns, New Economy voters, and well-educated voters, George W. Bush was winning solid support from states where incomes are low, a small percentage are exposed to college, the number of non-English speaking citizens are few, and commuting times are less than the national average. Bush's easygoing persona and image as a "regular guy" helped him in these places. But, so too did his devotion to traditional family values, which appealed to those who were tired of Clinton and wanted a respite from the values challenges they had to face during his two terms. In the bottom five states listed on table 5.4, voters often believe in Eternal Truths, are more religious, and have strong views about right and wrong. Bush and his fellow Republicans had a values message that appealed to these voters, many of whom were once reliable Democrats.

The Denouement

After the Florida mess was settled, Bill Clinton and Al Gore had a tense face-off in the Oval Office. According to press reports, Clinton criticized Gore for not utilizing him in the campaign and not giving enough emphasis to the administration's economic record. Gore countered that Clinton's infidelity undermined what should have been a winning campaign. A political partnership that was unusually close now lay in tatters, and staffers to both men argued their case in the media. Former Gore consultant Bob Boorstin was blunt: "Did we make mistakes? Yes. Would I say that Clinton was the only reason we lost? No. Would I say with absolute zero doubt in my mind that we would have won the election if Clinton hadn't put his penis in her mouth? Yes. I guarantee it. The guy blew it!"[128] Carter Eskew, another Gore consultant, agreed saying the Clinton scandals were "the elephant in the living room" that prevented Gore from making his case to disillusioned and angry swing voters.[129]

Ironically, while Clinton's sexual peccadillos greatly contributed to Gore's defeat and the Democratic Party's ongoing difficulties with traditional values voters, it was Clinton's adept handling of the economy that helped make a second Bush presidency possible. Prosperity meant that most Americans did not want to rock the boat with new, grandiose government programs. This hurt activist-minded Democrats, including Clinton, whose economic success left him unable to deal

TABLE 5.4 TOP FIVE AND BOTTOM FIVE STATES BY INCOME, EDUCATION, NON-ENGLISH SPEAKERS, COMMUTING TIMES, AND VOTE FOR PRESIDENT IN 2000

Median Income	Presidential Vote	College Education	Presidential Vote	Non–English Speakers	Presidential Vote	Commuting Times (in minutes)	Presidential Vote
Top Five States							
1. New Jersey ($54,226)	Gore	1. District of Columbia (41.1%)	Gore	1. California (39.5%)	Gore	1. New York (31.2)	Gore
2. Connecticut ($53,108)	Gore	2. Massachusetts (34.9%)	Gore	2. New Mexico (35.5%)	Gore	2. Maryland (29.2)	Gore
3. Alaska ($52,876)	Bush	3. Colorado (33.4%)	Bush	3. Texas (32.0%)	Bush	3. New Jersey (28.7)	Gore
4. Maryland ($52,436)	Gore	4. Connecticut (33.3%)	Gore	4. New York (27.5%)	Gore	4. District of Columbia (28.5)	Gore
5. Hawaii ($51,046)	Gore	5. Maryland (31.5%)	Gore	5. Hawaii (26.1%)	Gore	5. Illinois (27.0)	Gore
U.S. Median $41,343		*U.S. Median 25.1%*		*U.S. Median 17.6%*		*U.S. Median 24.3*	
Bottom Five States							
1. Kentucky ($32,843)	Bush	1. Mississippi (18.6%)	Bush	1. Arkansas (3.8%)	Bush	1. Wyoming (17.1)	Bush
2. Arkansas ($32,714)	Bush	2. Nevada (18.3%)	Bush	2. Kentucky (3.5%)	Bush	2. Nebraska (16.1)	Bush
3. Mississippi ($32,955)	Bush	3. Kentucky (17.2%)	Bush	3. Alabama (3.3%)	Bush	3. Montana (16.0)	Bush
4. Louisiana ($31,034)	Bush	4. Arkansas (16.6%)	Bush	4. Mississippi (2.9%)	Bush	4. South Dakota (15.6)	Bush
5. West Virginia ($28,569)	Bush	5. West Virginia (14.1%)	Bush	5. West Virginia (2.2%)	Bush	5. North Dakota (15.4)	Bush

Source: Eric Schmitt, "Census Data Show a Sharp Increase in Living Standard," *New York Times,* 6 August 2001, A1.

with larger problems. Pollster John Zogby explains: "Bill Clinton's tragedy is that he is one of the smartest men to occupy the White House, and he would have been, under different circumstances, a Franklin Roosevelt. But the American people clearly wanted Calvin Coolidge."[130]

For many Americans, George W. Bush fit the Coolidge model perfectly. Most saw the changes Bush wished to make more as changes in tone than in policy. Bush's lackadaisical lifestyle, and the fact that his father had already been president, made the transition from Clinton to Bush seem less jarring. But focusing on the economy or on Bush's cheery persona obscures the real message contained in the 2000 ballots—be they with a hanging chad, dimpled, or otherwise pregnant. That is, the cultural divisions between East and West, North and South, man and woman, straight and gay, gun owner and non–gun owner are unlikely to disappear, whatever either party or George W. Bush does or does not accomplish. The same geographic and cultural divide that was in evidence in 2000 is likely to persist in the 2002 and 2004 election contests. Instead of becoming the one nation George W. Bush longed for after the Supreme Court announced its decision in *Bush v. Gore*, the United States remains two nations, separated by a sharp geographic divide and an even sharper division when it comes to moral outlook. In many ways, the cultural gap resembles the social polarization described by Benjamin Disraeli in an 1845 novel titled *Sybil, or The Two Nations*. An encounter between the novel's hero Charles Egremont and an unnamed stranger produces a dialogue that could easily be replicated in twenty-first-century America:

> "Well, society may be in its fancy," said Egremont slightly smiling; "but say what you like, our Queen reigns over the greatest nation that ever existed."
>
> "Which nation?" asked the younger stranger, "for she reigns over two. . . . Two nations; between whom there is no intercourse and no sympathy; who are as ignorant of each other's habits, thoughts, and feelings, as if they were dwellers in different zones or inhabitants of different planets; who are formed by a different breeding, are fed by a different food, are ordered by different manners, and are not governed by the same laws."[131]

Unlike the British monarchy of the 1840s, George W. Bush has promised to "give it my all" in an attempt to bring the two nations together.[132] Like Richard Nixon, who in 1969 pleaded with Americans in a turbulent time to "stop shouting at one another,"[133] Bush wants to restore respect and civility to the political dialogue, but the partisan divisions produced by the voters are quickly being replicated at the elite level, as Democrats and Republicans find themselves deeply divided over the direction the federal government ought to take and the values that should predominate when making public policy. This phenomenon is described in the next chapter.

CHAPTER 6

The Father-Knows-Best President and the Return of Four-Party Politics

The twenty-first century will be the century of moral freedom.
—Alan Wolfe, *Moral Freedom*, 2001

TAKING THE PRESIDENCY after the long Florida recount, George W. Bush tried to govern like his model and Republican hero, Ronald Reagan. He muscled a ten-year, $1.35 trillion tax reduction through Congress in Reagan-like fashion, even beating the former president by several months in having a tax-cut bill on his desk. At a triumphant signing ceremony in June 2001, Bush acted as though the protracted postelection contest with Al Gore never happened. Of course, the reality was quite different. Bush knew that the landslide he had wished for in 2000 (and sincerely thought he would get) had vanished into the values chasm separating the blue states from the red ones. During the campaign, Bush exuded confidence that he would win in a landslide. He privately told Wisconsin governor Tommy Thompson in October: "I'll be the most surprised man in America if I don't win."[1] But while Bush was a forceful policymaker behind the scenes at the White House, at the onset of his administration his command of the presidential bully pulpit was considerably more muted. This was undoubtedly a result of Bush's penchant for verbal gaffes and a conscious strategy developed by his political team to draw a contrast with Bill Clinton (who never missed an opportunity to seize the spotlight). But Bush's reticence was also due to the values divide that he was disinclined to enhance. As one Bush voter put it, the new president seemed "toned down, quiet—almost *vice-presidential.*"[2]

In many ways, Bush's public profile is the mirror image of Bill Clinton's. While Clinton's personal morality was seen as reprehensible, his public policies met with broad approval. In Bush's case, two-thirds say he is honest, trustworthy, and has a strong personal character, but far fewer approve of his domestic policies.[3] Dick

Schrad, a city manager in Iowa, expresses sentiments felt by most Bush backers: "People in the heartland viewed Bill Clinton as a buffoon. I think George Bush has done a great deal to restore prestige, viability, and credibility to the office."[4] In fact, it is easy to like a president who travels to Capitol Hill and startles legislators by ordering his favorite lunch, a peanut butter and jelly sandwich. Yet, even as he appears to be down-to-earth, most Americans continue to believe that Bush does not understand their everyday problems. Pat McMahon, a New Hampshire homemaker, is particularly unhappy with Bush's handling of energy and environmental issues: "I don't like his energy policy. Drilling in wildlife areas in Alaska makes no sense. There are other ways of meeting our needs."[5] She is hardly alone. Two-thirds say that large business corporations, oil and gas industries, and wealthy people have too much influence in the Bush-Cheney administration, while an equal number believe that ordinary people have too little influence.[6]

Especially disturbing is the fact that the deep political and cultural divisions so evident in the Bush-Gore contest still persist. A 2001 CNN/*USA Today*/Gallup poll taken prior to the September 11th terrorist attacks found that if the election were rerun, the outcome would be another dead heat: 48 percent for Bush, 48 percent for Gore.[7] Moreover, when asked whether the country should go in the direction Bush wants to lead it or take the course offered by congressional Democrats, the result was another tie: 42 percent liked Bush's leadership; 43 percent preferred the Democratic approach.[8] The partisan stalemate is especially evident when citizens are asked to choose which party leaders they want to handle the most important issues of the day. George W. Bush has a decided advantage when it comes to dealing with international affairs and defense, both legacies from his father's presidency and issues on which the Republicans held large advantages during the Cold War.[9] He also does remarkably well on the education issue, running well ahead of more conservative Republicans who prefer the federal government to recuse itself from setting national education standards. But when asked about the environment, energy, prescription drugs, a patient's bill of rights, and Social Security, people prefer congressional Democrats. The Democrats' advantages on health care and Social Security are not surprising, since these programs have their antecedents in Franklin D. Roosevelt's New Deal, while their energy and environmental leads are momentarily reinforced by George W. Bush and Dick Cheney's close ties to the oil industry.

An anemic economy was only one reason for George W. Bush's inability to transform politics. The other—much more serious—dilemma Bush faces has to do with the present values divide. Clearly, his ability to muster an enduring Republican majority depends not just on his legislative successes but on his capacity to help citizens cope with shifting values. More than ever before, Americans are finding that what was once familiar is no more. As the definition of what constitutes a family changes, and the relationship between family and work becomes more complicated, a moral reassessment is taking place. To take but one example, twenty states currently permit gays to adopt children, and only Utah, Mississippi, and Florida have laws on the books prohibiting gays or unmarried couples from making this choice.[10]

Sociologist Alan Wolfe believes such moral reassessments will lead to an inevitable future: "The twenty-first century," he says, "will be the century of moral freedom."[11] Already, this rethinking of public and private values is contributing to a sense that individuals have innumerable choices in determining for themselves what it means to lead a good and virtuous life. But this new era of moral freedom makes it much harder for those in leadership positions to have their authority accepted with the deference to which they were once accustomed. Leaders of the American Roman Catholic Church, for example, find it difficult to impose their moral precepts on their flock in the authoritative manner they once did. As Pope John Paul II told the American bishops in 1987:

> It is sometimes reported that a large number of Catholics today do not adhere to the teaching of the Catholic Church on a number of questions, notably sexual and conjugal morality, divorce, and remarriage. Some are reported as not accepting the clear position [of the Church] on abortion. It has to be noted that there is a tendency on the part of some Catholics to be selective in their adherence to the Church's moral teaching. It is sometimes claimed that dissent from the magisterium is totally compatible with being a "good Catholic," and poses no obstacle to the reception of the Sacraments. This is a grave error that challenges the teaching of the Bishops in the United States and elsewhere.[12]

The result is a schism in which orthodox Catholics long for an era when church teachings were unquestioningly accepted while growing numbers of "cafeteria Catholics" pick and choose which doctrines they will or will not accept. In this new environment, church leaders must use the bully pulpit of their altars, along with other many other new media forums, to make their arguments. This does not mean that all Catholic teachings are rejected. For example, eight-in-ten Catholics believe that divorce represents a major threat to family values, and nearly half say it should be more difficult to obtain.[13] These beliefs are consonant with church teachings. But 84 percent also believe that divorce is only "sometimes wrong."[14] This unwillingness to condemn all divorces is yet one more example of how Catholics, like many other Americans, want their morality writ small.

In much the same vein, corporate executives can no longer issue edicts and expect that they will be unquestioningly followed. Instead, CEOs must develop new strategies designed to compete in the global marketplace where individual entrepreneurship is a valued commodity. Stan Davis and Christopher Meyer contend that in this new computer-connected economy of the Information Age, the "organization man" has given way to self-employed entrepreneurs of both sexes who move from job to job. Today, more businesses than ever before are staffed by free-lancers, consultants, contractors, and temporary workers. Although they may claim to be more independent than their parents, their success or failure nevertheless depends on the success of the larger enterprise they happen to work for at any given time. So prevalent are these temporary alliances that Americans now talk differently about their jobs. Once upon a time, those who left large corporations were said to "jump ship." These days, people "make moves."[15] Everywhere one looks, the old loyalties are no longer given the deference they once enjoyed, and employer-employee relations are considerably more transient. Laverne Eaton, a fifty-five-year-old grandmother, lovingly relates how the company to which she devoted thirty-two years of her life before retiring really "cared about us." In turn, she added, "we cared about them." Her son is currently employed by the same company, but the values exhibited by both employer and employee are considerably different. As Eaton describes it, "There's no loyalty, and people don't care about doing the job they're hired to do."[16] Even so, the greater sense of economic freedom Eaton's son and many others say they enjoy, even with all its insecurities, compliments the moral freedom Wolfe sees dominating in the twenty-first century.

Like religious institutions and large corporations, the federal government also has had to adapt to this new environment. During the 1990s, Bill Clinton and Al Gore promised to "reinvent government" by making it smaller and less bureaucratic. Their efforts met with some success as 272,900 employees and $58 billion were cut from the payrolls and 16,000 pages of rules and regulations were excised from the *Federal Register*.[17] But the Clinton-Gore promise to make government smarter, cheaper, and more modest did not by itself restore public trust. Like all large institutions, the federal government no longer commands the authority it once did. Back in the 1950s, when corporate thinking with its deference to authority figures dominated, 75 percent said they could depend on the government to do the right thing.[18] Half a century later, 69 percent say they trust government either just "some of the time" or "hardly ever."[19]

The invincible presidency that accompanied the 1950s era of the organization man is no more, thanks to Vietnam, Watergate, and various other presidential scandals. Nonetheless, presidents—like religious leaders and corporate executives—often long for the "good old days" when their leadership was given greater deference. Facing a storm of criticism in 1993 over gays in the military and health care, Bill Clinton lamented that he was not John F. Kennedy who had the Cold War to sustain him. "Gosh, I miss the Cold War," Clinton said, adding: "I envy Kennedy having an enemy. The question now is how to persuade people they should do things when they are not immediately threatened."[20] As the grandson and son of Establishment politicians, George W. Bush has expressed similar sentiments. Following the September 11th terrorist attacks, Bush undertook extraordinary measures to establish a shadow government outside Washington, D.C. But he did so without consulting the leaders of Congress, who presumably would be left in proverbial darkness if terrorists were to obtain and use nuclear weapons on the nation's capital.[21] In fact, Bush does not like to be challenged; he prefers a businesslike, crisp management style where decisions once made are promptly executed. In this, Bush is reminiscent of Dwight D. Eisenhower, a former four-star general, who also was accustomed to giving orders and having them unquestioningly obeyed.

By its nature, moral freedom breeds a morality-writ-small way of thinking that elicits considerable public skepticism toward all large institutions. But it also makes for a politics writ small. Today, most Americans view politics as far removed from the struggles that bedevil their daily lives. The old expression that there isn't "a dime's worth of difference" between the Democratic and Republican parties still holds true for most citizens, even as the policy differences separating the two parties have grown and the partisan rhetoric is far more strident. While most struggle to place their personal values in the larger context of classical liberalism—defining them as either expanding freedom, promoting more opportunity, or granting individuals greater equality—spokespersons for the two major parties often regard freedom, opportunity, and equality as mutually exclusive values. Thus, Democrats proclaim their fealty to the values of equality of opportunity, community, and tolerance. Yet, too often they show little regard for traditional families and the values they espouse. Republicans fill this void by proclaiming their reverence for traditional family values but frequently exhibit considerable intolerance toward those who either don't live in traditional families or wish to pursue alternative lifestyles. Americans want *all* of these values expressed, and they bemoan the "false choices" so often proffered by their political leaders. In 1991, E.J. Dionne Jr. lamented this failure of leadership in his well-received book, *Why Americans Hate Politics*: "Wracked by contradiction and responsive mainly to the needs of their various constituencies, liberalism and conservatism *prevent* the nation from settling the questions that most trouble it."[22]

A decade later, Dionne's observation represents an even more powerful truth. Liberals believe that good public policy will solve the current values crisis. "Got a problem with guns?" they say, "then change the gun laws." Conservatives also see politics and morality as inseparable. "Values in decline? . . . Post the Ten Commandments in public places." Today, more than ever before, those on the right share with those on the left a desire to use the broad legislative and judicial powers of government (since activists on both sides see all sorts of values deficits), and the content of the legislation they desire often tends toward more authoritarian approaches to governance.

The Father-Knows-Best President

Governing in this ideological atmosphere, George W. Bush has cast himself as a Father-Knows-Best president, wishing to convey 1950s-era moral lessons not just by his public persona and personal example but through executive action. During his first six months in office, the Bush-Cheney administration refused to give states the authority to expand family-planning services for poor women; reimposed a ban on abortion counseling at overseas health clinics; authorized a report questioning the effectiveness of condoms; proposed eliminating mandatory contraceptive coverage for federal employees; and boosted funding for abstinence-only sex-education programs, with most of the money going to evangelical Christian organizations.[23] Conservative commentator Andrew Sullivan likens the Bush-Cheney governing style to a Hallmark card: "The model of their masculinity is definitely retro—stern dads in suits and ties, undemonstrative, matter-of-fact, but with alleged hearts of gold."[24]

This form of values politics is small-minded and distorts politics as it was once commonly understood. In 1958, political scientist Harold Lasswell described politics as the art of "who gets what, when, and how."[25] Politics, it seemed, was nothing more than the allocation of federal dollars. During the Cold War, this dollars-and-cents politics led to the creation of a military-industrial complex whose objective was to bankrupt the Soviet Union into submission. The federal government spent $2 trillion on nuclear warheads, $1 trillion to control and defend these bombs, $375 billion for plutonium and uranium, and $20 billion keeping these things secret.[26] All of this money enhanced the get-something-for-me politics that Lasswell described. Nowhere was this me-oriented politics better illustrated than in the Charleston, South Carolina, metropolitan area where, in 1970, 35 percent of all payrolls were military-related. The list of defense installations located there included the Charleston Army Depot, the Marine Corps Air Station, the Marine Corps Recruit Depot at Parris Island, the Charleston Naval Shipyard, navy hospitals in Beaufort and Charleston, the Charleston Naval Station, the Naval Supply Center, the Naval Weapons Station, the Navy Fleet Ballistic Missile Submarine Training Center, the Polaris Missile Facility, the Charleston Air Force Base, and the North Charleston Air Force Station. The expenditures required to maintain these facilities totaled more than $385 million per year.[27] Charleston benefited from the longtime congressional service of conservative Democrat L. Mendel Rivers who, when he died in 1970, was chair of the House Armed Services Committee. But Rivers was only one of many who practiced the politics of plenty, and these artful practitioners prompted Daniel Bell to famously declare "the end of ideology" back in 1960.[28]

This sort of dollars-and-cents politics led many Americans to ask of their prospective leaders, "Whom do I trust with my pocketbook?" Today, that question has been supplanted by another, more personal one: "Whom do I trust with my kids?" The new values politics lacks the self-righteousness and confidence Americans often exhibited during the Cold War. Now many wonder about a myriad of questions to which the answers seem less definite: What is the nature of the contemporary family? Is marriage passé? What is the role of women at home and the workplace? How should men respond to the altered sex roles? How do gays and lesbians fit into the changing concept of what it means to be an American? Which truths remain immortal, and which ones are no longer valid?

These questions trouble many, and the answers citizens are forming to them are still embryonic. But their eventual responses to these queries—responses that undoubtedly will give new meaning to citizenship—are likely to be found outside the political arena. This is hardly surprising. After all, the civil rights revolution and the women's liberation movement, two of the most important social developments of the 1960s and 1970s, found sustenance outside traditional party politics. Oddly enough, the present values divide has not seen a rejuvenation of grassroots politics like that which energized the civil rights and women's revolutions. Instead, this new politics of values is intrinsically personal, as it raises profoundly individualistic questions each citizen must resolve for himself or herself. In the process, politics has contracted rather than expanded. As the realm of politics becomes smaller, party activists find themselves speaking with louder voices. The result has been the reemergence of what political scientist James MacGregor Burns once called "four-party politics."[29] This has happened even as the public square continues to find fewer people but ever-louder voices.

The Return of Four-Party Politics

In 1963, James MacGregor Burns described the emergence of what he called a "four-party politics" that had backing from very different quarters of the electorate. There was a Democratic presidential party still deeply rooted in the New Deal and Fair Deal programs of Franklin D. Roosevelt and Harry S. Truman. When John F. Kennedy spoke of "getting the country moving again," in 1960, most people knew what he meant. Besides closing the "missile gap" with the Soviet Union, Kennedy wanted to reinvigorate domestic policy to counter what he saw as the passivity of the Eisenhower years. Lyndon B. Johnson's Great Society largely completed this task. Thanks to the engorged Democratic congressional majorities following his 1964 landslide, Johnson had a string of legislative successes including Medicare (signed into law in Truman's presence); a Voting Rights Act that extended the franchise to southern blacks; an Elementary and Secondary Education Act, which created Head Start; and a War on Poverty that was Rooseveltian in reaching out to those previously left behind.

Until Johnson's presidency, the Democratic congressional party was decidedly more southern, conservative, and rural than its northern-based presidential counterpart. In 1949, Hubert H. Humphrey's first impression of the Senate "was that the people who ran it were the southerners or their allies." Humphrey noted that the southern influence was so pervasive that "the odor of magnolia was much stronger in Washington, D.C. than it was in Montgomery, Alabama, or Richmond, Virginia."[30] One of the most potent symbols of the established Dixiecrat rule was Virginia's Howard Smith. As chair of the House Rules Committee, Smith opposed the elections of Kennedy in 1960 and Johnson in 1964. With Smith and the Dixiecrat Republicans effectively blocking JFK's pleas to "get the country moving," Kennedy found some unlikely allies in his battle with the Dixiecrats. In 1962, the Students for a Democratic Society (SDS) blamed the southerners and their Republican allies for the governmental gridlock and demanded action:

> A crucial feature of the political apparatus in America is that greater differences are harbored within each major party than the differences existing between them. Instead of two parties presenting distinctive and significant differences of approach, what dominates the system is a natural interlocking of Democrats from southern states with the more conservative elements of the Republican party. This arrangement of forces is blessed by the seniority system of Congress which guarantees congressional committee domination by conservatives—ten of seventeen committees in the Senate and thirteen of twenty-one in the House of Representatives are currently chaired by Dixiecrats.[31]

As SDS noted, the seniority system often rewarded longevity rather than accomplishment. Southerners had few reasons to ally themselves with Kennedy and Johnson's Democratic presidential party, and any alliance they might have formed was terminated after passage of the civil rights laws and the rise of the New Left led by George McGovern during the Vietnam War.

Republicans, too, had their internal divisions. A Republican presidential party emerged after World War II that was dominated by northeastern internationalists strongly opposed to the isolationists, who previously controlled GOP politics. These so-called Modern Republicans, led by Dwight D. Eisenhower and Richard M. Nixon, believed that the New Deal could not and should not be repealed. As Eisenhower once memorably stated, "Should any political party attempt to abolish Social Security and eliminate labor laws and farm programs, you would not hear of that party again in our political history."[32] The Republican presidential party found growing support for its staunch anticommunism and resistance to the expansion of government in the burgeoning suburbs. Those who lived in the newly constructed Levittowns were well educated and employed in white-collar jobs. By becoming homeowners, many of these former New Deal Democrats no longer saw themselves as recipients of government largesse. Instead, they were taxpayers who looked upon government with a jaundiced eye and saw lots of money being wasted. The new Modern Republicans were spawned from the crowded byways that carried refugees from the inner cities to join the suburban station-wagon set in the suburbs.

THE FATHER-KNOWS-BEST PRESIDENT **179**

Even as the Republican presidential party was winning new converts, its congressional brethren were often mired in minority status thanks to a very different constituency and political outlook. Led by midwesterners, including Senate leaders Robert Taft (Ohio) and Everett McKinley Dirksen (Illinois), and House minority leaders Charles Halleck (Illinois) and Gerald R. Ford (Michigan), the Republican congressional party was more isolationist, parochial, small business–oriented, rural, and conservative than its presidential counterpart. Congressional Republicans resented easterners, whom they associated with the corporate values of size and greed found on Wall Street, while they themselves supposedly embodied the small-town virtues of Main Street. In presidential politics, the congressional Republicans intensely disliked New Yorker Thomas E. Dewey, and many backed "Mr. Republican," Ohio senator Robert A. Taft, for president in 1952. Speaking from the dais at that convention, Everett Dirksen, a Taft supporter, caused a near-riot when he shook a finger at Dewey and shouted: "We followed you before, and you took us down the road to defeat. Don't do this to us."[33] Republicans nominated Dwight Eisenhower anyway, but the intraparty split lasted for another decade, until Barry Goldwater took control of the presidential establishment away from the corporate-minded easterners.[34]

The four-party coalitions Burns identified are no more. The Republican takeover of the South is one reason. When the GOP captured control of Congress in 1994, the three House leaders (Newt Gingrich, Dick Armey, and Tom DeLay) represented districts located in Georgia and Texas respectively. For the first time since Reconstruction, a majority of House members from the Old Confederacy were Republicans. The party's standing in the South has held firm ever since. Former Wisconsin congressman Scott Klug, who retired in 1998 and was succeeded by a Democrat, says, "If you look at Democrats fifteen years ago, they were defined by the Northeast. Now you look at our [Republican] leadership, and it looks like we have lost the Civil War."[35]

The conservative southerners' leave-taking from the Democratic Party has made both congressional parties more ideologically pure. In 1998, a year marked by Bill Clinton's impeachment, 86 percent of Republicans in both chambers cast party-line votes. Democrats were not far behind with 83 percent of their members in lockstep. Such party hegemony is a sharp contrast to the days when Dixiecrats dominated Congress. In 1970, Republicans and Democrats had unity scores of 59 percent and 57 percent respectively.[36]

One reason for the increased ideological commitment is that congressional candidates are self-starters who recruit themselves rather than receiving invitations from their respective parties to seek office. Republican Dick Armey became a candidate in 1984 after watching the congressional debates on C-SPAN and thinking he could do a better job. The patrician sense of noblesse oblige that viewed public service as an honor and duty, a notion that inspired the political careers of Prescott Bush and George H.W. Bush, has largely disappeared. The constituencies and political cultures that animate each of the new congressional and presidential parties are examined below.

The New Democratic Congressional Party

Greater ideological homogeneity distinguishes the new Democratic congressional party from its Dixiecrat predecessor. Replacing the Dixiecrats are Democrats from New England, the Northeast, the upper tier of midwestern states, and the Pacific coast, who increasingly hold positions of power. Like their constituents, most believe in the idea of a morality writ small, and they oppose using the arm of government to impose their own sense of morality on others. But when it comes to big-ticket government spending programs, many are staunch liberals who do not share the general public's distrust of government. Most of these northern Democrats occupy safe seats that ensure a greater longevity than their districts have heretofore experienced. Barney Frank, for example, was first elected in 1980 and has had no serious competition since 1982, this despite being one of two openly gay members of Congress.[37] Likewise, Edward M. Kennedy, first elected in 1962, now ranks third in Senate seniority (behind the venerable Strom Thurmond and Robert C. Byrd) and has acquired a position of power that rivals that of the southern barons of yore. Kennedy doesn't have to worry much about getting reelected; in 2000, he received a whopping 73 percent of the vote, beating a token Republican challenger who almost did not get on the ballot and finished only a single percentage point ahead of the Libertarian Party candidate. Democrats run so strongly in Massachusetts that its entire ten-person congressional delegation consists of Democrats who are poised to acquire seniority and power akin to that of the southern barons of yore.

Four decades ago, Donald R. Matthews wrote that the seniority system's bias against urban liberals "tends to be self-perpetuating."[38] This is no longer true. Future Democratic control of both houses of Congress—whenever that occurs—will mean that northern and West Coast liberals will be the ones wielding power. In the Senate, Massachusetts's Kennedy, Delaware's Joe Biden, Connecticut's Joseph Lieberman, and Vermont's Patrick Leahy have already taken control of key committees away from conservative Republicans. Many of these committees were chaired by conservative southerners the last time the Senate was under Democratic control in 1994 (see table 6.1). The change has been dramatic both in temperament and in policy. Senate Armed Services Committee chair Carl Levin is a vocal opponent of George W. Bush's plan to deploy an antiballistic missile defense system, a position not shared by his Democratic predecessor, Georgia's Sam Nunn. Senate Judiciary chair Patrick Leahy has announced his opposition to conservative Supreme Court nominees like Clarence Thomas (whom he did oppose)

TABLE 6.1 DEMOCRATIC CHAIRS OF SELECTED SENATE COMMITTEES, 1994 AND 2001

Committee	1994 Chair	2001 Chair	First Election for 2001 Chair
Armed Services	Sam Nunn (Georgia)	Carl Levin (Michigan)	1978
Foreign Relations	Claiborne Pell (Rhode Island)	Joseph R. Biden Jr. (Delaware)	1972
Governmental Affairs	John Glenn (Ohio)	Joseph I. Lieberman (Connecticut)	1988
Health, Education, Labor and Pensions	Nonexistent	Edward M. Kennedy (Massachusetts)	1962
Judiciary	Joseph R. Biden Jr. (Delaware)	Patrick J. Leahy (Vermont)	1974
Rules and Administration	Wendell H. Ford (Kentucky)	Christopher J. Dodd (Connecticut)	1980
Small Business	Dale Bumpers (Arkansas)	John F. Kerry (Massachusetts)	1984

and Antonin Scalia (whom he did not, a vote Leahy regrets). Connecticut's Christopher Dodd, who chairs the powerful Rules Committee, is determined to advance Democratic issues on the floor. Joseph Lieberman, head of the Governmental Affairs Committee, is demanding that Vice President Dick Cheney surrender documents pertaining to his controversial energy task force. (Cheney has refused to comply.) Lieberman is a potential 2004 Democratic presidential contender, as is John Kerry of Massachusetts, whose Small Business Committee has a more liberal cast than that chaired by former Arkansas senator Dale Bumpers. Indeed, each of the Democratic chairs listed on table 6.1 could potentially form part of the 2004 Democratic ticket.

The rise of northern and West Coast Democrats to positions of influence is likely to persist. In 2000, almost all the Democratic gains in the Senate came from northern and Pacific states: Minnesota (Mark Dayton), New Jersey (Jon Corzine), Michigan (Debbie Stabenow), Washington (Maria Cantwell), and Delaware (Thomas Carper). The lone exceptions were Missouri, where the "Mel Carnahan line" represented by the late candidate's wife, Jean, won, and Florida, where Ben Nelson replaced Connie Mack.

The same phenomenon is occurring in the House, where northern Democrats are acquiring seniority and are poised to move into positions of power. The Democratic House leadership currently consists of Minority Leader Richard Gephardt (Missouri), Whip Nancy Pelosi (California), and Caucus Chair Martin Frost (Texas). In 2000, these members of Congress received near-perfect scores— 90, 100, and 100 percent, respectively—from the liberally oriented Americans for Democratic Action. If Democrats had assumed control of the House in 2001, many of the most powerful committee chairmanships would have fallen into the

TABLE 6.2   CHAIRS OF SELECTED HOUSE COMMITTEES, 1994, AND A HYPOTHETICAL
2001 DEMOCRAT-CONTROLLED CONGRESS

Committee	1994 Chair	2001 Hypothetical Chair	First Election for 2001 Chair	Percentage of 2000 Vote
Appropriations	William H. Natcher (Kentucky)	David R. Obey (Wisconsin)	1969	63
Financial Services[a]	Henry B. Gonzalez (Texas)	John J. LaFalce (New York)	1974	61
Education and the Workforce[a]	William D. Ford (Michigan)	George Miller (California)	1974	77
Energy and Commerce[a]	John D. Dingell (Michigan)	John D. Dingell (Michigan)	1955	71
Government Reform	John Conyers Jr. (Michigan)	Henry A. Waxman (California)	1974	76
House Administration	Charles G. Rose III (North Carolina)	Steny H. Hoyer (Maryland)	1981	65
International Relations[a]	Lee H. Hamilton (Indiana)	Tom Lantos (California)	1980	74
Judiciary	Jack B. Brooks (Texas)	John Conyers Jr. (Michigan)	1964	91
Rules	Joseph Moakley (Massachusetts)	Joseph Moakley (Massachusetts)/	1972	77
		Martin Frost (Texas)[b]	1978	62
Transportation and Infrastructure[a]	Norman Y. Mineta (California)	James L. Oberstar (Minnesota)	1974	68
Veterans Affairs	Sonny Montgomery (Mississippi)	Lane Evans (Illinois)	1982	55
Ways and Means	Dan Rostenkowski (Illinois)	Charles B. Rangel (New York)	1970	91

[a.] Committee was renamed.

[b.] Joseph Moakley would have headed the Rules Committee in January 2001 if Democrats had won control of the House. He died on 28 May 2001, and next in line to succeed him is Martin Frost.

hands of northern liberal Democrats (see table 6.2). This would be a remarkable change from 1994, when many of these same committees were led by southerners. For example, the House Ways and Means Committee would be chaired by New York's Charlie Rangel. While southerners would still have positions of influence, an increasing number hail from districts that are much more liberal than those represented by the Dixiecrats were. Martin Frost is one example. His Texas district is a Democratic enclave; Frost received 62 percent of the vote in the last election, and it was one of only ten congressional districts in the state to back Al

TABLE 6.3 HOUSE DEMOCRATIC FRESHMEN, 2001

Member	State and District
Mike Ross	Arkansas – 4
Mike Honda	California – 15
Adam B. Schiff	California – 27
Hilda L. Solis	California – 31
Diane Watson	California – 32
Jane Harman[a]	California – 36
Susan A. Davis	California – 49
Betty McCollum	Minnesota – 4
Wm. Lacy Clay	Missouri – 1
Steve Israel	New York – 2
Brad Carson	Oklahoma – 2
Jim Langevin	Rhode Island – 2
Jim Matheson	Utah – 2
Rick Larsen	Washington – 2

a. Previously served six years before giving up the seat to run unsuccessfully for governor of California in 1998.

Gore. But Frost's current leadership position and his potential ascension to chair of the Rules Committee hardly represents a restoration of Dixiecrat rule. Frost is a reliable liberal whose rating from the Americans for Democratic Action is 80 percent, while his lifetime rating from the equally conservative American Conservative Union is a paltry 16 percent. His Democratic colleagues on the Rules Committee, Tony Hall (Ohio), Louise Slaughter (New York), and Alcee Hastings (Florida), also share many of Frost's liberal views. Hall had a 75 percent score from the Americans for Democratic Action; Slaughter, 90 percent; Hastings, 80 percent. Like Frost, all won reelection easily: Hall, 83 percent (with no Republican opponent); Slaughter, 66 percent; Hastings, 76 percent.[39]

At levels well below that of committee chair, the Democratic ranks are being populated by new members from the East and West Coasts. During the 2000 election, Democrats picked up four congressional seats from California alone. Looking at the ranks of the fourteen Democratic House freshmen in 2001, only four fall outside the Northeast, upper Midwest, and West Coast Democratic strongholds (see table 6.3). Not surprisingly, most of these newly elected Democrats since the 1994 Republican takeover have values views akin to the morality-writ-small opinions of their constituents who live in Al Gore's blue states.

The New Democratic Presidential Party

The rise of northern and West Coast liberals in Congress presents several challenges to a Democratic presidential party that has been transformed by Bill Clinton. Rather than instinctively wanting more and bigger government, Clinton Democrats sought a "Third Way" between the old New Deal liberalism and its conservative do-nothing, let-the-private-sector-handle-it Republican counterpart. The Third Way called for more public-private partnerships among individuals, government, and business, the goal of which was to empower citizens to solve problems without interference from federal bureaucrats.[40] Government-run bureaucracies akin to those of the New Deal and Great Society eras were antithetical to the New Democratic thinking. As the party's 2000 platform stated, "Our fundamental mission is to expand prosperity, not government."[41] New Democrats believe that economic prosperity is inherently linked to deficit reduction, which inevitably led them to constrain government, not expand it. Thus, Al Gore promised to "pay down the debt every year until we can give our children the independence, self-sufficiency, and prosperity that will come when America is debt-free."[42] As one Gore adviser put it, "If you think of the last eight years, the [Democratic] party in government worked through all the biggies. It worked through trade; we are a free trade party. We worked through welfare reform; we are the party that reformed welfare. We worked through fiscal discipline, because we are the party that got rid of this deficit. So a bunch of cleavages actually have been settled by the process of governing."[43]

The result has been Bill Clinton's complete domination of the Democratic presidential party, as witnessed in the collective decisions of old-style, New Deal–minded Democrats such as Dick Gephardt, Paul Wellstone, and Jesse Jackson not to challenge Gore for the presidency in 2000. Only the iconoclastic Bill Bradley sought the Democratic nod, and, while criticizing Gore for supporting welfare reform, Bradley proved to be an inarticulate and reluctant defender of the old New Deal liberalism.

But Clinton's remaking of the Democratic presidential party incurred the wrath of congressional Democrats on issues such as free trade, welfare reform, and budget making. Of these, free trade was the among the most rancorous and is likely to have enduring consequences. Both Clinton and Gore were staunch free traders, and both eagerly sought passage in 1993 of the North American Free Trade Agreement. Vice President Gore confronted Ross Perot on the subject in a memorable 1993 appearance on *Larry King Live*. After that performance, the North American Free Trade Agreement won congressional approval, but only thanks to Republican, not Democratic, support. In 2000, Clinton favored giving China permanent normal trade relations, even though this hurt Gore with some congressional Democrats and many union households. Clinton's reliance on GOP support for his free-trade initiatives prompted Green Party candidate Ralph Nader to argue that the two major parties had been transformed into large corporate entities that were bought and paid for by special interests. Free trade in general, and commerce with China in particular, received few mentions in the

2000 Democratic platform, a testament to the rift between the two Democratic parties.[44] Welfare reform was another "wedge issue" separating Clinton from his fellow congressional Democrats. Most of the Senate and senior House Democrats voted against it. Budget cuts were also a continuous source of irritation to congressional Democrats who wanted to divert federal largesse back to their districts. In May 1997, House minority leader Richard Gephardt spoke for many of his fellow congressional Democrats when he denounced the balanced budget plan Clinton negotiated with the Republican Congress as "a budget of many deficits—a deficit of principle, a deficit of fairness, a deficit of tax justice and, worst of all, a deficit of dollars."[45]

In many ways, Third Way thinking is frequently at odds with the instinctive liberalism of the Democratic congressional party. In 1997, Richard Gephardt took aim at Clinton's willingness to listen to advice given by his conservative strategist Dick Morris: "Too often, our leaders seem enamored with small ideas that nibble around the edges of big problems."[46] Gephardt's championing of the old liberalism became more vocal as he climbed the congressional leadership ladder. First elected in 1976, the Missouri Democrat ran as a reformer who subsequently supported Ronald Reagan's tax cut and tax reform plans. As a backbencher, Gephardt often parted company with his fellow Democrats on such issues as abortion, busing, and raising the minimum wage. But as he sought more power within the Democratic caucus, his positions changed. He altered his stance on abortion from pro-life to pro-choice and supported increasing the minimum wage. In 1991, he led the opposition to the Gulf War Resolution and favored the elimination of funding for U.S. troops stationed in Saudi Arabia. After Bill Clinton's election in 1992, Gephardt fought for Clinton's economic stimulus plan and strongly supported the Clinton health care plan. Four years later, he was instrumental in passing a bill increasing the minimum wage. But at the very moment that Clinton moved to occupy the center with his New Democrat initiatives, Gephardt retreated into the opposition. He denounced the Clinton-backed North American Free Trade Agreement; he refused to give Clinton "fast track" authority for concluding trade agreements with Latin America; and vigorously opposed the welfare reform bill Clinton signed into law in 1996.

The clash of views between the two Democratic parties-in-government was muted by the budget surpluses that emerged after 1994, which, oddly enough, created their own brand of governmental liberalism. Both Clinton and Gore sought to protect the liberal successes of the past by placing Social Security and Medicare into their respective "lock boxes." But even with these two entitlements off-budget, there was still a lot of money to spend. In 2000, Al Gore and the congressional Democrats happily proposed a vast new public entitlement—a Medicare-run prescription drug program for seniors. Likewise, both Democratic parties wanted to allocate considerably more federal money for public school education. But while congressional Democrats have reluctantly concluded that balanced budgets are politically wise and economically beneficial, the Clinton-Gore presidential party starts with this premise.

At heart, congressional Democrats prefer an activist government, and they do not view public-private partnerships as a viable means of accomplishing their goals. Silently, many agreed with Ralph Nader, who saw Clinton's 1996 declaration that "the era of big government is over" as a capitulation to Republican thinking. Nader derided Clinton by nicknaming him "George Ronald Clinton" (a reference to Clinton's GOP predecessors, George H.W. Bush and Ronald Reagan).[47] California State Senate president pro tempore John Burton is equally critical: "I don't get this 'New Democrat' b—s—. There are only so many ways you can feed hungry people, or get jobs for people who don't have them, and get kids a good education."[48] Amy Isaacs, national director of the Americans for Democratic Action, says that her party's unwillingness to cut military spending in order to finance more domestic programs is alienating the party's rank-and-file liberals.[49] Many congressional Democrats privately agree, even as they were unwilling to publicly criticize Clinton and Gore during the last presidential campaign. In the coming years, disappearing surpluses, along with the emergence of trade as the primary foreign policy issue, are likely to enhance the fissures between the two Democratic parties. Those cracks will increase substantially the moment another New Democrat is elected president and Democrats hold majorities in both houses of Congress.

The New Republican Presidential Party

Like the Democrats, Republicans have their own intraparty tensions. The Republican presidential party clearly belongs to George W. Bush and his fellow governors, many of whom espouse what Bush calls "compassionate conservatism." By smoothing away the rough edges of conservatism, Bush and other like-minded Republicans seek to expand their party's appeal, especially to suburban women. Their premise is simple: winning elections is more important than remaining ideologically pure. Thus, Candidate Bush publicly considered pro-choice Republicans—including Pennsylvania governor Tom Ridge and New Jersey governor Christine Todd Whitman—as prospective ticket-mates. Although Bush eventually settled on the steadfastly conservative Dick Cheney, he continued to emphasize his "good fella," let's-not-leave-anyone-behind persona. Addressing a young black woman during an emotive appearance on *The Oprah Winfrey Show*, Bush explained how his newfound brand of "compassionate conservatism" included folks like her:

> WOMAN: As a twenty-five-year-old African-American woman with no children and no money, I qualify for broke, but I'm not poor. How do I fit into your platform, and the other millions of Americans just like me?

BUSH: Well, you fit into my platform by having a country that says the American dream is available to you. In other words, first and foremost, it doesn't matter how you're raised, what your background is. If you work hard, you can realize the greatness of the country. I don't know what your education background is like, but my vision says that every child is going to be educated in America. I want the public school system to hold out the promise for . . . every single citizen, so that when they get to be twenty-five years old, you can realize your dreams. See, I see America as a land of dreams and hopes and opportunities. And again, I don't know your personal circumstances, but I don't want anything to hold you back.[50]

Bush repeated this theme of inclusiveness in his Inaugural Address, saying that the promise of America means that "everyone belongs, that everyone deserves a chance, that no insignificant person was ever born."[51] A few months later, speaking at the dedication of the Pope John Paul II Cultural Center at the Catholic University of America, Bush elaborated: "In the culture of life we must make room for the stranger. We must comfort the sick. We must care for the aged. We must welcome the immigrant. We must teach our children to be gentle with one another. We must defend in love the innocent child waiting to be born."[52]

In making his pitch for a more inclusive Republican Party, Bush describes his so-called compassionate conservatism as "first and foremost springing from the heart."[53] Throughout his political career, Bush has frequently spoken from the heart, and he often uses this rhetorical device to admonish opponents. During the first presidential debate with Al Gore, for example, Bush related a visit with a man in Del Rio, Texas, whose home had been destroyed by a flood. Bush described how he "put my arms around the man and his family and cried with them"—an emotion that got the late Edmund Muskie into trouble when he shed a few tears on the steps of the *Manchester Union Leader* during the 1972 New Hampshire primary.[54] As president, Bush frequently uses the language of the heart to make his case. He advised senators to cast aside doubts about John Ashcroft and examine the nominee's "heart" before confirming him as attorney general. He similarly defended labor secretary–designate Linda Chavez, saying he wanted to shine a "light on her big heart."[55] Most famously, Bush described his heart-to-heart meeting with Russian president Vladimir Putin: "I looked the man in the eye. . . . I was able to get a sense of his soul, a man deeply committed to his country and the best interests of his country."[56]

At its core, compassionate conservatism seeks an activist, but restrained role for government. Bush's self-described brand of "focused and energetic government" includes programs designed to help "single moms struggling to feed the kids and pay the rent; immigrants starting a hard life in a new world; children without fathers in neighborhoods where gangs seem like friendship."[57] Unlike Newt Gingrich and the zealous Republican freshman class of 1994, Bush favored keeping the Departments of Education and Commerce, and even the controversial National Endowment for the Arts, intact. Bush even praised Lyndon Johnson's Great Society, which most conservatives have blamed for the country's present troubles: "My party has often pointed out the limits and flaws of the Great Society. But there were successes as well, and Medicare is one of them."[58] Bush consciously set himself apart from Gingrich-style conservatism, arguing that Republicans should not be naysayers but must articulate programs that offer people hope. Accordingly, he sought to rally "the armies of compassion" to assist the needy and create an environment where government could, on a limited basis, be a helpful partner to those less well off.[59]

George W. Bush's vision of the GOP as an army of compassionate conservatives was showcased in the 2000 Republican platform. How the party expressed its antiabortion views provides one illustration of the compassionate conservative approach to governance. While the platform unabashedly restated the party's pro-life stance and its determined opposition to partial-birth abortions, the Bush forces ladeled their positions with gobs of compassionate rhetoric:

> Our goal is to ensure that women with problem pregnancies have the kind of support, material and otherwise, they need for themselves and their babies, not to be punitive towards those for whose difficult situation we have only compassion. We oppose abortion, but our pro-life agenda does not include punitive action against women who have an abortion. We salute those who provide alternatives to abortion and offer adoption services, and we commend congressional Republicans for expanding assistance to adopting families and for removing racial barriers to adoption.[60]

To Bush, governing from the heart means forming more partnerships with private institutions, especially faith-based organizations. As governor, he created a pilot program establishing Second Chance group homes for unwed teenage mothers, some of them run by faith-based groups.[61] Bush took his cue from conservative thinker Marvin Olasky, who argued that the Great Society programs of the 1960s led to an explosion of the welfare rolls, which encouraged dependency on government. Olasky contrasted Lyndon Johnson's War on Poverty with the 1890s, when religious organizations created settlement houses designed to aid the poor in return for services rendered. Olasky called for a new back-to-the-future approach in helping the less fortunate: "Isn't it time that we start managing by results, even if that means returning social services to those private and religious institutions that emphasize challenging compassion?"[62] Conservative scholars Michael Joyce and William Schambra took issue with Olasky, writing that compassionate conservatism conjures up a "mushy, sentimental, soft-headedness that suggests a readiness to return to the days of well-intentioned government hand-outs, which make the giver feel good but did little for, and even harmed, the re-cipient."[63]

Bush was not deterred by such criticism, and he embraced Olasky's ideas for helping religious organizations as not only good governing but also good politics. In a time when values are being questioned and citizens long for some certainty, Bush offered a soothing voice and spoke with references to a compassionate Almighty. When referring to the poor, Bush did not sound like a harsh conserv-ative who blamed them for their poverty. Instead, he declared, "Abandonment and abuse are not acts of God, they are failures of love." Sounding more like a pastor than a politician, Bush noted that "some needs are hurts are so deep that they will only respond to a mentor's touch or a pastor's prayer." Accordingly, he promised that his administration would give religious organizations "an honored place in our plans and in our laws," adding, "When we see that wounded traveler on the road to Jericho, we will not pass to the other side."[64]

Still, not all conservatives welcomed George W. Bush's embrace of a compas-sionate conservatism laced with religious overtones. Pat Robertson, the founder and president of the Christian Coalition, warned of a "Pandora's box" being opened by making government funding available to Scientologists, the Nation of Islam, or re-ligious cults that employ "brainwashing techniques."[65] Undeterred, Bush created the White House Office of Faith-Based and Community Initiatives, and put the conservative political scientist and Democrat John J. DiIulio Jr. in charge.

Nonetheless, it is fair to say that most Republicans went along with Bush largely because his approach to politics was successful. Many congressional Repub-licans believe that compassionate conservatism does not threaten them because it is more of a media strategy than a governing one. Massachusetts Democrat Barney Frank sees few differences between Bush and the GOP congressional leaders:

> So far, compassionate conservatism is just words. Remember, John McCain is the one who threatened Bush, and Bush aligned with the party of [House ma-jority whip Tom] DeLay to defeat him. I don't see any signs that George W. Bush has any issue tensions with DeLay. On what issue? They have agreed with him on the tax cut. There is some debate over its political practicalities. But there is none over its ideological desirability. They don't disagree on gay rights. They don't disagree on the environment, on abortion. On what substantive issues do Tom DeLay and George W. Bush disagree? There may be a difference in style, because of the way you do it. But that's qualitatively different?[66]

Frank is correct to note that Bush has gone out of his way to make sure that few, if any issues, separate him from his fellow Republicans in the nation's capital. Yet, it is also fair to note that there is some fragility to their alliance. Unlike Bush, congressional Republicans are motivated more by issues than tactics. Making government smaller by getting rid of unwelcome cabinet departments and federal agencies, while at the same time adhering to traditional family values, remains at the heart of their thinking. These differences in outlook and attitude already have led to some grumbling. After voting for Bush's education reform bill, Tom DeLay expressed regret, telling conservative radio talk show host Rush Limbaugh, "I came here to eliminate the Department of Education." DeLay explained that his initial "yea" was cast only because he wanted to support a Republican president: "I'm ashamed to say it was just blatant politics."[67] Many Republican activists share DeLay's concerns. A survey of 400 delegates to the 2000 Republican National Convention found 79 percent favored eliminating the Education Department, while 83 percent opposed any federal role in setting educational achievement standards. Don Devine, vice chairman of the American Conservative Union which sponsored the survey, said, "There is an incredible kind of unanimity against some of the things Bush wants to do.[68]

As time passes, DeLay and his colleagues may not find a receptive audience at the White House for a conservative agenda that does not come with a compassionate modifier. Two of Bush's challengers for the 2000 nomination have already sided with congressional Republicans in arguing that conservatism does not need any qualifiers. Former Tennessee governor Lamar Alexander described Bush's compassionate conservatism as nothing more than "weasel words." Former vice president Dan Quayle was even more caustic: "I have ordered my staff to never—ever—utter the words 'compassionate conservative.' This silly and insulting term was created by liberal Republicans and is nothing more than code for surrendering our values and principles."[69] In 1999 Rush Limbaugh lamented Bush's emphasis on compassionate conservatism, and issued a warning: "The more he speaks, the more troubled I am becoming about his candidacy."[70] But remembering how useful an enemy Newt Gingrich was to the Democrats, Bush saw to it that no one in the Republican congressional leadership addressed his party's convention in prime time. Pat Robertson denounced the convention's gooey televised images as "Democrat lite."[71] Ever mindful of the tensions that could erupt between his party's presidential and congressional wings, George W. Bush used a line in his victory statement that seemed as equally directed to his fellow Republicans as it was to the mass television audience, "I was not elected to serve one party, but to serve one nation."[72]

The New Republican Congressional Party

Unlike the Bush-dominated presidential party, the Republican congressional party is much more responsive to the culture wars. Congressional Republicans overwhelmingly supported amendments to the U.S. Constitution to protect the flag, the Defense of Marriage Act, and overturning Bill Clinton's vetoes of bills banning partial-birth abortions. In 2001, the Republican-controlled House followed its conservative instincts by passing the Unborn Victims of Violence Act, which made it a federal crime to harm a fetus during an assault on a woman. The bill's foes described it as a backdoor attack on abortion rights, since the legislation defines the fetus as a separate person. Louise Slaughter, a Democratic congresswoman from New York, decried the measure: "The majority did not bring this bill to the floor to protect pregnant women. The majority brought this measure to the floor today to launch its battle to end a woman's right to choose." Steve Chabot, a conservative Ohio Republican, retorted, "The only people who have anything to fear from this bill are criminals who engage in violence against pregnant women and their unborn children."[73]

Gerald R. Ford is dismayed that congressional Republicans spend so much time debating the abortion issue. To Ford and his wife, Betty, who gained fame for her pro-choice views as First Lady, abortion is a private matter. According to the former president, "I'd like to throw the whole issue out of the partisan political arena. The less said about it, the better for the party."[74] Republican congressional leaders disagree, and in January 2001, they were delighted at the prospect of passing more conservative measures to their liking. Tom DeLay, for one, exulted, "We have the House, we have the Senate, we have the White House, which means we have the agenda."[75] DeLay and his colleagues believed that without the threats of a Clinton veto they would be able to transform their conservative values into law.

DeLay's enthusiasm was reinforced by the fact that, unlike their predecessors of the 1950s and 1960s, the House Republican leadership was uniformly conservative. The liberal-minded Americans for Democratic Action gave House Speaker Dennis Hastert, Majority Leader Dick Armey, and Majority Whip Tom DeLay perfect scores of zero in 2000. Not surprisingly, these men had lifetime ratings from the American Conservative Union of 92, 97, and 96 percent respectively. As they do for their Democratic counterparts, ideas count and principles matter to the conservative-minded congressional Republicans. In the early days of his presidency, Bush deferred to conservatives by proposing a tax-relief bill that ensured government would remain small. Although an education reform measure eventually found its way to his desk, Bush initially looked more like a Reagan-era Republican than the compassionate conservative he wanted to be. According to a CBS News/*New York Times* poll taken in the summer of 2001, 63 percent say Bush is a typical Republican (presumably of the hard-headed, corporate conservative type), while only 30 percent think of him as a different type of Republican (presumably a "compassionate conservative")[76]. Yet while Bush's task is to appeal to the entire country, the Republican congressional base is increasingly more

TABLE 6.4   HOUSE REPUBLICAN FRESHMEN, 2001

Member	State and District
Jeff Flake	Arizona – 1
Darrell E. Issa	California – 48
Rob Simmons	Connecticut – 2
Ander Crenshaw	Florida – 4
Ric Keller	Florida – 8
Adam H. Putnam	Florida – 12
C.L. "Butch" Otter	Idaho – 1
Mark Steven Kirk	Illinois – 10
Timothy V. Johnson	Illinois – 15
Mike Pence	Indiana – 2
Brian D. Kerns	Indiana – 7
David Vitter	Louisiana – 1
Mike Rogers	Michigan – 8
Mark R. Kennedy	Minnesota – 2
W. Todd Akin	Missouri – 2
Sam Graves	Missouri – 6
Dennis R. Rehberg	Montana – At Large
Tom Osborne	Nebraska – 3
Mike Ferguson	New Jersey – 7
Felix J. Grucci Jr.	New York – 1
Patrick J. Tiberi	Ohio – 12
Melissa A. Hart	Pennsylvania – 4
Bill Shuster[a]	Pennsylvania – 9
Todd Russell Platts	Pennsylvania – 19
Henry E. Brown Jr.	South Carolina – 1
John Abney Culberson	Texas – 7
Jo Ann Davis	Virginia – 1
Edward L. Schrock	Virginia – 2
J. Randy Forbes[a]	Virginia – 4
Eric Cantor	Virginia – 7
Shelley Moore Capito	West Virginia – 2

[a.] Won in 2001 special election.

southern, rural, and secure. Of the thirty-one freshmen Republicans in the 107th Congress, for example, ten hail from the Old Confederacy (see table 6.4).

The potential for intraparty dissension remains, as Bush seeks to recast his presidential party using words and phrases not often associated with the Republican Party. The extent to which such intraparty disagreements will occur, however, will largely depend on Bush's ability to institutionalize the changes he has wrought. For Republicans, the legacy of George W. Bush remains in doubt: Is the potential for intraparty disagreement unique to Bush, or will future Republican presidents seek to emulate Bush's compassionate conservatism? Only time will tell, but the answer will say much about the Bush years.

Big Questions, Small-Minded Politics

Prior to the 2000 election, Congressman David Price, a respected North Carolina Democrat, called for a "subdued partisanship."[77] But the passions that rule today's congressional parties make subdued partisanship an almost impossible goal. It is not only the issues separating the two congressional parties that makes bipartisanship more difficult to achieve, but it is also the demeanor of both parties. In March 2001, only one-third of House members showed up at a resort in Greenbrier, West Virginia, for the annual bipartisan retreat. Democratic minority leader Dick Gephardt stated the obvious, "Bipartisanship is over—not that it ever began."[78] Gephardt should know. His relationships with Speakers Newt Gingrich and Dennis Hastert have been almost nonexistent. Moreover, George W. Bush has done very little negotiating with congressional Democratic leaders. But, says Gephardt, the lack of civility at the top extends to those of a lesser rank: "Democrats and Republicans don't even make eye contact when they pass one another in the halls of Congress, unless it's to exchange furious glares."[79]

Rather than engaging in the hard task of governing, many congressional partisans find it more enticing to be sought-after guests on cable television programs such as *Crossfire, Hardball, Capital Gang,* and *The O'Reilly Factor* that promote entertainment value rather than political enlightenment. As Gephardt told his colleagues in 1998, "We are now rapidly descending into a politics where life imitates farce, fratricide dominates our public debate, and America is held hostage to tactics of smear and fear."[80] While these words were uttered in the passions swirling around Clinton's impeachment, the return of four-party politics, coupled with the polarization created by values-minded activists, means that governing in the morally free twenty-first century is more difficult than ever before. Reflecting on "the politics of personal destruction" that characterized the Clinton era, Gephardt observed that it caused citizens to hate their leaders and their government: "In time, they drop out and begin treating politics as just another form of gladiatorial entertainment; they start electing professional wrestlers as governors."[81]

Thus, we are likely to muddle along with a small-minded politics that avoids answering the most important questions of our time. To the extent these values questions are resolved, it is likely to be outside the realm of the very partisan four-party politics that characterizes the present era. Values will continue to matter more than ever before, but it is our politics that remains unable to cope.

CHAPTER 7

We're All Americans Now

This is the re-United States of America.
                —Jamie MacDonald, Boston dockworker, 11 September 2001

SEPTEMBER 11, 2001. This date, like so many other infamous ones in U.S. history, will be remembered long after the charred steel and ashes have been cleared from site of the World Trade Center, the damaged portion of the Pentagon, and the smoldering airliner debris left in rural Pennsylvania. In the minutes it took the terrorists to hit their targets in New York City and Washington, D.C., the world changed. By nightfall, nearly three thousand had perished. The death toll was especially staggering in New York, where the World Trade Center was transformed from a bustling hubbub of financial enterprise into the forbidding silence of a morgue. So great was the number of casualties that nearly one-in-five Americans either claimed to have known someone who was missing, hurt, or killed on that fateful day or had friends who lost loved ones.[1]

The effects were felt far beyond American shores. More than 100 Britons died, and another 500–700 were listed as missing, making the September 11th terrorist attack the worst in modern British history. Overall, more than eighty nations lost citizens, including 100 Japanese, 27 South Koreans, 50 Bangladeshis, 150 Mexicans, 9 Taiwanese, 7 Italians, and 7 Filipinos.[2] Reacting to the disaster, the French intellectual Dominique Moisi told the *Financial Times* of London: "All over Europe, not only in London but from Paris to Madrid, from Berlin to Rome, the terrorists who struck at America have recreated the strong sense of Western solidarity loosened by the end of the Cold War."[3] The French newspaper *Le Monde* expressed the sentiments of many Europeans in a headline that read, "We're all Americans."[4]

While many nations mourned their dead, Americans mourned something more: a loss of innocence. The sense of personal security that most citizens previously took for granted gave way to a somber reality that terrorism was about to become part of the American way of life. By midday on 11 September, all commercial airliners were grounded, and George W. Bush issued orders to shoot down any plane that refused to land. A few weeks later, as the terrorist threat intensified due to the spread of anthrax through the U.S. Postal Service, the U.S.A. Patriot Act became law. The new antiterrorist measure gave federal authorities enhanced powers to detain noncitizens, wiretap cell phones, intercept e-mails, and monitor Internet usage. It passed by overwhelming votes of 357–66 in the House and 98–1 in the Senate. These lopsided majorities were extraordinary, since Congress previously had refused to give the executive branch additional powers to pry into private lives, and its initial reluctance was supported by a plurality of Americans.[5] Now many Americans were willing to undertake additional security measures not even contemplated in the U.S.A. Patriot Act: 97 percent favored random searches of airline baggage; 85 percent would permit video surveillance of public places (including their street corners and neighborhoods); 65 percent would allow random searches of the mail; and an equal number favored regular police roadblocks to stop and search automobiles.[6]

In the wake of the September 11th attacks, Americans were tense. Many believed that a future terrorist strike was likely, and one in five thought it might even occur in their own hometown.[7] Another third planned to alter some aspect of their lives to lessen their chances of becoming the next terrorist target,[8] and an equal number said they were either "a little nervous" or "very nervous" about boarding an airplane.[9] The travel and tourism industries felt the immediate effects of the national jitters, as vacation plans were cancelled and business trips postponed. Forty-two percent said they thought about a future terrorist attack during the course of a "routine day."[10] Of course, "routine days" following 11 September had become a distant memory. To take but one small example, the phrase "homeland security," once considered a redundancy, suddenly became the "in" vocabulary of the moment, and President Bush appointed Pennsylvania governor Tom Ridge to head the new Office of Homeland Security.

The sobering realization that the war against terrorism would be long and difficult was particularly jarring to the young. Across the country, students of all ages, who were largely unaccustomed to adversity, were suddenly and unexpectedly confronted with the face of death. Jessie Kindig, a Barnard College sophomore, expressed a commonly held sentiment: "We grew up with nothing bad ever happening to us. Not the Bay of Pigs, not the Cold War, not the threat of nuclear terror."[11] An MTV viewer from Bowling Green, Kentucky, e-mailed the network, writing: "My generation has seen nothing like this in our lifetime, and it will be something that we will never forget. Our parents can remember where they were when President Kennedy was shot, and our grandparents can tell us what they were doing when Pearl Harbor was bombed. It is sad that our generation now will be able to look back in twenty years and say, 'I remember where I was when the World Trade Center collapsed.'"[12] Chelsea Clinton was unusually expressive in recalling her memories of that fateful day:

> I woke up that Tuesday morning feeling good about where I was in my life and happy about where I was going. Now that sense of security is gone, and since the 11th, for some moment every day, I have been scared. Not by a sense of immediate, immense danger, but by something more subtle and corrosive: an uncertainty about my place in the world—where I am emotionally, psychologically, and sometimes even physically. . . . I do not think it is out of place to divide my life into before and after the 11th. For the first time a single day now means more than just twenty-four hours—it implies a whole new world.[13]

For many who belonged to the now renamed Generation 9-11, what once passed for normal now seemed either out of place or totally irrelevant.[14] One man dressed in the baggy pants and clothes of the hip-hop culture told an MTV interviewer how he helped a pregnant lady lying flat on her stomach and covered with ash in the aftermath of the twin towers collapse. Instantly, the "gangsta" poses this young man (and others like him) had invented as a means of communicating his toughness were replaced by acts of kindness and compassion. According to him, the lesson was simple—be nice to those you meet: "I don't care how 'gangsta' people think they are."[15] Music executive Wilson Rogers believes gangsta rap is out of step with the post–September 11th marketplace: "When terrorists can be convinced of something so much they'll kill thousands of innocent people, well, the fact that I'm angry with my dad because he won't give me the car doesn't seem all that significant anymore."[16] Several gangsta rap releases were either postponed or shelved altogether.

Across the country, expressions of generosity and compassion became more commonplace. Seventy percent reported engaging in some form of charitable activity following the September 11th attacks, with 58 percent offering a financial contribution to those in need.[17] A nation that once "bowled alone" suddenly found neighbors who formerly did not speak to one another becoming better acquainted.[18] This was particularly true in neighborhoods where families were grieving the loss of a loved one. In one Washington, D.C., community, neighbors baked food for a victim's family and arranged a photograph book for her funeral. Many had not previously known the deceased, but after the Pentagon attack they were viewed by her survivors as extended family members. Amitai Etzioni, a longtime observer of American social habits, was struck by this rebirth of community spirit: "There has been an enormous return to community, in every conceivable way. People simply need to be with other people more."[19] According to one survey, 88 percent said the terrorist attacks had served to highlight what was really important in life, and 85 percent said that the attacks had brought the country closer together than ever before.[20]

Even television acted to enhance the growing sense of a national community, as millions gathered around the campfires of continuous network news programming. Not since the assassination of John F. Kennedy in 1963 had the country been so rapt by the horrific events unfolding before its eyes. As with Kennedy's assassination, for four days the major networks stuck to the tragedies in New York and Washington with few commercial interruptions.[21] Later, millions watched as the stars of music and film organized benefits that allowed the television audience to participate by contributing to those in need. The most successful of these was *America: A Tribute to Heroes*, which was simultaneously broadcast on all the commercial networks and raised an estimated $150 million.[22]

The constant televised replays of the compelling scenes of devastation in New York and Washington reminded Americans that they were being tested in ways that were even more daunting than the challenges previous generations faced. George W. Bush counseled a tuned-in public to find within itself the internal fortitude needed to insure victory: "You will be asked for your patience; for, the conflict will not be short. You will be asked for resolve; for the conflict will not be easy. You will be asked for your strength, because the course to victory may be long."[23] His message resonated across the values divide. Busta Rhymes, a popular rap artist, declared, "We all have to really come together and find within ourselves the common destiny. Which is to be able to persevere and succeed, to overcome this obstacle and to deal, to withstand, whatever we have to endure."[24]

Dave Sirulnick, an MTV executive vice president, thought that Rhymes and other pop artists captured a widespread youthful yearning to measure up to the their World War II "greatest generation" forebears: "Through pop culture, through movies like *Pearl Harbor* and *Band of Brothers* on HBO, there was a sort of a sense of what other generations had gone through. And so it was very fresh in young people's minds that they didn't have anything like this. They didn't have Vietnam. They didn't have Watergate. I think instantly people understood that this [new form of terrorism] was going to define their generation."[25]

The New Normalcy

After the September 11th attacks, 85 percent said the United States should return to business as soon as possible.[26] Despite such bravado sentiments, it was clear that while life would go on, it would be in an era that could only be described as the "new normalcy."[27] One manifestation of this new normalcy was the immediate transformation of the popular culture. On 11 September, the alternative music group System of a Down had the nation's Number 1–selling CD, *Toxicity*. One week later, the group's standing on the pop charts dipped to Number 11.[28] Rising to replace it was a CD featuring Celine Dion singing "God Bless America."[29] Clear Channel Communications, which owns 1,170 radio stations and has 110 million weekly listeners, issued a list of 150 songs it considered inappropriate for airplay. These included the Gap Band's "You Dropped a Bomb on Me," Soundgarden's "Blow Up the Outside World," the Beatles' "Ticket to Ride," the Drifters' "On Broadway," all songs by Rage Against the Machine, and even John Lennon's anthem, "Imagine."[30] MTV took to playing what it called "comfort videos": Lenny Kravitz's "Let Love Rule," Bob Marley's "One Love," Sting's "If You Love Somebody Set Them Free," and U2's "Walk On." Head programmer Tom Calderone explained, "This is a weird word to use, but we're trying to find videos that are soothing and compatible with what the country is feeling right now."[31] The major network executives were also astounded when compilations of *I Love Lucy* and *The Carol Burnett Show* scored big audiences among young viewers. Almost immediately, television programmers began scouring the vaults for more old "comfort programs" to repackage and re-air. Meanwhile, the contemporary sitcom *Friends* was extended for another season in the wake of its overwhelming popularity following the attacks.[32]

It was not only young people who were horrified by the events of 11 September and changed their listening and viewing habits. Citizens who had once treated politics so cavalierly, seeing it as little more than a spectator sport—and not a particularly entertaining one at that—suddenly found themselves listening to political leaders with attentive ears. According to one survey, 68 percent said politics had become "more relevant" to their lives.[33] Writer David Brooks reports that at Princeton University politics is everywhere. On one corner of the campus, the Princeton Peace Network hosts teach-ins and rallies and sings "We Shall Overcome," while nearby the Princeton Committee Against Terrorism sponsors rival events and sings "God Bless America."[34]

Astonishingly, as the horrific events of 11 September sank deeper into the national psyche, public confidence in government soared to levels not seen since 1968.[35] Public opinion surveys found 60 percent saying they trusted the government in Washington to do what is right "just about always" or "most of the time."[36] Correspondingly, those expressing a great deal of confidence in the military soared to 77 percent (a 27-point increase since 2000); 52 percent had a high confidence level in the executive branch (a 38-point increase); and 43 percent felt the same way about Congress (a 31-point gain).[37] But it was not just trust in the federal government that grew exponentially. Many viewed its intentions more benevolently. For instance, 57 percent *disagreed* with the statement, "I don't think public officials care much what people like me think." (Eight years earlier, 59 percent agreed.)[38] Vice President Dick Cheney marveled at the sudden shift: "One of the things that's changed so much since September 11 is the extent to which people do trust the government—big shift—and value it, and have high expectations for what we can do."[39]

One reason for this restoration of confidence was that government was the citizen's only defense against terrorism. As New York senator Hillary Rodham Clinton put it, "Only the government can respond to what we've confronted."[40] Many agreed with her. According to a Gallup poll taken shortly after the September 11th attacks, terrorism was overwhelmingly viewed as the country's Number 1 problem, and 50 percent believed government should do more to combat it.[41] Moreover, 56 percent wanted more government spending favored by the Democrats used to stimulate the economy; 32 percent preferred the tax-cutting approaches advocated by George W. Bush and the Republicans.[42] Clearly, the public desire for a more robust federal establishment was reflected in the actions undertaken by George W. Bush. Declaring a state of emergency on 11 September, Bush authorized $40 billion in emergency spending, with $20 billion earmarked for restoring New York City, and an additional $15 billion to bail out the faltering airlines. These measures (and others sure to follow) had more in common with Franklin D. Roosevelt's approach to governance than Ronald Reagan's. Also noteworthy was John McCain's proposal to quadruple the number of Ameri-Corps volunteers to assist in homeland security. Interestingly, the program had been begun by Bill Clinton in 1993 to promote a greater sense of public service among the young, and McCain, still constrained by his antigovernment, conservative ideology, had strongly objected to it.

These programs and proposals for an enlarged government put many conservative Republicans on edge. House whip Tom DeLay exerted his considerable energies to provide the votes needed to prevent a federal takeover of airport security. The Senate had earlier supported such a takeover by a vote of 100 to zero, and the measure was wildly popular with the public. Bush initially sided with DeLay but eventually bowed to public pressure and signed an airport security bill into law that added 28,000 employees to the federal workforce. Ed Feulner, president of the conservative Heritage Foundation, suddenly found himself at odds with the Bush administration over the airline bailout, the economic revitalization package earmarked for New York City, and portions of the antiterrorist U.S.A. Patriot Act. Grover Norquist, president of the Americans for Tax Reform, which had played a decisive role in helping Newt Gingrich obtain the Speakership, feared that in this new pro-government environment Bush would ignore conservatives and cut deals with unity-minded congressional Democrats. According to Norquist, "Wars are nasty things. They make governments grow. It's going to be our job as a center-right coalition to remind people to restore budget discipline."[43] Ideologically, it seemed, the world was turned upside down. The habitual contempt many Americans once exhibited toward government employees (many of whom belonged to unions)—an antipathy that had been building since the 1960s—dissipated completely as local police, fire, and emergency rescue workers were celebrated for their heroism.

Still, for all the positive outcomes in community building and restoring public trust in government, the events of 11 September exacted a severe emotional toll. Seven out of ten said they had either cried or had shown greater affection for their loved ones in the days following the tragedy.[44] Families drew closer and parents hugged their children more often. Some social commentators speculated that those planning divorces on 11 September awoke the next day with a sudden change of heart.[45] Among the Christmas 2001 letters I received was one that described a Catholic priest asking his parishioners during a Thanksgiving homily to give thanks publicly for the things that mattered most to them. Among the more surprising responses was that of one man who said, "I know it sounds strange, but I'm grateful for September 11th because it put me back in touch with what is important to me." Pollster Stanley B. Greenberg found those in focus groups expressing similar sentiments: "I think it's darn time that finally this country got back to caring about what's important, which is, you know, your family and home and self, and you know, stop being so materialistic."[46]

Adversity also brought nontraditional families closer. In New York, Republican governor George Pataki was persuaded to change that state's crime-victim assistance program, which required domestic partners to prove that a loved one provided 75 percent of the household income before state aid would be forthcoming. Matt Foreman, director of Empire State Pride Agenda, found his agency swamped with requests to assist grieving gays and lesbians on matters ranging from financial security to child custody. Foreman lamented, "What's still unavailable to gays and lesbians and their non-biological survivors are the far-reaching government funds—Social Security, workers' compensation. . . . We're not in *Leave It to Beaver* land anymore. There are all kinds of families who don't fit the government's definition of family, who need help and won't be able to get it."[47]

Inner transformations within homes were accompanied by a greater public expressions of spiritualism and religiosity. Responding to a question about the American dream after the terrorist attacks, 52 percent thought it could best be achieved through spiritual fulfillment; only 30 percent said it meant acquiring more material goods.[48] As one MTV viewer wrote: "Life isn't about fancy cars, beautiful homes, and tickets to a great concert. It is about the wonderful people in this world. Live life!"[49] Part of this new living meant attending a church, synagogue, or mosque. Surveys taken after 11 September showed that church attendance had spiraled to 51 percent—up ten points from a just a few months before—and 74 percent said they felt closer to God after the attacks.[50]

Accompanying this new spiritualism and religiosity was a rebirth of patriotism that sprang from deep within the hearts of citizens and provided the most visible evidence of just how profoundly the national psyche had changed. The American flag, once a controversial symbol in the values divide, became a symbol of unity. More than 80 percent reported displaying it in some form.[51] Along with raising the flag came a national chorus of patriotic singing. One of the most moving scenes occurred when a bipartisan congressional gathering spontaneously burst into a refrain of "God Bless America" on the steps of the U.S. Capitol. The song became something of a national anthem, much as it had been when the late Kate Smith sang it during World War II. Other patriotic tunes also found favor with the public. A compact disc titled *Sing America*, which had been previously released in 1999, suddenly began climbing the charts. The CD featured Cher singing "The Star Spangled Banner"; Linda Ronstadt performing "Back in the U.S.A.; James Taylor's vocals on the Stephen Foster standard, "Oh, Susannah"; and the Mormon Tabernacle Choir with a rousing rendition of "God Bless America."[52] George W. Bush quickly sought to capture this new patriotic spirit by urging veterans to speak to schoolchildren about duty and honor to the country. Laura Bush also urged children to be more patriotic. In a letter read in the nation's classrooms, the First Lady wrote: "We can be proud and confident that we live in a country that symbolizes freedom and opportunity to millions throughout the world."[53] Lynne Cheney, wife of the vice president, began writing an alphabet book titled *America: A Patriotic Primer.*[54]

Giving this new patriotism a lift were the tales of heroism and courage from firefighters, police, and hospital emergency workers who were among the first to arrive at the World Trade Center and Pentagon. A country that spent all of Campaign 2000 searching for heroes, and believing it had fallen short, unexpectedly found itself surrounded by them.[55] New York City Fire Department chaplain Mychal Judge had his story told again and again: the Franciscan priest was killed by falling debris while giving last rights to a dying fireman. Grieving firefighters carried Judge's body first to a local church and later to the firehouse where he had lived before they scurried back to the World Trade Center to rescue others. The courage of Todd Beamer—the doomed airline passenger who, along with three others, foiled an attempt to crash their hijacked plane into the U.S. Capitol, White House, or some other Washington-area target—was lauded. Facing certain death, Beamer recited "The Lord's Prayer" with an air-phone operator and told her of his intention to "do something" before ending the call with the words, "Let's roll." The fact that one hero was homosexual (Judge) and another heterosexual (Beamer) no longer mattered.[56] Nor did it matter that another of the heroic passengers was gay. So celebrated were the heroics of 11 September that rock musicians—not heretofore known to share many cultural affinities with police and firefighters—staged massive concerts to celebrate their heroism. Former Beatle Paul McCartney, who organized the Concert for New York, wrote a song for the occasion entitled "Freedom" that celebrated this value and those who sought to defend it.

The presence of so many extraordinary heroes gave rise to an enormous swelling of national pride. George W. Bush told of receiving a letter from a fourth-grade girl who wrote that while she did not want her military Dad to fight,

"I'm willing to give him to you."[57] Nowhere was the new patriotism more apparent than at that annual celebration of "the ideal American woman," the 2001 Miss America Pageant. For the first time since World War II, the pageant took on an unusually militaristic tone. Those gathered in Atlantic City to watch the event waved 13,000 flags, as the jumbotron at Caesar's Palace flashed a sign that proclaimed "One Nation, under God." Gone were the cultural disputes about premarital sex and divorce that disrupted previous pageants. Instead of debating different lifestyles, the unconventional was accepted and even celebrated. Many cheered for Miss New York, an Air Force reservist with plans to go on active duty in March—if not sooner.[58] The eventual winner, a somewhat more tradition-minded Katie Harman, saw her role as that of a patriotic (and values) unifier: "This is an opportunity for Miss America to rally the hopes of the American public. I want to make sure that this tragedy does not bring America down."[59]

Unlike her predecessors, Miss America 2001 did not have to preach about values. The same also held true for George W. Bush, who had planned his own fall campaign of values preaching: "Before September 11th, my administration was planning an initiative called Communities of Character. It was designed to help parents develop good character in their children and to strengthen the spirit of citizenship and service in our communities. The acts of September 11th have prompted that initiative to occur on its own in ways far greater than I could have ever imagined."[60] Even those who previously disagreed with Bush on values issues no longer wanted to argue the point. Suge Knight, founder of Death Row Records, was one: "We're supporting Bush, we're supporting the U.S.A. At this moment there's no such thing as ghetto, middle class, or rich. There's only the United States."[61] As Jamie MacDonald, a Boston dockworker, told a reporter on 11 September, "This is the re-United States of America."[62]

George W. Bush and the New "Us" versus "Them" Politics

Nowhere was the transformation of life after 11 September greater than at the White House. George W. Bush, whom many had dubbed "the Accidental President" after the Florida fracas, no longer found his legitimacy questioned.[63] Gone, too, were debates over the Social Security and Medicare "lock boxes," "fuzzy [budgetary] math," a patient's bill of rights, stem-cell research, and other skirmishes that threatened to place the second Bush presidency alongside the forgettable late-nineteenth-century presidents following the Civil War. Even Al Gore now referred to Bush as "my Commander-in-Chief," telling an audience of partisan Iowa Democrats, "Regardless of party, regardless of ideology, there are no divisions in this country where our response to terrorism is concerned."[64] From the sidelines, Bill Clinton also lent support, even as he longed to be at center stage. Confiding to a close friend, Clinton remarked that for a presidency to be great it must have a defining moment. As far as his own administration was concerned, Clinton lamented, "I didn't have one."[65]

For Bush, the terrorist attacks of 11 September thrust his heretofore unremarkable tenure deep into the arms of history. (In fact, the first arms to reach Bush were those of the Secret Servicemen who hustled him out of an elementary school classroom in Florida, where he had been reading to the children, and escorted him to two military bases before deeming it safe for him to return to the capital.) Like other presidents whose terms have been defined by historic challenges, Bush immediately realized that how he responded to this new strain of international terrorism would form his line in the history books. Showing his resolve to pass this test, Bush employed a familiar baseball analogy, saying to friends that the terrorists were not "going to steal home on me."[66] Publicly, Bush declared, "We wage a war to save civilization itself," and he repeatedly stated that overcoming the dangers posed by Osama bin Laden and his cohorts "is the purpose of my administration."[67]

The shedding of so much blood on American soil gave Bush an unparalleled opportunity to seize the bully pulpit. He did so with relish, as the struggle against bin Laden gave the presidency, to paraphrase Alexander Hamilton, a new burst of energetic administration.[68] No longer would *Time* issue a cover with a headline such as "The Incredible Shrinking Presidency," as it did in the waning days of the first Bush presidency.[69] The enlargement of the presidency back to near-imperial status was well-suited to the current Bush's Father-Knows-Best persona. Moreover, the secrecy needed to pursue the war in Afghanistan, along with the demise of virtually all political opposition, conformed nicely to mute Bush's instinct to stiffen when challenged. All of this proved to be a welcome balm to Bush, since prior to the war he had found his policies meeting with increased resistance. Only the day before the September 11th attacks, the Gallup Organization found Bush holding the lowest job approval rating of his young administration—51 percent.[70] Just three weeks later his approval jumped 39 points to 90 percent.[71] This score exceeded the previous all-time record approval posted by George H.W. Bush (89 percent) during the Persian Gulf War.[72] Moreover, in looking back at the 2000 election, few Americans had feelings of buyer's remorse. A Zogby poll found 67 percent saying they did not believe the country would be better off if Al Gore were president.[73] Similar percentages were happy that Bill Clinton was no longer in the White House, and that Dick Cheney instead of Joe Lieberman was vice president.[74] Looking ahead, one poll found Bush trouncing Al Gore in 2004 by a gargantuan 26 percentage points.[75]

Republicans rejoiced in these numbers. Tom Davis, chairman of the National Republican Congressional Campaign Committee, saw an opportunity "to reshape the image of the party from the top down."[76] The party was certainly in need of an image makeover. During the Cold War, Republicans portrayed themselves as muscular nationalists who would best protect the United States against the dangers posed by international communism. Their success in painting such a vivid portrait helped them to win seven of the ten presidential elections held from 1952 to 1988.[77] The three Democratic winners—John F. Kennedy, Lyndon B. Johnson, and Jimmy Carter—proved to be lonely aberrations in a string of Republican presidents. But with the Cold War over, the Republicans became increasingly mired in the moral absolutism described in chapter 3. Yet following 11 September, many reasoned that what had worked for the party during the Cold War would do so once more. Early polls gave some indication that history might indeed repeat itself. For example, when respondents were asked by the Gallup Organization which party they had more confidence in when it came to dealing with terrorism, 61 percent chose the Republicans; only 23 percent picked the Democrats. Republicans also posted gargantuan leads on handling national defense (65 percent to 24 percent) and foreign affairs (56 percent to 30 percent).[78]

Osama bin Laden also gave Republican leaders an unparalleled opportunity to recast U.S. politics by redefining who is "us" and who is "them." For years, Republicans had been skilled practitioners of us-versus-them politics. During the Cold War, the GOP helped create a worldview wherein the Free World was led by the United States (us), while those unfortunate enough to reside behind the Iron Curtain were led by the communist-run Soviet Union (them). Democrats, too, were no slouches at playing hardball politics. After Franklin Roosevelt's routing of Herbert Hoover in 1932 and Alf Landon in 1936, Democrats echoed Roosevelt's characterization of the Republican Party as nothing more than a bunch of uncaring, well-to-do "economic royalists" (them), while Democrats championed the forgotten "common man" (us).[79] Campaigning against Richard M. Nixon in 1968, Hubert H. Humphrey transformed what seemed to be a certain Republican landslide into a cliffhanger by using this brand of us-versus-them politics: "Our Republican friends have fought every piece of social legislation that has benefitted this country, they have fought against Social Security, they have been against all forms of federal aid to education, they have been against Medicare for our senior citizens, they have been against minimum wages. . . . You just name it, and I'll guarantee you that you will have found a majority of them in Congress against it."[80]

One reason why us-versus-them politics still flourishes is the willingness of many Americans to judge others by their purity of devotion to the classical liberal values of freedom, individualism, and equality of opportunity. Seizing on this love of liberty and its attendant values, George W. Bush sought to turn the terrorist war into the first new us-versus-them conflict of the twenty-first century. Using the earthy language of the Wild West, the president declared that he wanted Osama bin Laden "dead or alive."[81] But Bush did more than simply make bin Laden the most wanted man in the world. Rather, he sought public support at home by making the war against terrorism a campaign about defending traditional values. Addressing the nation on 11 September, Bush declared, "America was targeted for attack because we're the brightest beacon for freedom and opportunity in the world."[82] Later, standing before a joint session of Congress, Bush drew a bright line between the twisted thinking of the terrorists and those who loved freedom: "Every nation, in every region, now has a decision to make. Either you are with us, or you are with the terrorists. . . . Freedom and fear are at war. The advance of human freedom—the great achievement of our time, and the great hope of our time—now depends on us." As if to echo their commander-in-chief, military leaders at the Pentagon dubbed the Afghan war "Operation Enduring Freedom." In numerous speeches, Bush consistently portrayed the U.S. cause as one designed to enhance the values of freedom, religious tolerance, and a belief in progress, while castigating the terrorists as "evil-doers" who practice "a fringe form of Islamic extremism": "The terrorists' directive commands them to kill Christians and Jews, to kill all Americans, and make no distinctions among military and civilians, including women and children. . . . Afghanistan's people have been brutalized—many are starving and many have fled. Women are not allowed to attend school. You can be jailed for owning a television. Religion can be practiced only as their leaders dictate. A man can be jailed in Afghanistan if his beard is not long enough."[83]

Interestingly, Osama bin Laden likewise saw the struggle with George W. Bush and his "infidel" allies in values terms. In a videotape released from a mountain hideaway, bin Laden sought to rally the Islamic world: "These events have divided the whole world into two sides—the side of believers and the side of the infidels. May God keep you away from them. Every Muslim has to rush to make his religion victorious. The winds of faith have come. The winds of change have come to eradicate oppression from the island of Muhammad, peace be upon him."[84]

The Taliban rulers of Afghanistan also saw the American-led attack as a clash of two cultures. Mullah Mohammad Omar, the Taliban leader, contrasted the Western emphasis on materialism with the Taliban's religious piety: "Life can be led with just a few basics. The luxuries don't matter."[85] For years, the Taliban had been conducting its own war against modernity. Seizing power in 1996, Islamic clerics began their rule by hanging TV sets from trees and outlawing virtually all music and films.[86] Noting these actions, Italian prime minister Silvio Berlusconi cast the war as an ongoing struggle between Western modernity and Eastern traditionalism: "We must be aware of the superiority of our civilization, a system that has guaranteed well-being, respect for human rights and—in contrast with Islamic countries—respect for religious and political rights, a system that has as its values understandings of diversity and tolerance."[87] Americans also saw the war from a similar perspective. As one participant in pollster Stanley B. Greenberg's focus groups put it:

You know [in the United States] . . . you choose who you're going to marry, and you choose if you're going to have children, and you choose if you're going to go to school, and you choose to move out of state to get a better job, and you choose whether you get on a plane. And that's why a lot of people want to come here . . . because there's a lot of choices.

You could choose your religion; you don't have to be one thing or another. If you're a woman, you can walk down the street; you don't have to hide under a veil.[88]

The Global Reach of American Culture

As the respondent in Greenberg's focus group stated, Osama bin Laden's struggle against the United States represented a clash between modernity and traditionalism. For decades, American cultural habits—especially changes intended to give women and homosexuals equal rights—have long been derided in non-Western cultures. In 1998, bin Laden railed against the "American women soldiers" stationed in the Holy City of Mecca: "By God, Muslim women refuse to be defended by these American and Jewish prostitutes."[89] The greater presence of women in the military, and in all other aspects of American life, ran counter to the traditional Muslim view that women should assume a secondary role. One of the terrorists even took a towel to cover the exposed shoulder of a woman in a portrait hanging in his hotel room.[90] (Ironically, many of the attackers indulged in the hedonistic aspects of Western society, including drinking at sports bars and lap dancing at nightclubs. This was according to instructions later found in a terrorist training manual that advised, "When you're in the outer world, you have to act like them, dress like them, behave like them.")[91]

Yet, even as George W. Bush was successful in casting the new war as a struggle between good and evil, Americans continued to wonder, "Why do they hate us?" Even Bush publicly professed "astonishment" that bin Laden, the Taliban, and their supporters could have such profound hatred for the United States.[92] While part of bin Laden's and the Taliban's animosity was rooted in the long-standing U.S. support for Israel, much of it also stemmed from a deep dislike of American popular culture. For some time, the extraordinary reach of American culture was viewed by many Muslims as a threat to their religious beliefs and values. Back in the 1920s, Hasum al-Banna, founder of the Muslim Brotherhood, railed against a "wave of atheism and lewdness" he saw engulfing Egypt, a wave that "started the devastation of religion and morality on the pretext of individual and intellectual freedom." Al-Banna assailed Westerners for importing "their half-naked women into these regions, together with their liquors, their theaters, their dance halls, their amusements, their stories, their newspapers, their novels, their whims, their silly games, and their vices."[93] Scott Appleby, a historian at the University of Notre Dame, believes that the difference between the Western industrialized nations and Islam centers on the role of religion in public life: "Islamists reject secular modernity with its pornography, materialism, drug dependency, and high divorce rate. They would respect the U.S. much more if we did not separate God from governance—if we were in fact a Christian state."[94]

Today, the United States has been cast by a variety of Muslim clerics as representing "the great Satan."[95] Anthony Lobaido, an international correspondent for Worldnetdaily.com, describes how many Muslims see New York City as the Great Satan's culture capital: "All that is evil in the world can be found in New York: MTV, the United Nations, the U.N. abortion programs, the Council on Foreign Relations, Wall Street greed, Madison Avenue manipulation, and of course more AIDS cases than the rest of America combined."[96] Yet, even as American culture was being deplored by Muslim clerics, secular Muslims still cherished Marlboro cigarettes, wore Levi's jeans, played Michael Jackson's music, celebrated the heroics of Michael Jordan on the basketball court, and dined at fast-food eateries like McDonald's and Kentucky Fried Chicken.[97]

So dominant is American popular culture that the popular sneaker Reebok markets itself with the claim that on "Planet Reebok" there are no boundaries. Alfred M. Zeien, chairman of the Gillette razor company, says, "I do not find foreign countries foreign." During the 1990s, Ted Turner, founder of the Cable News Network, forbade correspondents to use the word *foreign* in their newscasts. In one sense, these executives are right to spot few differences on the world market, as globalization has increasingly come to mean Americanization. In China, for example, one can see the long arm of U.S. culture in the growing number of McDonald's, Starbucks, and Kentucky Fried Chicken outlets. (KFC serves more than 100,000 Chinese customers daily.) Shortly after the collapse of the Berlin Wall, former East Berliners could still gaze upon the stolid, overbearing statues of Karl Marx and Friedrich Engels facing toward Moscow but surrounded by American-based fast-food chains, international hotels, and a gaggle of neon billboards advertising products made by Panasonic, Coke, and Goldstar.[98]

Nowhere is the dominance of American popular culture more emphatic than in its occupation of theater screens across the globe. As one French observer put it, "Cinema used to be side salad in world commerce. Now it's the beef." On the opening day of the Steven Spielberg film *Jurassic Park* in France, the film ran in nearly one-quarter of the country's 1,800 movie houses. Iranian censors tried to overcome the onslaught of U.S. films, banishing most of them as "banal, opportunistic, and pseudo-revolutionary." Even so, *Driving Miss Daisy* and *Dances with Wolves* found receptive audiences.[99] In nearby Afghanistan, the Taliban unsuccessfully tried to downplay the popularity of the film *Titanic*, even as many Afghan men restyled their hair to resemble actor Leonardo DiCaprio's locks.[100]

American television possesses a similar global reach. MTV, the American-invented music cable television network, reaches 323 million households.[101]"I want my MTV" was a demand so widespread that MTV is now the largest network on the planet. But it was not only MTV that has enjoyed huge worldwide audiences. Syndicated network programs are also very popular in foreign lands. In Iran, for example, programs such as *Dynasty, Donahue,* and *The Simpsons* are beamed into homes thanks to the Star TV satellite company, even though the government has unsuccessfully tried to block its signal. Often, these shows have competed with "the man on the balcony" (a reference to the late Ayatollah Khomeini). In Russia, the *Wheel of Fortune* game show has been retitled *Field of Wonders,* where lucky contestants can receive Sony VCRs into which they may load Hollywood films if they give the wheel the right spin. Poland, too, has its version, dubbed *Kolo Fortuna,* which commands 70 percent of the Polish television audience on Thursday evenings. NFL football has even spawned its own French counterpart, where an American-born announcer can be heard to exclaim: "Alors, quelle finesse! Regardez le quarterback sneak de Dan Marino, ça marche vraiment parfaitement, n'est-ce pas?! Tiens! Touchdown! Eh, oui, je suis étonné! Quelle jeu! Quel grand show!"[102] In most world capitals, no translation is needed to stay in touch with current events, as CNN is just a click of the remote control. Across the globe, the American media has spectacularly succeeded in invading foreign lands in ways the U.S. military can only dream of doing.

Such overwhelming dominance often breeds resentment. For years, Canadians have complained that their southern neighbor has exerted undue influence on their country's culture. Back in 1986, Jeffrey Simpson, a columnist for the *Toronto Globe and Mail,* described the cultural behemoth the United States had become by envisaging its inversion:

> Imagine a movie-lover in St. Louis who checked the local paper and discovered that 97 percent of the films showing in his city were foreign. Or how about a book-lover in San Francisco who found that in every city store foreign authors had written 75 percent of the titles and that American books were consigned to an inconspicuous display quaintly called "Americana."
>
> Try to picture the vast record stores of New York filled with three foreign records for every American one. Think about watching television in Phoenix and finding three out of every four programs made not in the United States, but somewhere else. Consider the possibility that in Chicago three out of every four publications sold were foreign. This is what cultural life is like for Canadians.[103]

Simpson's complaint is one heard around the world. Following the U.S. domination of the Cannes film festivals in the early 1990s, French culture minister Jack Lang proclaimed an all-out war against Hollywood. Lang got French legislators to approve a domestic content law requiring that 60 percent of video programming be European and 40 percent of songs played on the radio be French in origin. An official in the Iranian Ministry of Culture and Islamic Guidance declared, "These programs, prepared by international imperialism, are part of an extended plot to wipe out our religious and sacred values." But the struggle against American dominance, dubbed "Jihad vs. McWorld" by political scientist Benjamin Barber, remains no contest. Even as France was passing its own domestic content laws, its government awarded Hollywood film star Sylvester Stallone the prestigious Legion of Honor.[104]

Twenty years ago, Charles Z. Wick, a former talent agent who was tapped by Ronald Reagan to be the director of the U.S. Information Agency, said, "I would hope that American pop culture would penetrate into other societies, acting as a pilot parachute for the rest of American values."[105] Wick's wish has come true. In Arab states, visa-seekers crowd U.S. embassies and shout "America, free!" even if these are the only English words they know.[106] They are hardly alone. One reason foreigners associate the United States with freedom is because of the American products they use and the means by which those products are marketed. Coca-Cola, for example, sells more than a soft drink; it sells a way of life. As one company executive in charge of sales in Kenya admitted, "There is a perceived way of life embedded in each bottle of Coke. Coke is modern, with it." A young Czechoslovakian concurred: "Coke equals America. America equals freedom."[107] Likewise, McDonald's sells more than hamburgers. Jim Cantalupo, president of the company's international operations unit, describes the foreigner's encounter with McDonald's as a plethora of choices, each one the symbol of a free society: "It's the drive-thrus. . . . It's the Playlands. . . . It's the smile at the front counter. . . . It's all those things. . . . The experience."[108]

For years, the Walt Disney Corporation sought to sell something more than a good time at its theme parks. As one early promotional piece for the first Disney theme park in Anaheim, California, put it: "Disneyland will be based upon and dedicated to the ideals, the dreams, and the hard facts that have created America. And it will be uniquely equipped to dramatize these dreams and facts and send them forth as a source of courage and inspiration to all the world."[109] Today, the Disney Corporation's reach is throughly global, as foreign guests stream into its theme parks in California and Florida, while Euro-Disney garners a somewhat smaller group of visitors in Paris. Moreover, its films are shown in movie theaters around the world, and its control of television markets has expanded thanks to its own cable channel network and its takeover of the American Broadcasting Company.

A Persistent Values Divide

But a culturally triumphant America overseas hardly mitigates the ongoing internal values divisions within the United States. Indeed, many Americans viewed the events of 11 September through the looking glass of the values divide. Former president George H.W. Bush denounced the American-turned-Taliban-sympathizer John Walker Lindh, noting that he was the by-product of "liberal Marin County hot-tubbers."[110] On the other side of the values divide was Katha Pollitt, a columnist for *The Nation,* who described having an argument with her thirteen-year-old daughter, a student who attends a high school located a few blocks from the World Trade Center. Her daughter, it seemed, wanted to fly the American flag, only to have her mother object: "Definitely not, I say: The flag stands for jingoism and vengeance and war."[111]

Those holding different cultural views from Bush and Pollitt also saw the terrorist attacks through the prism of the values divide. Reverend Lou Sheldon, chairman of the Traditional Values Coalition, objected to the policy of the Red Cross and other relief organizations to assist gays and lesbians who lost partners in the September 11th attacks: "They should be first giving priority to those widows who were at home with their babies and those widowers who lost their wives. . . . This is just another example of how the gay agenda is seeking to overturn the one man–one woman relationship from center stage in America, taking advantage of this tragedy."[112] Bill Bright, head of Campus Crusade for Christ, expressed the sentiments of many evangelicals when he called for a religious revival and repentance, noting that the events of 11 September presented "a golden opportunity for the church to serve its people." More than one thousand clergy signed Bright's letter, including former Republican presidential candidate Pat Robertson; James Merritt, president of the Southern Baptist Convention; Thomas Trask, general superintendent of the Assemblies of God; and James Dobson, president of Focus on the Family.[113]

Yet nowhere was the values divide greater than in the polarizing responses given to two leading figures in the culture wars, Hillary Clinton and Jerry Falwell. Appearing at the World Trade Center ruins shortly after the disaster, Clinton found herself shunned by police and firefighters as she accompanied George W. Bush who, in turn, was mobbed by admiring rescue workers. A few days later, the junior senator from New York confidently strode onto the stage at the Concert for New York, which was organized by several Clinton loyalists in the entertainment industry. Expecting a warm welcome from the crowd, Mrs. Clinton found herself loudly booed by police and firefighters sitting in the front rows. As the cops and firemen yelled, "Get off the stage! We don't want you here!" the former First Lady could hardly be heard above the din. Fireman Michael Moran, whose brother John was killed at the World Trade Center, said he jeered because of the "claptrap that comes out of her mouth!" Moran's disdain mirrored that of his colleagues: "She wants to spew her nonsense—she doesn't believe the things she says. She says what she believes will work in the moment."[114]

Indeed, many police and firefighters were upset that Hillary Clinton had denounced the police brutality in the Amadou Diallo slaying two years earlier. But much of their dislike had little to do with policy. In fact, Clinton had successfully lobbied President Bush for federal funds in the wake of the disaster. Rather, many police and firemen saw her as a pushy woman and carpetbagger whose independence, unconventional marriage, and acceptance of nontraditional lifestyles were things they abhorred. During the 2000 campaign, the New York Police Benevolent Association; the New York City Police Department Sergeants, Lieutenants, and Captains; and the New York City Correction Officers Benevolent Association, along with the Uniformed Firefighters and Fire Officers Associations endorsed her opponent, Rick Lazio.

Backstage, the Clintons were upset at the poor reception, and Bill Clinton lashed out at John Sykes, the chief executive of VH–1. According to news reports, the former president wagged his finger at Sykes and exploded, "We wouldn't have accepted your invitation to speak if we had known it would be this uncomfortable."[115] One confidante of Hillary's exclaimed: "How could we not know this would be the wrong forum for Hillary?! These are cops and firemen who listen to right-wing talk radio. They still think she killed Vince Foster, for Christ's sake!"[116]

Just as divisive was a television appearance by the Reverend Jerry Falwell on Pat Robertson's *700 Club* two days after the terrorist attacks. On the program, the two evangelical leaders discussed the tragedies of 11 September and speculated as to why they had occurred:

> ROBERTSON: We have insulted God at the highest levels of our government. And then we say, "Why does this happen?"
>
> FALWELL: What we saw on Tuesday, as terrible as it is, could be minuscule if, in fact—God continues to lift the curtain and allow the enemies of America to give us probably what we deserve.
>
> ROBERTSON: Jerry, that's my feeling. I think we've just seen the antechamber to terror. We haven't even begun to see what they can do to the population.
>
> FALWELL: The ACLU's [American Civil Liberties Union] got to take a lot of the blame for this.
>
> ROBERTSON: Well, yes.
>
> FALWELL: And, I know that I'll hear from them for this. But throwing God out successfully with the help of the federal court system, throwing God out of the public square, out of the schools. The abortionists have got to bear some burden for this because God will not be mocked. And when we destroy 40 million little innocent babies we make God mad. I really believe that the pagans, and the abortionists, and the feminists, and the gays, and the lesbians who are actively trying to make that an alternative lifestyle, the ACLU, People for the American Way—all of them who have tried to secularize America—I point the finger in their face and say, "You helped make this happen."
>
> ROBERTSON: I totally concur.[117]

The Falwell-Robertson exchange ignited a firestorm of protests. The Fox Family Channel, which broadcasts the *700 Club*, said it "in no way shares the views expressed by Reverend Jerry Falwell."[118] A White House spokesman called Falwell's remarks "inappropriate."[119] Lorri L. Jean, executive director of the National Gay and Lesbian Task Force, equated the attitudes held by Falwell and Robertson to those of the Taliban: "The terrible tragedy that has befallen our nation and indeed the entire global community, is the sad byproduct of fanaticism. It has its roots in the same fanaticism that enables people like Jerry Falwell to preach hate against those who do not think, live, or love in the exact same way he does."[120]

In response, Falwell and Robertson said their remarks were "taken out of context."[121] But in apologizing both remained stubbornly defiant. Falwell said: "Our choices have consequences. Our rebellion has results. In many ways, the results of recent days are a reflection of the crumbing foundation of America. It is time to reflect and repent."[122] Later, Falwell repeated his long-held view that the ACLU and other organizations "which have attempted to secularize America, have removed our nation from its relationship with Christ on which it was founded." Robertson agreed: "We have sinned against Almighty God, at the highest level of our government. . . . The Supreme Court has insulted you over and over again, Lord. They've taken your Bible away from the schools. They've forbidden little children to pray. They've taken the knowledge of God as best they can, and organizations have come into court to take the knowledge of God out of the public square of America."[123] Reverend Albert Mohler Jr., president of the Southern Baptist Theological Seminary, while not subscribing to the Robertson-Falwell apocalyptic view that the horrific events of 11 September were God's retribution for sin, said, "There is no doubt that America has accommodated itself to so many sins that we should always fear God's judgment and expect that in due time that judgment will come."[124] But the public uproar continued, and Pat Robertson subsequently resigned as president of the Christian Coalition.

The same values divide through which some viewed the events of 11 September also continued to shape electoral politics, which soldiered on despite the tragedy. Under laws peculiar to Virginia and New Jersey, those states elected new governors in 2001. While the terrorist attacks forced the candidates to suspend their campaigning temporarily, they hardly ameliorated the values divide that had characterized the bitter Bush-Gore contest of the previous November. One example occurred when Betty Barrett, age sixty-five, confronted Virginia Democratic candidate Mark Warner at a cosmetology class where she was getting her hair done:

BARRETT: Do you believe in abortion?
WARNER (pause): I believe in a woman's right to choose.
BARRETT: Do you believe in homosexuality?

WARNER: I don't believe in gay marriage.
BARRETT: Should gays be allowed in positions of authority?
WARNER: I think that we should make judgments based upon people's qualifications.
BARRETT: I've been impressed with you on TV. . . . And you've got a good face. [But] I have to vote for the other man.[125]

For his part, Warner avoided values issues, casting himself instead as a "fiscal conservative" who would clean up "the budget mess" in the state capital. Judy Maupin, a former member of the Republican National Committee, endorsed Warner, saying, "If you didn't know him and heard him speak, you'd swear he is a moderate Republican."[126] Besides sounding fiscally conservative, Warner took pains to identify himself with culturally conservative Virginians. He won endorsements from gun-rights "sportsmen" and vigorously courted the National Rifle Association, an organization he once spurned. Warner appealed to rural Virginians by casting himself as a bluegrass-listening good old boy, and even sponsored a NASCAR racing car. Instead of making guns and other cultural values issues in the campaign, Warner cited the poor economic conditions that were so prevalent in the rural parts of the state. One key Warner advantage was his lack of electoral experience (he had never held political office). Like Ross Perot before him, Warner sought to make his wealth an asset by claiming he was best-suited for troubled economic times and beholden to no one. (Warner had amassed a $200 million fortune selling cell phone licenses.)

Warner's opponent, former state attorney general Mark Earley, tried to capitalize on the tragedies of 11 September by emphasizing his law enforcement experience and recruiting New York City mayor Rudolph Giuliani to appear in his television commercials. George W. Bush, who was wildly popular in Virginia, also issued a statement endorsing Earley but refused to campaign for him—preferring to don his nonpartisan commander-in-chief's hat instead. But endorsements from these popular Republicans were of little use. Warner bested Earley by 6 percentage points, becoming the first Democrat to win the Virginia governor's mansion in twelve years.

Whereas Mark Warner eschewed values issues, New Jersey Democrat James McGreevey did just the opposite. McGreevey cast himself as the Anybody-But-Him candidate by reciting ad nauseam Republican Bret Schundler's positions on gun control and abortion. Schundler, a conservative who had upset the New Jersey Republican establishment by beating a more moderate primary opponent, supported laws making it easier for citizens to carry concealed weapons. Moreover, Schundler opposed abortion in every instance, save when the life of the mother was in imminent danger. Responding to the Democratic values attacks, Schundler compared himself to Mother Teresa and the pope, and suggested that the

TABLE 7.1   THE VALUES DIVIDE: VIRGINIA AND NEW JERSEY
            GUBERNATORIAL ELECTIONS, 2001

Democratic Advantages	*Republican Advantages*
Self-identified Democrats	Self-identified Republicans
Cities	Rural Areas
Women	Men
Liberals	Conservatives
Blacks	Whites
Hispanics	
Cares about you	Tax cuts
Education	Abortion
Economy	
Single/Divorced	Married with children

Sources: For Virginia: *Washington Post* poll, 22–25 October 2001; Roanoke College poll, 21–30 October 2001; and Mason-Dixon Polling and Research poll, 15–17 October 2001. For New Jersey: Quinnipiac University poll, 29 October–4 November 2001; Quinnipiac University poll, 23–28 October 2001; Chris Cillizza, "Democrats Claim Edge but Republicans Point to Pro-Incumbent Environment," *Roll Call*, 8 November 2001; Cliff Zukin, "Democrats Gaining Strength in New Jersey," *Star-Ledger/Eagleton-Rutgers* poll, press release, 4 November 2001; and Dan Balz and Thomas B. Edsall, "Capturing Center Key in Democratic Wins," *Washington Post*, 8 November 2001, A24.

Democratic candidate's tolerance for alternative lifestyles should be *the* campaign issue. Former Republican governor Christine Todd Whitman, whom George W. Bush tapped to head the Environmental Protection Agency, noted that Schundler's views on guns and abortion were at odds with those of most voters, including her own.[127] Other prominent Republicans, including former presidential press secretary James Brady, who was severely wounded in the 1981 assassination attempt on Ronald Reagan, also endorsed McGreevey. Even the Republican acting governor, Donald DiFrancesco, refused to back Schundler. Thanks to these internal party divisions and McGreevey's relentless emphasis on cultural issues, McGreevey and the Democrats won decisively. Once a pro-Republican state thanks to the party's conservative positions on taxes, New Jersey currently finds itself with an ever-growing number of self-identified Democrats.[128] One sign of the times can be seen in suburban, upscale Bergen County, which had a net shift of 50,000 votes from 1993 (when Christine Todd Whitman won by 30,000 votes) to 2001 (when McGreevey prevailed by 20,000).[129]

Although New Jersey and Virginia were on different sides of the electoral divide—New Jersey gave Al Gore a 16-point lead over George W. Bush, while Virginia gave Bush an 8-point victory—polls conducted in these states found the values divide alive and well. As table 7.1 shows, groups favoring Bush in 2000 continued to back Republican gubernatorial candidates while Democratic-identi-fiers who previously supported Gore had little change of heart, despite the near-unanimity of public support they gave Bush following the September 11th attacks.

A Rebirth of Tolerance?

Weeks after the tragedies at the World Trade Center and the Pentagon, it is clear that the events of 11 September changed the country in ways that are still sorting themselves out. It may be that the Democratic victories in Virginia and New Jer-sey will give a boost to divided government, as voters continue to care about ed-ucation, health care, and other issues on which Democrats have long-standing advantages. Yet, it may also be the case that the reinsertion of foreign affairs into presidential contests will give the Republicans a much-needed boost. Adding to the GOP hopes for a party realignment is a shift in the public's perception of the nation's moral climate. Unlike 2000, 64 percent of those polled after the Sep-tember 11th attacks say the nation's moral values are headed in the right direc-tion.[130] Most credit the Republicans for this improvement; correspondingly, the GOP has a two-to-one lead over the Democrats in handling the values issue.[131]

Notwithstanding this Republican values advantage, former House Speaker Newt Gingrich believes that the elections of 2002 and 2004 may not result in major gains for George W. Bush and his party: "The president has become both more powerful and less partisan, which is probably good for his reelection and probably not good for the Republican party. [Bush's] natural instinct will be to do everything possible to be leading the entire country, which is very different from Reagan, who was clearly the leader of the conservative wing of America."[132] If Gingrich is correct, it may be appropriate to compare George W. Bush to Dwight D. Eisenhower. Back in 1956, Eisenhower attempted to recast the Re-publicans as a "one-interest party" that was standing firm in the battle against communism.[133] Yet, Eisenhower's appeal for national unity in the face of the Cold War did not help Republicans in that election or in subsequent Cold War contests. Up until Eisenhower's reelection in 1956, never before had a political party lost the White House by landslide proportions (as the Democrats did) and won control of the Congress and the statehouses.

Ironically, September 11th appears to have fulfilled George W. Bush's desire to "change the tone" of partisan politics. As a presidential candidate, Bush cast him-self as an outsider who was unfamiliar with the war-room politics of the Clinton years. During the Clinton era, politics became a game of "gotcha," with scandal serving as the latest weapon in the partisan wars. Television news programs and Sunday talk shows that once enlightened voters on the issues were increasingly populated by ideologues from the right and left who acted as modern-day gladi-ators. Now, thanks to Osama bin Laden and the Taliban, Bush could play the part of a commander-in-chief who was above the newfangled party wrangling dominated by polls, consultants, and an obsession with public relations. Not willing to be left behind, Democratic congressional leaders emulated Bush by projecting themselves as co-leaders of a unity government. Former Democratic presidential candidate Bill Bradley welcomed the opportunity to clear away the "old ruts" of partisanship created by consultants and public relations specialists: "I hope this will get us out of message politics and into reality politics where language is not so much what pollsters have laid out for us but what we feel at the deeper levels of our conviction." Hillary Clinton wondered aloud if the country would ever return to "normal" partisan bickering, adding, "I hope not, if normal is the kind of political debate we've had for years."[134]

It may be, however, that the most important long-term political change is to give tolerance a boost. This may be particularly true among those belonging to Generation 9–11. Judy McGrath, president of MTV, says of her young viewers: "One of the things this generation likes to say about themselves is that they are diverse and they appreciate differences. Now it's going to be like, 'Let's see how well you're going to deal with this.'"[135] Of course, this was not merely a test for Generation 9–11 alone. Following the terrorist attacks, while nothing like the McCarthyism of the Cold War era appeared, there were instances of racial and religious discrimination directed at Arab Americans and Muslim Americans. The Federal Bureau of Investigation investigated ninety hate crimes committed against Arab Americans and Muslims in the days following 11 September. Representative John Cooksey, a Louisiana Republican seeking to oppose Democratic senator Mary Landrieu in the upcoming 2002 elections, said, "If I see someone come in that's got a diaper on his head and a fan belt [wrapped] around [it], that guy needs to be pulled over and checked."[136] Several Muslim women who remained faithful to their religious tradition by wearing the traditional hijab became objects of public abuse. An Arab-American Secret Service agent traveling from Baltimore to Texas during the Christmas holiday to protect President Bush was removed from a commercial airplane and detained for several hours.

Pollster Richard Wirthlin found that an astonishing 40 percent of survey respondents believe that Islam advocates murder and terrorism, while 44 percent say that the September 11th attacks represent the feelings of Muslim Americans toward the United States.[137] Correspondingly, John Zogby discovered that 55 percent were willing to restrict the immigration of certain ethnic or religious groups.[138] Moreover, the public was evenly divided when asked if they would favor deporting an innocent immigrant who either had a family member who was a proven terrorist or a friendship with one.[139]

At the same time, however, there were signs that the public collectively decided to reject Osama bin Laden's appeals to prejudice and embrace the value of tolerance. Sensing the shift in mood, George W. Bush favorably cited instances where tolerance triumphed over prejudice:

> I was struck . . . that in many cities when Christian and Jewish women learned that Muslim women, women of cover, were afraid of going out of their homes alone, that they went shopping with them, that they showed true friendship and support, an act that shows the world the true nature of America. Our war on terrorism has nothing to do with differences in faith. It has everything to do with people of all faiths coming together to condemn hate and evil and murder and prejudice. . . . I want to urge my fellow Americans not to use this as an opportunity to pick on somebody that doesn't look like you or share your religion. The thing that makes our nation so strong and that will ultimately defeat terrorist activity is our willingness to tolerate people of different faiths, different opinions, different colors within the fabric of our society.[140]

Bush's message of tolerance was echoed by others in his administration. Attorney General John Ashcroft met with Arab Americans, who relayed incidents of intolerance. Afterward, Ashcroft told reporters: "The Justice Department has received reports of violence and threats of violence against Arab-Americans and other Americans of Middle Eastern and South Asian descent. We must not descend to the level of those who perpetrated violence by targeting individuals based on race, religion, or national origin."[141] The secretary of education urged schools to preach tolerance to schoolchildren, a message reinforced by First Lady Laura Bush. Senate majority leader Tom Daschle, whose office received an anthrax-tainted letter, pointedly observed, "The overwhelming majority of people understand instinctively that the way we get through hard times is by turning to each other, not on each other."[142] The media reinforced the plea for tolerance preached by Bush and unity-minded Democrats. MTV educated its viewers on the traditions embraced by the Taliban, Islam, and Sikhs, while deploring signs of anti-Muslim and anti-Arab sentiments. The major broadcast networks likewise filmed public service announcements emphasizing the importance of accepting others with different faiths and cultural backgrounds.[143]

It should come as no surprise that prominent spokespersons from both parties would advocate tolerance. In his book, *Moral Freedom*, Alan Wolfe notes that tolerance is *the* primary moral underpinning of the twenty-first century. As one of Wolfe's interviewees explains, "I don't think anybody is better than anyone else. I really don't." This attitude is clearly some distance away from the nineteenth-century morality of Victorian England, not to mention the moral absolutism espoused by fundamentalist religious devotees of Judaism, Christianity, or Islam. Wolfe himself is emphatic: "Americans are not going to lead twenty-first century lives based on eighteenth and nineteenth century moral ideals."[144]

Yet, it may be that the events of 11 September have given tolerance an unexpected boost. Those holding favorable views of Arab Americans stood at 63 percent less than two weeks after the attacks, while 64 percent were favorably disposed toward Muslim Americans. Positive opinions of all Arabs and Muslims, whatever their nationality, stood at 50 percent and 52 percent respectively.[145] In addition, 55 percent said they opposed any policy that would single out Arab Americans for special scrutiny at airport check-ins, and 86 percent said they were either "very concerned" or "somewhat concerned" about the treatment Arab Americans and Muslim Americans might receive after the attacks.[146] Most strikingly, Americans were *more* tolerant of cultural diversity in the aftermath of the September 11th attacks than before. One survey, for example, found that opposition to the exclusion of "unpopular" books from public libraries rose from 64 percent to 71 percent.[147]

Throughout history, Americans have consistently portrayed themselves as possessing opposite characteristics from their enemies. During the Cold War, for instance, Americans drew a line between their adherence to democratic values and Soviet-style communism. In 1964, the *World Book Encyclopedia* explained the differences between communism and democracy, not in terms of philosophical works by each ideology's leading advocates but in the parlance heard around the dining room table: "In a democratic country, the government rules by consent of the people. In a communist country, the dictator rules by force and stays in power by force. A democratic government tries to act in a way that will benefit the people. . . . Under communism, the interests of the government always come first. . . . Communism violently opposes democracy and the democratic way of life."[148] Thus, when Ronald Reagan dubbed the Soviet Union the "evil empire," most Americans agreed with him.[149]

For many Americans, September 11th decisively answered the ever-present question, "What does it mean to be an American?" During the Cold War, being an American meant presenting oneself as the opposite of the country's enemy. Today, that same stance that says "I'm not my enemy" involves emphasizing the value of tolerance as the decisive contrast between freedom-loving American patriots and Osama bin Laden and his Taliban supporters. If a greater public emphasis on tolerance is an unintended consequence of the terrorist attacks, then its long-term consequences are likely to enhance Alan Wolfe's idea of a "morality-writ-small" that will predominate in the twenty-first century.[150] Such an enhancement of a morality-writ-small individual values structure need not be at the expense of respect for more traditional values, nor need it discourage religiosity. Indeed, many Americans may conclude that these values should be paramount in their personal lives. Yet, if more citizens are to embrace traditional married lifestyles or to attend a church, synagogue, or mosque with greater frequency, those who advocate this way of living must present their case differently. In short, they must not argue for their way of life as one that is girded in absolute moral truths per se. Rather, they must make the point that adherence to tradition is consistent with a positive outlook on life and brings with it certain distinctive benefits to individual well-being.

From a political standpoint, Democrats need to be more respectful of those whose family lives resemble the Ozzie and Harriet Nelsons and the Ward and June Cleavers of yesteryear. Though at present a minority of the electorate, this group of voters remains a potent force. Republicans, on the other hand, must emphasize the compassionate conservatism embraced by George W. Bush, which respects others instead of preaching to them. To date, Bush's compassionate conservatism remains unique to his persona and shows little promise of sustaining itself beyond his presidency. Thus far, neither party has been able to withstand the pressures from its more zealous supporters, whose rigidity prevents it from making a more universalist values pitch. Until this happens, it seems clear that while September 11th changed the country in profound ways, our politics remains deadlocked. Yet, even as that search for a new politics continues, one thing seems clear: We're all Americans now.

Notes

Introduction

1. Tom W. Smith, "The Emerging 21st Century American Family," paper presented at the National Opinion Research Center, University of Chicago, 24 November 1999, 31. In 1998, 67 percent of married couples had both spouses working outside the home.
2. William J. Bennett, *The Broken Hearth: Reversing the Moral Collapse of the American Family* (New York: Doubleday, 2001), 12.
3. Smith, "Emerging 21st Century American Family," 3.
4. Bennett, *The Broken Hearth*, 12; Smith, "Emerging 21st Century American Family," 29.
5. See Bennett, *Broken Hearth*, 12, and Smith, "Emerging 21st Century American Family," 23. Among men, 66 percent respond that their first union was a cohabitation; women, 64 percent.
6. California's white population is 49.9 percent as reported in the 2000 census.
7. See Richard M. Scammon and Ben J. Wattenberg, *The Real Majority* (New York: Coward-McCann, 1970), esp. 45–71.
8. James Q. Wilson, "A Guide to Reagan Country: The Political Culture of Southern California," *Commentary*, May 1967, 40.
9. Quoted in David Halberstam, *The Fifties* (New York: Villard Books, 1993), 509.
10. Bob Dole, acceptance speech, Republican National Convention, San Diego, 15 August 1996.
11. Quoted in Evan Thomas, "The Small Deal," *Newsweek*, 18 November 1996, 127.
12. Halberstam, *The Fifties*, 514.
13. "Gay Teacher's Disclosure Spurs a Debate," *New York Times*, 11 June 2000, 30.
14. Quoted in Michael Barone and Richard E. Cohen, with Charles E. Cook Jr., *The Almanac of American Politics, 2002* (Washington, D.C.: National Journal, 2001), 751.
15. Alan Wolfe, *Moral Freedom: The Impossible Idea That Defines the Way We Live Now* (New York: W.W. Norton, 2001), 186.
16. See John Kenneth White, *The New Politics of Old Values* (Hanover, N.H.: University Press of New England, 1988), 21.
17. Knute Rockne, "Gipp the Great," *Colliers*, 22 November 1930, 15.
18. Ronald Reagan, Address to the Graduates at Notre Dame University, South Bend, Indiana, 17 May 1981.

19. Ibid.

20. Quoted in Stephen E. Ambrose, *Nixon: The Education of a Politician, 1913–1962* (New York: Simon and Schuster, 1987), 541–42.

21. Ronald Reagan, remarks on arrival at West Lafayette, Indiana, 9 April 1987. Representative J.C. Watts once used the same story; see J.C. Watts, "Response to President Clinton's State of the Union Address," Washington, D.C., 4 February 1997.

22. Quoted in Paul D. Erickson, *Reagan Speaks: The Making of an American Myth* (New York: New York University Press, 1985), 2.

23. Quoted in James MacGregor Burns, *Roosevelt: The Lion and the Fox* (New York: Harcourt, Brace, and World, 1956), 283.

24. Ibid.

25. See Jake Tapper, "Joe Lieberman's Blank Slate," *Talk*, November 2001, 160.

26. V.O. Key Jr., *The Responsible Electorate: Rationality in Presidential Voting, 1936–1962* (New York: Vintage Books, 1966), 7.

27. Ibid., 2–8.

28. Walter Lippmann, *The Phantom Public* (New York: Harcourt, Brace, 1925), 56–57.

29. Later Wilson modified his view, writing that "*somebody must be trusted* in order that when things go wrong it may be quite plain who should be punished." See Woodrow Wilson, *Congressional Government* (Boston: Houghton Mifflin, 1885), 213.

30. Quoted in J. Joseph Huthmacher, *Massachusetts: People and Politics, 1919–1933* (New York: Atheneum, 1969), 162.

31. These were Texas, Florida, North Carolina, Tennessee, Kentucky, Virginia, and Maryland. See John Kenneth White, *The Fractured Electorate: Political Parties and Social Change in Southern New England* (Hanover, N.H.: University Press of New England, 1983), 10.

32. Cited in Michael Barone, *Our Country: From Roosevelt to Reagan* (New York: Free Press, 1990), xii.

33. Transcript of forum conducted by the Americans for Responsible Government, Madison Hotel, Washington, D.C., 1 October 1985.

34. See Katherine Shaver and Mike Allen, "Federal Agent Accuses Pilot of Discrimination," *Washington Post*, 28 December 2001, B1; and "Pilot Barred Arab-American Secret Service Agent," CNN/AllPolitics website, 27 December 2001.

35. Paul F. Lazarsfeld, Bernard R. Berelson, and Hazel Gaudet, *The People's Choice* (New York: Columbia University Press, 1940); Bernard R. Berelson, Paul F. Lazarsfeld, and William N. McPhee, *Voting: A Study of Opinion Formation in a Presidential Campaign* (Chicago: University of Chicago Press, 1948).

36. Lazarsfeld, Berelson, and Gaudet, *People's Choice*, 174–75; and Lazarsfeld, Berelson, and McPhee, *Voting*, 125–26.

37. Angus Campbell, Gerald Gurin, and Warren E. Miller, *The Voter Decides* (1954; reprint, Westport, Conn.: Greenwood Press, 1971), 85.

38. "Transcript of Bush News Conference," *Washington Post*, 10 November 1988, A41.

39. Committee on Political Parties, *Toward a More Responsible Two-Party System* (New York: Rinehart and Company, 1950), v, 17–18.

40. Ibid., 30.

41. Gerald M. Pomper, "Toward a More Responsible Two-Party System? What, Again?" *Journal of Politics* 33 (1971): 929–32.

42. Norman H. Nie, Sidney Verba, and John R. Petrocik, *The Changing American Voter* (Cambridge, Mass.: Harvard University Press, 1976).

43. Anthony Downs, *An Economic Theory of Democracy* (New York: Harper and Row, 1957), 40.

44. See Martin P. Wattenberg, *The Rise of Candidate-Centered Politics* (Cambridge, Mass.: Harvard University Press, 1991), 17–20.

45. Ronald Reagan, acceptance speech, Republican National Convention, Detroit, Michigan, 17 July 1980.

46. Transcript of the Reagan-Carter presidential debate, Cleveland, Ohio, 28 October 1980, in David Broder, Lou Cannon, Haynes Johnson, Martin Schram, and Richard Harwood, *The Pursuit of the Presidency, 1980* (New York: Berkeley Books, 1980), 399.

47. See Voter Research and Surveys exit poll, 3 November 1992. H. Ross Perot got 25 percent of these voters and George H.W. Bush received a paltry 14 percent.

48. Downs, *Economic Theory of Democracy*, 36.

49. See, among others, Robert S. Erikson, Joseph Bafumi, and Bret Wilson, "Was the 2000 Election Predictable?" *PS: Political Science and Politics* 34, no. 4 (December 2001): 815–19.

50. *Washington Post* poll, 18–22 December 1998.

51. National Commission on Civic Renewal, "A Nation of Spectators: How Civic Disengagement Weakens America and What We Can Do About It," University of Maryland, College Park, June 1998.

52. See Wolfe, *Moral Freedom*.

53. James Davison Hunter, *The Death of Character: Moral Education in an Age without Good or Evil* (New York: Basic Books, 2000), xiii.

54. Andrew Kohut, "Deconstructing Distrust: How Americans View Government," press release, Pew Research Center for the People and the Press, 1998.

55. Cited in James Davison Hunter, *Culture Wars: The Struggle to Define America* (New York: Basic Books, 1991), 195.

56. See Oscar Handlin, *The Americans: A New History of the People of the United States* (Boston: Atlantic Monthly Press, 1963), 297.

57. Quoted in Hunter, *Culture Wars*, 177.

58. Ibid., 195.

59. Theodore Roszak, "Youth and the Great Refusal," *The Nation*, 25 March 1968, 402–3.

60. Ibid., 406.

61. Students for a Democratic Society, "Port Huron Statement of Students for a Democratic Society," Port Huron, Michigan, 11–15 June 1962.

62. Roper Organization poll, September 1939.

63. Roper Organization poll, 11–19 January 1974.

64. Princeton Survey Research Associates poll, 3–4 February 1994.

65. See especially David Frum, *How We Got Here: The '70s, The Decade That Brought You Modern Life* (New York: Basic Books, 2000).

66. Quoted in Norman Mailer, "By Heaven Inspired," *New Republic*, 12 October 1992, 24, 30.

67. Gallup poll, 1–4 April 1977.
68. Peter J. Boyer, "Gore's Dilemma," *New Yorker*, 28 November 1994, 108–9. Emphasis added.
69. Ibid., 109.
70. Quoted in Howard Fineman, "The Man to Beat," *Newsweek*, 30 August 1999, 29.
71. See White, *New Politics of Old Values*, 2d ed. (1990).
72. "Transcript of Hart Statement Withdrawing His Candidacy," *New York Times*, 9 May 1987, 9.

Chapter 1: Four Stories for Our Time

1. See David Goodman, "A More Civil Union," *Mother Jones*, July/August 2000, 50.
2. See Pamela Ferdinand, "Vermonters Rise to Sort Out Law on Marriage," *Washington Post*, 6 February 2000, A3.
3. The Vermont Supreme Court held in *Baker v. Vermont* that "the State is constitutionally required to extend to same-sex couples the common benefits and protections that flow from marriage under the Vermont law." The state legislature took the marriage statutes and added the words "or partner in a civil union" wherever the words *marriage* and *spouse* appeared. The law won Senate approval on a vote of 19–16 and House passage by a vote of 79–68. Democratic governor Howard Dean signed the bill into law on 26 April 2000. The new "civil union" statute allows same-sex partners to transfer property, make medical decisions for each other, inherit estates, oversee one another's burials, protect child care and custody rights, and file joint state tax returns.
4. Quoted in Ferdinand, "Vermonters Rise," A3, and Goodman, "A More Civil Union," 50.
5. Debra Rosenberg, "State of the 'Union,'" *Newsweek*, 23 October 2000, 56.
6. Michael Powell, "Riled Up in Old Vermont," *Washington Post*, 17 October 2000, C1.
7. "Archdiocese of Boston, Bishops of Boston Province issue statement on Vermont 'Civil Unions Bill,'" *The Pilot*, 9 June 2000. Retrieved from http://www.rcab.org/pilotstories/pilot060900/Bishops/CivilUnion.html.
8. Quoted in Ferdinand, "Vermonters Rise."
9. Quoted in Hanna Rosin and Pamela Ferdinand, "Gays Achieve Breakthrough in Vermont," *Washington Post*, 17 March 2000, A1.
10. Quoted in Carey Goldberg, "A Kaleidoscope Look at Attitudes on Gay Marriage," *New York Times*, 6 February 2000, 16. By 2001, three thousand gays and lesbians had received civil union licenses. Ironically, terminating a civil union is more difficult than receiving a license. While residency is not required for a civil union, to end the arrangement one partner must stay in Vermont for six months in order to obtain a "divorce." See Tammerlin Drummond, "The Marrying Kind," *Time*, 14 May 2001, 52.
11. Ibid.
12. Edward Hoagland, "How It Became So Very Uncivil," *Washington Post*, 29 October 2000, B1.
13. Rosenberg, "State of the 'Union,'" 56.

14. See Malcolm E. Jewell, "The State and Local Elections: Politics Beyond the Beltway," in William Crotty, ed., *America's Choice 2000* (Boulder: Westview Press, 2001), 170, 172.

15. Quoted in Ross Sneyd, "House Readies to Explicitly Outlaw Gay Marriage," *Burlington Free Press*, 16 March 2001, A1.

16. Quoted in Nancy Remsen, "A State Divided," *Burlington Free Press*, 13 September 2000. Retrieved from http://www.burlingtonfreepress.com/news/3000h.htm.

17. Quoted in Benjamin Soskis, "State's Right," *New Republic*, 11 June 2001, 25.

18. Under Vermont law, if no gubernatorial candidate receives 50 percent of the vote, the election is to be decided by the State House of Representatives.

19. Voter News Services exit poll, 7 November 2000.

20. See "Transcript of the Second Bush-Gore Presidential Debate," CNN, October 11, 2000.

21. "Transcript of the Cheney-Lieberman Vice Presidential Debate," CNN, October 5, 2000.

22. Gary Bauer, "Fuzzy Morality," *New York Times*, 8 October 2000, WK15.

23. Voter News Services exit poll, 7 November 2000.

24. Zogby International, press release, 23 August 2001.

25. Kenneth Jost, "Gay-Rights Update," *Congressional Quarterly*, 14 April 2000, 312.

26. Ibid., 309.

27. *Bowers v. Hardwick*, 478 U.S. 186 (1986).

28. *Powell v. State of Georgia* (1998). Until 1961, all states prohibited sodomy.

29. Gallup poll, 10–14 May 2001.

30. Frank Newport, "American Attitudes Toward Homosexuality Continue to Become More Tolerant," Gallup press release, 4 June 2001.

31. *Washington Post*/Kaiser Family Foundation/Harvard University poll, 29 July–18 August 1998.

32. Gallup Organization/*USA Today* poll, 30 September–1 October 1998.

33. Quoted in D'Vera Cohn, "Census Shows Big Increase in Gay Households," *Washington Post*, 20 June 2001, A1.

34. James Sterngold, "An Unlikely 'Don't Tell' Target: Lawmaker May Face Discharge," *New York Times*, 26 August 1999, 1.

35. Chris Moeser, "Military Inquiry Targets Lawmaker; Reservist Steve May Focus of Gay-Policy Rule," *Arizona Republic*, 13 August 1999, SD1.

36. See E.J. Montini, "Straight Talk from a Gay Patriot," *Arizona Republic*, 28 September 1999, B1.

37. Steve May, interview, *Larry King Live*, CNN, 30 August 1999.

38. May had already disclosed his homosexuality, but the army was unaware of it.

39. May, interview, *Larry King Live*.

40. Peter Slevin, "'Unlimited Potential,' but Not in This Army," *Washington Post*, 17 October 2000, A3.

41. May made an unsuccessful run for the State Senate in 1996 and during that campaign was "outed" by a campaign operative.

42. Scott Thomsen, "Gay Reservist, Lawmaker Calm Amid 'Don't-Ask-Don't-Tell' Storm," *Associated Press*, 2 October 1999.

43. May, interview, *Larry King Live.*

44. Slevin, "'Unlimited Potential,'" A3.

45. Quoted in Thomsen, "Gay Reservist, Lawmaker Calm," and Sterngold, "Unlikely 'Don't Tell' Target."

46. Steve May, telephone interview by author, 19 March 2000.

47. May disclosed his homosexuality in 1996 during his first unsuccessful run for office. May's sexual orientation was not much of an issue in his 1998 campaign.

48. Eileen L. Norton to the Commander, 63d Regional Support Command, letter, 7 February 2000.

49. Quoted in Sterngold, "Unlikely 'Don't Tell' Target."

50. May, telephone interview.

51. Associated Press, "Gay Legislator in Army Faces Inquiry on Speech," *New York Times*, November 1999, 22.

52. Bob Barr, interview, *Larry King Live*, CNN, 30 August 1999.

53. Oliver North and Steve May, interview, *Larry King Live*, CNN, 18 September 2000.

54. Ibid.

55. Quoted in Thomsen, "Gay Reservist, Lawmaker Calm."

56. Jerry Falwell, interview, *Larry King Live*, CNN, 30 August 1999.

57. Quoted in Vanessa Williams, "Clinton Concedes 'Don't Ask, Don't Tell' Policy Hasn't Worked," *Washington Post*, 12 December 1999, A26.

58. Robbie Sherwood and Chip Scutari, "Army Ends Effort to Boot May," *Arizona Republic*, 16 January 2001, A1.

59. May, telephone interview.

60. Ibid.

61. *The Starr Report: The Findings of Independent Counsel Kenneth W. Starr on President Clinton and the Lewinsky Affair with Analysis by the Staff of the Washington Post* (New York: Public Affairs, 1998), 20–21.

62. "The Shaming of the President," BBC broadcast, 14 September 1998.

63. Quoted in Adam Cohen, "We Fight Like Cats and Dogs," *Time*, 28 September 1998.

64. Quoted in John Vinocur, "Behind the Ridicule, the French May See Peril in Too Much Truth," *International Herald Tribune*, 9–10 January 1999, 1.

65. BBC, 10 o'Clock News, 11 January 1999.

66. BBC World News, 10 January 1999.

67. "Transcript of Remarks by Vaclav Havel," CNN, 16 September 1998.

68. "Clinton Leaves Office with Mixed Public Reaction," Gallup press release, 12 January 2001.

69. George Washington, Farewell Address, 17 September 1796.

70. Forrest McDonald, "Presidential Character: The Example of George Washington," in Philip G. Henderson, ed., *The Presidency: Then and Now* (Lanham, Md.: Rowman and Littlefield, 2000), 8.

71. Gallup poll, 4–7 February 1999.

72. NBC News/ *Wall Street Journal* poll, 26 February–1 March 1998.

73. Zogby International poll, February 1998.

74. Yankelovich Partners poll, 4–5 October 2000.

75. William J. Bennett, *The Death of Outrage: Bill Clinton and the Assault on American Ideals* (New York: Free Press, 1998), 9.

76. *Washington Post*/Kaiser Family Foundation/Harvard University poll, 29 July–18 August 1998.

77. Peter Baker, *The Breach: Inside the Impeachment and Trial of William Jefferson Clinton* (New York: Scribner's, 2000), 18.

78. Quoted in Megan Rosenfeld and Michael Colton, "Portrait of Monica," *Washington Post*, 14 September 1998, B1.

79. Quoted in John B. Judis, "Washington Possessed," *New Republic*, 25 January 1999, 15.

80. Quoted in Ronald Brownstein, "Pushing the Moral Pendulum," *Washington Post*, 31 December 1998, B5.

81. Peter D. Hart Research Associates poll, 16–20 March 1999.

82. Hillary Clinton, interview, *Today*, NBC News, 27 January 1998.

83. Senator Joseph I. Lieberman, "Remarks on the Senate Floor," Washington, D.C., 3 September 1998.

84. "Public Attentiveness to Major News Stories, 1986–1999," Pew Research Center for the People and the Press, press release.

85. Peter D. Hart Research Associates poll, 16–19 March 1999.

86. Alan Wolfe, *Moral Freedom: The Impossible Idea that Defines the Way We Live Now* (New York: W.W. Norton, 2001), 188.

87. Gertrude Himmelfarb, *One Nation, Two Cultures* (New York: Knopf, 1999), 98.

88. See Alan Wolfe, *One Nation After All* (New York: Viking, 1998), especially 275–322, and Alan Wolfe, "The Pursuit of Autonomy," *New York Times Magazine*, 7 May 2000, 54.

89. Quoted in Edward Rothstein, "Same Old Story," *New Republic*, 25 January 1999, 13.

90. Ibid.

91. ABC News poll, 9 September 1998; NBC News/*Wall Street Journal* poll, 16–19 June 1999; Peter D. Hart Research Associates poll, 16–20 March 1999.

92. Fox News/Opinion Dynamics poll, 18 August 1998.

93. The Gallup data cited here can be found in "The 2000 Presidential Election—A Mid-Year Gallup Report," press release, 22 June 2000.

94. See Dan Merkle, "Gore's Sunny Forecast," ABC News.com, 28 August 2000; and Adam Clymer, "And the Winner Is Gore, If They Got the Math Right," *New York Times*, 4 September 2000.

95. See "2000 Presidential Election—A Mid-Year Gallup Report."

96. Cited in Karlyn Bowman, "Gore Getting Over Clinton Fatigue as Race Enters the Homestretch," *Roll Call*, 14 September 2000.

97. Quoted in Robert G. Kaiser, "Political Scientists Offer Mea Culpas for Predicting Gore Win," *Washington Post*, 9 February 2001, A10.

98. Ibid.

99. Hart and Teeter Research Companies poll, 3–5 November 2000.

100. Gallup poll, 10–12 March 2000.

101. Wirthlin Worldwide poll, 7–10 July 2000.

102. Cited in Nancy Gibbs, "It's Only Me," *Time*, 19 March 2001, 22.

103. See "2000 Presidential Election—A Mid-Year Gallup Report" and *New York Times*, 17–19 July 2000.

104. *Washington Post*/Henry J. Kaiser Family Foundation/Harvard University poll, 7–17 September 2000.

105. Voter News Services exit poll, 7 November 2000. Whites backed Bush by a margin of 54 percent to 42 percent; those who were married backed Bush by a 53 percent to 44 percent margin; those who had children under age eighteen also backed Bush by 52 percent to 45 percent; those who attended religious services more than weekly backed Bush 63 percent to 36 percent; those who attended weekly supported Bush 57 percent to 40 percent.

106. Ibid. Those who were not married supported Gore 57 percent to 38 percent; gays backed Gore 70 percent to 25 percent; African Americans gave Gore a whopping 90 percent of their votes to a mere 9 percent for Bush; Hispanics voted 62 percent for Gore to 35 percent for Bush; those aged 18–29 backed Gore 48 percent to 46 percent; first-time voters supported Gore even more strongly, 52 percent to 43 percent; those who seldom attended church services gave Gore 54 percent of their votes to Bush's 42 percent; those who never attended church voted 61 percent for Gore to 32 percent for Bush.

107. See Tom W. Smith, "The Emerging 21st Century American Family," paper presented at the National Opinion Research Center, University of Chicago, 24 November 1999, 1, 3.

108. Tennessee's placement in the Bush column made Gore eligible to join a small and dubious club that includes major-party nominees who lost their home states. James K. Polk lost his home state of Tennessee in 1844; Woodrow Wilson lost New Jersey in 1916; Alf Landon lost Kansas in 1936; Adlai Stevenson lost Illinois in 1952 and again in 1956; and George McGovern lost South Dakota in 1972. Richard Nixon also technically fits this category, having lost New York in 1968 to Hubert H. Humphrey. Nixon had moved to New York from his native California just a few years earlier.

109. Cited in Edward Sidlow and Beth Henschen, *America at Odds: An Introduction to American Government* (Belmont, Cal.: West/Wadsworth, 1998), 309.

110. Wolfe, *One Nation After All*, 239–40.

111. Harwood Group, *America's Struggle Within: Citizens Talk About the State of the Union* (Washington, D.C.: Pew Center for Civic Journalism, 1996), 8.

112. Quoted in E.J. Dionne Jr., *They Only Look Dead: Why Progressives Will Dominate the Next Political Era* (New York: Simon and Schuster, 1996), 90.

113. Blum and Weprin Associates poll, 13–16 March 2000.

114. Gallup poll, 9–11 March 2001.

115. Quoted in Jeff Adler and William Booth, "Five Wounded in Month's Second California School Shooting," *Washington Post*, 23 March 2001, A3.

116. Nancy Gibbs and Timothy Roche, "The Columbine Tapes," *Time*, 20 December 1999, 50.

117. Ibid., 42.

118. According to a 9–11 March 2001 Gallup poll, 65 percent believe that it is very likely or somewhat likely that school shootings can happen in their community.

119. Blum and Weprin Associates poll, 13–16 March 2000.

120. See Nancy Gibbs and Julie Grace, "The Littleton Massacre," *Time*, 3 May 1999. The story was later disputed, and Valeen Schnurr was credited with having spoken these words of faith.

121. Bill Clinton, State of the Union address, Washington, D.C., 27 January 2000.

122. Tom DeLay, "Why Kids Murder Kids," *Washington Post*, 27 March 2000, A27.

123. Wirthlin Worldwide poll, 7–10 July 2000.

124. *Washington Post*/Kaiser Family Foundation/Harvard University poll, 29 July–18 August 1998.

125. George W. Bush, announcement speech, Cedar Rapids, Iowa, 12 June 1999.

126. Al Gore, announcement speech, Carthage, Tennessee, 16 June 1999.

127. Ben J. Wattenberg, *Values Matter Most: How Republicans or Democrats or a Third Party Can Win and Renew the American Way of Life* (New York: Free Press, 1995), 13.

128. Dan Balz, "Picking Up Votes in a Maze of Ideals," *Washington Post*, 5 October 1998, A1.

129. Associated Press, "'In God We Trust' Now Required in Mississippi Classrooms," CNN.com, 23 March 2001. Retrieved from http://www.cnn.com/2001/US/03/23/school.religion.ap/index.html.

130. Quoted in Wilson Carey McWilliams, *Beyond the Politics of Disappointment?* (New York: Chatham House, 2000), 65.

131. Quoted in "Notebook," *Time*, 19 March 2001, 17.

132. Gibbs, "It's Only Me," 22.

Chapter 2: Whose Country?

1. Alexis de Tocqueville, *Democracy in America*, ed. Richard D. Heffner (New York: New American Library, 1956), 117–18.

2. Cited in Richard Morin and David S. Broder, "Worries about Nation's Morals Test a Reluctance to Judge," *Washington Post*, 11 September 1998, A1.

3. *Mrs. Doubtfire*, Twentieth-Century Fox, 1993.

4. See Ellen Nakashima and Al Kamen, "Bush Picks as Diverse as Clinton's," *Washington Post*, 30 March 2001, A27.

5. See Mike Allen, "Hughes Keeps White House in Line," *Washington Post*, 19 March 2001, A1.

6. Stan Davis and Christopher Meyer, *Blur: The Speed of Change in the Connected Economy* (Reading, Mass.: Addison-Wesley, 1998), 7.

7. Quoted in Richard Rovere, *The American Establishment and Other Reports, Opinions, and Speculations* (New York: Harcourt, Brace and World, 1962), 3.

8. Ibid., 9.

9. Ibid., 20. Even losing tickets had a similar pairing: Alf Landon (non-Establishment) with Frank Knox (Establishment), Wendell Willkie (Establishment) with Charles McNary (non-Establishment), Thomas E. Dewey (Establishment) with John Bricker (non-Establishment), Adlai E. Stevenson (Establishment) with John Sparkman (non-Establishment), Stevenson again with Estes Kefauver (non-Establish-

ment), and Richard M. Nixon (non-Establishment) with Henry Cabot Lodge (Establishment).

10. Quoted in David Brooks, "The Organization Kid," *Atlantic Monthly*, April 2001, 49.

11. See Richard M. Nixon, *RN: The Memoirs of Richard Nixon* (New York: Grosset and Dunlap, 1978), 454–55.

12. "Agnew's Hour," *Newsweek*, 23 February 1970, 24.

13. Quoted in David S. Broder, *The Party's Over: The Failure of Politics in America* (New York: Harper and Row, 1972), 111. Emphasis added.

14. The Beatles, *The Beatles Anthology* (San Francisco: Chronicle Books, 2000), 356.

15. It can be argued that Lyndon B. Johnson and Hubert H. Humphrey signaled the end to the Establishment's influence with their election in 1964. Nelson A. Rockefeller, an Establishment throughbred, became vice president in 1975, and that was only by a presidential appointment. George H.W. Bush was an Establishment type paired with the non-Establishment Ronald Reagan. Bush put the son of an Establishment newspaperman on the Republican ticket in 1988. Bill Clinton (definitely non-Establishment) ran with the son of an Establishment type, Albert Gore Jr. in 1992 and 1996. While George W. Bush and Dick Cheney can lay claim to the Establishment, their outlooks run counter to many of the Establishment's orthodoxies.

16. See David Gergen, *Eyewitness to Power: The Essence of Leadership, Nixon to Clinton* (New York: Simon and Schuster, 2000), 86–87.

17. David Brooks, *Bobos in Paradise: The New Upper Class and How They Got There* (New York: Simon and Schuster, 2000), 20.

18. Emily Eakin, "More Ado (Yawn) About Great Books," *New York Times Education Supplement*, 8 April 2001, 24.

19. Allan Bloom, *The Closing of the American Mind* (New York: Simon and Schuster, 1987).

20. See Eakin, "More Ado (Yawn) About Great Books," 24.

21. Gallup poll, 25–28 October 2000; 10–14 January 2001; 26–28 March 2001.

22. Zogby International, press release, 17 April 2001. The poll was conducted 26 February–2 March 2001, and it found 43 percent favoring a three-year moratorium on legal immigration, 40 percent who said a suspension would be harmful to the state, and 16 percent had no opinion.

23. Patrick J. Buchanan, *The Death of the West* (New York: St. Martin's, 2002), 3.

24. Arian Campo-Flores, "A Town's Two Faces," *Newsweek*, 4 June 2001, 34.

25. See Eric Schmitt, "Whites in Minority in Largest Cities, the Census Shows," *New York Times*, 30 April 2001, A1.

26. Quoted in Alan Wolfe, *One Nation After All* (New York: Viking, 1998), 133. In 1987, Governor Bill Clinton signed legislation making English the official language of Arkansas. Congress has yet to pass such a law.

27. Robert J. Dole, Address to the American Legion Convention, Indianapolis, Indiana, 4 September 1995.

28. George W. Bush, Address to Congress, Washington, D.C., 27 February 2001.

29. See Mike Allen, "Bush: Respect Mexican Immigrants," *Washington Post*, 6 May 2001, A7.

30. George W. Bush, *A Charge to Keep: My Journey to the White House* (New York: HarperPerennial, 2001), 237.

31. *Alexander v. Sandoval*, 532 U.S. 275 (2001), 24 April 2001. The five justices in the majority were Scalia, Rehnquist, O'Connor, Kennedy, and Thomas. A dissenting opinion was filed by Justices Stevens, Souter, Ginsburg, and Breyer.

32. See Eric Schmitt, "U.S. Now More Diverse, Ethnically and Racially," *New York Times*, 1 April 2001, 18.

33. See Jim Yardley, "Non-Hispanic Whites May Soon Be a Minority in Texas," *New York Times*, 25 March 2001, 18; Dana Canedy, "Florida Has More Hispanics Than Blacks, Census Shows," *New York Times*, 28 March 2001; and Michael Janofsky, "Arizona Owes Growth Spurt Largely to an Influx of Hispanics, *New York Times*, 28 March 2001.

34. William Jefferson Clinton, "Erasing America's Color Lines," *New York Times*, 14 January 2001.

35. See David Margolick, "Brother Dearest," *Vanity Fair*, July 2001, 96.

36. George Bush, Address to the Republican National Convention, Philadelphia, Pennslyvania, 2 August 2000.

37. John Zogby, "John Zogby's Twenty-First Century Trends," Internet document, January 2001. See http://www.zogby.com

38. See F. James Davis, *Who Is Black?: One Nation's Definition* (University Park: Pennsylvania State University Press, 1991).

39. See Vinay Lal, "A Political History of Asian Indians in the United States," *Diaspora*. Internet site: http://www.sscnet.ucla.edu/southasia/Diaspora/roots.html.

40. See William Booth, "California's Ethnic Diversity Grows," *Washington Post*, 30 March 2001, A3; and D'Vera Cohn and Darryl Fears, "Multiracial Growth Seen in Census," *Washington Post*, 13 March 2001, A1. The national multi-race figure is 2.4 percent.

41. Associated Press, "San Diego Council Bans the Word 'Minority,'" CNN.com, 3 April 2001. Retrieved from: http://www.cnn.com/2001/US/04/03/minority.vote.ap/index.html

42. Quoted in Stan Grossfeld, "'It's a Good Life,'" *Boston Globe*, 6 May 2001, E1.

43. Ibid.

44. Schmitt, "Whites in Minority," A1.

45. Dale Russakoff, "Census Finds Diversity Spreading to Suburbs," *Washington Post*, 9 March 2001, A14.

46. D'Vera Cohn and Carol Morello, "Northern Virginia's Growth Outpaces State's," *Washington Post*, 9 March 2001, A1.

47. Cohn and Fears, "Multiracial Growth Seen in Census," A1.

48. Schmitt, "Whites in Minority," A1.

49. Russakoff, "Census Finds Diversity," A14; Genaro C. Armas, "Census Highlights Varied Racial Mix," *Boston Globe*, 9 March 2001, A3.

50. Chuck Taylor, "Ricky Martin: Stoking Latin Fires," *Billboard*, December 1999.

51. D'Vera Cohn, "Shifting Portrait of U.S. Hispanics," *Washington Post*, 10 May 2001, A1.

52. Frank Davies, "High Court Hears 'English-Only Case," *Orange County Register*, 17 January 2001, 1.
53. See Darryl Fears and Claudia Deane, "Biracial Couples Report Tolerance," *Washington Post*, 5 July 2001, A1.
54. *Washington Post*/Henry J. Kaiser Family Foundation/Harvard University poll, 29 March–20 May 2001.
55. *Loving v. Virginia*, 388 U.S. 1 (1967).
56. Ibid. After their convictions, the Lovings moved to Washington, D.C., which permitted interracial marriages.
57. Gallup poll, 24–29 September 1958.
58. National Opinion Research Center poll, April 1968.
59. Rovere, *American Establishment*, 11.
60. "A Marriage of Enlightenment," *Time*, 29 September 1967, 30.
61. Brooks, *Bobos in Paradise*, 14.
62. Cited in James Davison Hunter, *Culture Wars: The Struggle to Define America* (New York: Basic Books, 1991), 73.
63. The number of Muslims is in dispute partially due to the U.S. Census, which does not ask one's religious affiliation. For more on the varying numbers, see Bill Broadway, "Number of U.S. Muslims Depends on Who's Counting," *Washington Post*, 24 November 2001, A1.
64. Muslim immigration to the United States has come in five waves: (1) 1875–1912, (2) 1918–22, (3) 1930–38, (4) 1947–60, and (5) 1967–present. See Yvonne Haddad Yazbeck, *Islamic Values in the United States: A Comparative Study* (New York: Oxford University Press, 1987), 14.
65. U.S. State Department, "Islam in the United States: A Tentative Ascent, A Conversation with Yvonne Haddad." Retrieved from: http://www.usinfo.state.gov/usa/islam/hadad.htm
66. Christina A. Samuels, "Scarf Covers Virginia School in Religious Debate," *Washington Post*, 3 February 2001, B1.
67. See Peter Whoriskey, "Boom Bolsters Indian Community," *Washington Post*, 27 May 2001, A1.
68. See Patricia Leigh Brown, "With an Asian Influx, a Suburb Finds Itself Transformed," *New York Times*, 26 May 2001, A1.
69. Cited in Lal, "Political History of Asian Indians."
70. Cited in Whoriskey, "Boom Bolsters Indian Community," A1.
71. Cited in Patricia Digh, "Companies Make an Effort to Accommodate Religion," *Career Journal*, 10 September 1999 Retrieved from http://www.careerjournal.com/hrcenter/shrm/features/19990910-digh.html, and the U.S. State Department, "Islam in the United States," fact sheet. Retrieved from: http://www.usinfo.state.gov/usa/islam/fact2.htm
72. Quoted in "Soka Gakkai Buddhists Are Diverse Group in Search of Peace and Harmony," *Huntsville Times*, 21 October 2000.
73. Cited in Digh, "Companies Make an Effort."
74. "A Colorado Push for 'In God We Trust,'" *Washington Post*, 7 July 2000, A14.

75. Quoted in Joseph I. Lieberman, *The Power Broker: A Biography of John M. Bailey, Modern Political Boss* (Boston: Houghton Mifflin, 1966), 22.

76. U.S. Department of Commerce, Bureau of the Census, *Historical Statistics of the United States: Colonial Times to 1970* (Washington, D.C., 1975), 105–6.

77. See Daniel Chauncey Brewer, *The Conquest of New England by the Immigrant* (New York: G.P. Putnam and Sons, 1926), 120.

78. Steven Greenhouse, "Unions Hit Lowest Point in Six Decades," *New York Times,* 21 January 2001.

79. Peter D. Hart Research Associates poll, 14–17 September 2000.

80. See Frances Cairncross, *The Death of Distance* (Boston: Harvard Business School Press, 1997).

81. Roberta Fusaro, "Congress Sees E-Mail Flood During Trial," *Computerworld,* 2 February 1999.

82. Blum and Weprin Associates poll, 13–16 March 2000.

83. Cited in Wolfe, *One Nation After All,* 133.

84. Jack Hitt, "Does the Smell of Coffee Brewing Remind You of Your Mother?" *New York Times Magazine,* 7 May 2000, 74.

85. G.K. Chesterton, *What I Saw in America* (New York: Dodd, Mead and Company, 1922), 7.

86. Remarks by the president and First Lady in a national television address on drug abuse and prevention, Washington, D.C., 14 September 1986.

87. Bill Clinton, State of the Union address, Washington, D.C., 3 February 1997.

88. Jesse Ventura, interview, *Hardball with Chris Matthews,* CNBC, 6 October 1999.

89. See Norman Vincent Peale, *The Power of Positive Thinking* (New York: Prentice-Hall, 1952), Robert H. Schuller, *Move Ahead with Possibility Thinking* (Garden City, N.Y.: Doubleday, 1967), and Robert H. Schuller, *Success Is Never Ending, Failure Is Never Final* (Nashville, Tenn.: T. Nelson Publishers, 1988)

90. Michel-Guillaume-Jean de Crevecoeur, *Letters from an American Farmer, 1782,* in Henry Steele Commager, ed., *Living Ideas in America* (New York: Harper and Brothers, 1951), 21.

91. Princeton Survey Research Associates poll, 31 July–17 August 1997; Gallup poll, 10–14 January 2001.

92. Cited in Bill Broadway, "Good for the Soul—and the Bottom Line," *Washington Post,* 19 August 2001, A1.

93. Brooks, "Organization Kid," 40.

94. Cited in Karlyn Bowman, "The Family Dinner, Alive and Well," *New York Times,* 25 August 1999.

95. Quoted in Wolfe, *One Nation After All,* 99.

96. Interestingly, a 1950 Gallup poll found 4 percent had dinner before 5:00 P.M.; 11 percent at 5:00; 14 percent at 5:30; 2 percent at 5:45; 34 percent at 6:00; 2 percent at 6:15; 13 percent at 6:30; 11 percent at 7:00; 7 percent after 7:00; and 2 percent said no special time, it varies. Gallup poll, 29 June–4 July 1950.

97. Bruskin, Goldring Research poll, 16–18 October 1992; Peter D. Hart Research Associates poll, 14–17 September 2000.

98. See Jill Andresky Fraser, *White-Collar Sweatshop: The Deterioration of Work and Its Rewards in Corporate America* (New York: W.W. Norton, 2001), 76–77.

99. Peter D. Hart Research Associates poll, 12–16 April 2000.

100. Fraser, *White-Collar Sweatshop*, 3–4.

101. Louis Hartz, *The Liberal Tradition in America* (New York: Harcourt Brace Jovanovich, 1955).

102. The phrase "the American dream" was coined during the Great Depression by James Truslow Adams in *The Epic of America* (Boston: Little, Brown, 1935), 174.

103. Cited in Beatrice Gormley, *President George W. Bush: Our Forty-Third President* (New York: Aladdin Paperbacks, 2001), 81.

104. Hart and Teeter Research Companies poll, 20–24 February 1997; ABC News poll, 30 April–6 May 1996.

105. Wolfe, *One Nation After All*, 317–18.

106. Hart and Teeter Research Companies poll, 29–30 October 1997.

107. Gallup poll, 25–26 January 2000.

108. Gallup/CNN/*USA Today* poll, 15–17 December 2000; Gallup/CNN/*USA Today* poll, 5–7 May 2000; NBC News/*Wall Street Journal* poll, 9–12 September 1999; ABC News poll, 16–22 August 1999.

109. Cited in Everett Carll Ladd Jr., *The American Polity* (New York: W.W. Norton, 1987), 67.

110. Roper Organization poll, October 1986.

111. Cited in "Zogby Poll Views Young America for Korean Readers," Zogby International press release, 30 March 2001.

112. Quoted in Rick Marin, "Is This the Face of a Midlife Crisis?" *New York Times Sunday Styles*, 24 June 2001, 1.

113. Ibid.

114. David Noonan, "Wall Street's New Pitch," *Newsweek*, 12 March 2001, 48.

115. Richard B. Wirthlin, "Responding to Shifts in Employee Values," *The Wirthlin Report*, March 2001, 1.

116. Zogby, "John Zogby's Twenty-First Century Trends."

117. See Broadway, "Good for the Soul—and the Bottom Line," A1.

118. See Diana Leafe Christian, "An Alternate Version of the American Dream," *Boston Globe*, 4 March 2001, E8.

119. Blum and Weprin Associates poll, 13–16 March 2000.

120. *Washington Post* poll, 7–17 September 2000.

121. See Peter Carlson, "'My Wife and Kids': Make Room for Everydaddy," *Washington Post*, 28 March 2001, C1.

122. Opinion Dynamics poll, 23–24 June 1999.

123. Cited in Everett Carll Ladd Jr., *The Ladd Report* (New York: Free Press, 1999), 112–13.

124. Quoted in Robert Lane, *Political Ideology: Why the Common Man Believes What He Does* (New York: Free Press, 1962), 69.

125. Chesterton, *What I Saw in America*, 4.

126. Eric Hoffer, *The True Believer* (New York: Harper and Row, 1951), xi.

127. Gary Wills, *Inventing America* (New York: Vintage Books, 1978), xxii.

128. For a greater elaboration, see John Kenneth White, *Still Seeing Red: How the Cold War Shapes the New American Politics* (Boulder: Westview Press, 1998).

129. Daniel J. Boorstin, *The Genius of American Politics* (Chicago: University of Chicago Press, 1953), 14.

130. Gallup Organization poll, 4–9 April 1968.

131. Hartz, *Liberal Tradition in America*, 58.

132. Quoted in Thomas E. Cronin, *The State of the Presidency* (Boston: Little, Brown, 1980), 161.

133. See especially Seymour Martin Lipset, *American Exceptionalism: A Double-Edged Sword* (New York: W.W. Norton, 1996).

134. Gallup poll, June 1938.

135. Gallup poll, 30 July–4 August 1950.

136. Quoted in Lipset, *American Exceptionalism*, 291.

137. Quoted in Morton J. Frisch, ed., *Selected Writings and Speeches of Alexander Hamilton* (Washington, D.C.: American Enterprise Institute, 1985), 316.

138. Dwight D. Eisenhower, acceptance speech, Republican National Convention, San Francisco, 23 August 1956.

139. John Kenneth Galbraith, *The Affluent Society* (Boston: Houghton Mifflin, 1958), 18–19.

140. Roper Organization poll, 22–29 August 1987.

141. "Proceedings of the State Conference on Immigration in Massachusetts Industries," *Bulletin of the Department of Education*, 5 November 1920.

142. Cited in Edward B. Fiske, "With Old Values and New Titles, Civics Courses Make a Comeback," *New York Times*, 7 June 1987, 1.

143. National Opinion Research Center, General Social Surveys, 1996 poll. Reported in *The Public Perspective*, February/March 1997, 9.

144. Roper Organization poll, May 1992.

145. *Washington Post*/Henry J. Kaiser Family Foundation/Harvard University poll, 29 July–18 August 1998.

146. Hart and Teeter Research Companies poll, 7–10 December 2000.

147. Quoted in Morin and Broder, "Worries about Nation's Morals," A1.

148. The no-marriage rule was imposed in 1949 after Miss America Jacque Mercer got married and divorced during her year-long tenure. The current rule asks contestants to affirm the following: "I am unmarried. I am not pregnant, and I am not the natural or adoptive parent of any child."

149. Ann Gerhart, "Miss America Relaxes Rules for Its Ideal," *Washington Post*, 14 September 1999, C1.

150. Ann Gerhart, "Pregnant Pause for Pageant," *Washington Post*, 15 September 1999, C1.

151. Gallup poll, 10–14 May 2001.

152. Gallup poll, 18–20 May 2001.

153. Cited in Gerhart, "Pregnant Pause for Pageant," C1.

154. Gallup poll, 10–14 May 2001.

155. *Washington Post*/Henry J. Kaiser Family Foundation/Harvard University poll, 29 July–18 August 1998.

156. See D'Vera Cohn, "Married-with-Children Still Fading," *Washington Post*, 15 May 2001, A1.

157. Eric Schmitt, "For First Time, Nuclear Families Drop Below 25% of Households," *New York Times*, 15 May 2001, A1. See also E.J. Dionne Jr., "The Myth of the Fading Family," *Washington Post*, 23 May 2001, A21.

158. Barbara Kantrowitz and Pat Wingert, "Unmarried, with Children," *Newsweek*, 28 May 2001, 48.

159. Schmitt, "For First Time, Nuclear Families Drop," A1.

160. See D'Vera Cohn, "Census Shows Big Increase in Gay Households," *Washington Post*, 20 June 2001, A1.

161. See Cohn, "Married-with-Children Still Fading," A1.

162. Data acquired from John Zogby, "Love, Sex and Romance," Zogby International polls, 2000.

163. See "Zogby Poll Views Young America for Korean Readers."

164. Kristen Wyatt, "Carter Cuts Southern Baptist Tie," *Washington Post*, 21 October 2000, A4.

165. Quoted in Hunter, *Culture Wars*, 112–13.

166. Ibid., 50, 64.

167. Ibid., 144, 148.

168. Ibid., 181.

169. See People for the American Way, www.pfaw.org.

170. Zogby International poll, 2–6 May 2000.

171. Quoted in Wolfe, *One Nation After All*, 99.

172. Dan Quayle, Address to the Commonwealth Club of California, San Francisco, 19 May 1992.

173. See Ariel Kaminer, "What Do We Talk About When We Are Paying Someone to Listen," *New York Times Magazine*, 7 May 2000, 79.

174. Quoted in Sharon Waxman, "Sex on TV: Study Finds More, Sooner but Safer," *Washington Post*, 7 February 2001, C1.

175. "*Survivor* Viewers Want to See Jerri Voted Out Next," Gallup press release, 14 March 2001.

176. Dan Quayle, *Standing Firm* (New York: HarperCollins, 1994), 247.

177. Wolfe, *One Nation After All*, 11.

178. Robert Bork, *Slouching Towards Gomorrah: Modern Liberalism and American Decline* (New York: Regan Books, 1996), 139.

179. Quoted in Hunter, *Culture Wars*, 311.

180. Robert J. Dole, "State of the Union: The Republican Response," Washington, D.C., 23 January 1996.

181. Quoted in Hunter, *Culture Wars*, 64.

182. *Washington Post*/Henry J. Kaiser Family Foundation/Harvard University poll, 29 July–18 August 1998.

183. Quoted in Morin and Broder, "Worries about Nation's Morals," A1.

184. Princeton Survey Research Associates poll, 13–14 April 2000; *Washington Post*/Henry J. Kaiser Family Foundation poll, 7–17 September 2000; Princeton Survey Research Associates poll, 24 August–10 September 2000.

185. Gallup poll, 14–19 February 1958.
186. Gallup poll, press release, 1 March 2001.
187. Quoted in Hanna Rosin, "In Unexpected Ways, Issues of Faith Shape the Debate," *Washington Post*, 29 October 1998, A1.
188. NBC News/*Wall Street Journal* poll, 13–15 October 2000.
189. Gallup poll, 5–10 December 1963.
190. CNN/*USA Today*/Gallup poll, 18–19 August 2000.
191. Gallup poll, 11–20 March 1988.
192. Public Agenda Foundation poll, 4–25 November 2000. Emphasis added.
193. *Washington Post*/Henry J. Kaiser Family Foundation/Harvard University poll, 7–17 September 2000.
194. Quoted in Wolfe, *One Nation After All*, 68, 54.
195. "Americans More Religious Now than Ten Years Ago, but Less so than in the 1950s and 1960s," Gallup press release, 29 March 2001. The index measures the respondent's belief in God; the ability of the respondent to state a religious preference; whether the respondent is a member of a church; whether the respondent attended church in the past seven days; the importance of religion in the respondent's life; whether the respondent believes that religion answers problems; whether the respondent places a high level of confidence in organized religion; and whether the respondent gives a high rating to the ethical standards of the clergy.
196. *Washington Post*/Henry J. Kaiser Family Foundation poll, 29 July–18 August 1998.
197. Blum and Weprin Associates poll, 13–16 March 2000.
198. Quoted in Daniel Bell, "The New Class: A Muddled Concept," in B. Bruce Briggs, ed., *The New Class?* (New Brunswick, N.J.: Transaction Books, 1979), 186, 170.
199. Henry James, letter (1872) in biographical note to *Letters of Henry James*, ed. Percy Lubbock (1920), vol. 1.
200. Quoted in D'Vera Cohn and April Witt, "Minorities Fuel Growth in Maryland Suburbs," *Washington Post*, 20 March 2001, A1.
201. Quoted in Gary L. Rose, *Connecticut Government at the Millennium* (Fairfield, Conn.: Sacred Heart University Press, 2001), 81.
202. Executive Order 10980, signed 14 December 1961.
203. Executive Order 11126, signed 1 November 1963.
204. Lyndon B. Johnson, Commencement Address, University of Michigan, Ann Arbor, 22 May 1964.
205. Quoted in Garry Wills, *Nixon Agonistes: The Crisis of the Self-Made Man* (Boston: Houghton Mifflin, 1970), 50.
206. E.E. Schattschneider, *The Semi-Sovereign People: A Realist's View of Democracy in America* (reprint, Hinsdale, Ill.: Dryden Press, 1975), 15.
207. Jean Bethke Elshtain, *Democracy on Trial* (New York: Basic Books, 1995), 38.
208. Dwight D. Eisenhower, *Mandate for Change* (Garden City, N.Y.: Doubleday, 1963), 46. Emphasis added.
209. Irving Kristol, *Neoconservatism: The Autobiography of an Idea* (New York: Free Press, 1995), 486.
210. *Washington Post*/Henry J. Kaiser Family Foundation poll, 7–17 September 2000.
211. Barney Frank, interview by author, Washington, D.C., 20 December 2000.

212. Alexis de Tocqueville, *Democracy in America* (New York: Alfred A. Knopf, 1989), 2: 215–16.

213. Wilson Carey McWilliams, "The Meaning of the Election," in *The Election of 2000*, ed. Gerald M. Pomper (New York: Chatham House, 2001), 192.

214. Ibid.

215. Vaclav Havel, "The State of the Republic," *New York Review of Books*, 5 March 1998, 42.

216. Gallup poll, 28–29 December 1998.

217. Gallup poll, 2–5 February 1979.

218. See Wirthlin, "Responding to Shifts in Employee Values," 4.

219. Mary Ann Glendon, *Rights Talk: The Impoverishment of Political Discourse* (New York: Free Press, 1991), x.

220. Quoted in Wolfe, *One Nation After All*, 290–91.

Chapter 3: Republicans and the Politics of Virtue

1. Quoted in Leon D. Epstein, *Political Parties in the American Mold* (Madison: University of Wisconsin Press, 1986), 18.

2. Committee on Political Parties, *Toward a More Responsible Two-Party System* (New York: Rinehart, 1950), 15.

3. See, for example, John Kenneth White and Jerome M. Mileur, eds., *Challenges to Party Government* (Carbondale: Southern Illinois University Press, 1992).

4. From "Strengthening the Political Parties," a position paper adopted by the Committee for Party Renewal in 1980 and presented to both national party committees.

5. Penn, Schoen and Berland Associates poll, 11–12 November 2000.

6. Alexis de Tocqueville, *Democracy in America* (New York: Alfred A. Knopf, 1989), 2: 96.

7. G.K. Chesterton, *What I Saw in America* (New York: Dodd, Mead and Company, 1922), 16, 17.

8. 1936 Democratic National Platform, as reprinted in the *New York Times*, 26 June 1936, 1.

9. Franklin D. Roosevelt, State of the Union address, Washington, D.C., 6 January 1941.

10. Lyndon B. Johnson, "To Fulfill These Rights," Commencement Address, Howard University, Washington, D.C., 4 June 1965.

11. Lyndon B. Johnson, "Remarks at a Fund-raising Dinner in New Orleans" (9 October 1964), in *Public Papers of the Presidents: Lyndon B. Johnson, 1963–1964* (Washington, D.C.: U.S. Government Printing Office, 1965), 1286.

12. Quoted in Theodore H. White, *The Making of the President, 1964* (New York: Atheneum, 1965), 382–83.

13. Hillary Rodham Clinton, Address to the Democratic National Convention, Chicago, 27 August 1996.

14. Hillary Rodham Clinton, *It Takes a Village and Other Lessons Children Teach Us* (New York: Simon and Schuster, 1996), 7.

15. H. Clinton, Address to the Democratic National Convention. Emphasis added.

16. See Arthur M. Schlesinger Jr., *The Cycles of American History* (Boston: Houghton

Mifflin, 1986). Republican Theodore Roosevelt is a notable exception. Stephen Skowronek believes that Bill Clinton was operating in an environment that was hostile to activist Democrats. See Stephen Skowronek, *The Politics Presidents Make: Leadership from John Adams to George Bush* (Cambridge, Mass.: Belknap Press, 1993).

17. Quoted in Robert Samuelson, "To Honor My Country," *Washington Post*, 4 July 2001, A19.

18. 1936 Republican National Platform, as reprinted in the *New York Times*, 12 June 1936, 1.

19. Alfred M. Landon, "Text of Governor Landon's Milwaukee Address on Social Security," Milwaukee, Wis., 27 September 1936. Retrieved from: http://199.173.224.3/history/alfspeech.html

20. See 1936 Republican National Platform.

21. Landon, "Milwaukee Address."

22. See especially Richard Ben Cramer, *Bob Dole* (New York: Vintage Books, 1995).

23. "Transcript of the First Presidential Debate," *Washington Post*, 7 October 1996.

24. Dole bowed slightly in this belief by accepting Jack Kemp to be his 1996 vice-presidential running mate. Kemp had been a longtime advocate of supply-side economics, which Dole had previously loathed.

25. Bob Dole, acceptance speech, Republican National Convention, San Diego, 15 August 1996. Emphasis added.

26. Herbert J. Storing, *What the Anti-Federalists Were For* (Chicago: University of Chicago Press, 1981), 16.

27. Quoted in Jean Bethke Elshtain, *Democracy on Trial* (New York: Basic Books, 1995), 9.

28. 1936 Republican National Platform.

29. "Landon's Message to Convention," *New York Times*, 13 June 1936, 7.

30. George H. W. Bush, acceptance speech, Republican National Convention, New Orleans, Louisiana, 18 August 1988.

31. Alexis de Tocqueville, *Democracy in America* (New York: New American Library, 1956), 194. Emphasis added.

32. *Olmstead v. U.S.*, 279 U.S. 849 (1925): 476.

33. Ronald Reagan, debate with Jimmy Carter, Cleveland, Ohio, 29 October 1980.

34. Public Opinion Strategies poll, 29–30 January 1992.

35. Peter D. Hart Research Associates poll, 16–20 March 1999.

36. "Landon's Message to Convention," 7. Emphasis added.

37. Tom Wicker, *One of Us: Richard Nixon and the American Dream* (New York: Random House, 1991), 686.

38. See John Kenneth White, *The New Politics of Old Values*, 2d ed. (Hanover, N.H.: University Press of New England, 1990), 61.

39. Ronald Reagan, State of the Union address, Washington, D.C., 25 January 1984.

40. Alexander Hamilton, "*Federalist* 68," in Clinton Rossiter, ed., *The Federalist Papers* (New York: New American Library, 1961), 414.

41. Although its members had never met Goldwater, they deemed him unstable anyway. Goldwater later sued for libel and won. See Michael J. Gerson, "Mr. Right," *U.S. News & World Report*, 8 June 1998.

42. "The Classics of Political TV Advertising I," Washington, D.C., video produced by *Campaigns and Elections* magazine, 1986.

43. Aaron Wildavsky, "The Goldwater Phenomenon: Purists, Politicians, and the Two-Party System," in Norman L. Zucker, ed., *The American Party Process: Readings and Comments* (New York: Dodd, Mead, 1968), 445.

44. For more on the Republicans and the Cold War, see John Kenneth White, *Still Seeing Red: How the Cold War Shapes the New American Politics* (Boulder: Westview Press, 1998).

45. "Robertson's Grand Design," *U.S. News & World Report*, 22 February 1988, 17.

46. Jerelyn Eddings, "A Republican Civil War: Can Dole Unite a Party Divided Over Abortion?" *U.S. News & World Report*, 8 July 1996, 38.

47. See Evan Thomas, Karen Breslau, Debra Rosenberg, Leslie Kaufman, and Andrew Murr, *Back from the Dead* (New York: Atlantic Monthly Press, 1997), 126–28.

48. John McCain, "Building a New Republican Majority," speech, Virginia Beach, Virginia, 28 February 2000.

49. Ibid.

50. See Mark J. Rozell, "The Christian Right in the 2000 GOP Presidential Campaign," in Mary Segers, ed., *Religion and Liberal Democracy: An American Perspective* (Lanham, Md.: Rowman and Littlefield, 2001). It should be noted that the loyalty oath was nonbinding; nonetheless, more independent-minded McCain supporters were put-off by it and chose not to vote.

51. Quoted in David Corn, "George W. Bush and Jesus Christ," *Commonsense*, 18 January 2001. See http://www.tompaine.com.

52. See Rozell, "Christian Right."

53. Paul Alexander, "John McCain's War on the White House," *Rolling Stone*, 7 June 2001, 42.

54. John Ashcroft, "We Have No King but Jesus," speech, Bob Jones University, Greenville, South Carolina, 8 May 1999.

55. Peter Perl, "The Gospel According to Tom DeLay," *Washington Post Magazine*, 13 May 2001, 14, 15.

56. "The Quotations of Chairman Helms: Race, God, AIDS, and More," *New York Times*, 26 August 2001, WK5.

57. Robert Aderholt, interview by author, Washington, D.C., 11 July 2000.

58. Quoted in "Perspectives," *Newsweek*, 23 April 2001, 17.

59. See Mark J. Rozell and Clyde Wilcox, *Second Coming: The New Christian Right in Virginia Politics* (Baltimore: Johns Hopkins University Press, 1996), 5.

60. Quoted in Nicholas Confessore, "Born Again," *American Prospect*, 13 August 2001, 10.

61. James Jeffords, statement announcing he is leaving the Republican Party, Burlington, Vermont, 24 May 2001.

62. Quoted in Benjamin Soskis, "State's Right," *New Republic*, 11 June 2001, 25.

63. See Michael Powell, "Jeffords in Step with New England," *Washington Post*, 27 May 2001, A5.

64. *Burlington Free Press*/WPTZ poll, 24 May 2001.

65. Quoted in Powell, "Jeffords in Step with New England," A5.

66. Robin Toner, "New England: Jeffords's Move Would Echo Trend Toward Inde-

pendence in the Region," *New York Times*, 24 May 2001, A1. Weicker's "A Connecticut Party" lost much of its influence after he decided not to seek reelection in 1998.

67. Michael Forbes, "Jeffords's Maverick Move," *Washington Post*, 25 May 2001, A39.

68. Quoted in Christopher S. Wren with Alison Mitchell, "Senator Makes Switch from GOP," *New York Times*, 24 May 2001, A1. McCain's remark parallels one made by Barry Goldwater in 1960 when Goldwater told conservatives at the Republican National Convention that they needed to "grow up" and take over the party machinery, which they did.

69. Michael S. Greve, "Federalism after the Election," *AEI Federalist Outlook, Number 4* (Washington, D.C.: American Enterprise Institute, December 2000).

70. Cited in Robert M. Eisinger, "Cynical America? Misunderstanding the Public's Message," *The Public Perspective*, April/May 1999, 47.

71. Barry M. Goldwater with Jack Casserly, *Goldwater* (New York: Doubleday, 1988), 385.

72. Quoted in Russell Baker, "Mr. Right," *New York Review of Books*, 17 May 2001, 8.

73. Cited in Bart Barnes, "Barry Goldwater, GOP Hero, Dies," *Washington Post*, 30 May 1998, A1.

74. Quoted in Stephen Shadegg, *What Happened to Goldwater? The Inside Story of the 1964 Republican Campaign* (New York: Holt, Rinehart, and Winston, 1965), 24, 28.

75. Quoted in Dana Milbank, "A Marriage of Family and Policy," *Washington Post*, 15 April 2001, A1.

76. Quoted in Thomas B. Edsall, "Conservatives Mobilize Against Gay Appointee," *Washington Post*, 12 April 2001, A4.

77. Ibid.

78. See Ben White, "Conservative Group Assails White House 'Trend' on Gays," *Washington Post*, 30 September 2001, A4.

79. Associated Press, "Bush Administration Broadens Overtures Toward Gays," CNN.com, 28 October 2001.

80. See Dana Milbank, "House Education Bill Got It Wrong for Some Critics on the Right," *Washington Post*, 7 May 2001, A4.

81. Dana Milbank, "Clear Break from the Right May Be Brief," *Washington Post*, 10 August 2001, A1.

82. "Only the Beginning," *Newsweek*, 20 August 2001, 19.

83. Clinton Rossiter, *Parties and Politics in America* (Ithaca, N.Y.: Cornell University Press, 1960), 11.

84. See E.J. Dionne Jr., "A Conservative Call for Compassion," *New York Times*, 30 November 1987, B12.

85. Cited in Rozell and Wilcox, *Second Coming*, 265.

86. Constance Morella, interview by author, Washington, D.C., 13 June 2000.

87. Paul Weyrich, letter to Free Congress Foundation supporters, Washington, D.C., 16 February 1999.

88. Cal Thomas and Ed Dobson, "Blinded by Might: The Problem with Heaven on Earth," in E.J. Dionne Jr. and John J. DiIulio Jr., *What's God Got to Do with the American Experiment?* (Washington, D.C.: Brookings Institution Press, 2000), 52.

89. Ronald Reagan, remarks at an ecumenical prayer breakfast, Dallas, 23 August 1984.

90. Quoted in David S. Broder, "A Prescient Assessment of Reagan," *Washington Post*, 9 December 1992, A23.

91. Weyrich, letter to Free Congress Foundation supporters.

92. Steve May, telephone interview by author, 19 March 2000.

93. Morella, interview.

94. Aderholt, interview.

95. Associated Press, "'Ten Commandments Judge' Sworn in as Alabama Chief Justice," CNN.com, 15 January 2001. Retrieved from: http://www.cnn.com/2001/ALLPOLITICS/stories/01/15/ten.commandments.jud.../index.htm

96. Associated Press, "'Ten Commandments Judge' Seeking Chief Justice Job in Alabama," CNN.com, 23 October 2000. Retrieved from: http://www.cnn.com/2000LAW/10/23/religion.judge.ap/index.html

97. Dole, acceptance speech, 15 August 1996.

98. Tucker Carlson, "Devil May Care," *Talk*, September 1999, 106. Ironically, King never asked Tucker the question, "What would you say to Governor Bush?" that prompted Bush's mocking response. Bush claimed to have seen the program and remembered this question, among others, as softballs lobbed by King at Tucker.

99. Peter D. Hart Research Associates poll, 16–20 March 1999.

100. Paul Koenig, "Does Congress Abuse Its Spending Clause Power by Attaching Conditions on the Receipt of Federal Law Enforcement Funds to a State's Compliance with 'Megan's Law'?" *Journal of Criminal Law and Criminology* 88, 2 (Winter 1998): 721–65.

101. Cited in *Texas v. Johnson*, 491 U.S. 397 (1989).

102. ABC News/*Washington Post* poll, 17–21 August 1989.

103. ABC News/*Washington Post* poll, 6–9 September 1990.

104. Princeton Survey Research Associates poll, 3–15 September 1996.

105. Louis Harris and Associates poll, 21–26 June 1990.

106. Patrick Brady, "At Issue: Should Congress Approve a Constitutional Amendment to Permit Laws Prohibiting the Physical Desecration of the Flag?" *Congressional Quarterly Researcher*, 25 June 1999, 561.

107. Quoted in Kenneth Jost, "Patriotism in America," *Congressional Quarterly Researcher*, 25 June 1999, 548.

108. "Senate Raises Flag Amendment Again," *Washington Post*, 28 March 2000, A4.

109. Center for Research and Analysis survey, University of Connecticut, 3–26 April 2000.

110. Senate Judiciary Committee Report to S.J. Resolution 14. Retrieved from http://thomas.loc.gov

111. Quoted in Dan Carney, "Beyond Guns and Violence: A Battle for House Control," CNN.com, 21 June 1999.

112. Sean Scully, "Ten Commandments Rider Passes," *Washington Times*, 18 June 1999, A1.

113. Quoted in wire reports, "House OKs Ten Commandments Bill," *Richmond Times-Dispatch*, 18 June 1999, A1.

114. Scully, "Ten Commandments Rider Passes," A1. Wamp's bill was defeated after other Republicans warned that it would give the federal government too much power over the mass media.

115. Robert Aderholt, press release, 17 June 1999.

116. Quoted in David Hess, "House Backs Ten Commandments Display," *Philadelphia Inquirer*, 18 June 1999, A1.
117. Aderholt, press release.
118. Quoted in Michael Barone and Grant Ujifusa, *The Almanac of American Politics, 1998* (Washington, D.C.: National Journal, 1997), 66.
119. Peter D. Hart and Teeter Research and Associates poll, 16–20 March 1999.
120. Gallup poll, 25–27 June 1999; Hart and Teeter Research Companies poll, 16–19 June 1999.
121. Hart and Teeter Research Companies poll, 16–19 June 1999.
122. Aderholt, interview.
123. Quoted in Hanna Rosin and William Claiborne, "Taking the Commandments Public," *Washington Post*, 8 February 2000, A3.
124. Quoted in David Pace, "Aderholt Asks House to Give States Right to Display Ten Commandments," *Daily Mountain Eagle* (Jasper, Ala.), 17 June 1999, 1.
125. Quoted in Michael Brumas, "House OKs Bill Allowing State Displays of Ten Commandments," *Birmingham News*, 18 June 1999, 1A.
126. Quoted in Scully, "Ten Commandments Rider Passes."
127. Aderholt, interview.
128. Morella, interview.
129. Quoted by David Brinkley, ABC News, 8 November 1988. Author's personal tape recording. Emphasis added.
130. Quoted in Dick Kirschten, "Second Thoughts," *National Journal*, 21 January 1995, 150.
131. Quoted in William Booth, "In a Rush, New Citizens Register Their Political Interest," *Washington Post*, 26 September 1996, A1.
132. William Claiborne, "Democrats Don't Have Lock on Hispanic Vote, Latino Leaders Say," *Washington Post*, 24 November 1996, A12.
133. Voter News Services exit polls, 7 November 2000.
134. Robert J. Dole, transcript, *This Week with David Brinkley*, ABC News, 17 September 1995.
135. "House Votes to Bar Gay Marriages Under Federal Law," CNN.com, 12 July 1996.
136. Quoted in Barone and Ujifusa, *Almanac of American Politics, 1998*, 254.
137. "House Votes."
138. "Senate Says No to Gay Marriage," CNN.com, 10 September 1996.
139. "House Says No to Same-Sex Marriages," CNN.com, 12 July 1996.
140. Princeton Survey Research Associates poll, 9–10 March 2000.
141. CBS News/*New York Times* poll, 10–12 January 1998; Hart and Teeter Research Companies poll, 17–19 January 1998.
142. Ibid.
143. CNN/AllPolitics, "House Passes Bill to Restrict Teen Abortions," 1 July 1999.
144. Quoted in David E. Rosenbaum, "House Passes Bill to Restrict Minors' Abortions," *New York Times*, 1 July 1999, A12.
145. CNN/AllPolitics, "House Passes Bill."
146. Bill Clinton, "Remarks on Returning Without Approval to the House of Representatives Partial-Birth Abortion Legislation," *Weekly Compilation of Presidential Documents*, 13 October 1997, 1545.

147. "The Prosecution's Opening Statements," *Washington Post*, 15 January 1999, A22.

148. "We Stand Poised on the Edge of a Constitutional Cliff," *Washington Post*, 11 December 1998, A28.

149. Quoted in Peter Baker, "Judge Orders Lewinsky to Cooperate," *Washington Post*, 24 January 1999, A18.

150. Quoted in Lars-Erik Nelson, "The Republicans' War," *New York Review of Books*, 4 February 1999, 6.

151. Gallup poll, Party Favorability Ratings, press release, November 1998. December 1992: Republican favorable, 62 percent; Democratic favorable, 73 percent (R-D= –11 percent). December 1993: Republican favorable, 73 percent; Democratic favorable, 68 percent (R-D= +5 percent). November 1994: Republican favorable, 70 percent; Democratic favorable, 55 percent (R-D = +15 percent). January 1996: Republican favorable, 61 percent; Democratic favorable, 62 percent (R-D = –1 percent). October 1996: Republican favorable, 63 percent; Democratic favorable, 70 percent (R-D = –7 percent). November 1998: Republican favorable, 57 percent; Democratic favorable, 68 percent (R-D = –11 percent).

152. Zogby International poll, February 1999.

153. Gallup poll, 24 May 2001.

154. Andrew Sullivan, "Going Down Screaming," *New York Times Magazine*, 11 October 1998, 48.

155. Ibid., 90.

156. Quoted in Thomas B. Edsall, "Spirit of the Body Politic Worries Religious Right," *Washington Post*, 12 November 1998, A6.

157. Peter D. Hart Research Associates poll, 16–20 March 1999.

158. Ibid.

159. CNN/*USA Today*/Gallup poll, 8–10 October 1999.

160. *Washington Post*/Henry J. Kaiser Family Foundation/Harvard University poll, 7–17 September 2000.

161. Peter D. Hart Research Associates poll, 16–20 March 1999.

162. The Mellman Group poll, 31 May–2 June 1996.

163. *Washington Post*/Henry J. Kaiser Family Foundation/Harvard University poll, 7–17 September 2000.

164. May, telephone interview.

165. Quoted in James Traub, "Newt at Rest," *New York Times Magazine*, 29 October 2000, 55.

166. See Alan Wolfe, *Moral Freedom: The Impossible Idea that Defines the Way We Live Now* (New York: W.W. Norton, 2001), 197.

167. Dan Balz, "Picking Up Votes in a Maze of Ideals," *Washington Post*, 5 October 1998, A1.

Chapter 4: Democrats and the Lingering Legacy of Bill Clinton

1. Bill Clinton, Remarks by the President at the Dedication of the Franklin Delano Roosevelt Memorial, Washington, D.C., 2 May 1997.

2. Quoted In Michael Waldman, *Potus Speaks: Finding the Words that Defined the Clinton Presidency* (New York: Simon and Schuster, 2000), 180.

3. Ibid., 181.

4. David Maraniss, *First in His Class: The Biography of Bill Clinton* (New York: Simon and Schuster, 1995), 437.

5. "Ronald Reagan and David Brinkley: A Farewell Interview," ABC News, 22 December 1988.

6. Quoted in Lou Cannon, "Why the Band Has Stopped Playing for Ronald Reagan," *Washington Post*, 21 December 1986, D1.

7. The Kennedy-Rossiter anecdote is found in Theodore C. Sorensen, *Kennedy* (New York: Harper and Row, 1965), 392.

8. Quoted in Edward Pessen, *The Log Cabin Myth: The Social Backgrounds of the Presidents* (New Haven: Yale University Press, 1984), 25.

9. Quoted in Bruce Oudes, ed., *From the President: Richard Nixon's Secret Files* (New York: Harper and Row, 1989), 565.

10. See, in particular, Kiron K. Skinner, Annelise Anderson, and Martin Anderson, eds., *Reagan in His Own Hand* (New York: Free Press, 2001).

11. Peggy Noonan, *What I Saw at the Revolution* (New York: Random House, 1990), 67.

12. Quoted in "Ronald Reagan and David Brinkley: A Farewell Interview."

13. See John Kenneth White, *The New Politics of Old Values,* 2d ed. (Hanover, N.H.: University Press of New England, 1990).

14. Richard B. Wirthlin, *Final Report of the Initial Actions Project,* 29 January 1981, 31. This document is unpublished. I am grateful to Dr. Wirthlin for the opportunity to peruse it and take notes from it.

15. Quoted in Everett Carll Ladd, *Where Have All the Voters Gone?* (New York: W. W. Norton, 1982), 111.

16. Richard B. Wirthlin, interview by author, Washington, D.C., 22 November 1988.

17. Quoted in "Flawed Vision," *Washington Post*, 21 August 1988, A22. According to the article, Reagan never received such a letter. Instead, the words had been penned nineteen years earlier by Mark Hawley in an essay printed in *Scouting Magazine* in 1969. Said Hawley, "It was part of a requirement for a Cub Scout badge, probably citizenship or something."

18. "Best Lines Slung from Tongues in '88," *Providence Journal*, 3 January 1989, B4.

19. Accounts of this session are taken from Donald Morrison, ed., *The Winning of the White House, 1988* (New York: Time, 1988), 219, and "How Bush Won: The Inside Story of Campaign '88," *Newsweek*, 21 November 1988, 100.

20. *Los Angeles Times* poll, 13–15 October 1988.

21. Garry Wills, "Introduction," in Morrison, *Winning of the White House,* 5.

22. Quoted in Hugh Heclo, "The Emerging Regime," in Richard A. Harris and Sidney M. Milkis, eds., *Remaking American Politics* (Boulder: Westview Press, 1989), 313.

23. KRC Communications poll for the *Presidential Campaign Hotline,* 1–5 November 1988.

24. Quoted in Wilson Carey McWilliams, *Beyond the Politics of Disappointment? American Elections, 1980–1998* (New York: Chatham House, 2000), 49.

25. "Excerpts from Interview with Clinton on Goals for Presidency," *New York Times,* 28 June 1992, 17.

26. David Kusnet, *Speaking American: How the Democrats Can Win in the Nineties* (New York: Thunder's Mouth Press, 1992).

27. Dan Balz, "Picking Up Votes in a Maze of Ideals," *Washington Post,* 5 October 1998, A1.

28. Quoted on the *MacNeill/Lehrer NewsHour,* PBS, 25 September 1992.

29. Bill Clinton, Acceptance Speech, Democratic National Convention, New York, 16 July 1992.

30. *Democratic Party Platform, 1996* (Washington, D.C.: Democratic National Committee, 1996), 17.

31. *Democratic Party Platform, 1992* (Washington, D.C.: Democratic National Committee, 1992), 7.

32. *Democratic Party Platform, 1996,* 17.

33. Cited in William Schneider, "Performance Trumps Character," *National Journal,* 31 January 1998, 231.

34. Gallup Organization poll, 10–11 November 1992.

35. Patrick J. Buchanan, Speech to the Republican National Convention, Houston, 17 August 1992.

36. ABC News/*Washington Post* poll, 26–30 August 1992.

37. CBS News poll, 18–19 August 1992.

38. ABC News/*Washington Post* poll, 4 October 1992.

39. CBS News/*New York Times* poll, 9–13 September 1992.

40. Hugh Scott, minority leader of the U.S. Senate, said in 1972 that the McGovernites favored the "three As," that is, "acid," "abortion," and "amnesty." See Ben J. Wattenberg, *Values Matter Most: How Republicans or Democrats or a Third Party Can Win and Renew the American Way of Life* (New York: Free Press, 1995), 27.

41. Quoted in Francis X. Clines, "Civics 101: Cultivating Grass Roots the Old Way," *New York Times,* 4 November 1992, B1.

42. Lynne Duke, "Clinton Chats with Reagan, Visits Suburban Mall," *Washington Post,* 28 November 1992, A7.

43. Voter Research and Surveys exit poll, 3 November 1992.

44. Quoted in Jeffrey Schmaltz, "Americans Are Sadder and Wiser, but Not Apathetic," *New York Times,* 1 November 1992, E1.

45. Matthew Robert Kerbel, *Remote and Controlled: Media Politics in a Cynical Age* (Boulder: Westview Press, 1995), 1.

46. Quoted in Evan Thomas, Karen Breslau, Debra Rosenberg, Leslie Kaufman, and Andrew Murr, *Back from the Dead: How Clinton Survived the Republican Revolution* (New York: Atlantic Monthly Press, 1997), 2.

47. "Clinton: 'I Do Not Believe She Was There Alone,'" *Washington Post,* 14 March 1998, A11.

48. Princeton Survey Research Associates poll, 29 July–1 August 1993.

49. Barney Frank, interview by author, Washington, D.C., 20 December 2000.

50. Allison Mitchell, "Stung by Defeats in '94 Clinton Regrouped and Co-opted GOP Strategies," *New York Times,* 7 November 1996, B1.

51. Office of the Press Secretary, "Transcript of Press Conference by the President," Washington, D.C., 18 April 1995.

52. Mitchell, "Stung by Defeats."

53. Quoted in Elizabeth Drew, *Showdown: The Struggle Between the Gingrich Congress and the Clinton White House* (New York: Simon and Schuster, 1996), 202.

54. Thomas et al., *Back from the Dead*, 23.

55. Bill Clinton, State of the Union address, Washington, D.C., 24 January 1995.

56. Ibid.

57. Quoted in Balz, "Picking Up Votes in a Maze of Ideals," A1.

58. Mark Penn and Doug Schoen, "Clinton: It is Simply a Matter of Packaging," October 1995 memorandum, reprinted in Thomas et al., *Back from the Dead*, 235–36.

59. Ibid., 236.

60. Quoted in Balz, "Picking Up Votes in a Maze of Ideals," A1.

61. Gallup Organization poll, 3–4 November 1996.

62. Gallup Organization poll, 15–17 September 1996.

63. CBS News poll, 27–29 October 1996.

64. See Bill Clinton, *Between Hope and History: Meeting America's Challenges for the 21st Century* (New York: Random House, 1996).

65. CNN/*USA Today*/Gallup poll, 28–29 August 1996.

66. CNN/*USA Today*/Gallup poll, 23–25 August 1996.

67. Bill Clinton, interview, *Meet the Press*, NBC, 9 November 1997.

68. Quoted in William Schneider, "Polls Save Clinton," CNN.com, 13 February 1998.

69. *Helena (Montana) Independent Record*, editorial, 18 August 1998.

70. Cited in Schneider, "Performance Trumps Character," 231.

71. Gallup/CNN/*USA Today* poll, 13–15 February 1998.

72. Ibid.

73. Gallup/CNN/USA *Today* poll, 18–19 March 1998.

74. Gallup/CNN/*USA Today* poll, 25–26 January 1998.

75. Fox News/Opinion Dynamics poll, 11–12 February 1998.

76. Michael Kelly, "At the White House, a Theory of Containment," *National Journal*, 31 January 1998, 205.

77. Quoted in *The Starr Report: The Findings of Independent Counsel Kenneth W. Starr on President Clinton and the Lewinsky Affair with Analysis by the Staff of the Washington Post* (New York: Public Affairs, 1998), 47.

78. Bill Clinton, State of the Union address, Washington, D.C., 27 January 1998.

79. ABC News poll, 27 January 1998; Gallup poll, 28 January 1998.

80. Jonathan Alter, "Playing the Gipper Card," *Newsweek*, 1 February 1999.

81. Gallup/CNN/*USA Today* poll, 25–26 January 1998.

82. Quoted in "Wanna-Be Watch," *National Journal*, 31 January 1998, 256.

83. Quoted in Richard L. Berke, "Republicans End Silence on Troubles of President," *New York Times*, 1 March 1998, 20.

84. Quoted in Thomas et al., *Back from the Dead*, 209.

85. Gallup/CNN/*USA Today* poll, 13–15 February 1998.

86. "Ken Starr's Reading List," *Washington Post*, 26 March 1998, B3.

87. "Burton Draws Fire for Clinton 'Scumbag' Remark," CNN.com, 22 April 1998.

88. See Peter Baker, *The Breach: Inside the Impeachment and Trial of William Jefferson Clinton* (New York: Scribner's, 2000), 16.

89. Quoted in Bob Woodward and Peter Baker, "Behind Calm Air, President Hides Rage Over Starr," *Washington Post*, 1 March 1998, A1.

90. *Los Angeles Times* poll, 27–29 January 1999.

91. Harris Interactive poll, 26 April–5 May 2001.

92. See Robert Lerner, Althea K. Nagai, and Stanley Rothman, *American Elites* (New Haven: Yale University Press, 1996), 91.

93. Spiro T. Agnew, speech, New Orleans, 19 October 1969.

94. Gallup/CNN/*USA Today* poll, 28 January 1998.

95. David Brock, "The Fire This Time," *Esquire*, April 1998, 64.

96. Hillary Clinton, interview, *Today*, NBC, 27 January 1998.

97. Quoted in Kelly, "At the White House, A Theory of Containment," 205.

98. Bill Clinton, Address to the Nation, Washington, D.C., 17 August 1998.

99. Jean Bethke Elshtain, "The Clinton Scandal and the Culture of the Therapeutic," in E.J. Dionne Jr. and John J. DiIulio Jr., eds., *What's God Got to Do with the American Experiment?* (Washington, D.C.: Brookings Institution Press, 2000), 102.

100. See Robert G. Kaiser and John F. Harris, "Shalala Rebuked Before Cabinet," *Washington Post*, 11 September 1998, A1.

101. *Washington Post*/Kaiser Family Foundation/Harvard University poll, 29 July–18 August 1998.

102. Opinion Dynamics poll, 12–13 August 1998; 12–13 February 1999.

103. Opinion Dynamics poll, 20–21 May 1998.

104. NBC News/*Wall Street Journal* poll, 26 February–1 March 1998.

105. Roper Starch Worldwide poll, 13 October–2 November 1998.

106. Associated Press, "Carter Denounces Clinton, Reaction to Scandal," CNN.com, 23 September 1998.

107. Quoted in Pessen, *Log Cabin Myth*, 7.

108. ABC News poll, 9 September 1998.

109. ABC News/*Washington Post* poll, 19–21 August 1998.

110. Gallup Organization poll, 14–15 September 1998.

111. CBS News poll, 11–13 August 1998; CBS News/*New York Times* poll, 13–14 December 1998.

112. CNN/*USA Today*/Gallup poll, 20–22 March 1998.

113. CNN/*USA Today*/Gallup poll, 11–12 August 2000.

114. Peter D. Hart Research Associates poll, 16–20 March 1999.

115. Tarrance Group and Lake, Snell, Perry, and Associates poll, 7–8 February 1999; Zogby International poll, 8–11 February 1998.

116. Quoted in Richard Morin and David S. Broder, "Worries About Nation's Morals Test a Reluctance to Judge," *Washington Post*, 11 September 1998, A1.

117. Clinton, Address to the Nation, 17 August 1998.

118. John F. Kennedy, Address Delivered to a Joint Convention of the General Court of the Commonwealth of Massachusetts, Boston, 9 January 1961.

119. "This Just In . . .," *Washington Post*, 24 February 2000, C3.

120. "Text of Kennedy's Speech: 'If We Stand Our Ground, We Can Prevail,'" *New York Times*, 30 August 1996, A13.

121. CNN/*USA Today*/Gallup poll, 5–7 January 2001.

122. Democrats had nineteen governors at the close of the 2000 campaign but picked up two additional seats one year later with the victories of Mark Warner in Virginia and James McGreevey in New Jersey.

123. Anna Greenberg and Stanley B. Greenberg, "Adding Values," *American Prospect*, 28 August 2000, 28.

124. "Illinois Democrat Swears to His Integrity," *Washington Post*, 28 September 1998, A11.

125. "Candidates Stressing 'Values' in Ads that Don't Name Names," *Washington Post*, 25 September 1998, A19. Bunning, Stenholm, and Campbell won. Hollister narrowly lost.

126. Quoted in Hanna Rosin, "Clinton Faces Test at Annual Prayer Breakfast Today," *Washington Post*, 11 September 1998, A34.

127. "Excerpts from Interview with Clinton," 17.

128. Clinton, remarks at the dedication of the FDR Memorial.

129. Todd S. Purdum, "Chelsea Clinton, Still a Closed Book," *New York Times*, 17 June 2001, 12.

130. Jean Bethke Elshtain, *Democracy on Trial* (New York: Basic Books, 1995), 21.

131. Robert D. Putnam, "Bowling Alone: America's Declining Social Capital," *Journal of Democracy*, January 1995, 68–72.

132. Army Special Counsel Joseph Welch to Senator Joseph McCarthy, congressional hearing, 9 June 1954.

133. Quoted in Paul Johnson, *A History of the American People* (New York: Harper-Collins, 1997), 937.

134. Thomas "Tip" O'Neill with William Novak, *Man of the House: The Life and Political Memoirs of Speaker Tip O'Neill* (New York: Random House, 1987), 333.

135. Cited in "Word for Word Political Sniping: When Senators Attack: 'Why I Oughta . . . ,'" *New York Times*, 11 June 2000, WK7.

136. Quoted in Richard L. Berke, "Lott Takes Parting Shot on Eve of Senate Power Shift," *New York Times*, 3 June 2001, 24.

137. CNN/*USA Today*/Gallup poll, 9–11 February 2001.

138. Princeton Survey Research Associates poll, 21–22 April 1999.

Chapter 5: Campaign 2000: One Nation, Divisible

1. George W. Bush, victory speech, Austin, Texas, 13 December 2000.

2. John J. DiIulio Jr., "Equal Protection Run Amok: Conservatives Will Come to Regret the Court's Rationale for *Bush v. Gore*," in E.J. Dionne Jr. and William Kristol, eds., *Bush v. Gore: The Court Cases and the Commentary* (Washington, D.C.: Brookings Institution Press, 2001), 321–23.

3. *Bush v. Gore*. A copy of the decision was obtained on the C-SPAN web site www.c-span.org

4. Reuters/NBC/Zogby poll, 13 December 2000.

5. Quoted in Anthony Lewis, "A Failure of Reason," reprinted in Dionne and Kristol, *Bush v. Gore*, 301.

6. Ruth Bader Ginsburg concluded her dissenting opinion with the words "I dissent," omitting the customary use of the word "respectfully."

7. Bob Dole, interview, *This Week with Sam Donaldson and Cokie Roberts*, ABC, 12 November 2000.

8. Quoted in David S. Broder and Matthew Vita, "Escalation of Warfare is Likely," *Washington Post*, 22 November 2000, A1.

9. Quoted in "Drums Along the Potomac," *Washington Post*, 3 December 2000, B2.

10. Quoted in John F. Harris, "McAuliffe Takes DNC Helm with Attack on Republicans," *Washington Post*, 4 February 2001, A1.

11. Quoted in Thomas B. Edsall, "Growing Rage Over the Recount Sharpens Conservative Rhetoric," *Washington Post*, 22 November 2000, A19.

12. See James W. Ceaser and Andrew E. Busch, eds., *The Perfect Tie: The True Story of the 2000 Election* (Lanham, Md.: Rowman and Littlefield, 2001).

13. Gore's total vote was 50,996,039 to Bush's 50,456,141. Reagan received 54,450,603 votes in 1984.

14. In Iowa, Gore held on to a slender 4,144-vote lead out of more than 1.25 million votes cast. New Hampshire gave Bush a 7,211-vote advantage out of more than 500,000 votes cast. In Oregon, Gore won by 6,765 votes out of more than 1.5 million votes cast. In Wisconsin, Gore edged Bush by 5,708 votes out of nearly 2.6 million ballots.

15. These were Florida, Iowa, Maine, Michigan, Minnesota, Missouri, Nevada, New Hampshire, New Mexico, Ohio, Oregon, Pennsylvania, Tennessee, Washington, and Wisconsin.

16. Voter News Services exit poll, 7 November 2000.

17. CBS News/*New York Times* poll, 12–14 February 2000.

18. ICR poll, 19–23 November 1999.

19. The "values voters" characteristics are cited in David S. Broder and Richard Morin, "Worries About Nation's Morals Test a Reluctance to Judge," *Washington Post*, 11 September 1998, A1.

20. Quoted in David S. Broder, "Seeking Character," *Washington Post*, 6 February 2000, B7.

21. Gallup Organization poll for *Newsweek*, 10–11 September 1992.

22. Zogby poll, January 2000 (ratings for George H.W. Bush were as follows: great, 17.4 percent; near great, 24.8 percent; average, 44.9 percent; below average, 9.2 percent; failure, 2.4 percent; not sure, 1.3 percent); Gallup poll, 4–5 June 1999.

23. George W. Bush, acceptance speech, Republican National Convention, Philadelphia, 3 August 2000.

24. Bill Bradley, *Time Present, Time Past* (New York: Knopf, 1996), xiii.

25. See Bill Bradley, *Values of the Game* (New York: Artisan, 1998), 113.

26. Bill Bradley, announcement speech, Crystal City, Missouri, 8 September 1999.

27. Dennis Rodman with Tim Keown, *Bad As I Wanna Be* (New York: Delacorte Press, 1996), 2.

28. Cited in Gertrude Himmelfarb, *One Nation, Two Cultures* (New York: Knopf, 1999), 82.

29. Bradley, announcement speech.

30. Ibid.
31. CNN/*USA Today*/Gallup poll, 8–10 October 1999.
32. Ibid.
33. Bradley, announcement speech.
34. Voter News Services, New Hampshire Democratic Primary exit poll, 1 February 2000.
35. John McCain, "Freedom Fighter: Barry Goldwater Had a Vision and a Will to Match," *Washington Post*, 30 May 1998, C1.
36. John McCain with Mark Salter, *Faith of My Fathers: A Family Memoir* (New York: Random House, 1999), 66–67.
37. John McCain, South Carolina debate, CNN, 15 February 2000.
38. John McCain, announcement speech, U.S. Naval Academy, Annapolis, Md., 27 September 1999.
39. Steve May, telephone interview by author, 19 March 2000.
40. McCain, announcement speech.
41. Cited in Michelle Cottle, "Open Season," *New Republic*, 21 February 2000, 23.
42. Cited in William Crotty, "The Election of 2000: Close, Chaotic, and Unforgettable," in William Crotty, ed., *America's Choice 2000* (Boulder: Westview, 2001), 31.
43. Cited in E.J. Dionne Jr., "The George W. Phenomenon," *Washington Post*, 27 October 1998, A23.
44. Cited in Ceci Connolly, "Candidates Stake Claims to Middle," *Washington Post*, 12 May 1999, A3.
45. Quoted in Thomas B. Edsall, "Candidates Find Virtue in Chastity as an Issue," *Washington Post*, 28 September 1998, A11.
46. See George W. Bush, *A Charge to Keep: My Journey to the White House* (New York: HarperCollins Perennial, 2001), 215.
47. See "Crevices," *New Republic*, 24 July 2000.
48. Cited in Rich Lowry, "It's Not Personal, Mr. Bush," *Washington Post*, 1 July 2001, B1. Bush knew what he was doing: 51 percent said that when a candidate speaks of a personal relationship with Jesus Christ, they are more likely to support that person for president. See CNN/Gallup/*USA Today* poll, 20–21 December 1999.
49. Quoted in Mike Allen, "Bush Uses Fourth to Extol Role of Faith," *Washington Post*, 5 July 2001, A2.
50. Quoted in Connolly, "Candidates Stake Claims to Middle."
51. Voter News Service exit poll, 3 November 1998.
52. Associated Press, "Bush Visits Jefferson Memorial," *New York Times*, 3 July 2001.
53. Bush, *Charge to Keep*, 19.
54. Transcript of first Bush-Gore Presidential Debate, CNN, 3 October 2000.
55. Bush, acceptance speech.
56. Ibid.
57. "Excerpts from Colin L. Powell's News Conference," *Washington Post*, 9 November 1995, A14.
58. National Commission on Civic Renewal, "A Nation of Spectators: How Civic Disengagement Weakens America and What We Can Do About It," University of Maryland, College Park, June 1998.
59. George W. Bush, "The True Goal of Education," speech, Gorham, New Hampshire, 2 November 1999.

60. Quoted in Connolly, "Candidates Stake Claims to Middle."

61. Bush, "True Goal of Education."

62. Ibid.

63. Dionne, "George W. Phenomenon."

64. George W. Bush, speech at Bob Jones University, Greenville, South Carolina, 2 February 2000.

65. Bush, "True Goal of Education."

66. See James Hatfield, *Fortunate Son: George W. Bush and the Making of an American President* (New York: Thomas Dunne Books, 1999). Hatfield claimed Bush was arrested for cocaine possession in 1972. The book was withdrawn after Hatfield failed to substantiate his claim. Bush denounced the rumor as "ridiculous and absurd." See Howard Fineman, "The Man to Beat," *Newsweek*, 30 August 1999, 29.

67. Quoted in Ann Gerhart, "Learning to Read Laura Bush," *Washington Post*, 22 March 2001, C1.

68. Fineman, "Man to Beat," 29.

69. Quoted in Nancy Gibbs, "I've Made Mistakes," *Time*, 30 September 1999, 32.

70. Quoted in Edward Walsh, "Bush Assails Gore on Fundraising," *Washington Post*, 15 September 2000, A18.

71. Bush, acceptance speech.

72. ABC News poll, 28–31 October 1999; CBS News/*New York Times* poll, 9–11 September 2000.

73. Fox News/Opinion Dynamics poll, 12–13 August 1998; Yankelovich Partners poll, 9–10 June 1999.

74. Princeton Survey Research Associates poll, 3–4 February 2000.

75. Princeton Survey Research Associates poll, 19–23 July 2000.

76. Fox News/Opinion Dynamics poll, 4–5 October 2000.

77. Zogby International poll, August 1999; CNN/*USA Today*/Gallup poll, 4–5 June 1999; CNN/*USA Today*/Gallup poll, 10–12 March 2000.

78. Gore ran an abortive campaign for the presidency in 1988.

79. Al Gore, announcement speech, Carthage, Tennessee, 16 June 1999.

80. Ibid.

81. Ibid.

82. Quoted in Bill Turque, *Inventing Al Gore* (Boston: Houghton Mifflin, 2000), 356, 360.

83. Al Gore, Commencement Address, University of New Hampshire, Durham, 22 May 1999.

84. Ibid.

85. See Melinda Henneberger, "Al Gore's Journey: Gore Has Explored a Range of Beliefs from Old Time to New Age," *New York Times*, 22 October 2000, A1.

86. Quoted in Calvin Woodward, "Candidates Struggle to Define When the Personal Should Become Political," CNN.com, 14 December 1999.

87. Al Gore, *Earth in the Balance* (Boston: Houghton Mifflin, 1992), 367.

88. *Capital Gang*, CNN, 2 September 2000.

89. Al Gore, acceptance speech, Democratic National Convention, Los Angeles, 17 August 2000.

90. Tipper Gore, *Raising PG Kids in an X-Rated Society* (Nashville; Abingdon Press, 1987), unnumbered first page.

91. Gore, *Earth in the Balance*, 265.

92. Transcript of Third Bush-Gore Presidential Debate, CNN, 17 October 2000.

93. Gore, *Earth in the Balance*, 14.

94. See Marjorie Williams, "Scenes from a Marriage," *Vanity Fair*, July 2001, 133.

95. Quoted in Turque, *Inventing Al Gore*, 21.

96. Joseph Lieberman, acceptance speech, Democratic National Convention, Los Angeles, 16 August 2000.

97. NBC News/*Wall Street Journal* poll, 10–11 August 2000.

98. Joseph Lieberman, transcript of remarks on the Senate floor, CNN, 3 September 1998.

99. Ibid.

100. Joseph Lieberman, statement at talk show campaign news conference, Washington, D.C., 26 October 1995.

101. Lieberman, acceptance speech.

102. Joseph Lieberman, "Vision for America: A Place for Faith," speech, Notre Dame University, 24 October 2000.

103. Princeton Survey Research Associates poll, 10–12 August 2000.

104. ABC News/*Washington Post* poll, 4–6 September 2000; CNN/*USA Today*/Gallup poll, 11–12 August 2000.

105. ABC News/*Washington Post* poll, 4–6 September 2000.

106. ABC News poll, 28–30 October 1999.

107. Fox News/Opinion Dynamics poll, 20–21 September 2000.

108. CNN/*USA Today*/Gallup poll, 6–8 October 2000.

109. CBS News/*New York Times* poll, 1–4 November 2000.

110. CBS News/*New York Times* poll, 20–23 July 2000; Greenberg Quinlan Research poll, 4–9 September 2000; Princeton Survey Research Associates poll, 24 August–10 September 2000.

111. NBC News/*Wall Street Journal* poll, 10–11 August 2000.

112. Greenberg Quinlan Research poll, 4–9 September 2000.

113. Arthur M. Schlesinger Jr., *The Vital Center: The Politics of Freedom* (Boston: Houghton Mifflin, 1949).

114. "Gay Issues, Characters, Join Prime Time," *Showbiz TV*, CNN, 16 October 2000. Retrieved from: http://www.cnn.com/2000/SHOWBIZ/TV/10/16/ga.TV/index.html

115. These were Wyoming, 69 percent; Idaho, 68 percent; Utah, 67 percent; Nebraska, 63 percent; North Dakota, 61 percent; South Dakota, 60 percent; Oklahoma, 60 percent; Texas, 59 percent; Alaska, 59 percent; Mississippi, 58 percent.

116. These were Washington, D.C., 85 percent; Rhode Island, 61 percent; Massachusetts, 60 percent; New York, 60 percent; Maryland, 57 percent; Connecticut, 56 percent; Hawaii, 56 percent; Delaware, 55 percent; New Jersey, 55 percent; California, 54 percent.

117. Voter News Service exit poll, 7 November 2000.

118. Quoted in Mary McGrory, "The Candidate's Blurred Images," *Washington Post*, 8 June 2000, A3.

119. See p. 228, note 108.

120. See John C. Green, James L. Guth, Lyman A. Kellstedt, and Corwin B. Smidt, "How the Faithful Voted: Religion and the 2000 Presidential Election," press release.

121. See Alan Wolfe, *One Nation After All* (New York: Viking, 1998), especially 275–322.

122. See David Brooks, *Bobos in Paradise: The New Upper Class and How They Got There* (New York: Simon and Schuster, 2000), 104.

123. Quoted in Henneberger, "Al Gore's Journey," A1.

124. Milken Institute. The top twenty New Economy states are Massachusetts (with a New Economy score of 92.3), which voted for Gore; California (85.5), Gore; Connecticut (83.7), Gore; Colorado (82.7), Bush; Washington (79.0), Gore; Maryland (78.2), Gore; New Jersey (74.7), Gore; New York (74.5), Gore; New Hampshire (71.2), Bush; New Mexico (70.5), Gore; Delaware (69.8), Gore; Utah (68.8), Bush; Virginia (68.0), Bush; Oregon (67.0), Gore; Vermont (64.3), Gore; Texas (63.3), Bush; Rhode Island (62.0), Gore; Arizona (60.8), Bush; Georgia (59.8), Bush; Minnesota (59.3), Gore. The New Economy Index is based on the percentage of the population aged twenty-five and older with a B.A. or greater; the percentage of the population twenty-five and older with an advanced degree, 2000; the number of doctoral scientists and engineers, 2000; exports as a percent of Gross State Product, 1999; federal research and development dollars per capita, 1997; industry research and development dollars per capita, 1997; academic research and development dollars per capita, 1997.

125. Quoted in William Booth, "Letter from California," *Washington Post*, 29 September 1999, A–7.

126. The 1948 Dewey states were New York, New Jersey, Pennsylvania, Michigan, Maryland, Connecticut, Delaware, Maine, Vermont, Indiana, Oregon, North Dakota, South Dakota, Nebraska, Kansas, and New Hampshire.

127. See Brooks, *Bobos in Paradise*, 43.

128. Quoted in Williams, "Scenes from a Marriage," 89.

129. Quoted in John F. Harris, "Clinton and Gore Clashed over Blame for Election," *Washington Post*, 7 February 2001, A1.

130. John Zogby, interview by author, Washington, D.C., 13 April 2000.

131. Benjamin Disraeli, *Sybil or The Two Nations* (Reprint, New York: Penguin Books, 1984), 12.

132. Bush, victory speech, 13 December 2000.

133. Richard M. Nixon, Inaugural Address, Washington, D.C., 20 January 1969.

Chapter 6: The Father-Knows-Best President and the Return of Four-Party Politics

1. Quoted in The Political Staff of the *Washington Post*, *Deadlock: The Inside Story of America's Closest Election* (New York: Public Affairs, 2001), 17.

2. Quoted in Dan Balz and David S. Broder, "For Some Voters, President Has Yet to Prove Himself," *Washington Post*, 5 August 2001, A1. Emphasis added.

3. ABC News/*Washington Post* poll, 26–30 July 2001.

4. Quoted in Balz and Broder, "For Some Voters, President Has Yet to Prove Himself," A1.

5. Quoted in David S. Broder and Dan Balz, "Bush Gets High Approval Ratings in Poll," *Washington Post*, 2 August 2001, A4.

6. ABC News/*Washington Post* poll, 26–30 July 2001.

7. CNN/*USA Today*/Gallup poll, 3–5 August 2001.

8. ABC News/*Washington Post* poll, 26–30 July 2001.

9. See John Kenneth White, *Still Seeing Red: How the Cold War Shapes the New American Politics* (Boulder: Westview Press, 1998).

10. See Hanna Rosin, "Florida Ban on Gay Adoptions Upheld," *Washington Post*, 31 August 2001, A4.

11. Alan Wolfe, *Moral Freedom: The Impossible Idea that Defines the Way We Live Now* (New York: W.W. Norton, 2001), 195, 199.

12. Pope John Paul II, statement to the American bishops, Los Angeles, September 1987.

13. Institute for Social Inquiry, Roper Center poll, 11–24 March 1997; National Opinion Research Center poll, 1 February–25 May 1996.

14. Institute for Social Inquiry, Roper Center poll, 11–24 March 1997.

15. Stan Davis and Christopher Meyer, *Blur: The Speed of Change in the Connected Economy* (Reading, Mass.: Addison-Wesley, 1998), 148, 151.

16. Quoted in Wolfe, *Moral Freedom*, 27.

17. Al Gore, *Common Sense Government* (New York: Random House, 1995), 14.

18. Cited in Dan Balz and Richard Morin, "A Tide of Pessimism and Political Powerlessness Rises," *Washington Post*, 3 November 1991, A1, A16. The 1958 results are contained in the National Election Study (NES), which has been conducted every other year since 1952 by the University of Michigan.

19. *Los Angeles Times* poll, 3–5 March 2001.

20. Quoted in Ann Devroy and Jeffrey Smith, "Clinton Reexamines Foreign Policy Under Siege," *Washington Post*, 17 October 1993, A1; and Richard Reeves, *Running in Place: How Bill Clinton Disappointed America* (Kansas City, Mo.: Andrews and McMeel, 1996), 94.

21. See Edward Walsh, "Daschle Calls for Sharing of Plans," *Washington Post*, 4 March 2002, A-4.

22. E.J. Dionne Jr., *Why Americans Hate Politics* (New York: Simon and Schuster, 1991), 11.

23. See Ceci Connolly, "Administration Promoting Abstinence," *Washington Post*, 30 July 2001, A1.

24. Andrew Sullivan, "Who's Your Daddy?" *Time*, 18 June 2001, 92.

25. Harold D. Lasswell, *Politics: Who Gets What, When, How* (New York: Meridian Books, 1958).

26. Figures cited in Jim Carrier, "Bomb Blues," *Denver Post*, 13 July 1995, A1. The Energy Department still houses 280 million pages of classified information. See Stephen I. Schwartz, "Atomic Audit: What the U.S. Nuclear Arsenal Has Cost," *Brookings Review*, Fall 1995, 17.

27. See White, *Still Seeing Red*, 133–34.
28. Daniel Bell, *The End of Ideology* (Glencoe, Ill.: Free Press, 1960).
29. James MacGregor Burns, *The Deadlock of Democracy: Four-Party Politics in America* (Englewood Cliffs, N.J.: Prentice-Hall, 1963).
30. Hubert H. Humphrey, interview for the Lyndon B. Johnson Oral History Collection, 17 August 1971.
31. Students for a Democratic Society, "Port Huron Statement," Port Huron, Michigan, 11–15 June 1962.
32. Quoted in Fred I. Greenstein, *The Hidden-Hand Presidency: Eisenhower as Leader* (New York: Basic Books, 1982), 50.
33. Quoted in Herbert Brownell with John Burke, *Advising Ike* (Lawrence: University of Kansas Press, 1993), 117.
34. For more on this, see Rick Perlstein, *Before the Storm: Barry Goldwater and the Unmaking of the American Consensus* (New York: Hill and Wang, 2001).
35. Quoted in John B. Judis, "The Hunted," *New Republic*, 17 and 24 April 2000, 34.
36. "Party Unity Background," *Congressional Quarterly Weekly Report*, 9 January 1999, 92.
37. The other is Republican Jim Kolbe of Arizona, who was outed after supporting the Defense of Marriage Act in 1996.
38. Donald R. Matthews, *U.S. Senators and Their World* (Chapel Hill: University of North Carolina Press, 1960), 165.
39. In 2002 Tony Hall announced his retirement from Congress in order to become the U.S. representative to the United Nations Agencies for Food and Agriculture.
40. Third Way thinking has reshaped Britain's Labour Party, led by Prime Minister Tony Blair, and Germany's Social Democratic Party led by Chancellor Gerhardt Schröder.
41. *The 2000 Democratic National Platform: Prosperity, Progress, and Peace* (Washington, D.C.: Democratic National Committee, 2000).
42. Ibid.
43. Quoted in Thomas B. Edsall, "Gore Campaign Crafting a Centrist Platform," *Washington Post*, 7 July 2000, A1.
44. The platform promised to fight for free-trade agreements that "protect the environment and . . . labor standards." See *Democratic Party Platform, 2000* (Washington, D.C.: Democratic National Committee, 2000).
45. Quoted in Michael Barone and Grant Ujifusa, *The Almanac of American Politics, 1998* (Washington, D.C.: National Journal, 1999), 835.
46. Richard A. Gephardt, speech to the John F. Kennedy School of Government, Boston, 2 December 1997.
47. See Ken Silverstien, "Candidate Nader," *Mother Jones*, July/August 2000, 63.
48. Quoted in Mark Shields, "California's Comeback Kid," *Washington Post*, 22 March 1998, C11.
49. See Edsall, "Gore Campaign Crafting a Centrist Platform," A1.
50. George W. Bush, interview, *The Oprah Winfrey Show*, 19 September 2000.
51. George W. Bush, Inaugural Address, Washington, D.C., 20 January 2001.
52. George W. Bush, Remarks by the President at the Dedication of the Pope John Paul

II Cultural Center, Catholic University of America, Washington, D.C., 22 March 2001.

53. Quoted in Alison Mitchell, "Bush Draws Campaign Theme from More than the Heart," *New York Times*, 12 June 2000, A1.

54. Transcript of the first Bush-Gore presidential debate, CNN, 3 October 2000.

55. See Rich Lowry, "It's Not Personal, Mr. Bush," *Washington Post*, 1 July 2001, B1.

56. George W. Bush and Vladimir Putin, news conference, Ljubjana, Slovenia, 18 June 2001.

57. See George W. Bush, "A Culture of Achievement," speech, Manhattan Institute Luncheon, New York, 5 October 1999, and George W. Bush, acceptance speech, Philadelphia, 3 August 2000.

58. Quoted in E.J. Dionne Jr., "Fighting on Gore's Ground," *Washington Post*, 8 September 2000, A33.

59. See George W. Bush, "Foreword," in Marvin Olasky, *Compassionate Conservatism: What It Is, What It Does, and How It Can Transform America* (New York: Free Press, 2000), xi, xii.

60. *Republican National Platform, 2000* (Washington, D.C.: Republican National Committee, 2000).

61. See Olasky, *Compassionate Conservatism*, 8–9.

62. Marvin N. Olasky, *The Tragedy of American Compassion* (Washington, D.C.: Regnery Gateway, 1992), 224.

63. Quoted in David Brooks, "One Nation Conservatism," *Weekly Standard*, 13 September 1999, 24.

64. Bush, Inaugural Address.

65. Pat Robertson, "Mr. Bush's Faith-Based Initiative Is Flawed," *Wall Street Journal*, 12 March 2001.

66. Barney Frank, interview by author, Washington, D.C., 20 December 2000.

67. Quoted in "Washington Wire," *Wall Street Journal*, 27 July 2001, A1.

68. "A Lesson from the Right," *Washington Post*, 19 July 2000, A7.

69. Quoted in E.J. Dionne Jr., "Construction Boon: It's No Accident That the GOP Is Being Rebuilt by Its Governors," *Washington Post*, 14 March 1999, B4.

70. Rush Limbaugh, interview, *Meet the Press*, NBC, 10 October 1999.

71. Pat Robertson, interview, *Face the Nation*, CBS, 1 October 2000.

72. George W. Bush, victory speech, Austin, Tex., 13 December 2000.

73. Juliet Eilperin, "Unborn Victims Act Wins in House," *Washington Post*, 27 April 2001, A1.

74. Quoted in Thomas M. DeFrank, "Ford Urges Bush to Select Pro-Choicer as Running Mate," *New York Daily News*, 17 July 2000, A1.

75. Juliet Eilperin, "DeLay Sees Opportunity of a Lifetime for Republicans," *Washington Post*, 7 December 2000, A23.

76. CBS News/*New York Times* poll, 14–18 June 2001.

77. David Price, interview by author, Washington, D.C., 25 October 2000.

78. Quoted in Michael Barone and Richard E. Cohen with Charles E. Cook Jr., *The Almanac of American Politics, 2002* (Washington, D.C.: National Journal, 2001), 896.

79. Richard Gephardt, *An Even Better Place: America in the 21st Century* (New York: Public Affairs, 1999), 18.

80. Ibid., 9.

81. Ibid., 11.

Chapter 7: We're All Americans Now

1. Princeton Survey Research Associates survey, 13–17 September 2001.

2. See "Losses Mount Around the World," CBS News.com, 13 September 2001, and "Countries Start Counting Their Citizens' Death Toll," *Agence France-Presse*, 14 September 2001.

3. Quoted in R.W. Apple, "No Middle Ground," *New York Times*, 14 September 2001.

4. See Nancy Gibbs, "Mourning in America," *Time*, 24 September 2001.

5. Opinion Dynamics poll, 9–10 May 2001.

6. Zogby International tracking poll, 7 November 2001.

7. Zogby International tracking poll, 3 November 2001.

8. See "Tuesday Briefing," Gallup press release, 25 September 2001.

9. Zogby International tracking poll, 3 November 2001.

10. Zogby International tracking poll, October 24, 2001.

11. Karen W. Arenson, "A Generation Unfamiliar with Feeling Vulnerable," *New York Times*, 14 September 2001.

12. "Audience Response to the Attacks," MTV.com, 12 September 2001. A Gallup poll (26–27 November 2001) found 72 percent saying that the September 11th attacks would have a greater historical significance than the Japanese bombing of Pearl Harbor.

13. Chelsea Clinton, "Before and After," *Talk*, December 2001/January 2002, 100, 142.

14. Barbara Kantrowitz and Keith Naughton, "Generation 9-11," *Newsweek*, 12 November 2001, 46.

15. Quoted in Jim Rutenberg, "MTV, Turning Serious Helps Its Generation Cope," *New York Times*, 2 October 2001.

16. Quoted in David Segal, "All Together Now," *Washington Post*, 24 September 2001, C1.

17. Wirthlin Worldwide poll, 5–8 October 2001.

18. See Robert D. Putnam, *Bowling Alone: The Collapse and Revival of American Community* (New York: Simon and Schuster, 2000).

19. Quoted in Donna St. George, "After a Death, a New Way of Life," *Washington Post*, 28 October 2001, A1.

20. *Time*/CNN poll, conducted by Harris Interactive, 19–20 December 2001.

21. See Lisa de Moraes, "Wall-to-Wall Coverage Close to Setting a Record," *Washington Post*, 15 September 2001, C7. A CNN/*Time* magazine poll found two-thirds saying the events of 11 September would define a generation the way the Kennedy assassination did. CNN/*Time* poll, 7–8 November 2001.

22. "Millions from the Stars," CBS News.com, 26 September 2001.

23. George W. Bush, Radio Address of the President to the Nation, Camp David, Maryland, 15 September 2001.

24. Quoted in Rutenberg, "MTV, Turning Serious."
25. Ibid.
26. See Lydia Saad, "Americans Anxious, But Holding Their Heads High," Gallup press release, 1 October 2001.
27. See among others Robert Sullivan, "New York's New 'Normal,'" *Time*, 2 October 2001.
28. See Segal, "All Together Now."
29. See Nekesa Mumbi Moody, "'God Bless America' Debuts on Top," Associated Press, 25 October 2001.
30. See Neil Strauss, "After the Horror, Radio Stations Pull Some Songs," *New York Times*, 19 September 2001.
31. See Segal, "All Together Now."
32. See Teresa Wiltz, "Playing in the Shadows," *Washington Post*, 19 November 2001, C1.
33. See Dan Balz and John F. Harris, "Shock of War May Have Changed the Tone in Politics," *Washington Post*, 14 October 2001, A3.
34. See David Brooks, "The Organization Kid Revisited," Newsweek.msnbc.com, 4 November 2001.
35. See Frank Newport, "Trust in Government Increases Sharply in Wake of Terrorist Attacks," Gallup press release, 12 October 2001.
36. Gallup poll, 5–6 October 2001.
37. See Tom W. Smith, Kenneth A. Rasinski and Marianna Toce, "America Rebounds: The Public's Response to the September 11 Attacks," *The Polling Report*, 5 November 2001, 6.
38. Gallup poll, 5–6 October 2001.
39. Quoted in Bob Woodward, "A Test of Government's Trustworthiness," *Washington Post*, 25 October 2001, A31.
40. Quoted in Balz and Harris, "Shock of War."
41. See Gallup poll, 8–11 November 2001; 5–6 October 2001.
42. See "Tuesday Briefing," Gallup press release, 6 November 2001.
43. See John F. Harris and Dana Milbank, "For Bush, New Emergencies Ushered in a New Agenda," *Washington Post*, 22 September 2001, A3.
44. See "Tuesday Briefing," Gallup press release, 25 September 2001.
45. See Nancy Gibbs, "We Gather Together," *Time*, 19 November 2001, 36.
46. Quoted in Stanley B. Greenberg, "'We—Not 'Me,'" *American Prospect*, 17 December 2001, 25–26.
47. See Hank Stuever, "The Bomb with a Loaded Message," *Washington Post*, 27 October 2001, C1.
48. Zogby International survey, 12–15 October 2001.
49. "Audience Response to Attacks."
50. Zogby International tracking poll, 5–7 October 2001. Church attendance stood at 41 percent in February and May, 2001. See "Tuesday briefing," Gallup press release, 25 September 2001. *Time*/CNN poll, conducted by Harris Interactive, 19–20 December 2001.
51. "USA Today Snapshots," *USA Today*, 19 October 2001, 1A. According to this survey conducted by Luntz Research Company, 3 October 2001, 64 percent displayed

the flag from their home; 29 percent wore it on an article of clothing; 28 percent placed it on an automobile.

52. Segal, "All Together Now."

53. See Dana Milbank, "Bush Makes a Pitch for Teaching Patriotism," *Washington Post*, 2 November 2001, A2.

54. Lynne V. Cheney, *America: A Patriotic Primer* (New York: Simon and Schuster, 2002).

55. One Gallup poll found 90 percent of the respondents ranked firefighters first for their ethics and honesty. They were closely followed by nurses (84 percent) and the U.S. military (83 percent). See Gallup poll, 26–27 November 2001.

56. See Stuever, "The Bomb with a Loaded Message"; and Jesse Green, "Requiem of a Heavyweight," *Talk*, December 2001/January 2002, 78–81.

57. George W. Bush, Address to the Nation Announcing the Bombing of Afghanistan, Washington, D.C., 7 October 2001.

58. See Hank Stuever, "Miss America the Beautiful," *Washington Post*, 22 September 2001, C1.

59. Hank Stuever, "Our New Miss America: Of Thee She Will Sing," *Washington Post*, 24 September 2001, C1.

60. George W. Bush, press conference, Washington, D.C., 11 October 2001.

61. Quoted in Segal, "All Together Now."

62. Quoted in Kenneth Auchincloss, "We Shall Overcome," *Newsweek*, 24 September 2001, 19–20.

63. See, for example, David Kaplan, *The Accidental President: How 413 Lawyers, 9 Supreme Court Justices, and 5,963,110 Floridians (Give or Take a Few) Landed George W. Bush in the White House* (New York: William Morrow, 2001).

64. Quoted in Dan Balz, "Gore Pledges to Back Bush, Calls for Unity," *Washington Post*, 30 September 2001, A3.

65. Quoted in "Notebook," *New Republic*, 15 October 2001.

66. Quoted in Frank Bruni, "For Bush, a Mission and a Defining Moment," *New York Times*, 22 September 2001.

67. George W. Bush, address to the nation, Atlanta, 8 November 2001.

68. See Alexander Hamilton, *Federalist* No. 70. Hamilton's famous line reads, "Energy in the executive is a leading character in the definition of good government." He continued, "It is essential to the protection of the community against foreign attacks." Alexander Hamilton, James Madison, and John Jay, *The Federalist Papers*, ed. Clinton Rossiter (New York: New American Library, 1961), 423.

69. "The Incredible Shrinking President," *Time*, 29 June 1992.

70. Gallup poll, 7–10 September 2001.

71. Gallup poll, 21–22 September 2001.

72. See David W. Moore, "Top Ten Gallup Presidential Approval Ratings," Gallup press release, 24 September 2001.

73. Zogby International survey, 17–18 September 2001.

74. Zogby International poll, 8–10 October 2001.

75. Gallup poll, 2–4 November 2001; CNN/*USA Today*/Gallup poll, 5–6 October 2001.

76. Quoted in E.J. Dionne Jr., "A New and Improved George W.," *Washington Post*, 12 October 2001, A33.

77. See John Kenneth White, *Still Seeing Red: How the Cold War Shapes the New American Politics* (Boulder: Westview Press, 1998).

78. CNN/*USA Today*/Gallup poll, 11–14 January 2002. See Richard Benedetto, "Democrats Lose Advantage with Voters in Latest Poll, *USA Today*, 15 January 2002.

79. Quoted in James MacGregor Burns, *Roosevelt: The Lion and the Fox* (New York: Harcourt, Brace, and World, 1956), 274.

80. Quoted in Theodore H. White, *The Making of the President, 1968* (New York: Atheneum Publishers, 1969), 359.

81. George W. Bush, Remarks to Employees at the Pentagon, Arlington, Virginia, 17 September 2001.

82. George W. Bush, Address to the Nation, Washington, D.C., 11 September 2001.

83. George W. Bush, Address to a Joint Session of Congress, Washington, D.C., 20 September 2001.

84. "Text of Bin Laden Remarks," *Washington Post*, 8 October 2001, A12.

85. Quoted in Maureen Dowd, "All that Glistens," *New York Times*, 3 October 2001.

86. See John F. Burns, "America Inspires Both Longing and Loathing in Arab World," *New York Times*, 16 September 2001, A4.

87. Quoted in "Perspectives," *Newsweek*, 8 October 2001, 17.

88. Quoted in Greenberg, "'We—Not 'Me," 26.

89. "Bin Laden's Obsessions," *New York Review of Books*, 15 November 2001, 4.

90. Jodi Wilgoren, "A Terrorist Profile Emerges that Confounds the Experts," *New York Times*, 15 September 2001.

91. Quoted in Johanna McGeary and David Van Biema, "The New Breed of Terrorist," *Time*, 24 September 2001, 31.

92. Bush, press conference, 11 October 2001.

93. Quoted in Benjamin R. Barber, *Jihad vs. McWorld* (New York: Ballantine Books, 1996), 210.

94. Quoted in Kenneth L. Woodward, "A Peaceful Faith, a Fanatic Few," *Newsweek*, 24 September 2001, 68.

95. See Stanley Bedlington, "Not Who You Think," *Washington Post*, 29 October 2001, B2.

96. Quoted in "Notebook," *New Republic*, 8 October 2001, 11.

97. See Burns, "America Inspires both Longing and Loathing."

98. See Barber, *Jihad vs. McWorld*, 24, 23, 5, 6.

99. Ibid., 90, 92, 94.

100. Burns, "America Inspires Both Longing and Loathing."

101. Cable Network Profiles," MTV.com, 1 November 2001.

102. Barber, *Jihad vs. McWorld*, 207, 102, 101.

103. Jeffrey Simpson, "Living Beside a Cultural and Economic Colossus," *New York Times*, 24 August 1986, E3.

104. See Barber, *Jihad vs. McWorld*, 91, 207, 92–93.

105. Quoted in "Pop Goes the Culture," *Time*, 16 June 1986, 73.

106. Burns, "America Inspires Both Longing and Loathing."

107. "Pop Goes the Culture," 71, 73.
108. Quoted in Barber, *Jihad vs. McWorld*, 128–29.
109. Ibid., 134.
110. Quoted in Lloyd Grove, "Who's Gonna Spill about Bill and Hill?" *Washington Post*, 28 February 2002, C–3.
111. Katha Pollitt, "Pull Out No Flags," *The Nation*, 8 October 2001.
112. Quoted in "Notebook," *New Republic*, 22 October 2001.
113. "'Sin' Led to Attack, Evangelical Group Says," *Washington Post*, 22 September 2001, B9.
114. Quoted in Matt Drudge, *The Drudge Report*, 23 October 2001.
115. Lloyd Grove, "Hillary's Knight in Shining Anger," *Washington Post*, 2 November 2001, C3.
116. Quoted in Drudge, *The Drudge Report*, 23 October 2001. For her part, Hillary Clinton said, "I have gotten used to being in situations in political life, either vicariously or on my own, where that just happens sometimes." See Frank Bruni, "Clinton and Schumer: Show Us the Money," *New York Times Magazine*, 16 December 2001.
117. See Lisa de Moraes, "The TV Column," *Washington Post*, 15 September 2001, C7; and Gustav Niebuhr, "U.S. Secular Groups Set Tone for Terror Attacks, Falwell Says," *New York Times*, 14 September 2001.
118. De Moraes, "TV Column."
119. Laurie Goodstein, "Falwell's Finger-Pointing Inappropriate, Bush Says," *New York Times*, 15 September 2001.
120. Quoted in "Falwell Apologizes to Gays, Feminists, Lesbians," CNN.com, 14 September 2001.
121. De Moraes, "TV Column."
122. "'Sin' Led to Attack," B9. Falwell's son, the Reverend Jonathan Falwell, wrote a fundraising letter saying that "Satan has launched a hail of fiery darts at Dad." The younger Falwell asked for a special Vote of Confidence gift of at least $50 or $100. See Peter Carlson, "Jerry Falwell's Awkward Apology," *Washington Post*, 18 November 2001, F1.
123. "Falwell Apologizes to Gays."
124. Goodstein, "Falwell's Finger-Pointing Inappropriate."
125. Quoted in Craig Timberg, "Businessman Warner Charged Up to Make the Sale," *Washington Post*, 21 October 2001, C9.
126. Quoted in Carol Morello, "Warner Blurs Political Labels," *Washington Post*, 26 October 2001, A1.
127. Quoted in David M. Halbfinger, "In Polls and in G.O.P., Schundler Is Paying a Price for His Missteps," *New York Times*, 30 August 2001.
128. See Cliff Zukin, "Democrats Gaining Strength in New Jersey," *Star-Ledger*/Eagleton-Rutgers, press release, 4 November 2001.
129. See Dan Balz and Thomas B. Edsall, "Capturing Center Key in Democratic Wins," *Washington Post*, 8 November 2001, A24. McGreevey won 55 percent of the vote in Bergen County to Schundler's 44 percent.
130. Opinion Dynamics poll, 19–20 September 2001.

131. IPSOS-Reid poll, 28–30 September 2001.
132. Quoted in Balz and Harris, "Shock of War."
133. Dwight D. Eisenhower, acceptance speech, Republican National Convention, 23 August 1956.
134. Quoted in Balz and Harris, "Shock of War."
135. Quoted in Rutenberg, "MTV, Turning Serious."
136. Quoted in "Notebook," *New Republic*, 8 October 2001, 11.
137. See "America Reponds," *The Wirthlin Report*, September 2001, 2–3.
138. Zogby International tracking poll, 7 November 2001.
139. Zogby International tracking polls, 6 November 2001.
140. Bush, press conference, 11 October 2001.
141. Quoted in James J. Zogby, "Arab-Americans Are Defended," *Washington Watch*, 1 October 2001.
142. Ibid.
143. See Rutenberg, "MTV, Turning Serious."
144. Quoted in Alan Wolfe, *Moral Freedom: The Impossible Idea that Defines the Way We Live Now* (New York: W.W. Norton, 2001), 82–83, 95–96.
145. Zogby International tracking data, 23 September 2001.
146. Ibid.
147. See Robert Putnam, "Bowling Together," *American Prospect*, 11 February 2002, 21.
148. *The World Book Encyclopedia* (Chicago: Field Enterprises Educational Corporation, 1964), 724b.
149. Ronald Reagan, Remarks at the Annual Convention of the National Association of Evangelicals, Orlando, Florida., 8 March 1983.
150. See Alan Wolfe, *One Nation After All* (New York: Viking, 1998), especially 275–322.

Index